THE LAST QUARTER

A TRILOGY

MARTIN FLANAGAN

ONE DAY HILL

1970
First published by Allen & Unwin, 1999

Southern Sky Western Oval
First published by Penguin Group (Australia), 1994

The Game in Time of War
First published in Picador by Pan Macmillan (Australia), 2003

This edition published by One Day Hill Pty Ltd
PO Box 1448
Camberwell East 3126
Victoria Australia
Web: www.onedayhill.com.au

ISBN 9780975770894

Design and Layout: Guillaume Roux
Cover art: Ainsley Walters

Set in Palatino
Printed in China by Bookbuilders Pty Ltd

A catalogue record is available from the National Library of Australia.

When I was born
a poem ran to meet me
with a ball in its hand;
its name was Johnny Greening.
He was 16, the year before he went to Collingwood;
he played for Parklands High.
Footy in Burnie when I was a kid was very good.
Five or six of those in the school competition
Would "go to Melbourne" and make it in the big time.
Burnie was coastal industrial,
Moe or Morwell by the sea.
Lots of tough kids.
I played in that competition, too,
Scared out of my wits half the time,
But it meant I saw the best of those kids play,
The ones who made it, the ones who didn't.
And I saw them close up.
Crosswell came down from Launceston to play.
At 17, very possibly the best schoolboy footballer in Australia,
a highjumper's leap,
an intellectual's cool appraisal of the game,
an actor's passion for the glory of the stage.
I saw Rodney Oborne.
I remember him as a blue flash parting a pack
In the under 14s.
I knew too well the world through which they ran,
Its hard bumps and collisions,
Its cruel fists that cut others down
But these were the ones
Who could vault the menace and be gone.
This book is dedicated to all those young men
Who have thrilled me with their skill and daring
Putting words in my mouth that had to be shouted.

1970

1970

Sport is drama. Occasionally, it tilts over and becomes something more; what happens is that the memory of an event acquires a life of its own and goes careering down the years, unstoppable, ruthlessly refining itself in the public memory. Peter McKenna meets it twice a week, Syd Jackson four times, perhaps because he's black. The question usually goes, 'Are you Syd Jackson? Did you play in the 1970 grand final?'. After a few beers and in playful mood, Syd has been known to answer, 'No, I'm Lionel Rose', but mostly Syd admits to his identity. Mostly, he says, such contacts are good. But then Syd played for Carlton, and Carlton won. One year, before a grand final, I was watching an all-night telecast of past finals; Peter McKenna was one of the hosts. McKenna played full-forward for Collingwood in an era of great full-forwards and his record stands with the best of his peers, but here he was saying there's nothing in losing. 'When we [Collingwood's 1970 grand final team] meet, we've got nothing to talk about.' There was no doubting the emptiness in his voice. I began to wonder: what happens to people whose lives get tangled up in legend?

The first person I contacted was Ron Barassi. In so far as the myth of the 1970 grand final has a name, it's his. With his team trailing by 44 points at halftime, it is said that Barassi instructed the Carlton players to handball at every opportunity; they did, won by ten points and thereby revolutionised the game. Before this match, it is further said, football was a static game of fixed positions and man-on-man contests. The myth of the 1970 grand final, in its simplest form, is that it was when the modern game was born, the progenitor of the one we see today where no positions are fixed and the field of play is one large fluid mass with individuals running near marathons each match.

Barassi I'd met a couple of times before, most significantly in Sydney in 1995. In his 60th year, Barassi had gone north in answer to an SOS from the AFL, SOS meaning Save Our Swans. The Sydney experiment was on the edge of collapse. Barassi's partner from his glory days at North Melbourne, Ron Joseph, worked out the back, trying to recreate Sydney as a genuine football club and not a marketing operation, while Barassi ordered the team and was paraded before the Sydney media as the game's elder statesman. As a coach, he appeared to have lost his famous fire but he brought wisdom to the role, gathering the team around him so that by the end of his term it was stealing wins. As an ambassador, he was an undoubted success, in part because, as a person, Barassi is worth meeting. He's an individual thinker; not many people are. Although his name is synonymous with sport, he appreciates that it frequently approaches absurdity. At the same time, what he has to say about Australian football is lucid and revealing. In Sydney, Barassi told me the major reason Australian football didn't break into Sydney in the 1890s was because most of the sports masters in the Sydney private schools were English and they favoured rugby as evidence of the imperial tie. When I got back to Melbourne, I checked press reports of the committee meetings at the 1908 Jubilee of Australian football in Melbourne. He was right.

Denis O'Callaghan, who played on the halfback flank for Collingwood in the 1970 final, always liked Barassi. In those days, as part of the match-day program, players and officials from both clubs would meet at a function after the game. O'Callaghan recalls Barassi always seeming pleased to meet with players from other clubs. 'He seemed to me to be on about something larger and to have the interests of the game at heart.' By 1977, when North Melbourne won its second premiership under him, Barassi stood alone—in the popular imagination, at least—as *the* coach in Australian football, a fiery furnace in technicolour shirts who jabbed his finger into players' faces and confronted them like an apparition from hell. In the words of Carlton centre halfback John Goold, Barassi was 'a pretty furious fellow back then'. In the late '70s, when David Williamson wrote *The Club*, a comic drama about a Melbourne football club suspiciously like Collingwood trapped in a historical dilemma, the coach who promises to redeem the club's fortunes is called Rostov. By then, it had to sound foreign—like Barassi.

An account of his 1977 season at North Melbourne by John Powers, entitled simply *The Coach*, examined his methods in detail, but, even so, I had no real understanding of Barassi's drive until one of his former players, Brent Crosswell, wrote an article about playing chess with him. Crosswell favoured carved sets and classical strategies. Barassi played with a cheap magnetic set and demanded another game immediately he lost. As a player, his most famous quality was his determination, jaw clenched, limbs flung wide. Ian Robertson remembers Barassi in his early days at Carlton initiating a table tennis competition and making it to the final with a dislocated arm in a sling. Then, in *Public Lives, Private Passions*, a book about the wives of famous men, I came across an interview with his second wife. Cherryl Barassi is of Jewish and Aboriginal descent. She is a strong and original thinker who lists Kafka as one of her influences and is seriously committed to the environment. She made living with Barassi sound comic—at home with what she calls the commander type, the sort who never says thank you or sorry. In her view, the legendary determination so feted in Barassi the footballer becomes the blindness which results in him bursting through a door of their Richmond hotel and breaking the ribs of the barman standing on the other side and then, two weeks later, doing it again. But when she attends one of his public appearances and hears him talk, she also sees a man who expresses his inner truth.

When I rang Barassi and told him my intention to write on the 1970 grand final, he exploded, 'Oh no, not again!'. He then said he'd meet me if I brought a piece of paper saying he could edit the final product. I didn't think that was a possibility. There was a short silence, then he agreed to meet in a St Kilda café the following morning. In Sydney, I had managed to ask him a couple of questions he hadn't been asked before. We had been discussing the future of Australian football, an indigenous game whose origins were a direct consequence of cultural isolation, in the world of global entertainment. Barassi has always believed the game's best defence is a national competition. But what if the game did become extinct, I asked—what would be lost? He said something about not being able to look his grandchildren in the eye and then fixed his gaze on a point near the ceiling, grin on his face. He looked like an angler wrestling with a mental fish. What would be lost, he eventually said, would be the best code of football in the world. He quoted, verbatim, a statement by an American baseball coach asked, in the 1890s, whether he thought American football would catch on. He thought not; it was too complex, a university game. But he had recently toured the world and seen an Australian game which in its highscoring and attacking play would be well-suited to the demands of the American public. Barassi's mother, who was of English and Irish descent, was the daughter of a mine manager, and one of Barassi's forays outside the world of football was as a venture capitalist, assessing the commercial worth of inventions. Barassi believes Australian football is a world-class sporting invention.

Barassi arrived at the café slightly late, looking energetic. After greeting me warmly, he sat down, fixed his pale green eyes on mine and again inquired as to my purpose. It helped that I had read the column he had written on the game, with the assistance of journalist Scot Palmer, a few days after the match. It was novel journalism, a stream of consciousness account of the match which gave a clear sense of the pace and temperature of his thinking. (*2.00 Too many well-wishers in the room. Bert, get the place cleared . . . Righto fellers into the coach's room. Come on Serge you're always last. The door slams shut and I face 20 expectant, tense young men . . .)* 'The first thing that has to be understood,' he said, leaning forward, 'is that I didn't invent handball—Len Smith did.' Barassi's father—the name is of northern Italian extraction—was a farm worker who played for Melbourne from 1936–40. When Ron Barassi senior was killed at the battle for Tobruk, his former Melbourne team-mate, Norm Smith, became Barassi's mentor. Together, as coach and captain, they made Melbourne great, sharing a total of six premierships. Len Smith, a lesser-known figure, coached Fitzroy and later Richmond in the '60s before heart illness prematurely terminated his career. A lot of ideas in football today—padded goalposts, free kick when the ball goes out on the full, restricted area around the centre bounce—are Len Smith's. With lowly Fitzroy, he also developed the philosophy of 'play-on' football—of seeking to move the ball as quickly as possible and thereby overcome the height advantage regularly held by other teams. The mechanism by which Smith sought to achieve this was handball.

Beyond that, however, it was true—he didn't have anything to say he hadn't said a dozen times before. He became more enthusiastic when I said I would attempt to talk to all the players. 'You have to talk to Bert Thornley,' he said with a gust of enthusiasm. 'He's a terrific bloke.' After Barassi, the second bestknown name associated with the 1970 grand final is Teddy Hopkins. Brought on at halftime, Hopkins, Carlton's 19th man, kicked four goals. This was before the days of the interchange bench; players taken from the field were not permitted to return. Bert Thornley is the person Hopkins replaced. 'Bert was having a horror day,' said Barassi, 'but who's to say he wouldn't have fired in the second half?' I sensed the decision might still trouble him. I had one last question. What did he remember of the day other than the game? 'Isn't that amazing?' he said. His big face was beaming and he was looking at the ceiling again. 'Not a bloody thing.'

See the Barrackers Are Shouting

Memory, its absence and distortions, are a large part of this story. Collingwood halfback flanker Max Richardson can remember virtually nothing of the 1970 grand final but he concludes that Collingwood must have had the Melbourne rooms because he recalls turning left at the top of the race. But then he claims to have no interest in the past. 'There are only two days,' he says with a sweeping gesture, 'today and tomorrow.' Perhaps another reason for his limited recall is that he was involved in later Collingwood disappointments. Max Richardson captained Collingwood in the 1977 grand final. On that occasion, Collingwood led a North Melbourne team coached by Barassi by 27 points at three-quarter time and were fortunate to escape with a draw through a last-minute goal by Twiggy Dunne.

In a period of public indignity and torment that lasted more than three decades, Twiggy Dunne's goal stood as Collingwood's sole, ambiguous moment of honour. When I first came to Melbourne in the mid'80s, Twiggy's giant size 12 boots, wrinkled and dipped in bronze, sat in a trophy case just inside the door at Victoria Park. To the right of the boots and sundry other items of memorabilia was a full-length portrait of Jock McHale, the brewery foreman who won nine premierships for Collingwood in a coaching career that spanned 38 years. The epitaph beneath the painting declares McHale's period of service to be a 'World Record'. When Colin Tully arrived at Collingwood from Bendigo in 1965, that's the attitude he recalls meeting—as far as anyone knew, or for that matter cared, Collingwood was the best football club in the world. The reverse image of this hubris is to be found in the sorry environment from which the club emerged.

When Collingwood Football Club was formed in the 1890s, the suburb was the worst slum in Melbourne and otherwise known for rats, foul air and illegal gambling. Big 'Jerker' Jenkin, Collingwood's first ruck in the 1970 grand final, has a magnificent photograph of Collingwood's 1901 team beneath his house. Collingwood finished second that year. Even from a distance of nearly 100 years, their capabilities are evident. Of roughly uniform height, the young men of the Collingwood Football Club are strong, supple athletes, broad of shoulder with clear, unforgiving eyes. On the end of the front row is a player something like Collingwood's 1990 premiership player Michael Gayfer—lean but knobbly, slightly bent back. 'He was still around the club when I arrived,' says Jerker, identifying him with a builder's broad forefinger. His name was Mr Rush and he was a wizened little fellah in a long coat. One day he said to Jerker, 'Football's a funny game. It can take you so high and bring you so low.'

Peter McKenna, like Twiggy Dunne, grew up in Melbourne's northern suburbs loathing Collingwood because everyone else barracked for them. Walking into Victoria Park, though, he 'smelt the history'. Famous faces stared down at him from every wall; many former greats were still around the club. Debonair Jack Regan, the great fullback who duelled at high altitudes with South Melbourne ace Bob Pratt, was club secretary. Colin Tully has fond memories of former captain and then chairman of selectors Harry Collier. When Tully's prodigious and usually reliable kicking went astray, Collier quietly took him aside and suggested he do two laps of Victoria Park bouncing the ball on the white line as he ran. One lap with the left hand, one with the right. 'The action's the same as dropping the ball onto your boot,' he said. The two laps done, the young player found his former assurance had returned. Tully thrived on a culture that was both egalitarian ('I never saw anyone turned away') and, in its own way, Spartan. Tully listened to the stories told by the trainers, men who had been at the club 30 or 40 years. They remembered the '30s when the Collingwood players wore their boots without stops during the week and with stops on Saturdays because they only had the one pair. Grimly tough, one of their number, Alby Pannam, was remembered for bypassing a handshake offered by a young opponent, instead grabbing and squeezing his testicles. Tully was also told no matter how badly he was hurt, a Collingwood player always got back to his feet. 'You didn't have to move around, but you did have to get up.' In one of his first games, against Hawthorn at Glenferrie Oval, Tully was knocked out running beneath a pack. The giant hands of Ray Gabelich restored him to his feet. 'You can stand up, Nugget,' he heard Gabelich say.

No club ever had truer colours. The Collingwood world view was a simple matter of black and white, Them and Us. Former rover Wayne Richardson shrewdly points out that the present AFL club which most resembles the old Collingwood is probably Adelaide. The grace of the Adelaide players is matched only by the gracelessness of its supporters. Imagine if Adelaide, not content with having conquered the competition in 1997–98, went on to win four premierships in a row because that's what Collingwood did between 1927 and 1930. Formed during one social depression, Collingwood peaked during the next. In the course of the '30s, a critical decade in the history of Australian sport that saw the emergence of iconic figures like Bradman, Phar Lap, Hubert Opperman and Walter Lindrum, the club won another two premierships to establish itself as the model of excellence in Australian football. In so doing, it acquired a ferocious following throughout the country. As a club, it cared for nobody's view but its own and in 1958, when it won its 13th premiership, it confidently established a league record over its principal rival, Melbourne, the toff's club from the top end of town.

Blond defender Peter Eakins came to Collingwood from West Australia at the beginning of 1970. When asked what playing for Collingwood meant, he replies, 'Reilly's ditch'. He can't remember who took him to pay his respects to the drain which ran a few hundred metres to one side of Victoria Park, but having seen it in all its septic glory he was told that if you were born on this side of the ditch you were Collingwood, if you were born on the other side you weren't. He was then driven to a local factory and introduced to the manager. Notwithstanding the fact that a large proportion of his employees did not speak English as their first language, the young player was bluntly informed that if Collingwood lost on Saturday the factory was not a happy place to be the following week and productivity suffered.

Twiggy Dunne was the first Collingwood player I interviewed. He still works at Collingwood and we met at Victoria Park. Anyone who saw the 1998 production of *The Club* at the Melbourne Theatre Company will be able to imagine the scene, the set for that particular production being a work of football art in its own right. The audience found themselves looking down on a playing field as green as a billiard table and, beyond it, the memory of an industrial landscape. Written by David Williamson, a Collingwood supporter, the play is a comic drama about a football club wedged in the past, unable to move. One of the catalysts for change is a young, effortlessly talented, dope-smoking recruit from Tasmania who has no apparent respect for the game's authorities or traditional ways. Twiggy Dunne went along to see the MTC production. I asked him what he thought. Not too far from the truth? He grinned and looked away. 'Not too far,' he said. When I look at Twiggy Dunne, I see the First AIF . . . a tall lean individual in a slouch hat, laconic, unaffected, standing with three mates and a donkey in front of the pyramids. Twiggy was one of Collingwood's best in the 1970 grand final. There's a photo of him with his hands on knees minutes after the siren has sounded, not once but a long tooting succession of them. He is being thanked by coach Bob Rose whom, it is said, has tears in his eyes. Twiggy's father was buried the day before and most of his team-mates attended the funeral; he's often wondered if that had an effect on them.

Twiggy is one of those who recalls supporters, some of them people he had never seen before, in the Collingwood rooms at halftime, victory written all over their loud, jubilant faces. The presence of these supporters—how many of them there were and exactly what they were doing—is still a sore point. Some of the Collingwood players remember them vividly; others not at all. Twiggy also believes fitness was a problem, not just in 1970 but over a period of years when Collingwood was regularly run down in finals. 'You have to have stamina to play those games,' he says. Not just fitness, but the ability to absorb blows. In the third quarter of the grand final, when Dunne was over the ball in a pack, Carlton back pocket Barry Gill hit him like a car. The bump, entirely fair and within the rules, threw his body 45 degrees to the angle it had been on. Then Vin Waite landed on him with his knees. Awarded a free kick, Twiggy got up, but he was limping; there was still more than a quarter to go. Early in his career, he says, training was much as it had been in Jock McHale's day; by the end, Collingwood were in the hands of Tom Hafey, a fitness fanatic. That's what intrigues Twiggy about Barassi. You never hear stories about him flogging sides, like Hafey did, keeping them out on the track until 7.30 at night, but they always ran on in finals, always had vigour at the end. 'He must have known something,' mused Twiggy. Twiggy was also the first person I spoke to about Johnny Greening.

'I was a good friend of John Greening's,' he said simply.

In 1970, Johnny Greening was Collingwood's 19-year-old prodigy. He had arrived at Victoria Park from Burnie, a tough industrial town on the northwest coast of Tasmania, at the age of fifteen. He grinned a lot, went to the races when he should have been at school and had not a single doubt about his ability. 'He had enormous confidence,' says Peter McKenna. 'He believed he could beat anyone—and he could.' One day, going to a match at Waverley in the team bus, he informed McKenna that he expected to pass Ted Whitten's record for the most number of VFL games played, much as if he were commenting on the weather. In 1972, with half a Brownlow in his pocket, his brilliant career was effectively ended when he was hit behind the play against St Kilda at Moorabbin. Unconscious and bleeding from the mouth, there was a fear he would die on the ground. Eventually, Johnny Greening did return to the game. Twice—Twiggy is deliberate about the number—he thought Greening was back to what he had been before, a player of seemingly unlimited ability with the confidence to match; but it wasn't to be.

Twiggy didn't have a lot more to say, but before I left Victoria Park he took me into the boardroom with its felt-green walls, polished wood and memorabilia. One item is an ornate certificate given to a player leaving for Tasmania in the early years of the century; given under the seal of the Collingwood Football Club, it attests to his manly behaviour. That's what club president Tom Sherrin told the players in the rooms after the 1970 grand final. They would face the defeat like men.

We are the Navy Blues

Geographically, Carlton is only two suburbs away from Collingwood but in cultures the two clubs are far apart. In 1970, Collingwood still stood by its tradition, a potent combination of rigid pride and 19th century trade unionism fuelled by the rage of the industrial underclass. By contrast, Carlton was well along the road to reinventing itself as a middle-class club. In the early '60s, Carlton had been beset by internal difficulties. The battling Blues, as they were called, did most of their fighting off the field. The club hadn't won a premiership since 1947, and in 1964 it finished tenth, its lowest ever position. The next year, it was taken over by businessman and former dentist George Harris. Even Harris's friends describe him as arrogant. Other descriptions include forceful, energetic and dictatorial. The ambit of his intentions was immediately apparent: he succeeded in luring to Carlton the captain of the Melbourne Football Club and heir apparent to coach Norm Smith, Ron Barassi.

What needs to be understood is the deeply

conservative nature of Australian society at that time. Barry Humphries described Australia around this time as 'an exotic lump of the Home Counties that had somehow slipped its moorings and drifted into Southeast Asia'. In the 1966 census, 3 million of Victoria's population of 3.2 million were listed as British. For the purposes of the Act the word British was also taken to mean Irish, but even more remarkably the definition of British included (a) those born inside Australia and (b) those born outside Australia. As far as the census was concerned, Aboriginal people simply didn't count. The conservative government of Sir Robert Menzies had been in power federally since 1949 and few people saw significance in the fact that it had begun sending 'military advisers' to South Vietnam. In Victoria, Sir Henry Bolte's conservative government had recently hung a man. Australia was a colonial power, with control over New Guinea, and the country's leading magazine, *The Bulletin*, a relic of 1890s nationalist radicalism, had taken the slogan 'Australia for the White Man' from its banner only three years earlier. The only visible ethnic groups were Greeks and Italians, and the ring of censorship around the country excluded not only *Lady Chatterley's Lover*, but also *Peyton Place* and Ian Fleming's *The Spy Who Loved Me*. Melbourne was a uniform, suburban society, its sense of diversity limited to the division between Catholic and Protestant. In Sydney, the same forces were shaping the political consciousness of an ambitious, unimaginative young conservative named John Howard, but Melbourne did have a sizable kink in its character, a winter passion which amounted to a sort of folk opera. It was football and Barassi's action amounted to a revolution in its values. A player of his commanding stature was declaring that his pre-eminent belief was not loyalty to the club or, as was said in those days, to the guernsey.

Within a decade, only traditionalists would talk in those terms; those at the cutting edge, like Barassi, would speak instead of professionalism. In 1964, however, Barassi saw Carlton's offer as representing the chance for him to stand or fall on his own efforts. He had seen the confusion and ill feeling generated by the passover of the coaching mantle to Smith from his predecessor at Melbourne, Checker Hughes. The pair had ended up having a public dispute on the boundary line during a game. Having satisfied himself that Carlton was soundly administered—what he calls the first prerequisite for success—Barassi accepted the club's offer. His aim, he said, was to mould the perfect team. 'No-one has achieved this yet,' he said at the time, 'but if you aim high enough, I think you have a better chance of success'.

By establishing order and winning Barassi from Melbourne, George Harris—in the words of John Nicholls—created the conditions for the Carlton Football Club 'to be reborn'. When John Nicholls (also known as Big Nick) speaks, you listen. There are several good reasons for this. One is that he doesn't speak often, at least not in public. The second is that he is a football legend. True, the word legend is battered and exhausted from overuse, but I advance the following testimony in support of its application in this case. Most people list Alex Jesaulenko as one of the all-time greats. He says Nicholls is the best player he has seen or played with. Why? 'Because he could have two marks and four kicks and still win a game.' Former Collingwood captain Des Tuddenham is not alone, even among former Collingwood players, in saying Nicholls has the best football brain of anyone he has met. For nearly two decades, Nicholls influenced matches, indeed seasons, with the silent knowingness of his play. Bert Thornley says he never heard Nicholls raise his voice. Syd Jackson calls him the General and says he could tell you what to do with a glance. Even the umpires talked about his chilling stare. As a player, Big Nick was a ruckman of only moderate height who combined bulk with craft and surprising agility, palming with his left hand while reserving his right to dispense justice to those who incurred his wrath.

Len Thompson played his first game for Collingwood in the 1965 preliminary final and was immediately recognised as embodying that most devastating double, a giant talent in a giant frame. The following year, Nicholls' right fist caught the teenage ruckman on the jaw at a boundary throw-in, knocking him out. Not surprisingly, there are two versions of the story. As Thompson tells the tale, and he is an excellent football anecdotalist, he took the opportunity presented by the 1971 interstate trip to Perth to ask Nicholls, then his Victorian captain, why he had hit him. 'You made a mistake that day, Thommo,' Thompson has the big man replying. 'You started to beat me.' Thompson sees it as an act of respect; Nicholls had spotted his potential. 'The great players see what has to be done to make things happen—or not happen,' he says. The other version of the incident comes from Carlton rover, Adrian 'Gags' Gallagher. Gallagher owns the Royston Hotel in Richmond, a nicotine-stained establishment with lots of old men with wrinkled faces and fags hanging from their bottom lips standing around the bar and a few yellowing items of football memorabilia randomly arranged on the walls. Someone has drawn on a photograph of Barassi in his North Melbourne days and there seems to be no clear distinction between the barmen and the patrons as they move from one side of the counter to the other. All this is familiar to me, and when Gags appears I have the feeling of having met him in a previous life, a pub somewhere on the west coast of Ireland. Our short chat lasts several hours. He is a small grey-haired man with a grin that keeps working to the front of his face even when he is being serious. Gallagher had played in junior representative teams with Thompson. Seeing Big Nick bleeding from a cut beneath his eye, he attempted to warn Thompson and received a reply something like, 'Get out of the way you little runt or I'll give you one as well.' (Lee Adamson remembers Thompson being a 'physically aggressive player' in junior footy). Gallagher's account ends with Thompson being carried from the field, big legs dangling over the end of the wire stretcher. Thompson went on to win many major honours, including five Copeland trophies (Collingwood's best and fairest) and a Brownlow medal, but coach Bob Rose believes the incident had an inhibiting effect on his career.

Some compare Big Nick's presence on a football field with Tony Lockett's—a combination of power and grace, coloured by a sense of menace—but in addition to being a football legend Big Nick is also a Carlton legend. This may seem like a non-distinction but there is a point to be made. To enter conversation with Big Nick via the doorway of football is to meet someone whose every thought is directed towards the interests of his club. When Jackson and Thornley arrived at Carlton in 1967 from West Australia, they immediately noted how Nicholls silently moved to include them, attending a barbecue at their house. Barassi was always grateful for the way Nicholls stepped aside as leader when he came across from Melbourne. As far as the other Carlton players were concerned, a significant moment in Barassi's early coaching career was when he publicly chastised Nicholls for knocking the ball on and not marking, and Nicholls accepted the criticism. Everyone accepted Big Nick's authority; Big Nick accepted Barassi's. According to Adrian Gallagher, Carlton's chain of command went all the way down. If you broke what Gallagher calls the team ethic, the person you answered to was Nicholls' Italian mate, Sergio Silvagni. Robert Walls has a memory of Serge at a halftime break with his hands round Brent Crosswell's throat. Its officer in the rear was Goold, a Victorian centre halfback who had gone within a few votes of winning a Brownlow medal. Gallagher, who won Carlton's best and fairest in 1970, defends the system. 'Everyone has to keep the team rules,' he said. Doesn't that inhibit the most talented players? 'No. When you get into a situation where everything's equal like a grand final, it's then set up for the best players to give that little bit more.'

The new Carlton was unambiguously about ambition and success. Eighteen-year-old Phil Pinnell was deeply impressed by the interest George Harris took in his education while 20-year-old David McKay observed that reserves players were second-class citizens. Even a place in the seniors did not assure you of respect; that came if and when you played well in finals. Barassi's brand of corporate conservatism extended to the personal appearance of his players—beards were banned, the length of hair and sideburns strictly regulated. On the training track, he demanded total commitment. He had a saying: 'Training doesn't make perfect—perfect training makes perfect.' Winning, says Neil Chandler, Carlton's 19th man in 1970, is a matter of psyche. Chandler says Barassi made training so unremittingly intense, the games themselves were sometimes easier. He also taught that games were often won and lost in the last five minutes. Under Barassi, Nicholls says Carlton developed the ability to win from behind, but he was assisted in his endeavours by Harris's administration. When he arrived, the club had possessed a core of capable players; in the seasons that followed, Carlton complemented them with a series of exceptional recruits. In '67, Alex Jesaulenko, born in Yugoslavia of Ukranian parents, was persuaded to come down from Canberra. Jesaulenko, who hadn't played the game until he was 14, says now he had no idea what he was getting himself into. The following year, Carlton secured Crosswell and Jackson. Jackson, the only Aboriginal player in the league during his career, amazed his new team-mates by kicking boomerang goals from the pockets. No-one had seen the like of him: fast, squarely built, every movement charged with skill and a scarcely subdued volatility. At the same time, the club had the good fortune to have a quality centre half-forward emerge from its junior ranks in Robert Walls. Gradually, the pattern for several decades of success was established, a combination of navy blue stability with strands of individual brilliance.

Carlton's teams had always been tough and hard to beat, but now they acquired an additional characteristic. In Jesaulenko's words, 'they were good when they were cocky.'

Initially, Big Nick was no more interested in discussing the 1970 grand final than Barassi had been. Eventually, however, having agreed to do so, he instructed me to be outside the publishing firm where he works at 8.15 the following morning. He then revised our appointment to 8.05 and insisted on giving me a detailed explanation on how to find the place. I confess to having been mildly apprehensive about our meeting. Big Nick is a man of mystery; an aura of respect surrounds his name in the football world yet little is known about him. An anonymous writer once observed that he had 'an inner reserve which forbade familiarity'. We had spoken once before—in 1987—when I was writing an article on the then Carlton captain, Stephen Kernahan, who was being described as the most valuable footballer in Australia. He probably was, but the term angered Nick. 'That's the sort of nonsense you people in the media think up,' he said. He detailed two instances of mistakes Kernahan had made in recent games, one of which resulted in Carlton 'handing over' the ball. 'You never hand over the ball,' he said. At the time, I had wondered at the vehemence of his response. Now, however, he met me with a handshake and a grave look, then suggested we sit outside in his car. In his 60th year, Big Nick has the manner of a retired police superintendent, measured and earnest.

The first thing Nicholls told me was that 1970 was not Carlton's year. Barassi was the best coach he had worked with, but by 1970 his methods were wearing thin. (Phil Pinnell describes Barassi as 'the best and the worst thing' to have happened to his football career. 'In the end, I was so scared of making a mistake I didn't do anything)'. Carlton had peaked in 1969, Nicholls said, but had lost that year's grand final to Richmond. Furthermore, he informed me, if either Richmond or Hawthorn had been 44 points up at halftime in the 1970 grand final, Carlton would not have won. What do you need to win a grand final, I asked. 'Luck,' he said squarely. 'If the two teams are evenly matched, you have to have luck.' Then he added, 'And you have to have a steely resolve to stick to a game plan.' Game plan is part of what this story's about and it's not that Collingwood didn't have one. They had the slickest in the business. It revolved around delivering the ball to full-forward Peter McKenna by the quickest means possible, usually passes from the flying feet of centreman Barry Price and rover Wayne Richardson. Relative to the other great full-forwards of the day, McKenna lacked strength in the air, but he led like a hare and kicked drop punts of unerring accuracy. In three years—'70, '71, '72—McKenna kicked 407 goals and saw off a succession of brutally hard defenders, not least Carlton's Wes Lofts. Collingwood coach Bobby Rose says McKenna never fought back when hit. 'People thought it was a weakness, but they were wrong. He just kept kicking goals.' Big Nick's response to the threat posed by McKenna was to 'pressure' Richardson and Price—that is, to break down Collingwood's game by interrupting McKenna's supply of the ball. Barassi's response was to try and introduce a system of play which denied them the advantage of their height.

Nicholls said Collingwood had been Carlton's natural foe for as long as he could remember. For many years, in terms of membership, they had been Melbourne's two biggest clubs. Barassi had brought another dimension to that rivalry. At Melbourne in the '50s and '60s, Barassi had met Collingwood's reputation for hardness head on. He believed 'the Colliwobbles' did exist—that is, that the image and substance of the famous club were two different things—while George Harris brought another energetic response to the issue. He was openly contemptuous of Collingwood supporters and deeply resentful of the fact that he was invariably sat among them when Carlton played at Victoria Park.

One who thrilled to the possibilities of the new regime at Carlton was John Goold, full name John Crosbie Goold, great grandnephew of the first Catholic Archbishop of Melbourne. One of the characters of the postwar game, Goold played football like a man making a late dash for a role in *The Three Musketeers*, galloping off the halfback line, black curls flying, ball held rakishly in one long hand, his gait emphasised by the white ankle straps he wore at the base of his navy blue socks. Nowadays he is the marketing director of the Fresh Cheese Company of Australia and the Master of Hounds for the Ellerslie hunt, but back then Goold worked in women's lingerie, wore stockings at training and was known in the popular press as 'Ragsy'. A former scholar at Melbourne Grammar, people mistook Goold for a fop when, in fact, he revelled in the re-invention of the club initiated by Harris and Barassi. Football, to John Crosbie Goold, is about values, about an ethic of service. The club with the worthiest values, he believes, usually wins. His description of the Collingwood Football Club in 1970 is indulgent and self-satisfied. But if Carlton by this time was supremely assured of its ethic, it also had within its ranks a dissenter, a young recruit from Tasmania who was both part of football culture and outside it, who was familiar with the effects of marijuana but not much inclined to the drug because he found it nullified some part of his brilliant, hyperactive self.

Crosswell (1)

Ron Barassi's account of Brent Crosswell's career begins with him as a student at Scotch College in Launceston. A former Carlton player in that town had alerted the club to his talent. Accordingly, in 1967, on one of his regular visits to Tasmania to visit his mother, Barassi dropped in to see the 17-year-old and take him for 'a kick and catch'. So impressed was the coach by what he saw, he rang Carlton and said, 'Get the red carpet out for this boy.' Barassi enjoys floating the idea that a key person in Carlton getting Brent—he usually calls him Brent—was that foundation stone of Australian conservative politics, Sir Robert Menzies. Carlton had duly brought Crosswell and his parents to Melbourne for a match at Princes Park (now Optus Oval) which, as Barassi recalls, the Blues must have won because George Harris opened the drinks cupboard in the committee room, something he never did when they lost. Barassi arrived to find Menzies exercising his renowned charm and skills as an advocate on the Crosswell family. 'I've always thought Bob Menzies had something to do with bringing Brent to

Carlton,' he says. 'And within a couple of years, he (Crosswell) was a university-educated communist.' He laughs at that idea; really laughs.

A number of Carlton people from that period describe Crosswell in similar terms—as a communist or a perennial university student which, in those days, amounted to much the same thing. This surprises John Goold. 'Not everyone at Carlton appreciated Brent's intellect,' he says. 'He did something that was very unusual for the time—he asked questions.' 'From the moment he arrived,' says Alex Jesaulenko of Crosswell, 'he had a lot to say.' Jesaulenko's early memory is of a young man pumping iron and looking at himself in mirrors. 'He was a character, and every football club needs characters.' No-one seems to have doubted Crosswell had the prerequisites to become a great player. During his schooldays, he had been a champion high jumper and it had also been suggested by former English Test cricketer Frank Tyson that he might one day play cricket for Australia. Barassi believed Crosswell's physique was just about ideal for an Australian footballer and, according to wingman Gary Crane, the only flaw in his game was that he sometimes had difficulty gathering the ball when it was directly beneath him, at his feet. With Jesaulenko, Crosswell was the quickest Carlton player over ten metres; over 20 metres, according to Nicholls, Crosswell won by five. Crosswell also met Jesaulenko's measure of a great player—he had the capacity to alter the pattern of a match. In 1968, Carlton won its first premiership under Barassi and its first in 21 years. Playing in the centre with an injured shoulder, 18-year-old Crosswell was, in Barassi's view, one of Carlton's best.

Unfortunately, success in sporting terms had never been quite enough for Crosswell. A former schoolmate recalled seeing him amuse himself by pretending to drown when he was leading the field in a private school swimming carnival, one hand waving dolefully above the water as he sank towards the bottom like the upturned hull of the *Titanic*. David McKay remembers the night when Crosswell, having tired of successive victories in the sprints, announced that he would race the rest of the squad running backwards. 'And he won!' says McKay. 'Give me a grey day at the Western Oval,' Crosswell once declared, 'and I wasn't worth a cracker. Give me 100 000 people at the MCG and I was Hercules.' It was true; he had twin instincts. He wasn't a mere player; he was also a performer, one who expanded to the scale of the occasion. With time, he even acquired a stage name. It originated in the fact that he never remembered anyone else's name and called everyone Tiger. Soon enough, the name rebounded and became his own—Tiger Crosswell. A Tasmanian Tiger, I have always fancied, much discussed but little known and, like the old thylacine, calculating in his appearances. Some years later, when the pair were at North Melbourne, 'Gags' Gallagher suggested to Crosswell in a humorous moment that he approach the committee and advise them that as he was a big occasion player he start the season at the halfway mark and build up for the finals. To the considerable surprise of both Gallagher and the committee, he did so.

Crosswell not only had an innate sense of theatre, he had a wit and vocabulary to match. One can imagine him on the set of *Vanity Fair*, magnificent in the uniform of a young officer, trading badinage with the beautiful

Becky Sharp in a corner. Peter McKenna, who roomed with Crosswell on an interstate trip to Hobart, returned uncertain whether he was brilliant or crazy. 'But I do know he was terrific company.' McKenna describes Crosswell as 'the most different' person he met in football. Phil Pinnell, who admired Crosswell, agrees and adds, 'Different in every way.' Kevin Hall's view is that the two people at Carlton who weren't intimidated by Barassi were Crosswell, 'because he had too many words', and Gallagher, because no-one or nothing could wipe the grin off his face. In a 1980 interview, by which time Crosswell had participated in Barassi's inglorious return to the Melbourne Football Club, the player said: 'I certainly never believed that football performed the sorts of services to society that Barassi and the committee men at Carlton argued . . . that people involved in physical contact sports have got the edge on someone who isn't, they've been blooded, they're more reliable, they've got the inner resources, they're able to extend themselves.' There was reason in what he said—both Barassi and George Harris would experience humiliating public lows in their business careers—but the difference between player and coach went beyond their social and political philosophies.

Len Thompson recalls a day at Victoria Park when he had been detailed to follow Nicholls who had stationed his light-moving bulk in one forward pocket. Crosswell was in the other. Carlton was losing. As Thompson tells the story (Crosswell says he has no memory of it), the runner arrived panting at Crosswell's side. 'Tiger,' he said, 'the coach says we need a lift—go on the ball.' 'Tell the coach to get fucked,' replied the young player. The runner, momentarily taken aback, retorted, 'I bring the messages out. I don't take them back.' Back to the bench he trotted, returning like a steel-tipped boomerang seconds later to repeat the coach's demand. The young player repeated his. As the runner departed, Big Nick spoke from the forward pocket: 'Brent, go on the ball.' He did, and for 20 minutes, in the Collingwood ruckman's view, he succeeds in altering the balance of play. Thompson recalls, in particular, two fine marks. When he then returned to the pocket, the runner was immediately out again. Same message. Why stop? Barassi never stopped—that was the quality, above all others, which distinguished him as a player. Even now, big mouth twisting with emphasis, Barassi says, 'Brent Crosswell could have been one of the greatest *ever*.'

The tortured relationship between the legendary coach and his temperamental star provided more than a decade of headlines. Crosswell claims that if he came in at halftime and saw that Barassi was in one of his rages, he would hide in the toilets. Gallagher says he often joined him and that Bert Thornley's mistake in the 1970 grand final was not getting in there quickly enough. But when asked if Crosswell was a serious footballer, John Goold replies, 'My oath.' Under crossexamination, Goold does admit that Barassi's rigid code of discipline did frustrate the more gifted players and their ability 'to express themselves'. The 1970 grand final is Ron Barassi's finest hour. Best on ground in the match was Brent Crosswell. When I asked Crosswell about the myth of the modern game and Barassi's part in it, he replied, 'If Barassi gave an instruction at halftime to handball at all costs, I didn't hear it.' Then, with impeccable timing, 'Perhaps I was in the toilet.'

Bobby Rose

Bobby Rose's speech is plain and untutored, his manner courteous. The face is red and slightly battered, but he meets me with a bright, determined grin. 'You have to be strong,' he said, when I asked him his philosophy. 'You have to be positive. If you sit down in the corner and let things overwhelm you, they will.' In 1972, his son, Robert, was rendered paraplegic by a car accident at a time when he was on the verge of playing Test cricket for Australia. The day we met, Robert Rose was again gravely ill following postoperative complications. Adversity has been Bobby Rose's lifelong companion. I first observed him in 1985 when he returned to Collingwood as coach after the New Magpies' administration had taken the club to the edge of bankruptcy. In his first game back, Collingwood lost to North Melbourne; afterwards, Rose said young people today accept defeat too easily. He never has. 'I always wanted to have another go,' he says, grinning and loosely swinging a right hand in the memory of a punch. Barassi's grin is a man glimpsing new horizons; Rose's is like fierce sunshine after heavy rain.

A child of the Depression, Rose grew up in the Mallee during a period of prolonged drought when most of the district's men were away at war. When his father fell ill, he supported the family—or, as he says, kept his brothers in shoes—with the purses he made as a professional boxer. He was scarcely sixteen when, visiting Melbourne for a bout at Festival Hall, he accepted an invitation to train at Victoria Park. The greenness of the grass dazzled him. Few ovals in the Mallee had grass; players wore leather bars across their boots instead of stops to give them a grip in the red dirt. His gear had holes in it, something Lou Richards never let him forget, but his most potent memory of that first night was the figure of the Collingwood coach, Jock McHale. For a youth who had prematurely accepted the responsibilities of manhood, McHale must have represented the pinnacle of male achievement. When Collingwood lost, McHale didn't speak; Rose says he didn't have to. He stood at the top of the race and each player, in passing him, would have to look into his pale blue eyes. As a player, Bobby Rose would do anything rather than disappoint Jock McHale.

He was seventeen when he started playing for Collingwood. He remembers the day the club entered his soul, a cold, wet Saturday. Arriving early at Victoria Park, he found supporters already there, some with coverings, some without, and realised these were people for whom Collingwood was the best and perhaps only thing in their lives. Collingwood was a larger version of family. The bond was only deepened by the fact that four of his brothers also played there and, in the 1970 grand final, the Collingwood runner was his brother

Colin. In ten years as a player, Rose won the Copeland trophy four times including 1953, a premiership year. Unfortunately, his playing days preceded television, but Barry Price says there are old-timers at Collingwood who see parallels in style between Rose and Nathan Buckley. Buckley is one of the consummate skill players of his generation. Rose was similarly blessed but Barassi adds to the picture, crediting Rose with genuine toughness in addition to balance, coordination and wonderful kicking skills. When Barry Price arrived at Victoria Park in 1965 from Ararat, he was led to understand that Bobby Rose was the greatest footballer Collingwood had ever produced.

Price, the sportsmaster at Melbourne's Scotch College, combines a shy grin with a schoolmaster 's quiet authority. Even so, one could easily miss his depth of feeling. Price was widely respected by his team-mates, even the wild ones like Lee Adamson who says Price was 'a ball player who took no nonsense'. He had to be both quick and brave; opponents like Big Nick came looking for him with arms swung high or the weight of their knees at the bottom of a pack. Price admired Rose and the respect was soon mutual, Rose suggesting he experiment with drop punts, instead of the old stab pass, as a means of delivering the ball quickly and accurately. By 1969, when Price won the Copeland trophy, he had displaced Colin Tully as Collingwood's centreman. Having met by the Scotch College oval, we shift to Price's office. He handles a footy as we speak, moving it about in his hands, instinctively feeling its possibilities. Price believes Australian football is a great game and has worked to re-establish it within the the culture of his school. Scotch

College now has an 1858 Club, that being the year of the first recorded game which was played between Scotch and Melbourne Grammer on the slope above the MCG. Every two years, the school also sends an underage team to the Northern Territory to play an Aboriginal or Tiwi Island side.

Price disagrees with the perception that Bob Rose lacked innovation as a coach. Collingwood had won its last premiership, in 1958, by catching Melbourne on a wet track and subduing them with force. Ruckman Hooker Harrison had harassed and nullified Barassi while Murray Weideman held fort at centre half-forward. Price says Rose substantially altered the culture of the club, building a team around skill, speed and height, employing tall wingmen, Greening and Dean, and playing three ruckmen—Thompson, Jerker Jenkin and Big Bob Heard. This enabled Collingwood to implement what was called an umbrella defence, the tall players dropping back and outmarking opposition forwards. The team was, however, conventional in its structure. It had two other distinguishing characteristics. The first was its youth—at 27, Des Tuddenham was its oldest player. The second was that most of the players had barracked for Collingwood as kids. They more or less had to, as part of the Collingwood tradition was that it didn't pay for recruits. As far as the club was concerned, the reward for the individual lay in being chosen to represent it.

In 1964, Rose's first year as coach, Collingwood went within four points of winning the premiership. In 1966, they lost to St Kilda by a point. To all outward appearances, neither defeat caused the club's Olympian self-belief to waver, but in fact there was a doubter—

Bobby Rose. He nurtured deep anxieties about Collingwood. During the years when he was coaching at Wangaratta, he had come to realise how out of date the club's recruiting policy was. He also saw that its glory days were a lot further in the past than most people realised—Collingwood had won only two premierships since the '30s. Rose believed Collingwood desperately needed to win another if it was to retain its place at the forefront of the league. Over a period of six years, through industry and the persuasive power of his own good name, Rose built a team which, by 1970, he believed was Collingwood's best since World War 2. He said as much publicly, and of course the Collingwood fans believed him. Rose's team were young, swift and skilful. They surged in '69 but weren't accomplished enough to carry it off in the finals. Price says the players 'set themselves' for 1970. Not only would a premiership avenge Rose's two grand final defeats, many believed that in players like McKenna, Price, Thompson and the Richardsons, Collingwood had the ingredients to establish an era of supremacy. They were fortified by the fact that Collingwood finished the 1970 roster season on top of the league ladder with 18 wins and four losses, two games ahead of Carlton but with a vastly superior percentage (136 to 112), having kicked a succession of record scores in the course of the year. In Round 8, at Waverley, Collingwood defeated Carlton by 23 points; then, in the second-last round of the season, Collingwood had thumped its old foe by 77 points at Victoria Park.

Rose was popular with his players. Barry Price says that as a coach he spoke plain truths if required but basically sought to create a climate in which the young talents he had assembled could develop into more skilful and assured versions of themselves. He encouraged flair. In this, he was more liberal than Barassi, the man about to modernise the game.

The Teams

Ted Hopkins calls Carlton 'a crossroads club'. The inner-city suburb from which it arose was constructed in the 1890s for the Melbourne bourgeoisie, a rank of society which found its numbers drastically diminished by the depression of that decade and then relocated with the introduction of the electric tram system. The next phase of the suburb's history was as a home for successive waves of immigrants, beginning with Jews fleeing the pogroms of Eastern Europe in the late 19th century, and, 50 years later, southern Europeans, particularly Italians, seeking a new and better world. At the same time, the proximity of the Carlton ground to the University of Melbourne gave the club a body of support in the professional classes. Thus, in addition to being the club of new money with connections to the Liberal Party, Carlton was also the 'wog' club with supporters such as playwright Jack Hibberd and historian Manning Clark.

David McKay's career since leaving football has taken him as far afield as Kyrgyzstan, where he went in the early '90s to help the former Soviet republic set up an employment service, but, in 1970, he was a reserved farmer's son from Newlyn with a wry appreciation of human nature. He enjoyed going to training at Carlton as much as, if not more than, the matches. Such a diversity of people, not only around the club but in the team. McKay recalls the night at training he made an error in executing a pass. Barassi snapped at him, 'Twenty push-ups for that error, McKay.' Then, looking past McKay, the coach added, 'And you can do 20, Bruce Doull, for wandering round like a lost soul.' Bruce Doull is the Leunig man who became a champion footballer. He rarely, if ever, spoke. Crosswell once peered deeply into his pale blue eyes and concluded that Bruce Doull was a feeling. In the 1970 grand final, then aged 20, Doull was Carlton's reserve.

Unofficial Carlton historian Ian Collins once said that for as long as he could remember Carlton believed a cross-section of personality types was good for a team. Imagine a single team containing Goold and Crosswell, the only Aboriginal player of the day in Jackson, Gags Gallagher, his stuttering, humorously inclined mate from Tassie, big Percy Jones, Alex Jesaulenko, a club legend like Nicholls and his Italian offsider, Sergio Silvagni. I began to wonder: was it a trick of perception or was it correct to say that the Collingwood players seemed quieter and more modest —more uniform— than their Carlton counterparts? Or was that because I was viewing the Collingwood players from the common dismal perspective of defeat? Sooner or later, I met the loss in every one of them.

As far as Len Thompson is concerned, 1970 is one of a spectrum of Collingwood grand final defeats, beginning in '65 and ending in '77. Before the 1977 grand final, he was so het up by the attitude of some of his younger team-mates he bit the head off a customer in the pub he was managing. His then wife told him to take a few days off. She pointed out that younger members of the team couldn't be expected to take the game as seriously as he did. You only learn from experience, she said. I don't remember Len Thompson ever playing badly in a grand final; he just didn't win one for the club. Thompson's misfortune was to intersect with the club of destiny just as it was beginning to look for individual saviours. A sense of disappointment surrounds his pink face like a high altitude cloud. Three months after we spoke, his decision to sell his football memorabilia, including his Brownlow medal, was made public.

McKenna was more circumspect, perhaps because he works in the media, but I was left in no doubt that the defeat still lived in him. With his Beatles haircut and affable demeanour, McKenna had been the most popular Collingwood player of his day, bringing a new generation of supporters to Victoria Park. He admits feeling that he failed the supporters. 'I think most Collingwood players of that time do.'

Centre halfback Ted Potter lives in Orbost where he teaches physical and outdoor education. Jerker Jenkin, a Friar Tuck of a footballer, had described Potter to me as 'a skinny, bearded recluse'. When I put this to Potter he laughed in a gentle, good-natured way and said the beard had gone and he was heavier than he was in his playing days. Potter was also highly regarded by his team-mates. Each week, in Jerker Jenkin's words, he got 'a bastard of a job'; it was an era of great forwards and each Saturday Potter had to check one of them. Rose says Potter is one of the players from that era that would hold his own in the modern game. Although an ungainly kick, he was athletic and rigidly self-disciplined. Rose calls him a 'stopper '. The coach remembers Potter taking Darrell Baldock, Royce Hart and Jesaulenko in successive weeks and breaking even. 'At Collingwood,' says Thompson, 'we never saw Baldock play a good game because of Potter.' Alex Jesaulenko says three goals on Ted Potter was a good day's work. Unfortunately, in the 1970 grand final, Carlton's young giraffe of a centre half-forward, Robert Walls, got away from him, tearing open the Collingwood defence in the second half with fierce, inspired, angular runs. The effect of his play was that Potter was forever in pursuit of him and he cramped well before the end of the match but had to be left on the field.

Potter never complained. Thompson remembers him wheezing with asthma during a halftime break. Each week, on the football field, Potter gave everything for the team because football was a team game, but if he hadn't been playing football he would have been snow skiing. He was a teetotaller not much given to socialising, preferring to spend time in the bush, walking, fishing, looking for gems. His housemates, Tully and Wayne Richardson, would wake in the night to the grinding sound of his gem cleaner. In the end, Potter gave league football away at the age of 26. He admits the anxiety, the weight of responsibility, got to him. Potter's father had died when he was a boy, and he had been brought up, in country Victoria at Rutherglen, by his mother. She told him that when you played sport you did your best and when it was over, it was over. That's what bothers Ted Potter about the 1970 grand final—it's not over.

He doesn't know how many times he's thought about Jesaulenko's famous mark and how easily he could have prevented it by moving across and blocking his path. 'I thought Jerker was big enough,' he says. I ask Potter if he's glad he played league football. There's a pause. It's as if he is slightly surprised that anyone other than himself has ever had the thought. 'I have asked myself that question,' he says.

When I rang Terry Waters, Collingwood's captain on the day, he immediately asked, 'Is it [the article] going to be negative?' That would depend on what I was told, I said, but by now I was certainly interested in the consequences of the defeat. 'The consequences are not great,' Waters replied elegantly. 'It's just that they keep returning to haunt you.' Formerly an industrial chemist, Waters is now a principal in a transport business. Polished and articulate in manner, he has the sort of head one sees on busts of Roman governors. John Goold describes Waters as 'a good fellow'. As a player, he was renowned for his high marking—whatever the weather or the state of the game, Waters went for them. Some said too often, but he also took marks of a sort that No-one else could or did. He had been Collingwood's best player in the 1966 grand final and an All-Australian. He, too, implied the 1970 final kept reappearing in his mind, demanding to be replayed. 'Every time you think about it, you kick yourself for an incident here or an incident there that might have had some influence on the game.' He swayed as he said it, like a cup of tea being stirred by an invisible spoon.

Then, when I was at risk of lapsing into generalisations about the Collingwood team, I met Des

Tuddenham. It wasn't easy to do. These days, Tuddy's in demolition. He makes it sound like he's knocking down half Melbourne and, even if he's not, he will if he gets the chance. I'd ring him on his mobile, he'd say he was too busy and tell me to ring back the following day. We'd agree on an hour. When I rang back, I'd be met by the sound of din and commotion. 'Talk to you now?' a voice would shout. 'I can't talk. I've got three trucks here.' Some days he called me Merton. 'Ring me back tomorrow, Merton.' Merton did. We finally arranged to meet at his apartment in South Melbourne on the night of the Australian Open tennis final between Thomas Enquist and Kafelnikov. Tuddy had gone. Not much of a match, we agreed; no real engagement, two professionals passing one another at a polite distance.

Although each of the Collingwood players had said something memorable to me about Tuddenham, usually with a grin, nothing had prepared me for the experience of actually meeting him. He was much smaller than I expected, a red brick of a man with a limp like a soldier wounded in war. It's a football injury. Classical music was flooding through the house. His mother had a fine singing voice and played the piano for an hour each evening. He wishes now he had listened more often. He opened a bottle of fine white wine and, when it was empty, he opened another. Tuddenham's nature has brought him its share of troubles, but one of his impulses is generosity. He's helping a former Collingwood player down on his luck; furthermore, he's dirty on another old team-mate who could help and hasn't. Meeting Des Tuddenham after meeting the other members of Collingwood's 1970 team is like driving past a set of guide posts and suddenly finding yourself passing through the Arc de Triomphe, a giant structure with a black hole at its centre. The hole in Tuddenham's case is not an absence of thought or feeling—many of his judgments about the game and those who have played it are surprisingly subtle and, no less than Crosswell (whom he admired), he had an instinct for the theatre of the game. No, in Des Tuddenham's case, to an extent that seems unnatural, the black hole is a total absence of fear. Tuddenham is a twin. He says his brother Basil had more talent than he did as a footballer but was a worrier. Perhaps Basil got Des's nerve ends as well as his own. In the blackness of their absence is a laugh like a blazing red fire.

Of Irish Ballarat stock, Tuddenham had arrived at Collingwood in 1963 and played with the remnants of the '58 side. Murray Weideman, Tarzan in a black and white guernsey, was his hero. Tuddy says Bob Rose's insistence on no drinking after Tuesday night saw Weideman leave the club prematurely. 'We wouldn't have lost in '64 if we'd had the Weed,' says Tuddy emphatically. 'No way.' At 23, Tuddenham was captain of Collingwood—the youngest captain, he says, in the club's history. Twiggy Dunne loved Tuddenham for his 'sheer Collingwoodness'. Bob Rose says even by the standards of the '30s, Tuddenham was tough. Robert Walls gives the Carlton perspective when he says Tuddenham was someone you always kept an eye out for on the football field. 'He'd cut you in half,' he says drily. Len Thompson says Tuddenham had no idea of his size. 'He thought he was six foot six, 15 stone and powered by a V–8 engine'. He describes him as a lunatic on the training track. Barry Price remembers Tuddenham's knees clicking as he ran past because so much cartilage had been removed from them. Tuddenham ran before games and during games; between seasons, he ran professionally. He was in no doubt that Collingwood lacked fitness. Never one to stand back, he told Rose he would take over the club's fitness training. 'I told him he could do the rest of the coaching'. The offer was not taken up.

Tuddy believes he should've coached Collingwood after Bob Rose. Would've won three premierships, he says. Tuddy's word for himself is leader. 'No use denying what you are.' Barry Price had described his first game to me, standing in the race at Victoria Park, preparing to follow this glistening block of muscle with a torrent of words rushing from his mouth onto the field. At the appointed moment, the rest of the team entered the arena in the usual restrained manner, the one suggesting reserves of mental and physical strength. Not Tuddy. 'He bolts,' says Price, making a shooting gesture with his hands. Crosswell played on Tuddenham early in his career and observed that much of his play was pre-planned. He predicted the path of the ball then ran to meet it. This meant he hit goalsquare packs like a truck, smashing defensive walls that would normally stop a player twice his size. Crosswell tried the technique but found there was a catch. If you guessed wrongly, your momentum carried you past the point of no return. Thompson says Tuddy 'used to get his sights fixed'. He recalls him lining up Carlton centre half-forward Mark McClure and charging. McClure went to ground; Tuddy got lower and lower in his approach to the target, eventually tripping and breaking his arm. Tuddenham would happily spend an afternoon damaging, and being damaged by, the competition's other hard men, such as Footscray's E.J. Whitten, then drink with them until midnight. To him, that *was* the game, a belief readily absorbed by Lee Adamson. In the 1966 grand final, Tuddenham led Collingwood to within one point of victory. Then, at the beginning of the 1970 season, the captaincy was taken from him. Thinking about it, he still shakes his head with bewilderment. How could Collingwood have been so stupid?

In a sense, Bob Rose's career was a portent of the problem. The greatest player in the history of the club had left Collingwood at the age of 27—in his prime. Collingwood's policy of one wage for all, a legacy of its days as a club for industrial labourers, meant a champion like Rose received the same money as a first gamer. One great player after another—Rose can list them—left the club at the peak of their powers, usually after marrying and acquiring young families. Ace full-forward Ron Todd went to Williamstown in the VFA and kicked 1000 goals. Rose went to Wangaratta, from where he observed the recruiting strategies being employed by other clubs, particularly St Kilda and Richmond, who were building premiership teams. Recruiting was to become the bane of Rose's life. Player after player melted through his hands because he was unable to offer them financial inducements. With Tuddenham as captain, his cause acquired a vocal and active supporter. 'Dick Clay went to Richmond for a car,' says Tuddenham. 'With the money going through Collingwood social club each Saturday night, we could have bought him a Rolls Royce.' In the words of John Nicholls, looking on from Carlton, when the Collingwood committee finally bowed to the inevitable at the end of 1969 'the matter was badly handled'. The club moved to lure West Australian Peter Eakins to Victoria Park. To gain his signature they offered him a sum of money—perhaps $7000 a year, No-one seems to remember. What is remembered vividly is that it was more than they were paying their captain. Tuddenham, along with vice-captain Len Thompson, struck. For this public violation of the club's creed, Collingwood stripped Tuddenham of the captaincy. Tuddy says he wasn't the same player after that and Barry Price agrees. The red flame no longer burnt up the whole ground; instead, it pursued its own paths. There is no doubt in Des Tuddenham's mind as to who should have captained Collingwood in the 1970 grand final. Himself.

A night with Tuddenham is an experience worth having. Not only is he a generous host, he talks without restraint. Totally without restraint. It is like entering a canyon with large vivid drawings on the walls. Our evening concluded with me showing him the team lists for the grand final and inviting him to comment. When asked to do this, most of the other players made small remarks about their peers, their kicking or marking. Tuddy took a more strategic view. My second-last note for the evening reads, 'Should've beaten these cunts by ten goals.' The last is, 'Should've knocked out Hopkins.'

The Umpire

Don Jolley sits in a wheelchair as he has done for more than 20 years since being paralysed in a car accident. He's still got a life, he says, still got children and grandchildren. Jolley was the sole field umpire in the 1970 grand final. No problem with memory here. Jolley has a word for everyone who played. 'The first one to handball was Serge [Silvagni]. He was in the back pocket. I said to him, "What the bloody hell are you doing?" He said, "I've been told to handball and that's what I'm doing".' I drop some names in front of Jolley, letting them land like bread on the surface of a pond with fish in it. Goold? 'Stirred them up, got them started. Had a stare.' McKay? 'Could he mark or what!' Nicholls? 'Ole Crystal Eyes, we called him. One look from him and you'd drop dead.' Potter? 'Underrated. He was quiet but he was a real redhead.' Jolley remembers the day Potter split Big Nick's eye and sent him from the field. That was in 1969. There was a total of seven or eight reports from both sides; George Harris got them all off because the umpire had so many report cards to fill in they were late filing them. In those days, there was only one umpire and no video.

To some extent, Jolley let the game regulate itself. 'I'd say to the players, "If you give one, you'll get one, but after that you're up and I don't like going out Monday nights".' Jolley says Crosswell is the best player he saw under pressure. 'I had him in his first game. The boy's come out and gone Biff! Bang! Bong!, hitting blokes. I said, "I'll have a word with you thanks, son".' I give him more names. Greening? 'Best talent we never really saw.' Walls? 'Cool, calm, collective.' Robertson? 'Last bloke to kick a drop kick on the MCG—he let one go on the members' wing in 1972.' Silvagni? 'Only bloke I ever saw who always got his kick away.' The list goes on and on. It's like a chant; in fact on the field, when he was umpiring, he often sang. One day as Nicholls rumbled past, he said to Jolley, 'Even if you're not embarrassing yourself, you're embarrassing me.' Jolley likes to see the humorous side of life. The funny thing about the 1970 grand final, he says, is that he's a Collingwood supporter.

The Day

The sun rose a few minutes after six. The world's attention is directed towards the Middle East and the bloody purge of PLO forces within his country by King Hussein of Jordan. In Melbourne, the most advertised movie on television is a gentle English comedy called *The Tichfield Thunderer*, but the competing genies of the time are reflected in the city's smaller movie houses, a film on the Woodstock concert at the Palladium, an R-rated Swedish film (*Never Before So Clearly Told . . . The Facts of Life and Love*) at the Embassy, a film about the 1917 Bolshevik Revolution at the Twin. Australia is entering a period of dramatic change. In March, nine Australian soldiers died and 29 were injured near Nui Dat. Two months later, Melbourne witnessed its first moratorium march, a crowd of more than 100 000 people mobilising in their opposition to the Vietnam War. Earlier in grand final week, a committee of inquiry had warned the American president, Mr Richard Nixon, that the radicalisation of America's youth on university campuses across the nation may have serious long-term implications. At the same time, the leader of the opposition in Australia's federal parliament, the Labor Party's Mr Whitlam, drew loud accusations of treason when he issued legal advice to young men seeking to avoid military service in Vietnam. In the Northern Territory, in an incident reported in only a minor way, an elder of the Gurindji people, Mr Mick Rangiari, warned that his people will take the land leased by the Vestey company whether the government grants it to them or not. The Whitlam government, which will explode onto the scene like a technicolour bomb with its proposals to end conscription, initiate land rights and implement no-fault divorce (to name but a few), is just two years away. Melbourne now has an international airport (Tullamarine), although domestic flights continue to operate through Essendon.

The day's top is 64 degrees Fahrenheit (temperatures have not yet been converted to Celsius). In the course of the morning and early forenoon, the MCG has swollen to a size not seen before or since. Syd Jackson is in the Carlton team, on a half-forward flank. Against Collingwood, his opponent is invariably Lee Adamson, a lean, hungry defender who thrives on what he calls aggression. He sucks it into his body like hot red oxygen and plays his own version of the game. In the second semi-final, Adamson was reported for charging Jackson and Jackson was reported, by four umpires, for striking his opponent. At the tribunal, Jackson alleged that Adamson had subjected him to racial abuse, the first reported instance of such a claim in the history of the game. The case was dismissed. Adamson now says everyone knew the allegation wasn't true, that George Harris made it up. At the time, says Carlton centreman

Ian Robertson, it was seen as another case of George Harris's ingenuity, of his ability 'to come up with something new'.

In the second semi-final, Collingwood came from three points down at three-quarter time to defeat Carlton by ten points. That match drew a crowd of 112,000. Now, a fortnight later, an additional 10,000 people have squeezed into the ground. Peter Smith, Norm Smith's son, has queued since dawn to obtain a seat for Barassi in the members' stand. Another of the Carlton coach's unorthodox views is that the game is best watched from above, rather than sitting, as tradition dictates, on a bench with the trainers. Smith manages to secure five seats in the first row of the members' stand, left-hand side. Melbourne wins the reserves, defeating Richmond by two points. In the Carlton change rooms, Barassi takes the players into the smaller team room. No-one else is admitted. Not trainers, not committee men. Now, he says, it's just us and them. The players describe the noise as they ran down the wired-in races in the northern stand as a cushion of sound. Like their feet aren't touching the ground.

The First Half

The replay is in black and white. No centre square. Waters, as captain, wears number one—a Collingwood tradition. Streamers fall through the air like long tears, tears of joy, tears of agony. The Channel 7 commentators are Mike Williamson, Alan 'Butch' Gale and Ted Whitten. The pace is immediate, so is the threat. Tuddenham kicks past, possibly through, the tumbling, bowlegged ball of blue that is Sergio Silvagni. Immovable in the packs, Silvagni is also dropping back to cover McKenna's leads. Constant noise, loudest when Jackson touches the ball. *Boo!* In the members' stand, at Barassi's instruction, Peter Smith follows McKenna, Thompson and Price, plus the Collingwood runner, through binoculars. Nineteen-year-old Johnny Greening bounds into the game, dodging an opponent and bouncing the ball on the hard centre wicket. It comes back to him badly, wobbling unevenly; he takes it as easily as if it were waiting on a plate. Like a ballet of malign intent, arms are flung high at every intersection in the play. Thompson rushes Jackson. He dodges, then dodges again as Greening arrives with outstretched arm. Waite misses Tuddenham; Tuddenham doesn't miss Waite. With his first touch, Crosswell displays confidence, dodging an opponent, taking two bounces. Minutes later he comes from the side to take a wonderful mark at centre halfback. From the outset, he has it all—leap, timing, sureness of touch. Minutes later he almost takes another at the opposite end of the ground. He appears to be running where he wishes, leaving O'Callaghan free on the halfback line.

Thompson, deposed as vice-captain along with Tuddenham, is in number 28. Mike Williamson says a big rumour swept Melbourne during the week that Thompson wouldn't play in the grand final unless he was given more money. 'It's not true,' says Williamson. The boy, as he calls him, has a rash on his leg. Williamson calls the eruptions pimples; Thompson and his opponent David McKay both call them boils. Thompson hasn't trained properly for five weeks because of a thigh strain; liniment, used in an attempt to get him out on the track, has inflamed his fair skin. He has plenty of the ball early but fumbles. He also runs around a lot, expending precious energy. McKenna's first score is a point. 'He's the star of this game,' says former Fitzroy captain Butch Gale. 'Along with Jesaulenko.' In the second semi-final, Jesaulenko kicked eight and McKenna kicked nine. Jezza creates Carlton's first score, a point, by squirming through a pack—it's like watching a man squeeze his fist through a sleeve woven from wire—and knocking the ball to Crosswell. By that stage, the 22minute mark of the first quarter, Collingwood has three goals six on the board.

In the ruck, Big Jerker is leaping early and leaping

late but the effect is that Nicholls is unable to find a commanding rhythm. Jerker changes with the versatile Twiggy Dunne who proves remarkably effective as a tap ruckman. The rovers, Wayne Richardson and Gallagher, do battle. Richardson is the more obvious talent, precision passes off either foot from standing starts. Gallagher is busy and brave, head over the ball. A blow from Tuddenham knocks the breath from his body but he runs on, grinning. Late in the first quarter, Richardson is involved in a collision with Goold. He gets up holding his leg, alleging Goold has run at him. Shortly afterwards, he limps past the camera. It is the first of Collingwood's bad omens.

Collingwood win the first quarter because they have more individual winners. Casually skilful players like Max Richardson and Con Britt intersect gracefully with play, their taller team-mates like Jenkins and Waters drop back and out-mark the Carlton forwards. From Collingwood's viewpoint, the game is going according to plan. Barassi responds by swapping Jesaulenko and Walls and Big Nick introduces his own disincentive scheme, a backhander catching Price. Minutes later, Nicholls flattens Con Britt with a high tackle. Players rush to the scene. Greening runs at Nicholls, David in pursuit of Goliath. Tuddenham tussles with Goold, who is always high on his list of targets, mocking him by patting his long hair. Mike Williamson laughs, 'Look at Tuddy.' In the next passage, Jerker Jenkin tries to even up, but he has none of Nicholls' covert finesse. Carlton begin to hold their own in general play, they're just not scoring; McKenna has four goals, Jesaulenko none. Crosswell makes Gallagher's second goal, slithering through a pack in the forward pocket, backhanding the ball into the goalsquare. A Jesaulenko goal is disallowed, thereby denying Carlton due reward for their first sustained period of play.

At the other end, Wayne Richardson goals with an almighty torpedo punt. Collingwood appear to have reasserted themselves. They attack again. McKenna has again worked himself free of full back Kevin Hall. He is running back with the line of flight, eyes on the ball. Coming from a roughly perpendicular position is Des Tuddenham. Tuddenham now says he was trying to lay out Carlton fullback Kevin Hall. Hall is more than prepared to believe this is the case, but the replay suggests Tuddenham had his eyes on the ball. The two Collingwood players collide heavily, the impact sending both to the ground. McKenna stays down, Tuddenham's hip having hit him in the head. Umpire Don Jolley notes that the Collingwood full-forward's eyes are spinning. Trainers assist him to his feet and he revives to kick another goal before halftime, but the most fateful incident of the match has occurred. Tuddenham, perhaps responding to McKenna's injury, takes a mighty mark, standing on Ian Robertson and then literally landing on his head after Robertson moves backwards and takes the Collingwood player's legs from beneath him. 'Good way to break your neck,' says Mike Williamson jovially. Tuddy's wife told Williamson on the way into the ground that he had a dream about the game. Collingwood win and he kicks six goals. That's Tuddy, says Williamson. He misses with that shot, but scores with another a few minutes later. The camera follows him as he runs back towards the centre. Look closely and you see the hint of a limp.

Ironically, it is in the wake of Collingwood's greatest setback that Carlton's resistance is at its lowest for the entire match. Collingwood press forward, firing away like kids in a shooting gallery, kicks going high and wide. Sitting on the trainers' bench beside the ground, Bob Rose begins to worry. Any team has only so much energy; Collingwood are spending plenty. Despite the difference, which now stands at seven goals, Carlton make another faint surge. At centre halfback, McKay is growing in confidence and he kicks the ball such distances that the game seems to change shape while it is in the air. Late in the quarter, he clears from centre halfback. Ruckman Graeme Jenkin is waiting at the front of the Collingwood defence. It is at this moment that Alex Jesaulenko finds his unique solution to Carlton's forward problems and the umbrella defence. It's called the Mark of the Century.

Jerker and Jezza

Big Jerker is a genial bloke, interested in people with a grin not far away. He says it's curious to think that had Collingwood kicked another two goals in a game in 1970, the 20 players would now be 'a closer group of men'. As it is, two of his best mates from footy are former Carlton players—Jezza and Syd Jackson. By trade, Jerker's a builder but I find him when he's on holiday and just back from the shack. On Monday, he starts work and he'll grin a bit less often but as he says, 'If you don't have a problem, you don't have a job.' After Tuddy, Jerker was the biggest presence in the Collingwood team, having stepped into the space left by the retirement of Ray 'Gabbo' Gabelich, the man who made the legendary run in the '64 grand final.

I meet Jerker at his ample home in Melbourne's northern suburbs. The house thumped to the beat of amplified music; his son, a personal trainer, was working out in the basement. When he'd finished, we visited the billiards room beneath the house. On the mantelpiece is a figurine of the famous mark, signed by both players. As sculpture, it's not particularly good. The bodies are straining apart. There was no strain in Jesaulenko's action—that's what made it so wonderful. The former gymnast alighted on Jerker 's back. 'It was that quick,' says Jerker, clicking two big fingers. It sent his 14stone frame sprawling. The next thing he remembers is the roar, a blast of sound as if from an explosion. Seven times Jerker played in front of crowds of 100,000; he says you can't imagine the effect the extra 20,000 had that day. Regaining his balance, he turned to find Jesaulenko had landed on one foot and was preparing to dispose of the ball.

Jesaulenko has no memory of the mark. 'I didn't remember it that day and I don't remember it now. It was just another mark. It only got bigger because the newspapers were there.' The mark was photographed from at least three different angles. Two of the shots are in Jerker 's billiards room. One has Ted Potter, straining backwards, hands spread, adjusting his sight to the altitude of the leap. That shot was taken from in front. Another, from side on, has Denis O'Callaghan standing in front of Jenkin looking up. When I asked O'Callaghan if he remembered that moment, his eyes glinted with humour. 'Oh, yeah,' he said. 'I remember saying, "It's yours Jerker—you're on your own".' Enter, at altitude and rising, multicultural Australia. My favourite photograph of the mark is the one taken slightly from the rear; it captures the smoothness of the flight. This is the one that has pride of place in Jerker's billiards room, signed by Jezza in large black print: 'To Jerker, Bad Luck. Lots of Love, Alex Jesaulenko 25'.

Halftime

Memories of what happened during the most famous halftime break in the history of the game vary. Len Thompson remembers raucous supporters—he says several hundred of them—that were 'somehow' admitted to the Collingwood rooms. He says the person who let them in should be shot. Twiggy Dunne remembers voices shouting, 'We've got 'em! We've got 'em! This is the one, this is our year!' He identifies one of the supporters as lawyer Frank Galbally. Fullback Jeff Clifton, who'd been positive and purposeful in the first half, dismisses as nonsense the story that champagne was flowing in the Collingwood rooms at halftime. So too—with barely suppressed anger—does Bob Rose. He sees it as being typical of the rumours that bedevilled his time as coach of Collingwood. Various players remember Rose moving to quell the euphoria, but Jenkin recalls 19-year-old Johnny Greening joining in the gleeful chorus and shouting, 'Crack the champagne, we've got 'em!' Jenkin and Thompson moved to calm Greening down. Thompson says you've only got to lose one of the various factors that combine to make a top sporting performance to lose the lot. Twiggy Dunne also recalls hearing mention of injuries—McKenna was concussed, Wayne Richardson had a bruised calf, Tuddenham a bruised hip. All three were senior players; Richardson and Tuddenham were also the two Collingwood rovers. Barry Price has since heard that Collingwood's fitness adviser thought the team look tired at halftime. Some players, like Colin Tully and Lee Adamson, have no memory of supporters in the rooms. Tully's account of the halftime break is deeply earnest. 'Bob Rose spelt it out for us. He said that Carlton would throw everything at us. We knew they would because they were a professional outfit and had a lot of pride.' Rose said the next fifteen minutes were the most important of the match.

By contrast, the mood in the Carlton rooms was one of shocked and sober silence. Jesaulenko had left the field thinking the task which now lay ahead of them was averting a defeat of the magnitude Carlton suffered at Victoria Park in the second-last round. So did Percy Jones. Kevin Hall, unaware of the extent of McKenna's injury, thought himself a chance to be replaced. Normally a ruck-rover or halfback, he had been selected at fullback to counter McKenna's speed; McKenna had already kicked five. Again, Hall was not alone in his thinking. When wingman Phil Pinnell, who had been well beaten by Robert Dean, saw Barassi approach, point and say, 'You're off', he stood up and removed his guernsey. So did Bert Thornley, the player beside him. Pinnell had to sneak into the team room to see which of them the coach meant.

Barassi had been in a terrible fury when he met the

team, grabbing the wooden table carrying the halftime drinks and upending it against a wall. Gary Crane, a man given to plain speech, says he was a raving lunatic. Barassi's version has him asking Hall and Robert Walls how many handballs the team had had in the first half. Both answers were wildly optimistic. 'Sixteen,' shouted Barassi, fixing them with the famous glare. 'A measley sixteen!' He told them to sit and think what they could individually do about the mess while the match committee retired to the room with the blackboard and worked out how to try and fix the team.

Barassi was initially dissuaded from swapping Hopkins for Thornley by Jack Wrout, Carlton's chairman of selectors, but he moved Goold to the wing, swapping him with the more defensively inclined Pinnell. Barry Gill, now the headmaster of Colac High School, remembers Barassi's initial outburst when he 'went off the air'. He says the period when Barassi and the match committee were locked up in the room with the blackboard was like sitting in the eye of a cyclone. Then, when the coach reappeared and summoned the team, he was 'almost a different man. He was cool and calm, he seemed to be in control. I think the players responded to that.' Gallagher says the trick in grand finals is to penetrate the surreal noise and excitement and find the truth of the day. For him, it came when Barassi said if the match continued as it had and Carlton lost by 14 goals, they would never be allowed to forget it. Why? Because the loss would be to Collingwood. Instinctively, Gallagher knew it was true. 'We had to take risks to save face,' he says. A number of the Carlton players say that—the second half was about saving face.

In terms of Barassi's career at Carlton, this was a late play. In 1970, the legend of the super-coach didn't exist. He was, in fact, in the process of losing his team and, by the following year, he had. 'At the ages of 16, 17 and 18, I thought Barassi was a god,' says Robert Walls. 'By the age of 21, in common with most of my team-mates, I'd had a gutful of him.' But, that day, Walls loved the man with the wild fire in his eyes. 'He could have closed down the game and stacked the backline,' says Walls. 'He could have organised a respectable defeat. But he didn't. He jutted out his jaw and made decisions.' His word for Barassi that day is bold. Ian Robertson remembers Barassi breaking the 44point deficit into two four-goal deficits—one for each quarter. Carlton had come from behind numerous times in the preceding seasons. Gary Crane remembers him speaking quietly. Risk was necessary to victory. They could make mistakes—once. He looked them in the eye: 'To win without risk is to triumph without glory.' In his subsequent career as coach and commentator, Robert Walls has shown himself to be both shrewd and uncommonly candid. 'If only one or two of the players hadn't believed him, it wouldn't have worked,' he says. Some accounts have Nicholls emphasising the need for handball as the Carlton players prepare to retake the field.

Vin Waite is one of the few players in that game who can remember in detail arriving at the ground. The big plumber from Drouin with the hammered-in nose parked his car near the ICI building, walked to the ground and watched the reserves. But of the halftime break, beyond hearing that Hopkins had replaced Thornley, he remembers not a thing. 'That's how intense it was.'

The Third Quarter

For two minutes, nothing happens. Then the first significant handball occurs, from Crosswell to Walls. Crosswell takes another mark on the half-forward line, falling backwards into a pack as he does; his feet have scarcely touched the ground when he handpasses to Walls, who storms past like a messenger boy on a motorcycle. In the goalsquare, Percy Jones misses the mark. The ball falls right, Hopkins goals. Within a minute, the scenario is repeated. Jesaulenko brings the ball in from the left flank with an elastic, airborne kick. Tully, Hopkins' opponent, wrestles with Jones. Again the ball falls to Hopkins, standing alone. Collingwood go forward and, from a set shot, Max Richardson boots the ball out of bounds on the full; his kick appears almost casual, like a golf shot at the end of a long day. Enter Kevin Hall, well-beaten by McKenna in the first half. He handballs over McKenna's head to Silvagni who kicks one of his flat shapeless punts. The ball is immediately driven back towards Collingwood's goal. Again, Hall handballs to Silvagni in what appears to be a repeat of a discredited tactic. This time, the ball pierces the Collingwood lines and reaches centre half-forward, where Walls again runs onto it and kicks long to the square. The ball spills free, this time to the right forward pocket. Jackson gets possession but cannot go left as the pack is in pursuit. Simultaneously, Jesaulenko displaces Tully, the one Collingwood player to Jackson's right, with a bump. In the small space thereby made available to him, Jackson swivels, drops the ball across his left foot and goals. Umpire Don Jolley says it's the best goal he's ever seen.

It's not Carlton's handball that's noticeable as much as their ability, and desire, to play on. Simultaneously, the Carlton players both increase the tempo of the game and employ a new pattern of teaming. None lead the way more obviously than John Crosbie Goold, his combination of high kicks and fancy dashes belying the seriousness of the shin injury he has carried into the match. Crosswell scores in the ninth minute. A minute later, Hopkins receives a handpass from Robert Walls and scores another—his third. Carlton add another pair of goals—Walls in the twelfth minute, Jesaulenko in the thirteenth. In ten and a half minutes, they have kicked seven goals, and the difference between the two teams is now four points. Thompson steadies the boat, goaling for Collingwood. McKenna kicks his sixth, Twiggy Dunne adds another. At the last break, Collingwood lead by 17 points. Bobby Rose had expected Carlton to challenge. At three-quarter time, he tells his team they have withstood the assault. He tells his players he believes in them.

At halftime, fuming volcanically, Barassi had nearly

fallen over leaving his seat in the grandstand. That was as his players expected, that and the fact that the first player he met would receive the full force of his temper. At three-quarter time, however, he met his players with something entirely unexpected. He praised them, said that regardless of the outcome he was proud of what they had done. Kevin Hall has since read a similar ploy in a Dale Carnegie book, but Barassi credits former umpire Harry Beitzel with having thought of it. He made it sound as if the game was over. His players, now scenting the possibility of a truly amazing victory, pressed forward to tell him that wasn't so. Barassi says he knew then they would win.

The Climax

The last quarter is different from the third. There is no explosive opening. The teams are once more matched. Hopkins, slightly off-balance, misses an open goal. 'The boy was running full pace,' says Butch Gale, excusing the error. Butch has the softest voice for a hard man; for a decade, he was to Fitzroy what Nicholls is to Carlton. He was also coached by Len Smith which means he knows all about play-on football; just before halftime, Butch said he thought Collingwood were slowing down. Making clever position, Thompson marks and goals. In both quarters of the second half, Thompson kicks the Magpies' opening goal but fatigue is now evident in all his movements. At the start of the third quarter, Crosswell saw exhaustion in his face and took energy from the thought that Collingwood were tiring. Throughout the second half, Crosswell continues on his solitary way. His mark in the third quarter is second only to Jesaulenko's as the best of the game, coming from behind, serenely riding the pack, taking the ball from the sky in passing. The game has many fine high marks. A minute or so after Thompson's goal, a pack of four or five thunders to meet a long ball coming into the Carlton forward line. They rise as one; in the middle of the pack, Collingwood fullback Jeff Clifton is carried upwards like a man in an elevator. Robert Walls says because the 'old game' was more predictable, players could position themselves for marks; as a result, there were 'more speccies'. Jesaulenko takes another in the final quarter worthy of comment. The pack jumps and lands, the ball ricochets in the air. Jesaulenko jumps again and, having got the ball, plays on; the other players, recovering from the impact of their airborne collision, are still finding their feet.

Collingwood defender Peter Eakins touches Robert Walls' artful shot from the right forward pocket on the line. Walls abuses the goal umpire, and is warned. Jolley speaks to him. Collingwood go forward, looking for McKenna, whereupon fullback Kevin Hall makes the first of three fateful interceptions and runs down the ground, answering attack with attack. Collingwood, by way of contrast, hold the ball when they win it and look upfield, waiting for opportunities to appear. 'Taking too much time, Collingwood,' drones Butch. He says it again, a minute later, and adds, 'I've got a terrible feeling.' He makes it sound like a slow creeping pain that starts at the bottom of your guts, a paralysing fear. Goold off, Chandler on. The Australian Light Horse has made its last charge on a football arena. The following day Goold enters hospital for surgery on a spur of bone in his leg. It took four injections for him to play, his left leg deadened from knee to ankle. Carlton's lesser players, like Percy Jones, are starting to appear.

He stands behind McKay, blocking Thompson's run at the ball, and Carlton's young centre halfback takes another of his nine marks. This is the match in which McKay will win the respect of the Carlton Football Club. Tully off for Collingwood, but it is Greening who is cramping. Potter cramped before the quarter began. Ricky Watt, Tully's replacement, is a lithe wingman; he soon gets into the play.

The quarter's climax is a plane of pure action lasting perhaps ten minutes during which hardly a free kick is given and the game is one continuous flow. This is Australian football at the highest level it can be played and suddenly the best talents—the likes of Jackson and Jesaulenko—are on display. Jesaulenko tries a soccer goal, taking the ball with an overhead kick. It misses but not by a whole lot. What can he not do? 'This is a wild finish,' says Butch. Jackson makes Hopkins' fourth and final goal, smothering the ball off Eakins' foot, pursuing it between two Collingwood defenders, straightening, handballing and covering up in the one split second as O'Callaghan crashes into him with hip and shoulder. Collingwood lead by one point. 'Will we be back next week?' asks Mike Williamson. 'Oo Michael,' says Butch. The 'oo' is large, like a boulder that could still roll either way. Pinnell cramps, McKay marks over Greening, who is now on the forward line, socks down. Greening appeals for a push. Not tonight, Josephine, says Jolley. Vin Waite, whose eyeballs have stuck out of his head like organ knobs since halftime, unloads Twiggy Dunne, having collected Wayne Richardson the previous quarter. Carlton's physical strength and greater experience are telling. Nicholls, eclipsed in the first half, is suddenly influential, kicking two goals. Collingwood still have individual winners, like Dean on the wing, they still create chances but Carlton have more rigour in their play. Now, for the first time, comes a chant of Carlton! Carlton! McKay finds it uplifting; most of his team-mates won't recall hearing it. Crosswell is in defence, in attack, somehow at both ends of action only a few kicks apart. A throwup occurs 20 metres in front of the Carlton goal. Crosswell's memory is that Percy Jones tapped it to him; in fact it is a poor bounce that lobs in his direction. He has no option but to stand and wait, and he has sighted Tuddenham on the other side of the pack. Collingwood's red bull has lowered his head and begun to charge; at the last moment, the Carlton player blocks and turns his back, waiting to be collected. Free kick for around the neck. 'Stupid!' shouts Butch. (Not a free kick, says Tuddenham, when I ask him.) Crosswell, flipping his long hair out of his face, goes back to take his kick, not unaware that the entire drama of the match is now concentrated upon him. His kicking has been the least reliable aspect of his game, but there is no doubt that he will score. There has been no doubt about him at any stage of the match. He doesn't attempt to kick it softly, to guide it through; the kick is confident and strong, the ball passing between the goals above post height. For the first time in the match, at the 25-minute mark of the final quarter, Carlton lead.

Greening off, Heard on. Big Bob Heard is the tallest man on the field and possibly the slowest. His era of football has passed and he is unsighted, but Bobby Rose's young team are not done for. Price, whose battle with Robertson is an advertisement for the days when centremen played wide of one another and taggers were unknown, wins the ball in the centre of the ground and heads goalwards. Everyone knows what he will do. His partnership with McKenna is the talk of the competition. No-one is sure which of them anticipates the other but, sensing what is about to happen, the cameraman splits to the Collingwood forward line. Yes, McKenna is on the lead, a clear pace ahead of Hall. Price finds him, the ball seems to stop in the full-forward's hands. It begins to come down, just as the defenders crash into him from behind. There is a moment when the players, including Sergio Silvagni, pause. The Collingwood story—which Don Jolley denies—is that he blew his whistle, but on the television Ted Whitten is shouting, 'Play on! Play on!' The ever-reliable Sergio Silvagni gathers the ball and boots it to centre half-forward. On the replay, four players run to meet it. Three are from Collingwood; the fourth is Jesaulenko. Will he get there before they close like a sliding door? He does—just—passing between them bent double; a step or two later, he kicks the ball at right angles to the line he is running with his left foot. Towards goal it bounces, spinning on its belly. For Kevin Hall, at the other end of the ground, the few moments it takes to bob towards the goal are a glimpse of eternity. Peter Eakins rushes back for Collingwood, but he arrives too late. The camera shudders. It is as if the stadium is bouncing. In that instant, as Jesaulenko's kick crossed the goal line, it seemed to Adrian Gallagher that the northern stand had lifted into the air.

Monday morning

In the *Age* on the Monday after the match, Percy Beames said the Collingwood players had failed Bobby Rose. 'This year, there was talk that they would not fail Rose again but they have.' Percy's prose is simple and direct. His lines are spoken rather than written, but they have the authority of someone who had both played the game and been observing it for decades. He couldn't recall a similar reversal in grand final history. The *Age* supplement carried some of the game's iconic photos, Barassi launching himself into the air as the final siren sounds, Bobby Rose a couple of minutes before, a wounded look on his face as if a hole has opened in his guts that he knows will never heal. After the match, when Rose met the press, he overturned custom by asking the first question. 'What went wrong?' he said. Jezza's mark over Jerker Jenkin was in the paper, as was an overhead shot of the ground: it looked like a doughnut with hundreds and thousands sprinkled over it. Remarkably little was actually *written* about the game. The only substantial interview was with Ted

Hopkins and the journalist was surprised to find that his jubilation was qualified. Hopkins said he was satisfied with his performance but next year he wanted to be in the 18. He had been on the bench no fewer than 12 times in the course of the 1970 season.

Few of the Collingwood players remember much about the aftermath of the match. Twiggy Dunne thought they might have gone back to Bob Rose's house and played billiards. They didn't; they went to the Collingwood social club. Of that Peter McKenna is certain because he joined his team-mates there about 11 p.m. McKenna says the 1970 grand final is like President Kennedy's death—everyone can tell you where they were on the day. In fact, most can give you two references—where they were at halftime and where they were at the end. The irony is that, having been knocked out, McKenna has no memory of the second half. After the game, he went home, slept for five hours and woke to the hard, inconsolable fact of loss. 'It hurt then,' he says, 'and it hurts now.'

Victory

By and large, for the Carlton players, 1970 became another bright button on the tunic of success. Having failed to make the finals in '71 under Barassi, they achieved what some regard as an even greater victory under Nicholls in '72, overcoming Richmond, the premiership favourites, in that year's grand final. Richmond had dealt with Carlton decisively two weeks earlier in the second semi-final, but Nicholls devised a strategy of all-out attack and then outscored the favourites in a skilful, highscoring game that saw major performances from Walls, Jackson and Doull. Crosswell, who missed through injury, watched from the old Southern stand behind a plume of smoke. By the end of the match he wished he were out on the field, Carlton had played so well. The scene was then set, in 1973, for one of the wildest and most violent grand finals of the postwar era. Again Carlton played Richmond, but this time Richmond won. Nicholls was concussed by an elbow to the head and Geoff Southby, one of the nominations for fullback of the century, was felled by a roundhouse right from Richmond's Neil Balme. Despite the loss, Carlton had established an enviable record. In six seasons, the club had played in five grand finals, winning three premierships.

Six years later, Carlton triumphed again, this time with Jesaulenko as playing coach. Again the hapless victim was Collingwood and again the margin was less than a goal, after a ball which appeared to be out of play was smacked back into the goalsquare by the outstretched arm of Carlton's Wayne Harmes. But a glorious chapter in the history of Carlton Football Club was about to end on a sour note. A rebellion against George Harris succeeded in ousting him as club president; Jesaulenko backed Harris. The resulting breach saw one of the club's greatest players transfer to St Kilda. Recalled by Carlton in 1989 as non-playing coach, Jesaulenko's relationship with the club was again ruptured when he was sacked by new president John Elliott. Asked to name someone in sport he admires, Jesaulenko nominates Melbourne basketball supremo Lindsay Gaze, a man whose long career in the sport has continued almost uninterrupted through the phases of player, coach and national coach. For whatever reason, it is a progression Jesaulenko has been denied and his relationship with his old club is a vexed one.

I finally met Jesaulenko in Carlton. Everyone says Jezza doesn't like talking footy, but in the end a workmate interceded on my behalf. I was sitting outside the University Café when I saw a slightly rotund, grey-haired man coming towards me. It was the walk that struck me; it was almost wary, as if he were heading into foreign territory. Jezza is that curious anomaly—a figure of Australian folklore who was a migrant to this country at a time when migrants were seen as being both new and strange. Without thinking, I was instantly familiar. 'Jezza,' I said, 'you're not like I expected.' He seemed to know what I meant. When people ask, 'Are you Alex Jesaulenko?', he often says, 'No, I'm his father.' 'People have an image,' he said, waving his right hand and briefly summoning a memory of the magnificent player a woman journalist once described as 'a balding Nijinsky'. Up close, his face is not unlike Marlon Brando's—flat grey eyes, small chipped nose—but the physical presence is less demonstrative. He sits, arms crossed. The voice is powerful but flat. Peter McKenna, who now works with him at Dick Pratt's Visiboard, says people never realised how *strong* Jezza was. What they saw was the balance and grace. Ironically, the man remembered for his effortless skills and relaxed approach to training placed little or no emphasis on skill in his training regimens as coach, even putting away the balls for long periods. Instead, he insisted on loads of physical work. In the event of a loss, the loads were increased in the manner of a punishment. David McKay remembers a night when the players ran a hundred 100metre sprints. Nor, it seems, did he bother much with tactics. Our discussion leads me to conclude Jezza doesn't overrate the importance of coaches. He says the most important job at a football club is recruiting.

Out of Carlton's 1970 side, four players went on to coach the club—Nicholls, Jesaulenko, Walls and Jones. All but Jones, who picked up the reins in the wake of Jezza's departure, achieved premierships. Since 1970, as club president John Elliott likes to remind people publicly, Carlton has overtaken Collingwood in the number of premierships won. That sort of talk wouldn't rest easily with Big Nick. The biggest mistake in footy, he says, is to think you're better than you are. 'That was Collingwood's mistake in 1970,' he says. Nicholls fears his club may be heading down a similar path, and, as always, there is reason in what he says. In its golden years, Carlton picked the best talent from around Australia. Now, in recruiting terms, the playing field is tilted in favour of clubs like Adelaide and West Coast which have whole states behind them. Carlton may never be that resource-rich again, particularly if its president continues to gratuitously insult Aboriginal Australians, the game's steadiest source of creativity for more than a decade.

As it was, the Carlton player who gave me the most emphatic reply when asked about the 1970 grand final was Syd Jackson. Was this the closest team he'd ever been part of? 'Christ, yes.' Syd is vice-president of the Carlton Old Players' Association. Gags Gallagher says it's like watching the Nawab of Pataudi when Syd walks through the Carlton social club. Gags wishes Jezza would go back more often; he's royalty, too. Why is Carlton's 1970 team so close, I ask Jackson. 'Because of everything we went through that day.' The lows of the first half, the exhilaration at the end. And the booing and the taunts. 'I think it was me they were talking about,' says Syd with the barest outline of a grin. 'I was the only person of that colour on the field.' Syd Jackson is a popular figure. Jerker says he's a champion little bloke. So do Waters and Tully. Late one night in Bendigo, Tully and Syd had a competition kicking drops over a fountain in the street. Syd plays golf now. 'It's a game which makes a man of you,' he says, then with a laugh, 'or makes you jump off tall buildings.' If he had his time over again, he would probably have been a golfer in the first place. I'm sorry to hear this because footy's my game and Syd was a great player. Lee Adamson used to whisper into his ear that he was scared but, on the evidence of the 1970 grand final, that's not true. Second quarter, forward flank—Jackson pursues the ball through a pack like a lizard, making the play, bodies crashing around him. They would have got him if they could. They would have got one another too, but Jackson was such an obvious target. And the goal he made for Hopkins at the end. Beat two Collingwood defenders and risked a third finding him as open as a door. Denis O'Callaghan was an old-style defender; he would have gone right through Syd and out the other side.

Big Nick had eyed me solemnly and said, 'Syd was a much-loved member of the team.' A number of the Carlton players—Goold, Jesaulenko—described Syd as 'a gentleman' and Nick had told me in some detail about a night in Syd's company, the quality of the food and wine. 'He had a short fuse,' Big Nick went on, 'but then we didn't know as much about racial insults in those days.' We certainly didn't. Syd Jackson is of the Stolen Generation. He was taken from his mother in infancy. Jackson, I have read, is not his real name; it was the name of the matron of the institution he was sent to. His father was called Tulloch, but that's not his real name either; it's the name of a Scottish landowner whose property he worked on at one time. What Syd did mention, in passing, is that his parents lived 'the traditional [Aboriginal] way'. Syd lives a world away, in Richmond, and we met at a café in Swan Street. I had read that Syd didn't meet his mother again until he was in his forties. 'Yeah,' he says shortly, 'a bit late.' Later he says he saw her twice, briefly, in his 20s, presumably when he went home between seasons. Syd was late returning from West Australia at the start of the 1970 season. There was talk of him not coming back at all. I asked him about Lionel Rose. Yeah, Lionel's a good mate and was back then. He understood how black players had to be consistently better than white players to be regarded as their equal.

Three years ago, Syd Jackson went on national television and said, in a slightly roundabout way, that Lee Adamson had not racially abused him in the 1970 second semi-final. 'At the time, it didn't seem to matter that much,' he says in a slightly weary way, 'but as the years went by it didn't seem fair.' Pretty much unconcerned either way is Adamson. He'd known all along he didn't say it. 'I was brought up not to be racist, all that matters to me is whether someone's a good bloke.' In fact, far from being aggrieved, he says you have to look at it from Syd's viewpoint. 'It was his chance to play in a grand final, in a premiership.' He looks at me earnestly. 'In that situation, you have to dig deep. I'm not saying I would have done what he did, but in his situation I certainly would have thought about it.' Adamson describes himself as 'a football person'. Fair-haired and scrawny, he'd run the length of the ground to enter a brawl, happily getting between players much bigger than himself to exchange punches. Nowadays, it's called whiteline fever. 'Besides,' he says, 'I might not have said that, but I said plenty of other things.' What sort of things? 'About him being a receiver and hanging out of the packs.' Irritated,

Jackson hit Adamsom at Waverley when the two teams first met in 1970; Adamson answered with a blow that broke his hand and left a large gash on Jackson's jaw. In the same match, Nicholls finally caught up with Tuddenham, who had dropped a Carlton wingman a season or two before. Tuddenham hit the ground with a bloody mouth. Adamson ran 40 metres and hit Nicholls with his already damaged hand. He received four weeks for striking Nicholls but missed eight with his broken fist. In the second semi-final, Adamson charged Jackson after seeing him give Tully 'a short right' in a pack. Jackson's answering blow, for which he was reported by four umpires, had just missed Adamson, shaving his jaw. 'If they hadn't come up with the claim of racial abuse,' says Adamson brightly, 'he was gone.' But Adamson didn't 'enjoy' the 1970 grand final. 'Couldn't after everything that had been in the press.' His way was to lean against his opponent, whisper in his ear, infiltrate his defences, but that day it felt like 120 000 people were listening. 'I couldn't play my natural game.'

My interview with Syd Jackson was a relatively short affair. Others joined us, including an academic from West Australia interviewing him about Aborigines in sport. What he didn't show me was his fire, and that's not something you can ask to see, but when we'd finished he wanted to take me round the corner to Gags Gallagher's pub to introduce me. He also said he'd ring Jezza to get him to talk to me. And he had a number somewhere for Bert Thornley. Was Thornley part of the 1970 victory? Oh yes, says Syd with a quick nod, so that I am in no doubt as to his meaning.

Off and On

Bert Thornley's a fisherman. He skippers boats with six-and seven-man crews off the northeastern coast of Australia and is away at sea for weeks on end. After a lot of inquiries and some detective work, I finally caught him when he was home from sea for a couple of days. Barassi enthuses about him for the same reason as he enthuses about Bob Rose: there's no malice or sneaking ill will about Bert Thornley. 'The interchange bench came too late for me,' is all he says. His stats at halftime were no worse than five other Carlton players, including Nicholls. In Thornley's case, playing as second rover in a side that wasn't getting a lot of forward play, he also lacked opportunities. On the replay, he looks a fit, strong player. Among the first to work with weights, he was bulky by the standards of the day. He was able to hold his own in the packs (and give Lee Adamson, tormentor of his house-mate, Syd Jackson, one under the ear in passing); but he wasn't quick. An Achilles injury soon after he crossed from East Fremantle prevented him from playing at his best in Victoria, but he still cherishes the opportunity Carlton gave him. He thrived on what he saw as the club's professionalism and commitment to excellence, and the intensity of the Victorian game. But the 1970 grand final was his last appearance at that level.

His replacement, Ted Hopkins, played only one more match. For the first round of 1971, he was again named on the bench. The following week his name was not to be found in either seniors or reserves. Hopkins, who had been at Monash University for the preceding three years, says he gave football away because he had a second 'quest'; he wanted to become a writer/publisher 'at the innovative end' of publishing. *Teledex*, one of his first works, was a book of poetry which opened like a contact book. He says he couldn't pursue both football and writing. Ted Hopkins has since returned to the game with a system of statistical analysis. Hardball gets, loose-ball gets, clangers, contested and uncontested possessions—these are his words, his ideas. He doesn't like his career being summed up by the Andy Warhol line about everyone in the modern world getting 15 minutes of fame, pointing out that he in fact played a total of 29 senior games, but, ultimately, his explanation of his fame isn't that different. He says humans use stories to place a frame of understanding over life's complexities and uncertainties. In his case, he was fitted with one of the oldest—the boy who came from nowhere to decide a big contest.

Before the game, David McKay saw Bert Thornley instructing a young friend in the use of a camera. He wanted mementoes of the day. Thornley says hearing he was being taken from the field was 'completely shattering . . . like having a ten-storey building fall on you.' He felt he'd done as well as anyone, but it's a point of pride to him that he stood and urged on his team-mates as they left the change rooms for the second half. 'Ultimately, you're there for the club. The club goes on forever, individuals come and go.' A few years ago, on the Gold Coast, he coached an under 8 football team. Footy, he taught them, is about team values and he prizes the towel the kids gave him at the end of the season. But Bert Thornley always had two sports, football and surfing, and after the 1970 grand final he went surfing. Far from the madding crowd, he sat on his board, felt the swell and fall of the sea, listened to a different roar. . .

Loss

There are those, in retrospect, who see inevitability in Carlton's victory. They were the club which had modernised efficiently. They had a coach who rode the crest of innovation in his era and a team drilled to meet the sort of challenge the grand final presented. What this analysis tends to overlook is how close Collingwood came to winning. The key play in the game is Price's pass to McKenna in the 27th minute of the final quarter. If the mark had been paid—and clearly some of the players, including Sergio Silvagni, thought that it had—Peter McKenna would have been an even money chance to convert. 'Straightest kick I ever saw,' says Adamson. Had that occurred, instead of trailing by four points Collingwood would have led by two and had everything to play for in the last scrambling moments. As it was, the ball rebounded and Jesaulenko kicked his magical goal, the one that bounced through. Was there luck involved, I asked Jesaulenko. 'Every time the ball bounces there's luck involved,' he replied. For Terry Waters, that kick, the idea of the luck of the bounce, sums up the game. He says words cannot convey the feeling in the Collingwood rooms after the match. 'I don't think anybody could believe it or wanted to believe it or could imagine how they were going to live with it.' The worst knowledge was that Collingwood could not have fielded a better side. In keeping with a tradition now lost to the game, Waters visited the Carlton rooms and publicly congratulated the club on its victory.

Peter Eakins is one of the Collingwood players who doesn't punish himself with thoughts about what might have happened. 'History's what did happen,' he says. Now back in West Australia running the Cottesloe Beach Hotel, Eakins retains a fond regard for the Collingwood Football Club but is at ease with the result. 'Footy's a great game and I loved playing it,' he says. 'But it's not the end of the world.' Eakins' son gave him a video of the match for his 50th birthday. He watched it and saw what too many have forgotten: Collingwood played well. There are spells in the second half when both teams are playing to maximum effect that are about as good as footy gets and a privilege to watch. Even in the final moments, Collingwood still had individual winners and players attacking—Eakins and Adamson were running from defence, Robert Dean (Bob Rose's nomination for best afield) was winning on his wing, Twiggy Dunne was continuing to weave in and out of the game in what Max Richardson calls his 'subtle, elusive way' while, in the centre, Barry Price was playing his best football of the day.

If the loss bears down as hard on McKenna as anyone, it is perhaps because he knows he could have won the match off his own boot. In his three previous outings against Carlton that season, he had kicked tallies of eight, nine and nine goals. That he was the form player in the 1970 Collingwood side is shown by the fact that he won that year 's Copeland trophy. When Tuddenham collected him at the 20minute mark of the second quarter of the grand final, he already had four goals to his name. Not that the former full-forward expects, or gets, much sympathy from Tuddenham. 'Six foot three and fourteen stone,' he says, his face one large rubbery grin. 'Get up, you big bastard.' If 1970 does not dominate Tuddy's thinking to the same extent it does some other Collingwood players, it's because he has a more darkly disturbing memory—the '66 grand final. He had the ball on Collingwood's half-forward line in the closing minutes and chose to kick to the square where two Collingwood forwards were matched with one St Kilda defender, fullback Bob Murray. Murray marked. Tuddenham could have, and possibly should have, run in and goaled—and, on that occasion, he was captain. Bob Rose admits that over the years the 1970 grand final has caused him much worry. His wife Elsie, a kindly, elegant woman, remarks in passing that 1970 'is the one we still cry about in the night'. 'Collingwood needed to win a premiership and, as coach, it was my duty to supply it,' he says. When he swings from the club to the individuals concerned, it's Tuddenham that he sees. 'Tuddy deserved to play in a premiership,' he says. 'As coach, I have to accept the blame for that.' It's a cruel word—blame—and he holds it to himself like a knife. This time there is no redemptive grin.

Rose wanted Tuddenham back as captain in '71; unrelenting, the committee reappointed Waters. In the event, Waters didn't see the year out. He and Rose had a disagreement, but 30 years later Waters has no interest in airing it. He simply says that after the disappointment of three grand final losses, he found it too hard to summon the necessary enthusiasm to mount another premiership campaign. He was replaced by Wayne Richardson. Meanwhile, the Victorian selectors saw fit to make Tuddenham the state captain and, after addressing the Victorian team during an interstate trip to Perth, he was approached by Essendon. After beginning 1971 in burning form, Collingwood faltered midway through the season and staggered into the final four on percentage. In the last home and away match of the year, however, they played Carlton at Carlton. Leading by precisely seven goals at halftime, Collingwood were overrun in the second half and lost by 19 points. 'We did it to them again!' says Barassi, beaming at the memory. (It's remarkable how many Collingwood players claim to have no memory of this match at all.) Again, Carlton's best was Brent Crosswell.

Less than one month after the 1970 grand final, Crosswell was back in the *Age* newspaper. From a distance of 30 years, the photo is scarcely to be believed. Tiger, shoeless and bare to the waist, is in silver flares and silver sunglasses; beside him, similarly attired, is a model whose ear he has no doubt been nibbling. The story says silver is the coming thing. The photo screams: Stereotype me as a footballer, if you can. The 1971 season hadn't begun when headlines shouted that Crosswell might never play again. He was in hospital with a rare blood disease. When Percy Jones and Gags visited him, Percy claims Tiger said all he wanted was to walk in a park and hear birds sing again. Crosswell returned to Tasmania, and press reports duly crossed the Strait to the effect that he had succeeded walking 60 metres with a stick. He made it back for the last two matches of the year. It struck some of his team-mates that whereas they were now beginning to be permitted to wear sideburns and slightly longer hair, Tiger had reappeared with a crew cut, thereby predating punk by a decade. The first headline triggered by his return was of 'another Barassi–Crosswell incident' at training. Crosswell was quoted as saying, 'I've just got back and he's on me already,' to which Barassi had replied, 'I've got 40 other players to train—not just him.' Nevertheless, Crosswell believes the game he played against Collingwood two weeks later was the best he played for Carlton. He destroyed them, but his relationship with Carlton had only another three seasons to run.

It intrigues David McKay that Crosswell is now capable of writing about football with such conviction and depth of feeling. 'At the time, he didn't seem at all interested in it.' Whereas other players packed their kits in ritual ways the night before the match, Robert Walls remembers Crosswell turning up to games with no gear whatsoever. Nicholls recalls a match at the Western Oval where Crosswell not only missed the team meeting but almost turned up too late to play. Carlton lost the match, Crosswell played poorly. That night, watching the evening news, Big Nick saw footage of a demonstration earlier in the day (that is, around the time of the team meeting) in the western suburbs at which a brick had been thrown. Crosswell was in the front row. Nicholls shakes his head. 'He was a good kid, there was no malevolence in him.' But, to him, Crosswell's priorities were all over the place, hopelessly so, and, at the end of 1974, Carlton let Crosswell go. 'That surprised me,' says Phil Pinnell, now the head of Wesley's middle school, 'because he was such a good player. But he was a loose cannon, and Carlton didn't like loose cannons.' Regarded by Carlton as a spent and largely wasted talent, Crosswell responded by being best afield for North Melbourne in its inaugural premiership win in 1975. Two years later, in the drawn grand final and its replay, he was again critical to North Melbourne's success, playing as a defender on Collingwood's principal forward, Peter Moore. Crosswell finished his career at Melbourne as part of Barassi's messianic return to his old club. The result was a disaster, the team proving demoralised and inept, its principal entertainment value being its core of football eccentrics, of whom Crosswell was one and a bulky punk with a shaved head and a jutting jaw named Mark 'Jacko' Jackson was another. 'Jacko was a commercially manufactured character,' says Len Thompson coolly. 'Tiger Crosswell was the real thing.'

Carlton's recreation of Collingwood's pain and humiliation in the last roster match of 1971 was Barassi's last as coach of the club. The 1971 season had begun for Barassi with a highly publicised disagreement on the training track with Gags Gallagher and, in the course of the year, the gap that had appeared between the coach and his players in 1970 widened. Barassi felt some of his players resented the blaze of personal publicity which had come his way in the wake of the grand final. Among the players there was a view that the legendary coach was not as singular in his devotion to the game. He was beginning to look at the world outside football, running an office equipment business that would eventually fail; before long, there would be talk of him entering politics for the Liberal Party. He even appeared at training in work clothes. When Carlton missed the finals (by percentage to Collingwood) at the end of '71, everyone seemed to agree the time had come for change and Barassi was photographed congratulating Carlton's new coach, John Nicholls. The week after his coaching career went into temporary hold, Barassi went to the MCG with 99 000 others and watched Collingwood feebly dismissed from the finals by Richmond. If Bobby Rose's heart wasn't broken before, wrote Barassi in his weekly newspaper column, it surely was now. Three weeks later, Rose, the man who had sought to create a new era for Collingwood, was appointed coach of Footscray. 'The 1970 grand final,' says Barry Price, 'had devastating consequences for our club.'

Realising that Collingwood was in crisis, Rose had met with president Tom Sherrin and said one of them should go. 'He [Sherrin] said, "Well, it won't be me".' McKenna remembers a final team meeting at the end of 1971 in a motel in Richmond at which 'Bobby told a few of us, including me, a few home truths about how we had played that year. I think he felt we had let him down.' Then, says McKenna, he was gone. So too was Tuddy, appointed captain-coach of Essendon. Then big Jerker also went to Essendon in a trade. McKenna says it never felt the same after they departed and, in 1975, the most popular Collingwood player of his generation chose to finish his career at Carlton. Adding to the club's sense of loss was the dreadful injury to Johnny Greening in 1972. If fortune had ever gone Collingwood's way, it now went against it—cruelly. I asked Terry Waters whether the the 1970 loss related to Collingwood's string of later grand final defeats, even though we were talking about different eras. He thought carefully before replying. 'They were different eras, but I think '70 did confirm in our minds the doubt as to whether as a club we could play finals football.'

Defender Denis O'Callaghan was one of Collingwood's best in the 1970 final, steady and unaffected throughout. Jerker says he would have made a good coach and Tuddenham agrees. He has a hard, precise football brain. He agrees that fitness was a problem and was one of the Collingwood players, like Price, who did extra training on his own. He also admired the discipline Barassi brought to his teams, believing that some of the flourishes performed by the Collingwood players were not always in the team's interest. As far as the grand final loss was concerned, O'Callaghan believes the team 'should have sat down and talked about it. We played some alright footy in the second half. We weren't that bad.' Collingwood, legendary club of old Australia, had chosen to deal with the loss in the way that losses were customarily dealt with in old Australia—get on with it, don't talk about it, don't admit the pain. Only, in this case, a vast chorus of imaginary pain had been swallowed along with the pain that was real.

A knee injury ultimately prevented fullback Jeff Clifton from fully realising the promise he displayed in 1970 when Butch Gale thought he was the most improved player in the competition, but his professional life prospered. A graduate in engineering from the University of Melbourne, he went building power stations in New Guinea. In the mid'80s, as part of a group attending a management seminar in Melbourne, he was challenged to speak about the worst experience of his life. He began, casually enough, talking about the 1970 grand final and was shocked by the scale and vividness of his recall. 'Suddenly, it was all there again.' He had to stop. Ted Hopkins, who perhaps understands the myth better than anyone, says that by the time the 1990 grand final came around, he was quietly barracking for Collingwood. 'The whole thing had become too depressing.'

Johnny Greening

Three last interviews—Greening, Crosswell and Tully—all in Tasmania. Johnny Greening I found through the Cooee Football Club. Cooee is a thin slip of sand on Burnie's western side. Its football team doesn't exist any more, lost in one of the many rationalisations of Tasmanian football of recent years, but its former great, Harold 'Tiger' Dowling, certainly still exists and Johnny Greening played for Cooee after he came back to Tasmania around 1980. I know because I watched him play. Initially, he captain-coached a Launceston club called City-South (now South Launceston) and I saw him there, too. Silk to watch, every movement polished and assured, but always with a frown on his face. At Cooee, among players he had gone to school with, he had no leadership responsibilities, and while there was more personality in his play there was still an inherent conservatism about his game. He let the game come to him and then responded. Only once did I see something of what the young Johnny Greening had been. Cooee, an exceptional team by local standards, played

Penguin, a gritty unrelenting rival from a few miles down the coast, in the match of the year. Cooee blasted them out of the park with a combination of strength and skill. That day, and that day alone, I saw Johnny Greening dance.

Johnny and his second wife, Bev Holman, were training racehorses at Spreyton, Tiger said. He rang back two hours later with a number. The paddocks were lush and green when I arrived and beheld a youthful figure with clear brown skin in shorts, walking towards a back shed. It was him, slightly humped but loose in his movements. Johnny Greening could run through a pack at full pace bent double. From a similar position, he could also leap onto a pack, take a mark and then fall off like a kid falling out of bed. At Victoria Park, they loved him. The judgment of the club was clear. Johnny played in 22, Bobby Rose's old number. Rose had seen Johnny as a 15-year-old; within twelve months, he had him at Victoria Park. For years, Greening was the youngest player around the place—just a kid, in Jerker's words. He couldn't enter public bars with team-mates, not that it bothered him. His business wasn't making friends, his business was football. 'I wasn't going to be a doctor or a lawyer when I was growing up,' says Johnny. 'I was going to be a footballer.' He was as young as six or seven when he realised his talent set him apart. At Collingwood, he was regarded as a loner, but one of the reasons he didn't talk football to people was because he didn't think about it like they did. Johnny saw league football as 'archaic'—ridiculously slow and run by people who were blind to the opportunities opening before it. Johnny laughingly went his own way. All the

Collingwood players recall the day, in what Johnny calls his first full year, that he kicked seven goals against Carlton at Princes Park before three-quarter time. Barry Price thinks he was on a forward flank. McKenna says, no, he was ruck-roving; he remembers him gliding through the centre, effortlessly dodging tackles, going bang, bang, bang, and the balls going over the full-forward's head. Johnny says, 'Tuddenham read me beautifully that day.' He means predicted his moves, had the ball waiting for him as he slid past.

Johnny was 19 when the 1970 grand final was played. How's his memory? Better than a lot of his team-mates. He recalls the exact temperature and gives it in Celsius—22 degrees. He remembers the supporters in the rooms at halftime. Johnny's word for the Collingwood rooms is eerie. Like they had a different sort of energy from the one required. Johnny's one of those, and they are to be found on both sides, who doesn't go along with the business about Barassi reinventing the game. He says it was a game Collingwood lost. Like Pinnell, Carlton's youngest player, Greening cramped before the match ended. Rose's first response, one that was certainly worth trying given the collapse of his forward line, was to put him up forward in a position that required less running. There's a moment late in the last quarter when Big Jerker Jenkin is despairingly trying to clutch a ball bouncing about his knees; Greening is a yard away, shouting, 'Give it to me, give it to me.' 'I would have turned on my left and gone pow,' he says. Pow means goal, six points, no doubt about it, but Jerker couldn't get the ball to him. Greening's cramps worsened; with a couple of minutes to go, he was taken from the field but Don Jolley says the change was badly handled and Collingwood played a minute, possibly longer, with less than 18 men. Like everyone else, Johnny's word for the mood in the Collingwood rooms after the match is devastation.

'It was a match that should have made us better,' he says. Instead, somehow, it made a team he calls brilliant worse. He recalls the late collapse in '71. The club started '72 with a new coach, Neil Mann. By then, Johnny Greening says he was three-quarters of the player he would have become. What he calls the incident occurred in the 12th round of that year. He remembers going to Moorabbin and Neil Mann saying, 'Another big one from you today, JG', something like that, and then nothing. None of the Collingwood players saw the incident, just turned and saw Greening unmoving on the ground, bleeding from the nose. He didn't regain consciousness for 16 days.
In his coma, Greening called out Barry Price's name. Asked to go to the hospital, Price was met by a figure in a wheelchair who recognised him but couldn't speak. 'It was a tragedy for John Greening,' says Barry Price slowly, 'and it was a tragedy for Australian football.'

How different would our sense of the game be if Daicos or Brereton had finished their careers at 21? Or Ablett or Jesaulenko? When Essendon next played St Kilda, Tuddenham went crazy, running round seeking vengeance and screaming, 'Today's Greening's day! Today's Greening's day!' Johnny did make it back. His return match, 18 months later, was against Richmond at the MCG; by all accounts, including his own, Johnny played a blinder, kicking five goals from the wing. Everyone thought he was his old self, but he wasn't. He says the skills were there but the motivation had gone. Others say the skills were there but not, like before, as one; what had previously been effortless now required great concentration. In all, Johnny Greening managed only a further eight senior games for Collingwood.

His sentences have a way of arriving at unexpected destinations which amounts to a sort of poetry. Before the incident, as he calls it, he was 'on a road with a rainbow at the end'. The football field was a blank sheet for him to compose on, his opponents 'were lambs to the slaughter'. And afterwards? 'Afterwards it never felt like that.' The old freedom had gone and, with it, the old certainty. His life unravelled, his first marriage failed. He says he now knows it's not uncommon for people who suffer 'head injuries' to suffer from depression. If he had his time over again, Johnny Greening would be a professional golfer or tennis player—more money, less risk—but in the early '60s those careers were on offer only to the lucky few. For a working-class kid, footy was basically the only way. Johnny Greening believes he was robbed of his career. I try and tell him there are people who played 200 league games whom No-one recalls; Johnny played until he was 21 and they're still talking about him. He half admits the thought, then waves it away. Jerker Jenkin had described Greening to me as an unusual bit of work and he was right—a middle-aged man who is youthful in manner and looks, who played his last game of football (for the local club, Spreyton, helping them to a premiership) at the age of 39, who is both genial and solitary, whose self-confidence is a cathedral with a hole in the ceiling the size and shape of a fist.

When I met Crosswell in Hobart the following day,

it became apparent that no-one in the 1970 grand final interested him more than Johnny Greening. He called him 'Collingwood's young champion'. Crosswell remembers being with a group of Carlton players and meeting Greening alone, late at night, in Sydney, after the two teams had played an exhibition match in that city. He liked Johnny's style, his mischievous humour, the way he took the game on his own terms. After the injury, the difference Crosswell noted was that Johnny's 'irony' had gone. Greening says it's the ability to think that makes the great players. 'Footy's about creating opportunities,' he said. Greening told me a coach at Collingwood—he wouldn't say who—told him not to turn so often onto his left foot. Johnny saw it as a way of wrong-footing opponents and moving the ball quickly. The coach saw it as confusing his teammates. In the first quarter of the 1970 grand final, he appeared beside an older player as he took a mark, called for a handpass and thundered towards goal. 'We were hot,' he says. 'We'd gone out there to kill the bastards.' As he ran back, the older player chided him for trying to play 'too fast'. 'I was 20 or 30 years ahead of my time,' says Johnny. Crosswell says talented individuals are often inhibited in team sports. They see things their team-mates can't. Sometimes, he says, they see things their coaches can't.

Crosswell (2)

Crosswell still says things which imply he's not seriously interested in football. But he looks serious when he says them. Maybe he's like an actor who lives a role when he plays it but is otherwise someone else. Crosswell says No-one played all that well in the 1970 grand final, it wasn't that sort of match, but I disagree. He did. Barry Gill summed it up best—not only did Crosswell have the ability to intersect with the game in a major way—for example, by taking a great mark—he could also think strategically. In the *Age* on the Monday after the match, Crosswell received fourteen of the fifteen votes cast by the newspaper's team of football writers for best-on-ground (second, on five votes, was Price), yet even then he was both within the game and outside it, planning his actions, executing them, withdrawing and thinking again. In defence, he plundered Collingwood's supply lines yet, in attack, he kept coming from unexpected positions. When he was absent from the contest, it seemed he was wholly absent, yet he was also Carlton's most visible presence over the whole of the game.

At my request, Crosswell showed me some clips of his playing days sent to him several years ago by the Seven Network. Most are of the later stages of his career. His chest is permanently expanded, fists clenched by his side. He is almost comic, either hitting or being hit, throwing his head in the air. This is Tiger Crosswell as most remember him. My favourite clip is when Tiger, on hands and knees, races an opponent, who is standing, to the ball; from the look on Tiger's face, you'd think it was an Olympic final. But the clips also include a mark from his very first game, against Geelong, at the age of 17. He comes from the side, like a high jumper to the bar, and climbs a goalsquare pack like a man vaulting a building in a single bound. The jump coincides perfectly with the arrival of the ball, which he takes from the air with a single grab. After he kicks the goal, the camera follows him, a skinny kid with sideburns and hands swinging like lead weights at the end of his arms. 'Look!' he shouts, 'I'm even walking like Barassi!'

Crosswell and I met in 1985 in the *Age* office. We were both in our first year of football writing; he was immediately positive and encouraging. Nor had I met anyone who talked football as he did, with the same penetration and emotional depth. If he was the football equivalent of an actor, he was one who had studied his part in detail. His first piece of writing to set Melbourne talking was about sex before games. It was like *Fawlty Towers* with erections, and dealt in part with the interstate trip on which he had roomed with McKenna. But it wasn't his best piece for the year. That appeared on grand final day when he wrote about

Vinnie Catoggio, a little Italian who started with Crosswell at Carlton and finished with him at Melbourne. Vinnie and Tiger used to piss off during the long pre-season training runs and hide among the rushes by Albert Lake. Crosswell claimed Vinnie made better duck calls than him because he was bilingual. Vinnie's first full senior game, at the age of 19, was the 1973 grand final, the one in which Carlton were belted by Richmond. It was one of those days when Carlton looked vulnerable to strength in the way that Collingwood had in 1970, and their good players were never able to find the space to play well. That year, wrote Crosswell, Silvagni, 'a player I respected', hit him in the side of the face with a piece of orange during the halftime break. In this, his one and only appearance at footy's summit, Vinnie Catoggio managed only two kicks and a couple of handballs. After the match, a Carlton official walking among the players, thanking them for their efforts, pointedly passed Catoggio by . . . Crosswell's story was about what happens when games get out of order, when people lose their perspective on winning and losing. He said it was uncivilised.

Three years later, Crosswell wrote another piece that etched itself into my memory. Only about 400 words long, it was written for a Bicentenary supplement in which a cross-section of the citizenry were asked to reflect on what it means to be Australian. Crosswell wrote about Goold, the great individualist from his time at Carlton. As a character, Crosswell might be seen as belonging to the Regency. Goold is from later in the century, around the time of Oscar Wilde, and almost equally unafraid socially. Crosswell's piece measured the ways the 'club' tried, unsuccessfully, to deal with such an individual. In the end, in a largely unspoken way, it became an issue of loyalty. Was it to himself or to the group? In the story, the final whispered judgment made of such a person is that he is un-Australian. Goold hadn't seen the piece and was mildly disconcerted when he heard the content of it. 'I thought I had more friends at Carlton than that,' he said. When Barassi went to North Melbourne, he tried to encourage Goold out of retirement to join him but a gentleman like John Goold does not swap clubs. In discussing Crosswell, however, Goold does say people don't realise how much further outside an outsider stood in those days.

'People at Carlton tended to see Brent for what he was not,' says Goold. He saw him as a conservative—like himself perhaps, of the landed variety, with a horse between his legs. Not quite. People habitually mistook Crosswell, whose progenitor had gone to Tasmania as a convict from Norfolk Island, for a scion of the aristocracy. Not at all. He was from the northern midlands, one of the island's oldest rural areas, but his father was a butcher. As a boy, Crosswell saw a group of men he knew and respected belittled by a local squatter. They accepted the bullying treatment. He determined then that he would never be spoken to like that by any figure of authority. I see Crosswell more as a gentleman bushranger, asking the squatter 's wife for one last indulgence as he leans forward to remove the brooch from her panting bosom. It was his skill at sport that earned him a place at a school for the sons of the rural aristocracy. He hated snobbery but, like Byron, another chap with a fondness for the classics, had considerable proficiency at boxing. That skill worked for him both at school and later on the football field, but what most people habitually confuse in discussing football, according to Crosswell, is courage and toughness. Far from being courageous, he says most acts of toughness, including his own, are born of fear. He will go through his tapes saying, 'That's a courageous act; that's not.' I put to him that football is more physically demanding now, but less violent. He disagrees. It's still violent, he says. It's just done in different ways.

But a football field is not the only violent place in our society, and a private school boarding house in the 1960s is not the only place you encounter snobbery and prejudice. For most of his football career, Crosswell was at university. Most people find it hard to carry the burden of one truth through their lives. Imagine carrying two—that of the athlete and that of the intellectual artist—in a highly polarised culture which insists the two are mutually exclusive. That's what gives his writing its special edge; his is the voice of a true outsider, someone who has never belonged to any of the groups or subcultures he has found himself in, but who writes nonetheless with insight and depth. There are people in the football world who grin and say of his football writing, yes, but Tiger writes fiction. If inquiring into a match played 30 years ago teaches you anything it's the subjective nature of individual memories but, putting that issue to one side, there is still the question of whether or not he writes good fiction. That is—does he reach truths otherwise left unspoken and unsaid?

Colin Tully

Sitting at Victoria Park, Twiggy Dunne told me he hadn't seen Colin Tully in 25 years. Some people thought he had returned to Bendigo, most were unsure of his whereabouts. In fact, he was south of Hobart in a small town called Margate. You get there via a slab of motorway. To the east is a silver-grey wedge of river as the Derwent opens to the southern ocean; to the west, low green hills, many of them with their native heads of hair. Once the roads that wove through this part of Tasmania were as pretty as a postcard. They were marketed as such, a rosy-cheeked maiden under every apple tree, but the apple industry has largely gone, a casualty of England's entry into the European common market, and Margate is now in the process of becoming a commuter suburb for the city of Hobart. Tully sells insurance from the back of the local real estate agent. I was slightly nervous about meeting him. No Collingwood player carries the burden of the 1970 loss more than Colin Tully.

He is a genial man, slightly plump but with a

sportsman's aplomb and composure. Most of the Collingwood players say he was the best sportsman in the club. But for football, it is said he might have played Shield cricket for Victoria (his cricket club was also Collingwood), but he was also good at golf, tennis — anything, it seemed. Sport continues to be a major part of his life. He has the highest grade of coaching qualification available from the Australian Cricket Board and until recently was president of the Channel Football Club, Margate's local team. The club wears St Kilda colours; a Channel guernsey, signed by all the players, is on the wall. When a couple of Channel's players were having trouble with their kicking, Tully quietly took them aside and suggested they run laps bouncing the ball off the white line, first with one hand, then with the other. It was something an old fellah called Harry Collier taught him at Collingwood.

We talk about Syd Jackson. They met again in Hobart several years ago. In the course of a long night, Tully displayed the tooth Syd had loosened with his fist in the course of the 1970 second semi-final. 'It's dead now, you bastard,' he said, wobbling the inert incisor about with a finger. Syd was abashed. He hadn't known it was Tully beneath him in the pack, he said, would never have done it if he did. He put down his glass and invited Tully to hit him back, to square up, to make it even. Tully was joking, but Syd wasn't. An eye for an eye, a tooth for a tooth, as a famous old book of tribal lore puts it. Syd told me his father practises Aboriginal law.

Colin Tully, self-imposed exile, is a Collingwood traditionalist. No-one gave me a more detailed insight into the culture of the club, but the conversation became more halting as we approached the 1970 grand final.

It's something he doesn't normally talk about. After Barassi, the biggest name associated with the game is Ted Hopkins. ('I played 150 games, he played half a game, but he's the one they remember,' Gary Crane had said.) That's why they also remember Colin Tully. Tully played on Hopkins, or, rather, he started the second half on him. Early in my inquiries, Len Thompson had leaned across the desk and told me that criticisms made of Tully for Hopkins' four goals were 'grossly unfair'. As a result, I had investigated the matter in some detail. Hopkins was an interesting player to study. Quick and lightly balanced, he played like a soccer striker. He didn't make his goals, but he certainly put them away. Once cracks appeared in the Collingwood defence, he was through them and gone. But in the hurly burly of play, when he is on roving duties, he is less assured, less certain in choosing options. The first goal, in the second minute of the third quarter, Tully says was his error. The kick is from Walls; Tully follows the line of the ball rather than his opponent. He goes left, the ball spills right to where Hopkins is waiting alone. Tully also accepts blame for Hopkins' second goal a minute later, but the question is whether he had any choice in the matter. Eakins has run down the ground and not got back. When the ball comes in high, Tully wrestles with Carlton's resting ruckman, Percy Jones. What should he have done? Let him mark? Again the ball spills to Hopkins.

The most contentious goal is the third, at the 10minute mark. Tully claims that Hopkins kicked this goal while he was on the ball—that is, when Tully was marking Carlton's other rover, Adrian Gallagher. The replay appears to support his contention. A minute earlier, Hopkins is clearly on the ball because he is at the centre bounce. Hopkins is running from the centre towards goal when he takes the handpass from Robert Walls. In the edge of the frame, the blurred figure of Tully can be seen with an opponent in short sleeves. Hopkins wore long. It is after he has goaled that Hopkins jogs back to the forward pocket. Simultaneously, Colin Rose, the Collingwood runner, appears and, having spoken to Tully, switches him and O'Callaghan. Tully admits he responded angrily, swearing at the runner. At three-quarter time, Tully says Bob Rose publicly blamed him for the three goals. Tully further believed he was 'dragged'—that is, taken from the field—after the blowup with the runner and before the third quarter ended. In fact, he was taken off midway through the last term, but still a clear five minutes before Hopkins scored his fourth goal, the one created so bravely by Jackson. Colin Tully never played football for Collingwood again.

Tully remembers the Collingwood rooms after the match. 'What had promised to be the best day of our lives had turned out to be the worst.' But for him the ordeal was only beginning. A version of history was being conceived and for the next 30 years he would be dragged along behind it like a man on a water ski. Truth? Who wants to know the truth? In bars, there was always a big mouth who wanted to remind him of Teddy Hopkins' four goals. Over the years, he has developed stock responses. 'How come the people who weren't there know everything? How come the people who were there don't talk about it?' Not a week has gone past in 30 years that he hasn't been reminded of the 1970 grand final, often when he least expects it. If he could erase any one day from his life, that would be the day. Sport's more than a game, of that he has no doubt. Like theatre, it's a place where people publicly invest their meaning and that is the riskiest of all investments. If he was a kid again and offered the chance to play league football, knowing what he now knows, would he do it? 'Fifty per cent of me would like the chance to change what happened. Fifty per cent says I don't want to go through anything like this again. I think I'd stick to golf and cricket.' Has he ever discussed any of this with the other Collingwood players? Never. He is struck by the thought. Never spoken . . . he is visibly enlivened by the idea. He thinks he'll ring Bubba Price and a few of the boys. When I get back to Melbourne I fax him a list of Collingwood phone numbers plus a copy of Crosswell's article on Vinnie Catoggio. He rings back the next day. The article is excellent.

On Your Feet

I end with Barassi for the same reason I began with him. The myth of the 1970 grand final is his. To what extent is it true? Did he, through a combination of audacity and forethought, reinvent the game in the course of the 1970 grand final? Some pretty good judges, like Robert Walls, believe he did. Walls compares handball counts in the 1968 grand final with those fifteen years later when Hawthorn were forging their reputation as the great team of the era. They increased fourfold. And, in the same period, the notion of football as a game of fixed positions was discarded. Barry Price says there was 'a definite change' after halftime in the 1970 grand final. Colin Tully is also in no doubt. 'I remember thinking during the third quarter, "This is an avalanche". In the backline, we didn't know whether to advance to meet it or wait back.' In the end, it's not so much a matter of handball statistics—handball was merely a mechanism. What Carlton did in a sustained way was simultaneously increase the tempo of the game and alter its pattern. That meant not only did the Carlton players have to possess a second method of play—Carlton had experimented with handball against Hawthorn at Glenferrie late in the season, coming from behind to win—they also had to be able to implement it in the most testing circumstance the sport could provide. It is this second ability which Barassi calls discipline.

But if that is victory, how is its alternative—loss—to be borne? 'If you want to know how loss is to be borne, look at Bobby Rose,' says Barassi fiercely. 'That game must be hell for him.' Few people can make the word hell sound so terrible, yet when the two men meet there is never a low blow, a slighting remark. Instead, from Rose, a grin and a sincere inquiry. The myth of the super-coach might be Barassi's, but his word for Rose is hero. What of Barassi's statement that Len Smith invented handball? My understanding of the history of inventions is that they rarely occur in single moments, are rarely the product of a single person's endeavours. Rather they represent trains of events, small incremental additions by various people and finally a moment when what is being experimented with rushes into being, like a geyser born of multiple pressures beneath the earth, and is thenceforth there for all to behold. In football, that day was the 1970 grand final and the implications of the change have been profound. In the '80s, I watched a Sydney Swans game on television with 'Butch' Gale. Dual Brownlow medallist Greg Williams was playing in the centre for Sydney. 'The rest are athletes,' said Butch, 'but Williams is a footballer.' He meant a player who basically lived on his skills, his abilities to anticipate an odd-shaped ball and then use it in a way which peeled open the game, not as an endurance athlete taught to kick and mark.

Alex Jesaulenko says once upon a time a good Australian footballer could turn around and do well in each of the other major football codes—as a kid in Canberra, he played them all—but the reverse was not true. A good rugby or soccer player was not necessarily a good Australian footballer. This simple equation proved, to his mind, which was the best game. He sees Australian football being taken over by 'people in business and acting', by the television industry. Soccer has had one rule change in 100 years, he says; each year, Australian football has another avalanche of change. Football is no longer run by football people, he says. 'One day, we'll be watching and we'll wonder if this is the same game we played.' Even Barassi, the Old Innovator, worries about football as it is now being played. With everyone rushing about in one large pack, there's not enough 'individual moments'. The 1970 grand final is studded with them, moments that became part of individual stories and memories. Television sports—one day cricket, for example—have little or no memory. They exist as a package of highlights together with a result; in no time, each merges into the next, a bright technicolour river whose course is directed by marketing men. But there is one player from 1970 who likes footy as it is now played—Johnny Greening. 'This is how I always knew it could be.' And, as he points out, the game is better policed.

Wayne Richardson wonders if there's as much feeling in footy these days. Richardson must be one of the last league footballers to have finished his career in the way that the most loyal clubmen once did, captaining the reserves to help develop the young players. Richardson loved his time at Collingwood.

His philosophy on the club's multiple disappointments in the '60s and '70s approaches the Oscar Wilde adage that the only thing worse than being talked about is not being talked about at all. 'I know one thing—it's better for Collingwood to lose a grand final by one point than finish eleventh.' It bothers him that there's fewer games at Victoria Park now, fewer people around the club. Even when it was falling over and losing grand finals in all sorts of different ways—fiercely, gallantly and finally, in 1980, grotesquely—there was one thing Collingwood never was. Ordinary. Richardson remembers when the suburb dressed up for its team. His fellow West Australian, Bert Thornley, says something similar—the 1970 grand final is a Melbourne story. 'Couldn't have happened anywhere else,' he says. Nor, I would suggest, at any other time. Strict chronology would insist that the infamous decade now remembered as the '60s ended when 1970 began, but in Australia the '60s were about to begin in earnest. The football world—for the most part, uncomprehendingly—contained the same conflicting forces that within a few years would both celebrate the coming of the Whitlam Government and hack it to pieces. These, too, would be large dramas (and, again, the name of the ubiquitous George Harris would figure among the dramatis personae). Australia was changing shape; cracks were beginning to appear in the myth of the monocultural nation. Look through them and you see Silvagni, Jesaulenko, Jackson, Crosswell. This game was played at an intersection in Australian history. Collingwood, the dragon in the imagination of 19th century Melbourne and the games first superpower, had been slain by a knight with a foreign-sounding name and a driving passion for modernity.

After his team failed to make a World Cup final in the '80s, French soccer legend Michel Platini said there is often more meaning in defeat than victory. Why? Because victory is a goal. Once it is achieved, new goals have to be found. David McKay remembers a feeling of shock the week after the 1970 grand final—something that had been so intensely meaningful one week before was no longer there. But for the losers it was. Losers are left with the agony of self-doubt. Some, like O'Callaghan and Max Richardson, say they came to terms with it years ago. Others, like Thompson, admit they haven't, but what is striking about Collingwood's 1970 team is that they remain—in most cases steadfastly—Collingwood men. Peter McKenna's word for what makes Collingwood special is loyalty. Colin Tully says it's even bigger than that but, when pressed, cannot put a word on it. 'I just love the word,' he says. Collingwood. After Jeff Clifton injured his knee he was bundled off to Fitzroy. Great bunch of blokes, he says, but as a club it didn't compare to Collingwood. If I were president of the Collingwood Football Club for a day, I'd give the 1970 team a cavalcade before a big game. It's time to bring them home. They've suffered enough for the club.

If Barassi did reinvent the game in the course of the 1970 grand final, it was a historic defeat at the hands of a highly accomplished side and, as Syd Jackson says, it wasn't until the last two minutes that anyone knew who was going to win. Twenty-seven years after the match, Barry Price sat with his family and, for the first time, watched the replay. It pained him anew to see the wasted opportunities, but he can now say he's proud to have played in the game. So he should be. Price carried

Collingwood's flag right to the very end. There is a classic encounter in the final minute when Price wins the ball in the centre of the ground. This is the moment Big Nick has both feared and foretold. He appears like a giant bear, arms extended to block Price's path. Price feints right, Nicholls covers; he feints left, Nicholls blocks him. Price goes right again, passes the Carlton captain and hammers the ball 50 metres upfield; but this time, perhaps because Nicholls' intervention wrong-footed him, McKenna isn't there.

Coming to Victoria in the mid-'80s, I saw a succession of dull, dispiriting grand finals that caused seasons to end on notes of thundering anticlimax. The league, which in its wisdom had previously tried to transfer the grand final from the MCG to the concrete wasteland of Waverley Park, had come up with the equally bad idea of a final five. The result was a series of mismatched grand finals in which one team was invariably fresher, mentally and physically, than its opponent. Some years the grand final was over within minutes of the start. It was like watching well-ordered drills at a passing-out parade. Afterwards, everyone congratulated the victor and No-one seemed to realise that the big loser was the game. Sport is drama. Drama occurs when individuals are confronted with obstacles which they must respond to in a naked and honest way and thus be revealing of themselves. These matches were the climax of the season, yet nothing was created or revealed, nothing occurred that enhanced the game or made it larger. Such is the power of the 1970 grand final that men who were young when it was played find the event pursuing them like a shadow through their middle age. This may never happen again, not in Australian football, nor even in Australian sport. That is why we should call on the players and the two coaches from 1970 to return to the stage, be upstanding and bellow our applause. They gave us a final that was truly grand.

SOUTHERN SKY, WESTERN OVAL

Introduction

This book was Terry Wheeler's idea. Wheeler liked ideas; his eyes danced with the possibilities they offered. 'Have you ever thought of writing a book on footy?' he said.

I had. A novel. About an Aboriginal player and a white player, about them getting to know one another through being in the same team. Then I'd visited Brent Crosswell in Hobart. He was also writing a novel about football, and his was better. True, more deeply felt. His book had an Aboriginal player in it, too. Crosswell said footballers and Aborigines had something in common: people who knew nothing about them thought they were stupid.

Crosswell had been a player, a magnificent one, but he also had a life outside the game. He made unprecedented utterances in the press, saying that he preferred the company of women to men. He went on sit-ins and moratorium marches. He was said to possess one of the game's great talents, but he was easily bored and sought novel ways to amuse himself. My favourite footage of him shows an incident in which, rather than stand up, he chooses to race an opponent to the ball on his hands and knees.

In the football world, Crosswell was an outsider, but in the outside world he was a footballer: he stood alone at the centre of Australian society. No one had better footy stories than Crosswell – some comic, some dramatic, some brilliant. He wrote as he played, but then he became ill with Mehniér's disease. It affected both his hearing and balance. His novel was no more than a few pages in a pad written in biro. He chose to read them to me; Tiger, as Crosswell was known, had always been a performer. 'Give me a grey day at the Western Oval,' he once declared, 'and I wasn't worth a cracker. Give me 50,000 people at the MCG, and I was Hercules.' And he was. Twice best on ground in grand finals.

The passage he read me was about a bloke trying to return to the game in his thirties and realising that part of him has gone, a part that was strong and youthful and certain. Listening to him read, I realised the extent to which I didn't understand the game. I'd been lulled into viewing it as a spectacle, as men running and crowds roaring and commentators discussing half-time stats. The tame had no inner life. I put my novel away, for the time being at least.

'I'm inviting you to record Footscray's premiership year,' said Wheeler when we met.

The media didn't know what to make of Terry Wheeler; to be honest, I wasn't always sure myself. As the first step towards winning the 1993 AFL premiership, he said, his players were going to jump out of an aeroplane shuddering through the air 1200 metres above Port Phillip Bay. If I were going to be part of the club in their premiership year, he thought it might help if I jumped too.

As luck would have it, I was interstate that weekend, in South Australia, opening an art exhibition for a Port Adelaide supporter who did me the favour of taking me for a beer in the Alberton Hotel. The paintings in the bar of the Alberton are as bold as red roses. They are of great South Australian players, representing their teams in premiership years. There is a painting of Malcolm Blight in his green-and-yellow youth at Woodville. His face is masked by shadow; the sun is above him. This is a portrait of an Australian hero. Richmond's national title in '73 is represented by a Tiger which is sleek and dangerous in a modern way: Neil Balme, just as I'll always remember him. The paintings extend around the four walls, ending above the cash register with the '91 and '92 AFL premierships. Suddenly, instead of people, there are corporate logos, instead of art, there are light, jokey cartoons of an Eagle and a Hawk. That's what worried people about the game: it was changing …

I accepted Wheeler's offer. I told him that if Footscray won the premiership it would be a bonus, but basically what he was offering me was a season on the inside, an opportunity to learn more about the game. The book would reflect that learning. He seemed to think that was a fair deal.

Wheeler

Terry Wheeler and I first met in April 1990 at the launch of *Too Tough to Die*, the story of the Fightback campaign which saved the Footscray Football Club in 1989. The venue was the Footscray Town Hall. A young bloke in overalls turned up in his lunch hour with a guitar and sang a song about the club. The Sunday before, Wheeler's born-again Doggies has won in Sydney for the very first time. Footscray had played with nerve and daring. A long-legged kid from Warrnambool named Leon Cameron had played his first game and been one of their best. I also noticed the presence of mind of their red-haired centreman, Simon Atkins, and a tackle the new captain, Dough Hawkins, laid on Merv Neagle when the Swans wingman attempted to burst through the centre of the ground in the second half and rally the home side. Dougie brought him down as if he were making off with the gate takings.

The coach had arrived at the book launch with his captain; they were together when we were introduced. Wheeler was bouncing on his toes, chest full of air, liquid brown eyes alive with good humour. 'So you're the writer,' he said.

A few weeks afterwards, Wheeler gave me an unsolicited insight into his thinking. This was unexpected – as a rule, Australian football coaches give nothing away. Footscray had just played and lost a nondescript match at the Western Oval, their home ground. In the course of the game, a youth with dark hair and a free-flowing stride named Kolyniuk ran at goal from outside the 50-metre line and scored. 'Imagine,' said Wheeler, 'if he thought like that all the time.' The following year, Footscray had its best win of the season at the MCG against eventual premier, Collingwood. In the last minute of the match, 'Billy' Kolyniuk swerved past his opponent after taking a mark on the wing, accelerated around the boundary with Collingwood's Graeme Wright in hot pursuit and goaled from the pocket. Billy won the game. When the siren sounded, Wheeler ran from the coach's box down on to the ground, eyes glinting with emotion. That was something else about Wheeler which was unusual. Australian football coaches ritually, habitually, talk down their teams; Wheeler talked his up. He said Footscray would win the 1992 night premiership. They didn't, and people laughed at him. But he also said they'd win sixteen roster matches. They did, and went on to play in three finals and finish third on the ladder. Wheeler was named 1992 AFL coach of the year, and ruckman Scott Wynd won the Brownlow Medal to add to Tony Liberatore's three years earlier. But still there were people who said Wheeler was bluffing.

In most cases, the link between player and coach is easily seen. Mick Malthouse's teams are as tough as teak and defensive by nature. Kevin Sheedy employs craft and craftiness (in cricket, he was a leg-spinner). Teddy Whitten employed every trick in the book. When he coached Williamstown in the VFA, he hosed down the visitor's rooms before they arrived so that they prepared for the game in a cold, dripping tomb. The truth was that I only knew Wheeler as a player by reputation, and his reputation was something about which he was sensitive. A succession of his opponents had been reported for striking him, thereby giving rise to the popular presumption that he had done something underhand to them first. Ben Bradley, the head trainer at Footscray, said he was an aggravating sort of play, but Ben also said he habitually waved away the trainers if he was injured or hurt. When I really thought about it, all I could recall of Wheeler as a player was a dark, blank face exploding out of the back pocket on a set of sturdy legs. I also recalled a newspaper story of the time quoting an umpire telling Wheeler of another such report, and him exclaiming, 'Oh no, not again!' as if it were the last thing he wanted. At very least, as a player, he had been vigorous and combative. As a coach, he was liable to quote *Jonathan Livingston Seagull.*

In the course of 1990, I did an interview with Wheeler and he told me some stories about growing up in Warburton, or Warby as he called it, 50 kilometres east of Melbourne. I liked his stories. He had an eye for detail and his portraits had a gently humorous tinge. Wheeler's Warburton was populated by characters like Mr Edwards, who owned the shoe shop in the main street and drove a white HR Holden, and Dick Treloar, the trainer, who carried a flask of green ginger wine in the back pocket of his white overalls for days when the fog descended on the Warburton ground from Mount Donna Buang around three-quarter time. He also told me a drily humorous story about the '84 bushfires, about staying and fighting the flames until the last, finally abandoning his new house, trudging across a paddock and nearly being shot by his own gun which had exploded in the heat. It was the story of the man who thinks he has lost the lot and suddenly finds he hasn't.

Wheeler's grandfather had been killed in World War I. His grandmother, still in her teens, had sought the comfort of the local Seventh Day Adventist congregation. Eventually, her son – Wheeler's father – had been forced to choose between religion and football. He chose football. Alan Wheeler loved the life of the Warburton Football Club and all that went with it. At various times, he was its president, treasurer and secretary. If anything, Wheeler's mother was stronger in the faith. Each Saturday, the family – mum, dad and the three sons, each of the boys with a regulation cow-lick hair-do – would be at the Warburton ground for the start of the reserves. Mrs Wheeler ran the kiosk, serving tea at three-quarter time in white china cups. She was from Condobolin in New South Wales; Her father had played footy in his youth across the border with Kotupna. Saturday afternoon inevitably led into Saturday night at the clubrooms, kids playing in the time-keeper's box or climbing through the manhole in the roof, women seated around the fire, men in the corners, the whole surrounded by photographs celebrating the history of the Warburton Football Club.

Wheeler was sixteen when he began playing senior football with Warburton. His father, as he remembers it, was always there. At Footscray, he helped Eddie Johns, the property steward, lay out the jumpers before the games. Then, in 1977, Alan Wheeler died of a heart attack. Five years later, in the space of twelve months, Wheeler's brother, Garry, was fatally electrocuted in a bush abattoir, and his grandfather died. That was when he came to believe there had to be more to life than met the eye. In the same year, having played 157 games with Footscray, mostly in the back pocket, he transferred to Victorian Football Association club Williamstown as captain-coach. Williamstown played in three grand finals under him, winning the premiership in 1986. In this period, his jousts with the equally determined Phillip Cleary (now playing in the Canberra league as the independent Member for Wills, but then captain-coach of Coburg) became part of VFA folklore.

In the course of my year at Footscray, I eventually saw a tape of the '85 VFA grand final between Williamstown and Sandringham which Willy lost by five points. Even Cleary said Wheeler was great. True, he flung his arms about in a way which discouraged his competitors, but he also met the ball with force and took it cleanly, and he was always either making the play or re-shaping it. That was one of his maxims: Know the game. Standing alone on the goal line, he marked the ball after Sandringham player miskicked a shot at goal from a distance of only 30 metres. Another maxim: Never presume. The 1985 VFA grand final is also remembered for the fact that Williamstown included a 14-year-old, Ron James, in their team. It was a highly audacious selection: he had never played senior football before. In the opening minute of the match, Ron James ran at goal, bounding the ball at least twice. He missed, but in the following year's grand final, which Williamstown won, he took six bounces and scored. In 1989, Wheeler returned to Footscray as reserves coach.

Wheeler was in Condobolin at the end of the 1989 season with his nine-year-old son when the news broke that Footscray was to be merged with Fitzroy. A man Wheeler had never heard of rang, identifying himself as the president of Footscray's new board.

'We're in a spot of bother down here,' said Peter Gordon. The voice was terse, abrupt. 'But we think we can get out of it. We've got a board and we've got a team. We want you to coach.'

In his playing days at Footscray, he and his team-mate and fellow student-teacher, Peter 'Spider' Welsh, had sat by the Maribyrnong River eating fish and chips, talking about the game and what makes teams hum. Wheeler had always imagined himself outlining his philosophy, at length, to a table of club directors.

'How long have I got to think about it?' he asked Gordon.

'About thirty seconds.'

Wheeler had to tell his nine-year-old son they were going back to Melbourne. The boy understood. It was about Footscray. The following day, twelve thousand people attended a rally at the Western Oval. There were supporters form other clubs, including South Melbourne. Wheeler had driven through the night to attend. 'I don't believe we own anything,' to told the crowd, 'I think we just hold it in trust for our children.'

Finding Footscray

'How do you find Footscray?' the wife of a Sydney recruit once asked Wheeler.

'Just drive over the Westgate Bridge', he replied, 'you can't miss it'.

I came to enjoy driving over the Westgate Bridge in the course of my year at Footscray. Ever so briefly, you're above the world. The bay is a broad blue curve to you left. On the horizon to the far north and west are small, hard lumps which signify mountains. Yet again, you are reminded that the land we live in is large and flat. Most days, the sky is overcast, but occasionally you catch long beams of afternoon light filtering through a silver hole in the cloud, touching a handful of houses in the grey streets below. The city is behind you, a lump of tall buildings and a tower in dark glass. Ahead is the West, a flat spread of houses, factories, storage depots, chimney stacks and power lines. This is Melbourne's other half, the part of the city started out of sight and out of mind on the other side of a swamp. The day of the Coode Island chemical fire, Hawthorn player Peter Schwab flew over the area in a news helicopter. Recognising the green shape of the Western Oval beneath him, he realised it was the only part of the western suburbs he knew. Footscray is only one of a dozen suburbs in the West, but Footscray Football Club is the West's only AFL team.

Take the Williamstown Road exit off the bridge and turn right at the lights. Williamstown Road is busy, big-trayed trucks and cars swapping lanes, but at its northern end is a Vietnamese eight-ball parlour; in its back corner, bathed in red light, sits Buddha. I believe in Buddha, in my fashion, and so does Lionel Rose in his. He had thirteen statues of him the day I visited his flat, as compared to only three boxing trophies. They stood in the corner, tall and gold and angular, with Japanese inscriptions. The flat was above a bottle shop on the road to Frankston. On the floor, beside an easy chair facing a window, was a red electric guitar. Across the road was light coastal scrub. Lionel liked Buddha because he smiled and wasn't a worrier. He rubbed his belly before he went for a punt.

An S-curve from Williamstown Road takes you out on to Geelong Road. The football ground and its large scoreboard pass on the left. Turn down Gordon Street which is also the back of the Doug Hawkins Wing. The pale stucco cement wall is old and water-stained. The houses on the other side of the street are single-fronted with tiny bull-snout verandahs. This is Footscray.

What do I know about Footscray? Initially, only things to do with football. Footscray is red, white and blue. It was admitted to the Victorian Football League relatively late, in 1925 (after 42 years and nine premierships in the Victorian Football Association). Only one premiership thereafter –'54. Team led by

Charlie Sutton, but its star player was E.J. 'Ted' Whitten, also known as Mister Football. Read all about him. Some say the best player ever, appointed captain-coach at the age of 23. Under Whitten, the club made the '61 grand final, but lost to Hawthorn. Then came the '70's and Footscray's years of turmoil. Dempsey, Quinlan, Templeton, Wilson and Round – each of them either a past or future Brownlow Medallist – left Footscray for other clubs. Bissett, McGhie and Sandilands went too. Footscray lost a generation of great players and, in so doing, acquired a reputation for serious political instability. The club divided over coach Bill Goggin. For a period, the social club and the football club were under the control of rival factions. In 1982, their one hundredth year of operation (but not their centenary year), the Bulldogs finished last. In 1985, an end-of-year players' trip finished at an airport in Hawaii after riotous behaviour on an international flight.

In 1984, however, Footscray had acquired Michael Malthouse, recently retired Richmond premiership player, as coach. Malthouse was fierce, proud and rigid. The following year, he coached Footscray to the preliminary final, its best result since '61. Doug Hawkins won the club's best and fairest and rover Brian 'Choco' Royal was in his prime, but it was Brad Hardie, a Western Australian in his first season of league football, who won the Brownlow Medal. Hardie was thick-set and pale with red hair; on the field he looked like a bread van surrounded by sports cars, but to say as much is to make the mistake a lot of people made in that first year and judge him on appearances.

As a player, Hardie was quick, nimble and extremely sure of himself. He operated out of the back pocket, but paid his opponent less attention than is customary for those in the last line of defence. That was because his instinct was to be in the first line of attack. Hardie was a play-maker. In the 1985 preliminary final, he gave the Dogs some of their best moments with his audacious play, but his critics said that he also cost them the match by giving his opponent, Hawthorn's ageing champion Leigh Matthews, too much space in the last quarter. The following year, Footscray found itself financially stricken, in part because of the recruiting spree which had assembled the '85 team, Captain Jim Edmonds joined the Brisbane Bears, leaving Malthouse with a diminished and diminishing pool of talent.

The coach saw out the decade, forging teams with his iron will and insistence on defensive play. These Footscray sides were known by an old name – the Scraggers. Eventually, perhaps inevitably, Malthouse and Hardie argued. Hardie too joined the Bears where he was largely used as a goal sneak. After a brief and even less productive affair with Collingwood, he went home to Perth, another talent squandered. That seemed to be the history of the club since '54: squandered talent. Footscray has won more Brownlow Medals than any other club – twelve if you count Bernie Quinlan, Barry Round and Brian Wilson, former Footscray players who won the medal at other clubs. Hawthorn, by comparison, has only won two, but since beating Footscray in the 1961 grand final the Hawks have won another seven premierships.

At the intersection of Gordon and Barkly streets is a long pale building made from rippled tin called the Drill Hall. Turn into Barkly Street: a large gravelled area with a couple of palm trees and the odd dark pine appears on the left. Drive in. A sign on the back of a modern brick grandstand declares: 'Welcome to the Home of the ICI Bulldogs'. A weathered but defiant fibreglass bulldog strains from the first entrance. This is the Western Oval. This is where people, myself among them, gathered on the morning of 3 October 1989 in response to the news that Footscray had been merged with Fitzroy. It was as if a bomb had gone off.

The Old Way

The old way into Footscray, Dynon Road, runs in a broad straight line from Arden Street in North Melbourne across industrial flatland – formerly swamp – eventually meeting the Maribyrnong River. That was one of Wheeler's sayings: 'You don't enter Footscray without crossing the Maribyrnong'. Batman, the so-called founder of Melbourne, had named it the Saltwater River, thereby distinguishing if from the Freshwater River (later the Yarra). The names mattered; sea water isn't for drinking. At the time, the Marin-Balluk people fished the Maribyrnong, using a system of stone traps, and regularly burnt off the tussocky plain to the west to invite game to feed on the growth which sprouted after the next rain. The Europeans saw the basalt plain as a potential quarry. The river they transformed into an industrial drain.

Abattoirs and boiling-down houses were assembling on the banks of the Maribyrnong as early as the 1840's. Chemical and manufacturing industries soon followed. By 1870, Footscray's stench was a joke throughout Melbourne. When the city fathers briefly toyed with the idea of up-grading Footscray's image by renaming it West Melbourne, a satirical magazine promptly translated the new name into Worst Smelldom. The council, then controlled by commercial interests, said the smell didn't matter and produced a succession of doctors who said it was not injurious to health. A contemporary newspaper account which found blood, offal, dead animals, excrement, rancid fat, black bubbling mud and the occasional fish gasping for breath in the Maribyrnong may have been trying to shock, but it is a fact that the Footscray Council continued welcoming noxious industries long after they had been banned from other parts of Melbourne. Footscray was never a pretty place, at least not to outsiders, but that was part of its pride. Applying for admission to the VFL in 1923, Footscray Football Club adopted the official civic line, declaring that Footscray was Australia's Birmingham, nothing to look at perhaps, but a place of industry and a city apart.

Footscray Football Club would never be party to the intense rivalries that characterised relations between the inner-city clubs like Richmond, Collingwood, Fitzroy and Carlton. Footscray Football Club's tribal conflicts were in the past, with VFA clubs like Port Melbourne. But the city of Footscray had a natural enemy in the city of Melbourne. The John Gent Stand at the Western Oval commemorates a town clerk described in his lifetime as a Footscray patriot; among those with whom he did battle on Footscray's behalf was no less a figure than Sir John Monash, then a civil engineer but previously one of the few outstanding generals of World War I.

Footscray always had its own leaders, like Pastor

Joseph Goble who gave the Christian faith new impetus after it had been used to lend respectability to the gross inequities and appalling poverty of the 1890s. Goble gave much of his small wage to the poor, and preached the brotherhood of man. He was known as Goble of Footscray. In the early years, Footscray also had its own gentry, but, like Australia as a whole, Footscray changed dramatically in the 1890s. The terrible depression of that decade had, by 1893, created 30 per cent unemployment. In Footscray, the figure was perhaps 10 per cent higher. Incidents of starvation were reported, as were gruesome suicides by men who could no longer support their families. Women pleaded in court for their children to be taken from them by the State. Visiting Footscray for a performance of Charles Dickens' 'A Christmas Carol', the premier of the day, J.B. Patterson, blamed the plight of the unemployed on their irreligious character.

James Cuming was a kindly, paternalistic employer and a keen patron of the Footscray Football Club who lived locally. Each week, during the worst of the depression, he supplied the soup kitchen run by the Footscray Ladies Benevolent Society with an abundance of provisions. But the depression, which followed a decade of reckless commercial behaviour uncannily like the 1980s, led to the introduction of class politics. In 1911, Footscray was the focus of a bitter national industrial dispute when H.V. McKay, maker of the Sunshine Harvester, took on, and defeated, the Agricultural Implement Makers' Union over his right to employ non-union labour in three local factories. The strike became a lock-out, but, after one month, the factory owners opened their doors to non-union labour.

Scabbing suddenly became and explosive issue in Footscray. The *Age* reported that men who returned to work were publicly harassed, as were their families. Footscray became a union town. In Footscray Park, a magnificent bronze bust was erected to honour the memory of Henry Lawson, the people's writer.

Cartoonist and artist Michael Leunig was born in the western suburbs. He has done football paintings. In a typical one, Us are playing Them, and all over the ground, men are leaping into the air in groups of twos and threes while a man with a French moustache is pirouetting madly through the middle of the field as if he has finally found the one place on earth where he is free to express himself. In the centre of the painting is an umpire, looking at the ball which is still to leave his hands, wondering at its mysterious hidden powers. Leunig's father, Bernie, played with Footscray reserves in the '30s. The players of his era were all workingmen – slaughtermen, fitters' labourers, members of the council asphalt gang – who arrived at training on their bicycles. 'All the young blokes in Footscray wanted to wear the guernsey,' says Bernie. Most worked Saturday morning – the slaughtermen killed until 11.30 – played footy in the afternoon and wore the smell of liniment like after-shave in the dance-halls around Footscray on Saturday night. Footballers, says Bernie, were popular with the girls. Sunday morning, it was back to the club for a barrel of beer. As an eighteen-year-old slaughterman, Bernie Leunig also witnessed the violence of the 1933 'chain' strike at Angliss's meatworks. More than one local business, given the choice of backing the workers or the employer, chose the workers. 'Not one local bloke scabbed on his mates,' says Bernie. Instead, non-union labour was brought in from country towns like Warrnambool and Shepparton. When one of the strikebreakers later arrived at the Western Oval as a recruit, the Footscray players refused to train with him. Charlie Sutton recalls hearing that Footscray forewent the opportunity to sign a centreman said to be even better than Brownlow medallist Alan Hopkins because he had crossed a picket line. 'Footscray's a workingman's club,' says Charlie. 'Always has been.'

The sweetness of the '54 premiership can only be imagined. When I asked Charlie Sutton his remedy for combating nerves in finals, he replied, 'Forget about yourself as an individual. Play for your guernsey and your supporters.' Embody the cause. During the Fightback, I received a poem, 'Requiem for Footscray', from a man named David Lumsden who lived in the outer suburb of Lower Templestowe but had grown up in the western suburbs. 'I don't really have an active interest in football,' he wrote, 'but I am saddened and have a strong feeling of loss.' The poem went, in part:

> 1954
> Pressed in with my parents
> At the Western Oval
> Evening
> Thousands of people
> Like VE Day, my father said.
> Filled with the heady feeling
> Of community
> The West had risen
> And was victorious …

Elsewhere, the poem says:

> In my childhood memories
> A fierce sense of loyalty
> Cross the Maribyrnong
> And you could feel it in the air
> The challenge …

But I'm going the other way, into Footscray. Its first tourist attraction, on a slight rise on the left, is a corrugated-iron mural depicting life in the western suburbs. The last panel features the Western Oval. The scoreboard says Collingwood 10.10 (70) to Footscray 18.24 (132); on the left is a giant figure in a Footscray guernsey who looks like he has just stepped out of the Beatles' *Yellow Submarine*. A few blocks away, Footscray College (formerly Footscray Tech) has a beautiful mosaic with a similar theme. The poet John Shaw Neilson lived in Footscray in the early decades of this century, bent and blind after years of working as a navvy in the bush. In the mosaic, Neilson is pictured not far from the Western Oval, and within hand-shaking distance of a smiling Doug Hawkins. Around the corner from Footscray College is a flower shop called the Bulldog Florist. I don't believe there is another flower shop in the English-speaking world called the Bulldog Florist ('When Footscray does well,' says Peter Gordon, 'the West is proud').

Footscray's next tourist attraction, continuing along Dynon Road, is Franco Cozzo's furniture palace. Franco Cozzo changed the way Footscray is spoken – to *Footerscray* – in the course of advertising beds which look like the sort of vehicle Mad Max would turn up in if he were taking Mae West to the drive-in. they have wings, mirrors, control panels and huge swirling bedheads in dramatic tones. The proud placard announcing Franco Cozzo's business has an Australian flag in the bottom right-hand corner and a signature declaring it to be the work of Bulldog Signs. Having passed Franco Cozzo's, you enter Footscray's business district which is almost wholly Asian in character. Saigon Travel Tours, Van Dzung Fashion Fabrics, Phong Mach Surgery, Dong Tanh unisex salon, Phillipine Videos, Klinika Philipino, Tiem Banh Golden Sweet Cake House.

In May 1989, football legend Ron Barassi was accused of racism after saying on radio that Footscray's poor attendances at the Western Oval were due to the influx of Vietnamese people into the area and the number of drug addicts transferring their activities from St Kilda to the western suburbs. He was advocating that Footscray leave the Western Oval. Barassi may have been careless in his phrasing – that is, grouping drug addicts with an ethnic group – but the fact remains that, by 1989, Footscray's attendances were the poorest of the eleven Melbourne teams. The club which appeared, forty years earlier, to have the resources to become the next Collingwood, the next great working-class power in the game was instead on the verge of extinction, fatally weakened by internal bickering and social changes beyond its control or imagining. Australia now has more people born overseas than any country in the world other than Israel, and most of them have been channelled into the western suburbs of Sydney and Melbourne. Footscray Football Club would never again know itself, or its supporters, as surely as it did in 1954.

Once, however, the club's existence was threatened from outside – that is, from the offices of the VFL in the city of Melbourne – it became a symbol of an older, larger struggle. Footscray people were being asked to believe that a club playing from Fitzroy's home ground (then Princes Park), in Fitzroy colours (with a slight modification in design), under the control of the Fitzroy coach and board of directors, represented Footscray. A ghost had been waiting by the Maribyrnong: the ghost of the old Footscray with its pride, its distinctive traditions, its sense of existing in opposition to Melbourne. Former Footscray mayor Lynne Kosky said the merger was yet another example 'of business making decisions for the people of the West'. Peter Gordon quoted the actor Peter Finch from the film *Network*: 'We're mad as hell and we're not going to take it any more.' A generation of older residents – particularly women – suddenly materialised and started working as volunteers. A pensioner, Irene Chatfield, agreed to take the VFL to the Supreme Court.

The club was given nineteen days to raise the $1.5 million necessary to eliminate the club's debt. Miracles were reported. A German in lederhosen and a St Kilda guernsey doorknocked North Altona and returned with bags overflowing with silver coins. The Footscray Cheer Squad marched down Barkly Street singing the club son. 'Sons of the Scray' (an Indian gentleman thought it was the national anthem), and had twenty and fifty dollar notes thrust into their hands by Vietnamese stall owners at the Footscray market. Footscray had already raised the necessary amount when chemical manufacturer ICI announced a major sponsorship worth $300,000. Alan Dalton, co-author of *Too Tough to Die*, believes the Fightback proved that while the ethnic composition of the West had changed, the old spirit remained. In his scholarly work *A History of Footscray*, Melbourne University historian John Lack wrote, 'Footscray, it seemed, had dissolved into a loose collection of ethnic communities, separated by language, and by customs, and by football codes … For many people, the red, white and blue of the F.F.C. had become the last sure identifier.'

But would the last sure identifier retain its grip?

Dynon Road becomes Hopkins Street and then Barkly Street. Barkly Street continues through the Footscray business district and then intersects with Geelong Road. Some of the older Footscray residents recall seeing flocks of sheep being droved down Geelong Road as late as the 1960s. On the other side of the intersection, like an old wooden ark on the edge of a bright, ever-shifting sea of change, sits the Western Oval.

Doug Hawkins

In the first week of January 1993, Footscray began playing practice matches at Skinner Reserve, a few kilometres past the Western Oval in Braybrook. Doug Hawkins, the captain of the Footscray Football Club, is a Braybrook boy. I once spent a day driving around the western suburbs with Dougie. He showed me the Housing Commission flat he grew up in and the street where he learned to kick torpedo punts to follow the curve in the road. He also showed me the deserted house in Braybrook where the homeless kids slept. We went inside. It was empty – bare mattresses, empty milk containers, glass from a shattered window across the floor. 'I understand these kids,' he said. 'I come from the same place they do.'

Dougie Hawkins was the bloke everyone in the western suburbs knew, the one with the wild, drunken past. But he had another name: Hawk. Hawk could spin and sway, stop and prop; the sun danced off his boots. He had power and poise: he could guide the ball along the boundary line through a stampede of feet, emerge intact, turn inside and score. He held his ground against bigger men. In the 1985 preliminary final, he worked the blunt force of Robert Dipierdomenico like a matador. At Footscray, they said Hawk was one of the best three or four players that had ever been at the club. But Dougie was 33 now and dancing on a dacron knee. He called himself an old bloke.

At the height of summer, Skinner Reserve was a shaved armpit of a ground, bare but for a scoreboard and a partially condemned grandstand. Some days, the temperature was well above 30 degrees Celsius. The heat was like the air which escapes from a recently stopped car when you lift the bonnet. Choco Royal had difficulty breathing. I had difficulty watching. Football seemed wrong at that time of year, unseasonable, out of place. Men in whites with zinc cream on their noses should have been playing cricket, a game with slow, easeful rhythms. Football was too fast, too furious, too unrelenting. Centreman Simon Atkins had to rub sunburn lotion into his scalp before taking the field.

But supporters still came to watch. At breaks, they clustered round their teams, like they used to in the old days. But in the old days, they heard what the coach said. Not any more, at least not in January. They didn't raise their voices. Wheeler was too busy issuing instructions, rearranging parts, tinkering with what he called his structure. 'Kick it high to centre-half-forward,' he told his players. 'I'll trust in our big blokes being able to mark it or our little fellows roving it from predictable knock-downs.' That was one of the first things I noticed about Wheeler: whether or not he had a premiership team, he planned as if he did.

Teams are designed, like cars, and Wheeler's team

had two key components. One was his 'first four', that is, the four players at the centre bounces – ruckman Scott Wynd, rover Tony Liberatore, centreman Simon Atkins and ruck-rover Leon Cameron. Wynd and Liberatore were Brownlow medallists, and Atkins – known as Axe – had been one of the Players of the Year in '92. Cameron was a gamble. Darren Baxter, Footscray's ruck-rover in '92, had played every game of the season, accumulating more than 500 possessions. At the end of the year, to the surprise of most (but not all), Wheeler had cleared him to Hawthorn. His replacement, twenty-year-old Leon Cameron, had played only three senior games in 1992, but Wheeler believed he was the more skilful player and a young man whose time had come. By adding a gifted and naturally offensive player to his first four, Wheeler also hoped to force opposition sides to reduce the attention they were paying to Axe. The other ingredient critical to Footscray's success was its set of four tall marking forwards: Coleman, Grant, Del-Re and Ballantyne. Wheeler hoped to make then interchangeable.

Ron Barassi's introduction of what is called the running game in, or around, 1970, revolutionised Australian football. The running game utilises the handpass as an offensive weapon, thereby providing teams with a means of by-passing taller, stronger, uglier opponents – particularly Tom Hafey's ferocious Richmond teams. In the mid-1980s, when Essendon's great dual premiership team started to falter, Kevin Sheedy added to the running game by insisting on versatility – that is, players who could play in a variety of positions. The effect was to vest more tactical power in the coach. The more positions each individual within the team can play, the more pieces the coach has to move about. Wheeler believed football was a players' game. He urged his players to wrest back control of the game, to make decisions for themselves. 'You don't win premierships with players who only do what they're told to do.'

Wheeler believed the pre-season parachute jump was an exercise in decision making. The Footscray players had been required to attend a sky-diving course at Pakenham aerodrome; what decision they made on the basis of the information they received from the instructors was their business. That was why he misled the media and brawled with them when they turned up on the day. The Jump was private. In the year I was at Footscray, I never heard mention of the two who didn't jump. I did hear, however, about the last two who did – Doug Hawkins and Mark Hunter. They watched from the Williamstown foreshore as the first group dropped through the sky, whooping and yelling. That decided Dougie. He kissed the photograph of his wife in his wallet, then made haste for Laverton air base with Hunter, whose wife was pregnant with their first child, beside him. Danny Del-Re was sitting slightly apart from the others when Dougie strode around the corner. 'I'm coming,' said Dougie. 'I feel better,' said Danny.

The first practice match I saw Footscray play was at Skinner's Reserve the Monday after the Jump. It followed what Wheeler called a floor session at the Western Oval. He sat in a tall canvas director's chair, and invited comments from the players, who were lying on their sides or sitting with their backs against the wall. I was surprised at how quiet and orderly they were as a group, but the exhilaration, the wild thrill of what they had done, was still evident among them. Dougie didn't mind admitting he was afraid. 'I don't like aeroplanes,' he said, 'and I don't swim in the sea because I'm shit scared of sharks.' Everyone laughed.

In 1992, one the eve of Australia Day, the Footscray players had climbed Mount Bogong in the dark and witnessed the dawn from its summit. That had been a symbol for the start of a new era in the history of the club, and the symbol had held its power: the team had duly made the preliminary final. In 1993, Wheeler had invited them to take the next step, to experience the wild splendour of playing in front of 100,000 people and competing for a place in history. With that in mind, they had overcome all manner of fears and objections, and stepped out of an aeroplane with the earth a distant blur beneath them.

The intra-club practice match Footscray played the Monday after the Jump was hard, intense and deeply personal. Best-on-ground? Doug Hawkins. The old bloke who didn't like aeroplanes and was shit scared of sharks was back in his element and clearly grateful to be so.

The President

One hot Saturday, I encountered Peter Gordon, the president of the Footscray Football Club, sitting with other Footscray supporters on the gravelly slope along from the condemned grandstand at Skinner Reserve. He was looking scruffy in casual clothes of vaguely fashionable intent. Freckled and slightly plump, he had gone pink in the heat. I had previously met Gordon and knew his manner: he thinks before speaking – the thoughts can be seen speeding past his eyes like a lane of fast-flowing traffic – and then expresses himself in a few short, abrupt phrases. The president speaks like a western-suburbs boy. One of his sons was with him. At least on of his sons was usually with him at the football, as was his wife Kerrie. She was the other co-author of *Too Tough to Die*, a quiet but independently minded woman who had organised a women's supporters group for the club which invited people like Moira Rayner, the Equal Opportunity Commissioner, dismissed in mid-1993 by the Kennett government, to speak.

When I next met Gordon, in the city, he was looking scruffy in a lawyer's suit and tie. The tie looked as if a kid in the playground had just tugged it from behind. I also noticed that he had crusts of blood on both ears. That day, a story on the back page of the *Herald Sun* newspaper quoted Gordon as saying that the Goods and Services Tax proposed by the Liberal Party at the forthcoming federal election was a threat to the survival of the AFL clubs in Melbourne. The chairman of the AFL Commission, Ross Oakley, was quoted as taking the contrary view, saying Gordon's views did not take into account the increased money football fans could expect to have after the abolition of payroll and sales tax, and income tax cuts. 'A lot of good that'll do unemployed people and pensioners in the western suburbs,' snorted Gordon. What really irked him was that the article identified him as a supporter of the Labor Party. Why, he asked, did the media never explore the connections between the Liberal Party and the AFL? Gordon claimed the AFL (and its predecessor, the VFL) had presided over the 'corporatisation' of football. In 1981, then VFL president Allen Aylett had been asked about the possibility of clubs being forced out of existence by the demands of a national competition. 'It's reasonable,' he said, 'it happens in every form of business.' But was business the essential character of football?

I asked Gordon about his ears. Burst blood blisters from burns sustained while watching football at Skinner Reserve. But the president was more interested in my companion whom he had identified as a graduate of Melbourne University and the son of a prominent Labor Party figure.

'Who do you barrack for?' asked Gordon.

'Geelong,' replied my friend.

'Where's your politics?' The challenge came with a grin, but was a challenge nonetheless. The president was a bulldog.

Peter Gordon grew up in the shadow of a petrol refinery, and the black effluent it blithely funnelled into the air was a source of discord in the family home. His father, Jack Gordon, was a quiet Catholic who worked for the same employer for 28 years and voted DLP after the Labor Party split in 1955. Once, walking past Melbourne Grammar in his blue overalls, Jack Gordon had a bucket of water flung over him by a bunch of kids. He may have forgotten the incident, but his son never did. When his wife wanted to ring the authorities and complain about the refinery, Jack Gordon forbad it. Eventually, they agreed that she could ring on an anonymous basis. The following night, her fifteen-year-old son rang the same number, identified himself and demanded to know what action had been taken in relation to his mother's complaint.

Doug Hawkins was Peter Gordon was real smart, and Dougie was right. The two novels which fashioned Gordon's youthful consciousness were James Joyce's *Portrait of the Artist as a Young Man* and Fyodor Dostoevsky's *Crime and Punishment*, two mighty books with one element in common: in both, the central character is a young man in revolt against the world. At university, Gordon deepened his political awareness by reading Marx. He also teamed with the only other student in the law faculty at Melbourne University from the western suburbs and set up the Western Suburbs Legal Service. He became so heavily involved in the voluntary practice that by the fourth and final year of his degree, he was pursuing it to the virtual exclusion of his lectures and tutorials. In 1980, he was employed as an articled clerk by Slater and Gordon, a left-wing firm which acted on behalf of workers and trade unions. Its famous advocate, 'Red' Ted Hill, had appeared in the Petrov Royal Commission. He told Peter Gordon that judges had no right to respect because they were part of the social problem, not the solution. What particularly impressed Peter Gordon was that Hill stood up in court and told judges they were part of the problem. Confront your enemy, said Hill.

Hill made a deep impression on Peter Gordon. So did another champion of the western suburbs, E.J. 'Ted' ('Mr Football') Whitten. Whitten had been skilful, versatile and aggressive - an aggressor, in my dictionary, being defined as someone who initiates hostilities. Gordon moved into the area of environmental law, quickly winning a string of cases in the western suburbs, and then toxic tort litigation. In 1985, he won the first common law action in Australia for a victim of mesothelioma, a cancer produced by contact with asbestos. The following year, Gordon was contacted by a Western Australian group caused the Asbestos Disease Society; shortly afterwards, in a small house on the outskirts of Perth, he was confronted with a room of dying men and grieving relatives, victims of what is said to be Australia's worst industrial disaster – the Wittenoom asbestos mine.

Peter Gordon persuaded his firm to fund the case. An early reversal in the wholesale legal warfare which followed almost bankrupted Slater and Gordon, but, in 1989, the same year as he orchestrated the Fightback campaign ('Dogs Lick VFL,' read the *Western Times*), Gordon negotiated a $25 million damages settlement for 330 Wittenoom victims. At the time, he was only 32 years old. Four years later, he was flying regularly to the United States advising legal firms in that country on suits launched by AIDS victims, a senior partner in Slater and Gordon, a member of the Melbourne committee of the Australian Republican Movement, and football's unofficial Leader of the Opposition. His critics said he tried to do too much, but there were also voices who said he was the man to take on the Victorian Premier, Jeff Kennett.

Peter Gordon respected Terry Wheeler's passion. He likened him to R.P. McMurphy, the character played by Jack Nicholson in the film *One Flew Over The Cuckoo's Nest*, in particular the scene in which McMurphy takes bets that he can break out of the asylum and go to a bar downtown. His plan is to lift a drinking fountain from its base and throw it through the hospital window, so that it takes the prison bars with it. He makes not one shuddering attempt but three. Finally, forced to accept the impossibility of the task, he stalks past the other inmates. 'I tried, goddamit,' he says. 'At least, I tried.' But Gordon and Wheeler were too unalike to be friends. Wheeler was an educator, Gordon a politically orientated lawyer. Wheeler was intuitive and operated on the basis of belief. Gordon was a man of strong beliefs, but his thinking was essentially pragmatic. The parachute jump gave Gordon sleepless nights. There was the issue of cost, of accidents and possible compensation. The president's politics had moderated since his student days. He now perceived that profit was essential to the club's survival. While Footscray remained in the black, the AFL had no pretext for tipping them out of the competition, and the club had duly recorded a profit in each of the three years since the Fightback.

Gordon wanted to make the western suburbs as wholly supportive of Footscray – as madly parochial – as Adelaide is with the Crows. The old social club in the John Gent Stand had been known to the players as the Pig-sty. Gordon's administration replaced it with a $5 million complex with a view from the top floor which extended to the distant Dandenong mountains. Gordon also brought baseball (the Melbourne Monarchs) and soccer (Brunswick Juventus) to the Western Oval to bolster its status as a sporting venue, and, through chief executive Dennis Galimberti, actively sought to reintegrate the club with the community which had saved it. Footscray sponsored the Western Region Alcohol and Drug Rehabilitation Centre and became involved in programs for the homeless and the unemployed. It initiated Care for Kids program which basically made footballers available as teachers' aids throughout the western suburbs. Dougie Hawkins was sent to Braybrook Primary School and put in a Grade 6 music class. At the same time, Wheeler set about re-creating his sense of a football club, taking the players to the Footscray Town Hall in Napier Street to see where Charlie Sutton had shown the premiership cup to 6000 supporters on grand final night 1954, inviting home the prodigal sons of the '70s – Bernie Quinlan, Gary Dempsey, George Bissett, Bones McGhie – and employing them as skills coaches. Football clubs are strange beasts with two heads, a coach and a president, and there were inevitable tensions between

Gordon and Wheeler, but on one thing they were agreed: a premiership was required to secure Footscray's future. 'We're not under threat at the moment,' said Gordon, 'but things can change.'

Super

In Footscray folklore, Steve Macpherson, known as Super, was second only to Dougie, perhaps because many of the incidents for which they were famous occurred while they were together. Super (named after the hamburger, Super Mac) had been recruited from Clarence in Tasmania at the age of 14 – along with his older brother Rod – after a carnival in Darwin at which he won a medal for being the best schoolboy footballer in Australia. He had come to Melbourne the following year. Looking back, he saw himself as having been a kid who lacked confidence and sought approval in the eyes of others. Dougie was someone he immediately felt at ease with (everyone immediately felt at ease with Doug Hawkins), but these were Dougie's drinking days. Sometimes, in the rooms, Dougie and Super played at fighting. Dougie threw big loopy lefts and looked around grinning, as if he was worried someone might take them seriously. Super had a quiet humour in his eyes too, but his style was a whole lot deadlier. He kept walking forward, parrying, opening up his friend for the big punch he never threw. Super's father, a merchant navy man from Glasgow, had done some boxing. He had been a reserved man.

Super was candid about his life. In 1983, he broke the jaw of a Collingwood player in a practice mach, an incident which led to him receiving a five-match suspension and being sued in the civil courts. The crowds started telling him he was an animal, which wasn't what he wanted to hear. The following year, he was charged with assault after an incident in a Torquay bar during a training camp. The crowd response to him worsened. He found it easiest to become the sort of person they said he was; if they were going to call him names, he'd make sure they said them with feeling. Whole chunks of seasons began disappearing through suspension. He also found that the only person who could live Doug Hawkins' lifestyle and still play league football was Doug Hawkins. Super's body started registering the toll with injuries. I recall a mark I saw Super take in 1985 when Footscray defeated Hawthorn at Princes Park, running with the flight of the ball. It was the act of a young man careless with skill and courage. But Steve Macpherson didn't become the player he should have and, at the start of 1991, Wheeler told him the only position for which he was being considered was the back pocket and that the was sixth in line for it. 'You're going to have to find something,' said the coach.

People had been throwing him books for years on subjects like self-esteem and personal growth. Super began reading them. He also began working for the club, running its Care for Kids program. The days when it was of some value to schools having footballers kick end-to-end in the playground for half an hour had gone. But league footballers could be of use as male role models, particularly in areas with a high incidence of single-parent families. He found adolescent boys listened when he talked about fear. He noticed how small girls without fathers often wanted to hold his hand. He saw that it helped if he and Phil Krakouer went along when a busload of kids were taken to the musical, *Oliver*. At 27, Super had the thoughtfulness of a leader, and a natural authority within the club. The Footscray players had been advised to take no part in Fightback as it could prejudice their chances of being picked by the new club. Dougie was wary. Super wasn't. He stood at the microphone at the Fightback rally and sang a version of 'American Pie' which included the line, 'This is the day that Footscray didn't die.'

Super wanted to be the next captain of Footscray. He was shrewd, he had fire and hard football sense, but he could no longer be sure of his body. He was recovering from an operation to his right shoulder when we met. His left shoulder had previously been operated on. He missed Footscray's first match in the pre-season competition – against Carlton, under lights, at Waverley, in the Foster's Cup – so I sat with him in the stand. Super said it was a game of hurt.

The Foster's Cup

On the day of the Fightback rally, a Church of Christ minister named Ian Corlett approached Wheeler and offered to help in whatever way he could. Ian had spent twenty years working in the Kensington Housing Estate and coached junior sides in the Footscray District Football League. Three months later, on New Year's Day 1990, Ron James was killed in a water ski-ing accident. The young man who had played in Williamstown's grand final side at the age of fourteen had since graduated to Footscray. His death was a major blow to the club at a time when it was struggling to find new life and momentum. Wheeler sensed that a number of the players were in a state of shock and unable to express their feelings. For the first time, he wondered if the job was too big for him. With the utmost caution, the coach introduced Ian to the life of the club, personally monitoring his initial contacts. Three years later, Ian went most places with the players; he even jumped out of aeroplanes with them. Super said Ian was someone 'you could open up to'.

Before the Foster's Cup match against Carlton in March 1993, Wheeler told Ray Green, the team manager, that I had the same access as Ian Corlett. 'The same as Ian!' bellowed Greenie. Greenie was a sergeant-major. It was Greenie who got the boys, as he called the players, into uniform. On match day, they wore navy blazer, dark trousers, denim blue shirt and club tie. Dougie Hawkins remembered the first night he'd worn the tie to a club function. It made him feel nervous. But he didn't mind the change in the club. 'Footscray's more professional now,' he said. 'We know what it's been like for players at Carlton and Hawthorn all these years.' With Greenie's reluctant agreement, I entered the team room for the first time.

With the media, Wheeler's speech was formal and slightly awkward. He tended to speak in concepts which then had to be processed by the listener. The closer he was to the game, however, the simpler and more powerful his language became. That night, feeling flowed from him. During his pre-match address, I noticed Dougie swaying with the words, letting them work their way into his body. At half-time, everything was going to plan. The structure was holding, Footscray led by twenty points. I was intrigued to hear what Wheeler would say. He didn't. Bursting through the door of the coach's room, quivering hand aloft, he said, 'Okay. Any questions?' That was his half-time address: dealing with questions from the floor, clarifying instructions, keeping the machine, with its twenty parts, tuned and on course.

But the match was an omen. In the third quarter, Carlton challenged Footscray, not with any superior system but with vigour and zest. Basically, all they had was Kernahan on the forward line. The Dogs toughed it out but in the next round, against Fitzroy at Kardinia Park, they were overrun from the start. At half-time, with Fitzroy leading by fifteen points, Wheeler shouted at his players, 'Which Fitzroy player is cutting you up? There isn't one. You're being beaten as a team!'

Footscray rallied to lose by five points. I never saw Wheeler as angry again. 'What was that shit, Scottie?' he said, confronting his big ruckman. Wynd had kicked when he was supposed to handball. The Brownlow Medal suddenly didn't seem to count for a lot. Wheeler then rushed over to his captain and attacked him for giving away two needless free kicks. 'Your mind wasn't on the job!' Dougie's face reddened. The third player to feel the force of his blazing anger was wingman Nigel Kellett. He had hesitated when an opportunity presented itself on the half-forward line in the last quarter; Fitzroy had swept the ball away.

The players sat around on the changeroom floor, silent and morose. Wheeler faced them as a team. 'It is not your right to choose when you will represent the Footscray Football Club,' he thundered.

Afterwards, different players were summoned individually to speak to the match committee. Peter Foster and Scott Wynd were among them. No one was allowed to leave the rooms until all interviews were complete. 'It's like being at school,' muttered one of the younger players. I thought so, too.

The Question

The afternoon before the first match of the season proper – against Collingwood, under lights, at the MCG – I had a talk with Axe.

Axe had a poker face and eyes that saw everything. At an early team meeting I attended, Justin Charles, a young ruckman who played in the '92 finals, said, 'Go where Axe tells you. He knows where the ball's going to go.' Dougie was captain, but Axe was the mind at work behind Footscray's plays. Wheeler referred to him as the playing coach. 'I get dirty with blokes who don't think,' growled Axe. His square, pale, shuffling body seemed too slow for the task assigned him; his speed was in his hands and eyes. If Axe played well, the Footscray flow became a torrent. Once, during a break, when Wheeler was trying to organise better clearances from the centre, he asked Axe how much time he needed. 'A quarter of a second,' shot back Axe. It was a Footscray saying: how long do we need with the ball, Axe? A quarter of a second.

Axe was only 23, but he seemed a lot older. 'I'm

going back to Tassie as soon as I'm finished here,' he said. In his first two years at Footscray, he was home for the grand final. Home was Wynyard in northern Tasmania. The hills around his home are among the lushest in the land. Jutting into Bass Strait on the western side of the town is a flat headland called Table Cape. From the air, it looks like a neat carpet of greens, golds, and rich dark browns. They were Axe's colours. He had originally come to Footscray with his twin. It was Paul who wanted to come; Axe didn't. The club insisted they come as a pair, then, midway through their second season, cut Paul from the list. In a Tasmanian newspaper, Paul Atkins said no one would ever understand how much being cut from the list had hurt. Axe said Mick Malthouse thought Paul was having a bit much run. 'I lost a lot of confidence and motivation then.'

Axe played for Footscray in a long-sleeved guernsey, number 23. Paul played for the Burnie Hawks in a long-sleeved guernsey, number 32. 'Paul's louder than me,' said Axe, 'that's how people tell us apart.' As a joke, Paul once sat in on one of Malthouse's pre-match addresses as Simon. 'We must have won the week before,' said Axe, 'because Mick seen the funny side of it.' Once, when he was in his teens, Axe didn't come home. His mother was alarmed, but Paul sensed – correctly – that his brother was in no danger. Axe called it 'the thing twins have'. One night, at training, Wheeler saw Axe holding his hamstring and asked him if he had an injury. 'No,' he said, 'but I think Paul has.' Paul was in Tasmania. Wheeler wished he'd had both of them.

Axe was Wheeler's prize pupil. In 1992, Axe had 676 disposals, the third highest tally in the league, but by the end of the season the other teams were alert to him.

Each week, when he took the field, he met a tag – a shadow whose function was to block, frustrate and negate him. He had not been as prominent in the finals.

I asked Axe about the match at Geelong, I thought Footscray had tried. They just hadn't played well. Axe said playing on a Sunday in Geelong probably hadn't help, 'but if each of us could have found this much' – he indicated the smallest of fractions with a forefinger and a thumb – 'we might have won.'

'But if you try and it's not there, what more can you do?'

He grinned. His large pale face briefly looked young.

'That's the question,' he said.

II

The First Game

The season began with fireworks. Players from both teams congregated in the two races to watch the big iridescent dandelions pulsing to life in the night sky above the MCG, and I felt an excitement I hadn't known in years. It's called Seeing The Other Team Before The Game. The strangers with whom you are about to become intimately acquainted. The Collingwood players were in uniform – grey slacks, black short-sleeve shirts – but there was also an inner-city flashness about them. A number were sporting Depression haircuts, floppy on top and nothing around the edges. Watson, their young half-back flanker, had jug ears and a long solemn face. He looked as if he'd been recruited from Collingwood's 1930 premiership photo, and played like it too, as if he were blind to any form of human endeavour other than the pursuit of an odd-shaped leather ball. In the first quarter, he lined up Nigel Kellett.

Kellett was what Wheeler called a running kicker. He had a sprinter's pace, and the same finely tuned athleticism. His role was offensive: to make swerving runs through the opposition defence, scoring if possible. But first he had to collect the ball. He was at his most vulnerable, bent and stooping, the yellow ball bobbing away from his fingers, when Watson made his charge. Kellett saw him with a moment to spare, but the impact of the collision still lifted him off his feet; his body curled as it was thrown backwards through the air. I was standing next to Choco Royal.

'How did he get up after that?' I asked.

'He's tough, Nigel,' said Choco, nodding. 'He takes a lot of hits, playing on the wing.' Choco had missed the game through injury.

I turned, anxious for a second opinion, and found Chris Grant behind me.

No one at Footscray interested me more than Grant. Dougie said he was going to be a champion, and Dougie said the word champion should not be used loosely. Super said it was a pleasure to play twenty games of football with him a year, and I didn't hear Super say that about anyone else. Three floating fragments of bone had been surgically removed from Grant's ankle the previous week. Before the game, E.J. Whitten had shaken his hand and said, 'It hurts to miss the big ones, eh?' and Grant had nodded.

The young centre-half-forward's eyes were following the game, glittering with excitement. It took him a moment to focus on my inquiry. 'It only hurts for an instant,' he said, then his eyes darted back to the play. He was missing the game.

Two men fell in the first quarter. Libber backed into a pack and met Collingwood full-forward Saverio Rocca travelling like a lorry down an empty motorway.

The little rover's head bounced as it hit the ground. When a Footscray player tried to lift his body, it fell slackly from his arms. On the television, there was genuine anxiety in the commentator's voice. Libber didn't sham. He was carried past us on a stretcher, body inert, eyes glazed, head at an angle. Pert, the Collingwood full-back, was taken from the field shortly afterwards, concussed by a team-mate's knee. Pert had one of my favourite players in his Fitzroy days, flinging himself about like a soccer goalie, hanging suspended in the air. As a player, he was mean and conservative now. Maybe it was his coach. Or maybe it was the knee injury he had suffered. Wonky knees have caused many an angel in Australian football to fall to earth.

Axe began well in the centre, and when Axe did well Footscray prospered. They could start erecting their structure, relying on the tall marking forward which the critics said Footscray didn't possess. Axe was playing on Tony Shaw, a Collingwood captain in the Lou Richard street-urchin mould. Shaw would say anything to an opponent, usually with a sneer. Axe wore his red hair long, with a strip of ginger whiskers on his chin. In a previous game, Shaw had told him that as he hadn't had a haircut, he'd pull his hair out for him. Shaw was in the business of making his opponents look at him and not the ball, and there was a view that in the past, with Axe, he'd succeeded. But Wheeler, when I asked him, wasn't interested in the past. 'What about the future?' he said.

Axe had eight possessions in the first quarter. He directed play, congratulating Danny Del-Re after he completed a lead by crashing through a defensive wall. In the disarray, Footscray sneaked a goal. When Watson line up Axe, the Footscray centreman waited until the very last, then soccered the ball past him with his right foot so that the Collingwood player shot past having collected neither body nor ball.

Footscray surged. Matthew Croft was doing well on the half-forward line in only his seventh game of AFL football. Croft was tall and lithe. He played with initiative and daring, but before the match he'd been gripped with nerves to the extent that it affected his breathing. There were 60,000 people in the stands. The thump of the rock band during the pre-match entertainment could be heard in the concrete underbelly of the stadium. Wheeler had lain on the floor beside him. 'Imagine you're back in Mildura, Matthew. Can you see the trotting track? Can you see the cars? You're at home, you're running out on the ground, can you see it?' That was probably the question Wheeler asked his players more often than any other: can you see it? Croft said he could. 'Okay, Matthew,' said Wheeler, 'it's no different.'

In the second half of the quarter, a different pattern emerged. Footscray were generally solid in defence and controlling the centre square, but Collingwood's smaller players were collecting the ball as it came to ground and skimming into attack. At half-time, Collingwood were ten points ahead. It could have been seen as a significant reversal, but Wheeler assured them otherwise. 'The game is going exactly as we wish,' he said. His speech was slow and deliberate, like a man trying to speak over the sound of a fast-flowing river. 'I told you it would be won in that last fifteen minutes of the last quarter. We are positioned to do that.'

And Libber was coming back on to the field.

It seemed scarcely believable, but he was on his toes, responding to handballs fired at him from about one or two metres, when the team re-entered the rooms at half-time. The situation suddenly seemed redeemable. Collingwood had moved wingman Graeme Wright to the half-backline at quarter-time. Wright had been credited with 15 possessions for the term, enough for three men. His opponent, Rohan Smith, was young and gifted, but he lacked any instinct for defence. If Wright were countered, Footscray should be able to wrest back control of the game.

For a period, they did; ruck-rover Leon Cameron neatly side-stepping opponents, swaying through packs, kicking long off either foot, punishing Collingwood through the centre of the ground. But again, the further the quarter went, the more the flashing feet of Collingwood rover Tony Francis became the game's dominant image. At the start of the final term, Footscray again demonstrated its grand intent, pummelling the Collingwood defence with a sustained assault on goal which lasted most of the term. The lead had changed nine times in the course of the game, but ultimately Footscray could not secure a winning advantage. Danny Del-Re had managed four goals, but of Footscray's other forwards Hawkins, Coleman and Ballantyne had all been benched, as had centre-half-back Peter Foster. The final undeniable advantage was Collingwood's, but the winning margin, 20 points, did not reflect the life of the game.

Seven of Collingwood's 17 goals had come from a combination of free kicks and 50-metre penalties, and there were mutterings about the umpires capitulating, as usual, to the huge pro-Collingwood crowd.

Wheeler acknowledged the grievance, but he also listed four or five players whom he said would have to find more if they were going to be part of his plan, Standfield, Macpherson and Foster among them. 'The boat will go without you,' he said. He also criticised a young player for going to ground too often. 'Did you break your leg out there, son? You stayed down as if you had. This is a tough game. You've got to get up.' But he did not allow that defeat was total. Far from it. Footscray had accumulated 218 kicks and 111 handballs and Wheeler maintained that 300 possessions was sufficient to win a game of football. The problem, he said, was one of method.

Libber

How do you write a season? It goes so fast, at least to begin with. Like a rapid. Round 2 was Melbourne; the game was a scramble. Again, Wheeler's structure held for the first half. Again, Footscray were overrun at half-time. By the end of the match, Neitz and Schwarz, the Demons' two young forwards, were competing to see who could leap highest in the air. Footscray had nothing comparable at their end of the ground. Libber won it for them. He was awesome, accelerating into the base of packs, forcing the whole game and everyone in it to bend to the will of the smallest man on the ground (163 centimetres). His stats read 17 kicks, 16 handballs and four goals, including the last of the match. He laid one-third of his team's tackles. In 1992, he laid 136 tackles, 61 more than any other player in the league. 'I just love tackling.' He said, black eyes shining, when I asked him why he did it. Libber dropped them all, big and small. They usually made the mistake of thinking they could run over the top of him, then felt the man-trap spring shut around their thighs and drag them to earth.

Libber was a twin, like Axe. Fred Liberatore was the stronger, more passive one of the pair. Libber said playing footy was like playing with your brother. Libber was at ease talking about his family. His mother, one of 13 children, had been orphaned and spent her adolescence in a convent in Abruzzo, central Italy. Each Footscray home game, she stood on the fence beside the players' race, a tiny, daintily dressed woman fraught with passion and shouting at the umpires. Libber had tried to persuade his mother to watch from the grandstand but she wouldn't. His father watched the game from the other side of the ground on his own. He was the quiet one, the thinker. 'Dad's the rock,' said Libber. 'Mum's more impulsive.' Libber said he was like his mother. As a boy, Libber had won an under-13 best and fairest. In 1984, he won the Morrish Medal for the best and fairest player in the VFL Under-19 competition. In 1986 and 1988, he won the Gardiner Medal for the best and fairest player in the VFL reserves. But the board his mother had made for Libber's medals had a fifth peg in the middle. At a time when very few people believed her son could play AFL football, she believed he could win a Brownlow Medal.

I recalled the night he hobbled up to collect his Brownlow, leg in plaster. There was no doubting his pleasure, but there was also a calmness about him. It was as if other people were seeing, for the first time, what Libber had always known: he was a player. The story went that when Libber was cut from the North Melbourne list, the coach, John Kennedy, didn't even know who he was. Initially, Footscray didn't see much in him either. Mick Malthouse only played him in the wet. After being overlooked for a night match early in 1990, he had decided to leave Footscray. He'd even gone so far as to say goodbye to the club which, for Libber, meant saying goodbye to Dougie. Libber said Dougie was a huge part of Footscray. 'Don't go, mate,' said Dougie, 'Everybody loves you down here. You'd be first picked in my side.' Dougie said Wheeler was different from Mick as a coach, that he'd suit Libber. But Libber's mind was made up; he filled in the papers nominating himself for the draft. He was to drop them off at AFL House at two o'clock. Unbeknown to him, Choco Royal had been injured, thereby creating an opening in the side for a rover. Wheeler rang him at one o'clock, telling him he was in the side for that weekend's practice match. Libber believed in fate.

In the third game of the season, Footscray met Fitzroy at Princes Park. Initially, it went the same way as the Foster's Cup game at Kardinia Park. Fitzroy were busy and alert, racing to a 21-point lead by quarter-time. Axe was arguing with the umpires. One of them, Peter Cameron, warned Wheeler when they crossed during the break that he'd report his centreman if he didn't hold his tongue. On television, you could see Wheeler talking to Axe, both hands raised, and Axe shaking his head and turning away.

In the second term, Footscray held on and Wheeler made his first significant move of the season. He brought Keenan Reynolds, known as Crackers, out of defence and put him on a forward flank. Crackers was a Werribee boy, like Test cricketer Merv Hughes. He had a hot tuna tattooed on his breast and he liked a few beers the night before a game. He also like to say what he thought. When Wheeler showed edited highlights of the 1992 season intercut with scenes from the parachute jump, each of the plays he had selected was a forward move resulting in a goal. From the rear of the room, Crackers started interjecting, hand cupped around his mouth, 'Where's the fucken backmen?'

Crackers had spent his childhood watching games from the mayoral box at Windy Hill, two of his grandparents had been mayors of Essendon. At the age of 16, he'd seen Essendon's 1985 premiership team, said at the time to be the best in the history of the game. When he went to Essendon as a junior, he noted everything that Terry Daniher did at training. If it was good enough for the Essendon captain, it was good enough for Crackers. Six years later, Crackers' body quivered with muscle. He had a good leap and a sure pair of hands. In the Fitzroy game, Crackers gave the Footscray forward line what it had been lacking: a vital, vigorous, positive presence.

At half-time, Wheeler told his players that they were back in control of the match, despite being 23 points down. In the second quarter, they'd had 61 kicks (as opposed to 45 in the first), 16 marks (10) and 33 handballs (18). He acknowledged Crackers' contribution on the forward line and Bernard Toohey's work in defence. 'But we need more out of the centre,' he said. The first twenty minutes of the third quarter must have been how Wheeler dreamed it could be, Big Scottie rising above his opponent at the centre bounces, palming the ball right and left, and Axe, Libber and Leon Cameron meeting it at speed; in the case of Axe, taking it in one hand and slamming it on to his boot in the same stride. Axe's booming torpedo punts gave Footscray an immediate advantage. By three-quarter-time, the margin had been cut to three points.

The last quarter was frenetic, a desperate race to the line. Late in time-on, with Footscray ahead by four points, the ball lobbed into the Dogs' forward line. Dougie was having a lean day, his third in succession. Now he summoned a classic combination of courage and skill to secure the game for Footscray. The bodies rose in two tiers. Dougie's legs were taken from under him and his body seemed to drift sideways through the air, but he neither took his eye off the ball nor surrendered his position at the front of the pack. The ball hit his chest as surely as if he had been standing upright and alone in the middle of a paddock. The papers said it was one of those marks which only champions take, and the papers were right. His kick wobbled, but it was softly hit and didn't deviate too far from its intended path: that was experience. Fitzroy answered his goal, but the scoreboard at the end of the match showed Footscray winning by three points.

Wheeler was delighted.

'I don't like to you,' he said. 'At half-time, I thought you were getting back into it. You're a group who can make things happen.'

Footscray now had the by and, after that, Essendon. Essendon was the only team Footscray hadn't beaten in 1992. As the players filed into the showers I noticed Libber's back. Livid furrows had been clawed in his flesh; it looked as if he had been scourged. The scars would still be visible at the end of the season. I was learning what the players call pressure. Libber had won the match for Footscray against Melbourne. Against Fitzroy, he was, literally, a marked man.

The Quiet

Footscray was quiet to my way of listening. Maybe it was a question of personnel: Axe, Libber and Big Scottie were all reserved in their own way. Mark Hunter was humorous, but in the old Australian out-the-side-of-the-mouth tradition; you had to be standing beside him to hear it. Leon Cameron was a confident young man, but these were early days for him. From the outset, I'd been struck by the number of Footscray players who took nicknames from players at other clubs. Crackers was the only genuine extrovert among them but he didn't like big-heads so he played as if no one was watching. Dougie was the one the people came to see, but he wasn't having a good year, not getting enough of the ball, not influencing games when he did. But even in the old days, when he was making the grass sparkle, he was modest about it. He'd played the smaller crowd on the non-grandstand wing. That's why they named it after him.

Chris Grant was so modest he blushed whenever Greenie declared that he was going to win a Brownlow Medal. Greenie, who doubled as the weights coach, gloried in Grant's build in the way that architects glory in fine buildings they have constructed. His shoulder muscles bulged like plates in a suit of armour. In 1990, at the age of only seventeen, he had kicked 51 goals. As Wheeler was fond of saying, he was only a skinny kid from Daylesford, but he had solemn hands and an instinct which took him to the ball that crucial metre or so ahead of his opponent. Super said he held Footscray's forward line together that season.

I next saw him play the following year at Moorabbin. It was a most instructive match. Footscray were the better schooled side; its players were of the one mind, it had cleaner lines of operation, but St Kilda were more cunning and blessed with the odd brilliant individual. The St Kilda captain, Danny Frawley, spent the afternoon leaning on Grant like an old fence. The younger player couldn't shake his weight, couldn't lead or couldn't cut back. Since then, Grant had added 15 kilograms to his 192-centimetre frame. People said Grant had everything. He was nimble; he could dance on the spot. He could mark over the top of packs and take the ball as his feet. He was brave, uncomplaining and diligent. At the players' Induction Night, I'd noticed Wheeler introducing Chris Grant to Kelvin Templeton, making the connection between a champion of the past and a young player seen as embodying Footscray's future. There could be no greater defeat for Peter Gordon, Terry Wheeler or the new Footscray Football Club than Chris Grant having to be sold to salvage the club's finances of leaving to better himself elsewhere.

My first conversation with Chris Grant was about waking up in his home town, Daylesford. He was leaning on his crutches, watching training the Sunday morning of the bye. I'd woken one winter morning in Daylesford and seen the ice crack and melt and hang in sun-struck droplets from the branches of trees and telephone wires. 'It was pretty hard to come back,' he said, arching his back. Two weeks later, when he was out of plaster, we met in the changerooms. Sensing I wanted to speak to him, he stopped. He handballed to himself, knocking the ball lightly into the air and catching it as he dutifully answered my questions. He had been bored to tears not playing, he said. I asked him his favourite ground. 'This one,' he said, nodding towards the race, 'the Western Oval.'

I was astounded. The Western Oval had as good as ended my football writing career, or maybe it was Mick Malthouse's grimly defensive sides. I remembered a match against Geelong in the west which I spent under the awning on the Doug Hawkins Wing, watching the rain spill down from the roof. I had my sister with me. She recited the Gettysburg Address because she was bored and wanted to go home. Footscray advanced like an army of ants, Geelong eventually decided that if Footscray wanted the match that much they could have it. Surely, a player with Chris Grant's skills was made for the MCG.

'Why the Western Oval?' I asked.

He shrugged. 'It's home,' he said.

Footscray was Tony Campbell's second home. His parting of the ways with the Melbourne Football Club ultimately arose from the issue of whether or not he could participate in an exhibition bout of kick-boxing. In retrospect, he may not have helped his case by bringing a high kick to rest centimetres from coach John Northey's ear in a bid to demonstrate his mastery of the new sport. TC, as he was known, was something of a philosopher. He believed in what the American writer Ayn Rand called the virtue of selfishness. Two things motivated him – money and competition. As a kid, he had wanted to be a businessman not a footballer. 'Make no mistake,' he said, 'if it wasn't for the money, I wouldn't be playing league football.' At Caulfield Grammar, he had excelled in the shot-put and the high jump. It was an unusual combination which meant he combined strength with spring, but was not required to possess great stamina. TC was one of the last podgy footballers, but his self-belief was unassailable. He work his black hair oiled and parted down the middle and his pale plump face was usually tilted back in a way which suggested a mild arrogance. You could imagine TC driving in a Monte Carlo rally between the wars with a set of goggles on his head and wearing a pair of gloves. That's what the Footscray supporters called him – Gloves. When TC came to Footscray, he was told the club was looking to him to add some colour. Being a professional, he promptly obliged, wearing lime-green tights to training and gloves in matches. 'Gloves!' bellowed the commentators. 'Real footballers don't wear gloves!' The gloves, which came in three sizes and five colours, were marketed by Campbell Sports Equipment. TC had even received an inquiry from the DAFL, the Danish Australian Football League.

Journalists described TC as flamboyant. 'You mightn't believe it,' he said, 'but I'm not really. I'm actually a quiet person.' I did believe it. TC wasn't flamboyant; he was unashamed. And quiet. In fact, he was probably the quietest of them all.

History

On 17 April, the day that Footscray had the bye, Nicky Winmar raised his jumper and pointed to his torso after St Kilda had won a rare victory at Collingwood's home ground, Victoria Park. A nearby photographer said Winmar told a group of Collingwood supporters that he was black and proud of it. A later report claimed he said it took guts to win at Victoria Park, but the words hardly mattered. An Aboriginal man had unashamedly bared his skin before a violently abusive crowd. History had been made.

Periodically, the world of sport, and those in it, find to their bewilderment that they have leapt, like a bewildered frog, from the end of the news bulletins to the start. Suddenly, the grand, arcane, potty institution that is the Collingwood Football Club found itself in the witness box. Why did Collingwood have no Aboriginal players? Why did its supporters have the reputation for being the most racially offensive in the AFL? In a television interview, the Collingwood president, Mr Allan McAlister, succeeded in taking his club's position from bad to infamously worse by saying that Aboriginal players were welcome at Collingwood provided they behaved like whites off the field. The reporter, no doubt sensing he had a scoop of national proportions, gave Mr McAlister the opportunity to say more. In that respect, he rarely disappointed. He said Aboriginal players were welcome at Collingwood, 'provided they behaved like human beings'.

The Luritja word for fire is *Wura*. There were many who thought Allan McAlister should be tied to a stake in the City Square and have Wura tickle his toes. Certainly, his act of contrition was as public as that required of a medieval penitent. Accompanied by a batter of journalists and television crews, he made the journey few white Australians make, into the heartland of Aboriginal Australia, thereby experiencing for himself what it means to be in a cultured minority. In Darwin, he sat and watched as an Aboriginal dancer quivered a spear centimetres from his round, bespectacled, credulous face, and placed a curse on his beloved Magpies. Initially, he had been banned from Melville Island, home of the Tiwis, some of the most serious followers of Australian football the game has ever seen (when Hawthorn played a practice match in Darwin four years ago, Jason Dunstall was pulled aside at training by a crowd of Tiwis and introduced to the Aboriginal Jason Dunstall).

Melville Island is also the home of former Richmond champion Maurice Rioli. He took Allan McAlister fishing, after first explaining to him why Aboriginal people found what he said offensive. After three days, Allan McAlister returned to Melbourne a chastened man, having sensed, it seemed, both the magnitude of his offence and the fact that, in some part, it had been forgiven. The new Allan McAlister wanted the AFL to recognise the Aboriginal contribution to Australian football on grand final day.

In 1987, I made a journey similar to Allan McAlister's and attended the football carnival known among Aboriginal people as the Black Olympics, played at Yuendumu, on the Warlpiri tribal lands, 250 kilometres from Alice Springs. Thirty-two traditional or tribal Aboriginal communities from South and Western Australia as well as the Northern Territory were scheduled to attend. Only twenty-six came; the Pitinjatjara were initiating their young men and where the dreaming paths crossed roads, the roads closed. At Yuendumu, I met Ian King, the former Queensland Shield cricketer who organised the second Aboriginal cricket tour of England. Ian King said Australian football had parallels with the corroboree – the elements of flight and grace, the emphasis on male ritual. The best player I saw at Yuendumu, Dennis Jupurrula Nelson, was a classical Australian footballer: as light as a dancer on his feet, and bold and incisive in his actions. Like West Coast's Dean Kemp. But Dennis Jupurrula Nelson also had thick welts on his outer thighs – ritual mourning scars, 'sorry business'. Two of them, yet to heal, were like thin red fissures, seemingly bare to the muscle.

For two days, the football at the Black Olympics flowed swift and sure, with hardly a tackle. Someone said it was because the ground was too hard. I had come to the conclusion that football in the Land of the Honey Ant Dreaming was a form of athletics when, late on the second day, after perhaps fifteen or twenty games, two players abruptly exchanged a flurry of blows. In a blink, two hundred people were on the playing arena, confronting one another. This was the original one in, all in; in the bush, as in the city, footy is tribal. It is also one of this country's few cultural possessions which has been equally meaningful to black and white Australians for most of this century.

Peter Gordon asked me to address the issue of racism in sport at the president's luncheon before the Essendon game. It certainly wasn't a new problem. Johnny Mullagh was the star of the first Aboriginal cricket tour of England in 1867-68. At Lord's, against the MCC, he took five wickets and then scored 75 of his side's first innings total of 186. But, at York, Johnny Mullagh refused to retake the field because the Aboriginal players were not allowed into the refreshment tent during lunch. When he returned to Victoria, and the captain of the Apsley side called him a nigger, he waited until the next ball, hit a catch and left the field. In later life, Johnny Mullagh was described as 'humble, upright, quiet, retiring and civil'. When he died, the local newspaper overflowed with tributes to him. A painting, in which he was made to look Anglo-Indian, was hung in the Harrow Mechanics Institute. But Johnny Mullagh, real name unknown, had lived and died alone. He refused to marry a woman of his own race and believed no European woman would have him. Johnny Mullagh's life is but one instance of the human tragedy of racism.

I'd heard what was said over the fence to the Krakouer brothers and Nicky Winmar. The Krakouers were the best thing I'd seen in football. For a period, it seemed that they were engaging in a sort of creative anarchy, simultaneously unravelling the game and re-inventing it before our eyes. Winmar's full name was Nicky Elvis Winmar, and you could imagine him playing in a pair of blue sueded shoes. He could leap tall opponents in a single bound and was sharp and agile when the ball hit the ground. But the worst, most sustained racial abuse I've heard in a football match was directed at Chris Lewis on AFL grand final day, 1991. The whole match, it has to be said, was played in an atmosphere of pettiness and spite. Western Australia having positioned itself to take the premiership cup out of Victoria for the first time. The crowd was parochial in the extreme, and racism is only parochialism at a deeper, more sinister level. The hatred and contempt direct at Lewis that day rolled around the stadium like a lazy black beast.

The previous year, the Eagles had got to within one game of the grand final, and Lewis had been his young team's inspiration and guiding force. Knowledgeable sources declared him a champion, but his performances in that series inevitably brought hi under scrutiny. He was drawn into a vortex of grappling and wrestling which quickly escalated into fighting. His game deteriorated. At the end of 1990, he was the young man with the football world at his feet. Twelve months later, he was relegated to the forward pocket for the grand final with the home town crowd delighting in the sporadic, ineffectual nature of his play.

Doug Nicholls, the great Aboriginal Christian who represented Fitzroy in the twenties, said a footballer can preach a sermon by the way he plays the game. But there are not many Doug Nicholls in this world, black or white. Lewis was aggressive. He took the game to its limits and beyond, but others had done that before him and not been ostracised for it. The game gloried in its outlaws. But Lewis was a black outlaw. He was Jundamurra, or Pigeon as he is otherwise known. He did to them what they – or, rather, some of them – did to him. When Footscray played the Eagles in Perth in 1992, he rang among the Footscray players making mocking remarks about being working class. Eventually, he and Super came to blows.

The previous year, I'd gone to Lewis's home in a middle-class suburb of Perth. Outside was a maroon and grey four-wheel drive. Inside was a young man who liked didge with his rock 'n' roll, who spoke with feeling about his football club and team-mates, but who by preference sat in silence playing with his sister's baby on his knee. His girlfriend did the talking. We were discussing Aboriginal culture, and other people wanting to learn about it, when he interrupted. 'They don't want to learn,' he said wearily. During the 1990 finals, I'd watched Lewis train. He'd laughed a lot, and amused himself by practising 40-metre drop kicks from a standing start. He wasn't laughing any more, but he still said he'd meet anybody halfway.

The Winmar incident, and the torrent of opinion and comment it provoked, made the Essendon game seem slightly unreal to me. The match was played at the Western Oval and Footscray won by 46 points. Super said the feeling before the match was the best it had been since the previous year's finals. Scottie West, in only his third game, kicked six goals as a half-forward rover. However, two negatives came out of the match. Libber was reported for kneeing Gavin Wanganeen. He pursued the umpire back to the centre square, passionately proclaiming his innocence. It took him another quarter to get back into the match, but when he did he provided two memorable moments, the first when he tackled Mark Mercuri, grabbing him by the Guernsey, lifting him and carrying him across the boundary line like a bouncer ejecting a drunk. The other occurred a few moments later when he smothered a kick off the boot in a pack, gathered the ball as it spilled to the ground, stood in a tackle and speared a long looping handpass out to his left and into the arms of the running Leon Cameron. Goal. That was how it was meant to happen; in Wheeler's words, a classy agile player (Leon) teamed with a group of hard workers (Libber and Axe). The other negative was a serious knee injury – a torn medial ligament – to Steve Wallis. Wally had been the first player to greet me to the club.

After the match, the rooms were bubbling. The players, sweaty and exuberant, were clasping ice packs to their various trains and bruises. 'You've got to keep looking for the crack that'll blow a game open,' Wheeler was saying. 'You have to push to the limits, and you did that today.' The Dogs were back on track. A win in Perth suddenly seemed possible; in fact, anything seemed possible, including a premiership. I was standing beside Matthew Croft. After excellent performances in the Collingwood and Fitzroy games, he had been sidelined with a hamstring injury. Eventually, he would miss the whole year.

'Bet you wish you were one of them,' I said.

He tossed his head as if that were the last thing he needed to hear.

I mentioned it later to Wheeler, and he nodded. 'When you're not there,' said the coach, 'you're not there.'

Playing Away

I sat next to Shane Ellen on the plane to Perth. He was an unusual young man to be playing league football, or so it seemed to me. Detached. Even in the way he played. In the Essendon game, he came loping through a pack and casually leaned over and collected the ball off the ground as if it were a handkerchief. He worked as a chef and was interested in dreams. 'What about you?' he asked. In Los Angeles, on the previous year's footy trip, he'd approached a cab driver for directions. 'You don't get shit for nothing here, man,' he was told. 'You want information, you pay for it.' Shane was good at accents. It was part of his subtle, mildly humorous way. I asked him how he saw Wheeler. He paused. 'An emotional man,' he replied, 'with a diverse mind.'

Shane Ellen was twenty years old and about to play his third game of AFL football. His first had been against Fitzroy in Round 3. He had emerged from the race at Princes Park and seen the Footscray banner tilting into the sky, and realised he'd been working towards this moment since he was nine. For the past five years, he had trained three nights a week. Sometimes, he had wondered if it was worth the effort. The Footscray players were milling beside the banner, waiting. Dougie called his name, 'Come here, Shane.' The captain put an arm around him, so that the young player's head was in the crook of his elbow, and the broke the crepe wall together. Shane Ellen's first game had been a long, hard, tortuous struggle, but Footscray finished with its nose ahead. Around the field, their players embraced. Again, Shane Ellen found himself near Dougie. The younger man couldn't believe the rush of feeling, the sense of closeness engendered by the victory. So this is what it's about, he thought.

Before that game, I'd been talking with Peter Foster. He was another of the so-called old blokes, along with Dougie and Choco, and the Sydney pair, 'Galaxy' Coleman and Bernard Toohey. Fossie had done just about everything in football, won a club best and fairest, represented the State, toured Ireland for a series of composite-rules Test matches and polled well in the Brownlow. For a decade playing at centre-half-back, Fossie had matched it with the biggest and the best. He was a powerfully built man. His face was constructed from slabs of pink flesh set around two piercingly blue eyes. He had hands the size of shovels and a thumping left foot, but he was cheeky too. He liked to run off his opponents, and advertise his dominance.

I asked him what distinguished footballers, one from another, over time. He thought before replying. 'The ability to overcome injuries,' he said. I thought of Leon Cameron. This was his year, it had to be. Darren Baxter had been cleared to Hawthorn to create a place for him. Initially, in the practice matches, Leon had played with energy but to no great effect; it was as if he were trying too hard. A high mark had eventually started him on his way; it was the best thing I saw in my time at Skinner Reserve. Leaning back like a high jumper, he slid across in front of an opponent, and caught the ball in flight. Each week, since then, he had been among Footscray's best. There was a seriousness about his game which belied his youthful looks. At an early age, he had been told, 'If you've got the ball, you're the one in control of the game', and that was how he played. But the slight frame that allowed him to bend away from opponents and angle through packs also made him vulnerable. He'd been unable to speak after the Melbourne game because of a whack across the larynx. After the Fitzroy game, he was holding his sternum and breathing with difficulty. Super was right; it was a game of hurt.

Libber had been cleared to play in Perth. Peter Gordon found an error in the way the charge was made. The case was dismissed, but Libber was still anxious to establish his innocence. He had run to meet me at Melbourne airport before we boarded. 'I didn't see him,' he said. I'd attended the tribunal hearing; Libber had entered the room pale-faced. It was the first time he had been reported since he started playing the game at the age of nine. The last instant of the incident with Wanganeen had been caught by a side camera; in the corridor, the press unanimously found Libber guilty, but the few frames captured by the camera were consistent with an involuntary leap. Libber felt Wanganeen had deliberately gone to ground.

We walked together to the bay the plane was leaving from. Most of the team had chosen reading material for the long flight like *Inside Sport* or *Picture* magazine. A number were reading the whimsical memoirs of former Melbourne underworld figure 'Chopper' Read. Libber had *The Milwaukee Murders*, but the picked up a novel I had with me, J.M. Coetzee's *Age of Iron*, and read a page or two. 'Gee,' he said, 'that's lovely writing.' Libber stood slightly apart from the group. He was older than most and a family man, but there was also a deeply introspective quality about him. The force which shone through him like a beacon on the football field was basically projected inwards when he was off it.

Libber said once you had won on another team's ground, it was just another football field. Until then, it was a foreign country. Footscray had never won in Perth. A victory over the reigning premier at home would establish the Dogs as genuine contenders, a team building on its momentum of the previous year. They had flown over on Friday night to acclimatise. On Saturday morning, they trained at West Perth Oval. In the afternoon, they went ten-pin bowling. Danny Del-Re proved himself to be the king of the pins, casually spinning the big black ball out of his hand like a bocce player, sending it curving down the alley, hitting strikes or collecting the ones and twos he didn't get the first time, then turning and laughing with embarrassment at his team-mate's applause and derision.

Danny had skill all right. I'd seen it in the practice matches, watched him sidestepping out of packs, casually pumping the ball 50 and 60 metres off either foot. But there was also a diffidence about him. The previous year, before the first final, he'd confessed to Wheeler that he was shitting himself about playing in front of 70,000 people. Wheeler had worked with him, helping him to identify the absolute essentials of his game. He persuaded Danny the crowd wasn't one of them and Danny promptly kicked eight goals. After the Winmar incident, Wheeler had spoken to his players about racism, explaining why it was wrong. It was Danny who rang him later wanting to talk about an exchange he had with an Aboriginal player on the field, asking the coach's advice.

Outside the ten-pin bowling alley, there was a blinding rain, for nearly ten hours, water poured from the sky by the tankful. Dougie and Mark Hunter rejoiced; the mud would slow down the quick legs in the West Coast side. But Subiaco Oval, when the team arrived at noon on Sunday, wasn't muddy; it was sandy. The couch grass was long, spongy and absorbent. The match had scarcely begun when the sun broke through the crowds, not a gentle warming sun, but a hot burning one that sucked the wetness from the earth and made the air moist and humid. It felt like Asia. In the first minute of the game, Shane Ellen was penalised for having a hand on Peter Sumich's arm. Sumich goaled and the crowd chanted, *'Soom-itch! Soom-itch!'* Footscray led at quarter-time, mainly because Grant was sparkling across the half-forward line in his first game for the year. But the contest was decided in the second quarter. Malthouse matched Grant with McIntosh, who attached himself like a leech to the young forward and sucked the life out of him. At the same time, the home team summoned their skill and experience to kill of Footscray's challenge. During this decisive phase of the game, Lewis was clever and innovative, making swerving runs through the Footscray defence, but once the game lost interest so, it seemed, did he.

Super and I had talked about Lewis in the bus on the way to the ground. 'I've heard he's a good block off the field,' said Super evenly, when I told him why I liked him, but he wasn't buying the idea of a code of conduct among players on the issue of racism. It cut both ways.

He asked Crackers, who was sitting in front of us, what he thought.

'I don't say nuthen to the Aboriginal blokes,' said Crackers, 'and they don't say nuthen to me.'

'I thought you were supposed to be a superstar, Grant,' yelled an Eagles supporter as the players left the field at half-time, but there was surprisingly little acrimony from the crowd. There was surprisingly little of anything, perhaps because the Eagles so rarely lose at home. There was no wild excitement, no hoarse roar swapping from one end of the ground to the other. It was more like an exhibition match. Behind the goal at the scoreboard end, two young couples lay on a rug, entwined in one anothers' arms anyone daring to occupy similar territory at Victoria Park would be a potential news item ('Daicos Kicks Ten – Two Die'). As it was, their activities continued until the third quarter when Sumich had a shot from the left-forward pocket and actually bounced the ball of the head of one of the young men involved. The only source of genuine excitement in the match, the only player who made the air blur, was wingman Peter Matera. He toyed with his opponents, tilting and swaying, inviting them to commit themselves so that he could be past them and gone. Matera was the Italian Nyungah, the Ferrari from the bush. A long time afterwards, they were Shane Ellen's two memories of Perth: the crowd chanting *'Soom-itch! Soom-itch!'* and Peter Matera splitting the Footscray defence and accelerating towards him, socks down, ball in hand, brown eyes levelled on the goals.

Footscray lost by 41 points. Their rooms after the match were dark and disconsolate. The club doctor was muttering about the poor light and sewing up a scalp which I recognised as Libber's. the little man was lying on a rub-down table, a sheet of plastic over his body. In five matches, I'd seen Libber knocked out, shirtfronted, given a black eye and have the flesh torn from his back. Now a gash in his head was being sewn up. The operation performed, he rose wordlessly and walked to the shower, towel around his waist. There was something awesome about Libber, a dignity, a stature. Later, I asked Shane Ellen when he became a footballer. 'What do you mean?' he replied. 'Kids who play under-nines are footballers,' I wanted to know when it became part of him. Libber and I had talked about that. Libber knew it was absurd to define yourself in terms of a game, but in his case he knew it was true. I tried, by way of explanation, to relate my conversation with Libber to Shane. 'Nothing I've done compares with Libber,' said the younger player quickly, and I had to let the matter drop.

Wheeler worried that he had got it wrong. It had been Danny's 50th game (and Bernard Toohey's 250th). The club had brought Danny's parents across. Maybe seeing his parents before the match had been too much. Danny had played his worst game for the year. The match also had an obvious sub-plot. It was the new

Footscray coach against the old (Malthouse). As players they had been similar. As coaches they could hardly have been more different. Malthouse thought in terms of competition, Wheeler opportunity. Malthouse's determination was epic and his legacy lived on at the Western Oval. Super was one of a number of senior players to quote him to me: 'Kill the body and the mind will die.' On this occasion, Malthouse had won. In another part of the rooms, lying face-down on the floor, was Scottie West. The hard men in the Eagles side had seen to it that the kid who kicked six goals the previous week wouldn't forget his first foray into their territory. Crackers had tried to protect him, as had big sedate Fish Standfield, but, at this level, a player can't be protected. When he stood up red-eyed, no one spoke. The youngster was allowed his emotion. It's an emotional game.

Losing at Home

I like to stand behind the goals. I like to see the interaction between forward and defender as the ball arrives, the forward seeking to judge its flight, the defender watching ball and man. Or the forward waiting for the moment to lead, to intersect with the play upfield, and the backman watching the ground at his opponent's feet to minimise his reaction times. Guy McKenna, from West Coast, actually looks ahead of his opponent so that he can't be sold a feint. It's eerie; eyes fixed on nothing, hand extended, using touch to keep in contact with his opponent. I love the individual drama of the game.

In Round 7, six days after the West Coast game, Footscray played North at the Western Oval and Wayne Carey, North's 21-year-old captain and centre-half-forward, was supreme. Crackers was one of the strongest players at Footscray, and he said Carey's strength was awesome. He held out opponents with a forearm and caught the ball in the flat of his free hand as if it were a pancake. He also had pace, mobility, balance. He marked from everywhere: in front, the side, over the top. By the end of the match, Grant was playing on him. Wheeler probably hoped that Grant would learn something from the experience because Carey was showing himself to be what everyone at Footscray hoped Grant would become – a great player. Good players consistently win their position; great players have spheres of influence and that day Carey's extended from one end of the Western Oval to the other. His team-mates, crushed and abject only three months earlier, were suddenly brimming with confidence and vitality. Maybe that's what hurt Wheeler so much about the defeat: people said North were playing like Footscray had in '92.

It was also a loss at home. There's a saying in football: even good sides struggle to win at the Western Oval. Long and thin-hipped, a flock of seagulls invariably littering the sky at the scoreboard end, the Western Oval is not attractive to the eye. Over the years, what had struck me as its most appealing feature was the Hyde Street Band, a collection of perhaps a dozen musicians – some fat, some tall, some skinny, some small – standing in random formation, dutifully adding their thin notes to the dull roar of the crowd before the game or at half-time. Nothing in Footscray reminded me more of the art of Michael Leunig than the Hyde Street Band.

The other factor which gave games at the Western Oval their unmistakably individual character was the wind. Dougie was regarded as the master of the wind. Usually, it blew from the north-west and it was no coincidence that the Doug Hawkins Wing was on the eastern side of the ground. 'Stand off it and see what it's doing,' he said, when I asked him how to play it. 'Don't get caught under the ball.' There were rules for playing the Western Oval. Towards the Geelong Road (or southern) end: don't centre the ball from the grandstand wing until you pass the John Gent Stand. To the Barkly Street end: keep your kicks below the level of the signs behind the goal. But local knowledge counted for nothing against North. Carey could not be subdued.

Footscray were thirty points down at half-time. Television commentator Dennis Cometti said the third quarter was the toughest he'd seen in five years. Certainly, it was Footscray's fiercest, most sustained assault for the whole season. Super rubbed brows with his opponent. Dougie made a bounding charge through the centre, like he was leading the Charge of the Light Brigade on foot. Afterwards, he said he didn't see North rover Anthony Rock. Everyone else said he went looking for him. Whatever, it was Dougie who was left on the ground. The trainers raised him to his feet. On TV, you saw Dougie focusing on the horizon past Mount Mistake (the Geelong Road end). 'I'll be right,' he muttered, and promptly rejoined the fray with his former vigour. But Wheeler was disappointed with his senior players. They couldn't control the game. They couldn't halt the slide. Libber and Axe had been checked by remorselessly close tagging, thereby nullifying Footscray at the centre bounces. In the last quarter, Axe had dropped a chest mark on the grandstand wing; when he won a possession shortly afterwards, the Footscray crowd gave him a derisive cheer. Wheeler was upset about that, too. 'Some supporters can be real bastards,' he said.

I had met him in his office before training. He was

holding a letter from a disgruntled supporter and shaking his head. It was a mixture of printing and handwriting, about three words to the line. It read as follows:

> MR WHEELER
> FOOTSCRAy FOOTBALL CluB HAS gOT THE WORST 3 FOOTBALLERS IN the AFL. AND I CAN't WAIT to see you make A Fool OF YOURSELF By Playing these Blokes. I Carn't BcliEvc you could Keep PLayING this BLOKEHE Is the worst FUCKEN PLAYER in HISTORY Of the game. PLAYER NO 1 Tony CAMPBELL NO 2 TONY CAMPBELL NO 3 TONY FUCKEN CAMPBELL HAVEN'T YOU GOT ANY TV REPLAY'S HE IS A DEAD Set EM BARASSSMENT MAN ON MAN SITUATIONS HE JUST GET FUCKEN KILLED AND HE ONLy GETS A KICK When SOMEBODy ELSe MAKes A MISTAKe FAIR DINKum I TH ougHT yOU HAD A good IDEA OF a FOOTBALLER THIS BASTARD WOULD NOT gET A GAMe WITH BuRRUM BUTTOCK 3RDS AND IF HE's NOT OVERWEIght tHAN HE MUST BE THe FATEST FACED PIg IN HISTORY. COME ON TERRy FOOTSCRAy HAS 15 PlAyERS IN thE 2NDS THAT WOULD KILL this Bloke. if yoU play hIM i CARN'T WAIT TO See hIM MAKe A FOOL of yOU. WATch Some TV REPLAys. hE's gOT 3 LEFT FEET (signed) A FOOTSCRAY FAN With A FOOTBALL BRAIN DANDENONG
> (rOGER the lODGER)

We went for a walk around the oval. The loss to North at home had dramatically reshaped the season in a way that the losses to Collingwood and West Coast hadn't. They were sustainable within Wheeler's grand plan. The North defeat wasn't. It suggested a fundamental flaw. The coach now had selection problems. Having chosen a player, Wheeler's instinct was to keep faith with him, but players in the reserves – particularly the older ones, like Choco and Fossie – now had grounds to argue with him. Both were players of reputation and neither was at all happy about being in the reserves. The parents of one young player had also contacted him and suggested that their son's career might have progressed better at another club, under another coach. That bothered him, too. 'How much do I owe the parents?' he asked. His face was creased, his eyes betrayed a lack of sleep.

'I don't think you should blame yourself too much,' I said, trying to be helpful. 'You haven't got the players to win the premiership.'

He winced and pulled away. Too late, I realised I shouldn't have said it. If he didn't believe what he said, how could he expect them to? And, at this level, if you didn't believe, you had no chance. League football had no place for the whimsical, not unless you were Gary Ablett, and no one could say for sure that he was.

When the players began arriving an hour or so later, I sat and watched as Wheeler strode around the ground, setting out the witches' hats. The deep wound was now masked by a grin and a genial greeting for each person that he met. To all appearances, the coach was a man at one with the world. It's lonely at the top.

The Old Footscray

Charlie Sutton was the old chief. As captain-coach of the 1954 premiership team, he stood alone in the history of the Footscray Football Club. 'They talk about all the money these boys get,' he said, nodding to the figures training on the oval. 'They'd play in a paddock for nothing.' Charlie used words sparsely, but to effect; he could still summon intensity. To play league football, he said, you needed 'a mad desire'. Charlie, who was built like a stump, had shirtfronted Collingwood's star centreman Marcus Whelan in front of the grandstand at Victoria Park. The wall of faces had jumped towards him. 'I thought the grandstand was coming over the fence at me,' he said, chuckling at the memory. Charlie said players today didn't know how to deliver a shirtfront. They jumped at the moment of impact. 'That's when you drop the shoulder,' he said. And follow through like a wooden club.

Charlie didn't offer his opinions unless asked. I asked often. 'You're an individual until you get the ball,' he said, when I asked him about football being a team game, 'then you become part of the team.' His pale eyes glinted when he spoke about the game but softened as soon as he stopped. Then he looked like everyone's uncle. There were two sides to Charlie. Humility in victory, courage in defeat. Raw, blazing, stop-at-nothing courage. Charlie said you had to be a bit of Jekyll and Hyde to play league football.

The new Footscray, created by Wheeler, was an institute of advanced football education based at the Western Oval. It had a chaplain, the AFL's first woman trainer, a string of specialist coaches and a player welfare program. Too academic, said the old-timers. 'Nice blokes don't win premierships,' said Charlie. The irony was that Wheeler had been a player in Charlie's mould. 'He was the club's first real tough back-pocket after Charlie,' said Ted Whitten Junior. 'If someone was there to be run through, he'd do it.' Ferret, as Ted Whitten Junior was known, had begun at Footscray the same year as Wheeler. He recalled the day 'a bloke from Geelong cleaned him [Wheeler] up'. In those days of one umpire and little or no television, footballers lived by their own laws, one of which was retribution. Wheeler didn't see the old way as wrong – justice, I gathered, was usually done – but he believed those days had gone. It was a different game now. More professional.

But Charlie's Bulldogs had roared. And laughed. When Jack Collins received an instruction to leave at the end of a club game and travel interstate to represent Victoria, Ted Whitten pinched his false teeth. I had the impression it was an earthier time. I kept listening for something at Footscray and not hearing it. How well, I began to wonder, did the players actually know one another? Super agreed it was a reasonable question.

The older blokes, like Choco and Fossie and Dougie, were bonded by the years. The younger ones, like Grant and Kretiuk, had water fights in the showers after training, but how well did they know one another as a team? As a whole? When I asked Bones McGhie at one of the trainers' Wednesday night barbecues, he exploded. 'They don't known one another! Players today don't know how to socalise!'

But the club was still Footscray, although it took people who had come from elsewhere to point it out to me because the best things about Footscray were unspoken. Ricky Jackson, who previously played at Melbourne, observed that Footscray didn't hurry players back from injury. Players were workers. He also noticed the absence of cliques. 'At Footscray, everyone's equal,' he said, 'from Dougie Hawkins to Scottie West.' Libber, who began with North Melbourne, had told me that Dougie was a huge part of Footscray, and it was true. At most clubs, no one is above the captain. At Footscray, no one was beneath him. 'How you going, old-timer?' Dougie would say to the boot studder, Ronnie Johns, putting his arm around him. Dougie always touched people when he spoke to them. 'The day he doesn't,' said Ronnie Johns, 'I'll know something's wrong with him.' Terry Wallace, who had a long career at Hawthorn followed by a single season at Richmond, said Footscray people were real, by which he meant without pretence. They were also, it seemed to me, uncommonly accepting.

Archie Selleck happened to accompany an acquaintance, Simon Beasley, to a Footscray training session in the early '80s. Beasley had since been and gone, having played 154 games with Footscray and kicked 575 goals. Archie, an enthusiastic amateur footballer, was still coming to training. He was even allotted his own guernsey – number 13. David Vuong was a young Vietnamese refugee who barracked for Melbourne. When Tony Campbell and Ricky Jackson came to Footscray from Melbourne, David Vuong came too. His knowledge of football etiquette was nil. He attended training and asked Shane Ellen if he could run laps with him. He tried to engage Glenn Coleman in conversation when Coleman, who was having a disappointing year (he'd been dropped after the Fitzroy game), was warming up in the rooms. 'You go back to Sydney?' asked David Vuong none too tactfully. He even wandered on to the oval as training was about to begin and asked the coach if he could have a kick with him. The trainers on the boundary line had traditional Aussie jokes with David Vuong, like telling him that Allen Jakovich was playing with Footscray next year, but no one told him to go away or sought to bar his entry.

Basically, no one at Footscray was better than anyone else. Nor was it in the nature of the place for individuals to project an image. I saw this as modesty. Wheeler saw it as lack of confidence. 'The background conversation in the western suburbs is, "I'm not good enough".' Was this, I wondered, why Wheeler and Peter Gordon were so public in their projections? Was it also part of the reason why Peter Gordon had brought Harry Beitzel to Footscray?

In the '60s and '70s, Harry's nasal chant and easy familiarity with the big names of the game had made him the king of football broadcasting, but Harry had since fallen on bad times. He had been declared bankrupt, charged with defrauding a Melbourne couple of their Soccer Pools winnings and attacked in withering terms in State Parliament. The ordeal had sapped Harry. He was quoted in a newspaper as saying that at one point he had even wondered if life was worth living. But Peter Gordon believed in him – even appearing to listen to his advice on matters relating to the supporters – and Harry had responded to this belief with gusto. The idea was that Harry would provide the western suburbs with its own coverage of Footscray games through community radio station 3WRB. To this end, he teamed up again with Tommy Lahiff, very possibly the oldest sports broadcaster in the world.

Tommy was 82. He looked like an army biscuits on legs, but he was still a Port Melbourne boy at heart. In Carlton's rooms after one of that club's grand final wins, he had refused to interview Malcolm Fraser because he was a politician, and a Liberal at that. He also took a swipe at a television journalist who smilingly made light of Harry's problems with the law. In the course of the year, community radio station 3WRB received a letter on Tommy's behalf which provided an insight into his origins.

> My Dear Mr Tom Lahiff,
> I am writing to you in reference to a game I umpired at Port Melbourne in 1946. When the game finished, I was taken off the ground by a trooper's horse. The game was Port and Coburg. At the three-quarter time interval, the police told me that if Port got beat there might be trouble. There was plenty of it. Port got beat by two points. The other umpires and myself never left the ground until 9 o'clock. I hope

> you remember as you were captain that day. The VFA sent me back again the next week to try me out. It was 100th game for me. I would like to see you sometime to talk about it. I could tell you a lot you don't know. By reading the press you are going alright, nice to write to you, wish you all the best. I am 83 now and still go for my run and swim down the beach at Seaford. I remain,
> yours faithfully,
> Syd Thomas

Harry read the letter out one night, on air. In addition to calling the seniors and reserves each week, Harry had started broadcasting live from the Footscray social club on Thursday nights. He called his new show 'Selectors' Table'. It began with a supporter chosen from the floor reading a paragraph or two from *Too Tough to Die* (Harry called it the Bible). The Footscray team for the big game (the big, of course, being the next game) was then read out (you heard it first on 'Selectors' Table') and discussed by the panel. Each week, a different player was detailed to join the panel, but Harry's particular stroke of showbiz genius was to cajole the club into making a member of the selection committee available. In addition to answering questions from the panel, the committee member was required to take them from the floor. A microphone was passed around the supporters and the lot was broadcast live. The show was preceded by a fine smorgasbord dinner provided at the bargain-basement cost of ten dollars. It ended with a phantom call of the big game by former captain Laurie Sandilands (patrons were free to boo the umpires, and did), details of the meat raffle and, for those who wished to stay, a round or two of Trivial Pursuit. 'Selectors' Table' was a sell-out.

On radio, Harry called Charlie Sutton 'Mister Footscray'. Charlie had captained the club for six years, coached it for nine and, in the late '70s, when the club was being torn apart by internal conflict, had returned as president. But Charlie always spoke as if there was one greater than himself – Whitten. Best player of all time, said Charlie, and no one at Footscray disagreed. Laurie Sandilands said the only player to come through the club in his time who rivalled Whitten for talent was Bernie Quinlan. Quinlan played within the rules and won a Brownlow Medal. Whitten made his own rules and became Mister Football. When Dermott Brereton destroyed Essendon in the second semi-final of 1989 with one quarter of unholy aggression, Whitten said it brought tears of joy to his eye. That was Mister Football's football.

Charlie said that in the early stage of his career, Whitten was unusually susceptible to being knocked out. It even happened one night at training when he was accidentally hit in the back of the head with the ball. His mother wanted him to stop playing so Charlie went and saw her. 'I promised her that he'd play centre-half-back, and after that he did.' Centre-half-back is less dangerous than centre-half-forward; you don't have to turn into the play once you get the ball. But it was hard to imagine E.J. Whitten ever being young and vulnerable. For a period, EJ, as he was known, had called the professional wrestling at Festival Hall and something of that sport's excess seemed to have entered his soul. He was nearly sixty, but every year he single-handedly put interstate football on the media map. Fists clenched, pale eyes bulging, he portrayed the agony and ecstasy of the Victorian cause. Followers from other states howled: with laughter when Victoria lost, with derision when they won. Choco Royal was in a Victorian team which became marooned in traffic on the way to Football Park in Adelaide. Forty-five minutes before the start of the match, the team was still inching towards the stadium. A hasty preparation was a sure prescription for defeat: EJ stepped from the bus and flagged down a police car. 'There's no show without us!' he bellowed. The police car responded by closing an oncoming lane of traffic and escorting the Victorian team, lights flashing, to the stadium. Climbing back aboard the bus, EJ punched the roof and launched into a song. The Vics won by ten goals. I asked Charlie why Whitten was so mad on interstate football. I always wondered if it was because at some point he privately despaired of further success with Footscray. 'Because it's the best football,' replied Charlie simply. 'And Whitten loved playing football.'

Charlie and Whitten had publicly accepted Footscray's merger with Fitzroy. At the time, I thought it was because the Footscray Football Club was no longer as they had known it. The city of Footscray was no longer as they had known it. Charlie seemed to view them in the way that working people once viewed Labor governments. But it was also the case that Charlie trusted the AFL, or the league as he called them. 'They have their weaknesses,' he said, 'but I think they're going in the right direction. Who else gives the clubs $1.2 million dollars a year? If private enterprise took over, they'd be getting a lot less.' This put him at odds with everyone else at Footscray whom I heard express a view on the subject, but Charlie was still part of the body of the club. After one of Footscray's losses, I found him in the race slapping the players on the back and giving them a brisk word of encouragement as they ran off the field. 'There's plenty who want to know them after a win,' he said. 'Not too many want to speak to them when they lose.'

Whitten I only saw twice after the opening match. Once was the night before Dougie's 300th when he spoke with humour and authority (Crosswell said he was the best football raconteur he'd heard). The other occasion was one evening at training, when he was standing on the boundary line with Charlie. He wasn't that big a man for the impact he is supposed to have had on matches, but you could sense the effect he had on others. Charlie was standing beside him, feet apart, chest out. Whitten had been skilful, versatile and aggressive – Bones McGhie said no one intimidated him – but former commentator Mike Williamson also described him as the most entertaining player he had called. There was no match, Williamson said, that Whitten couldn't bring to life. Whitten had a sense of football as theatre. He was the exception who proved the Footscray rule, the western-suburbs boy who unashamedly projected an image.

Charlie and Whitten were discussing training, lamenting the lack of man-on-man work. 'Teddy'd do more in ten minutes than some of these blokes do in an hour,' Charlie was saying. 'You'd have to pull him off the track.' Then he said to me, 'Have you met Ted?' and to Whitten, 'Martin's writing a book on us.' I sensed it was a formality he could have done without, but he extended his hand. Dougie Hawkins had told me about the E.J. Whitten handshake. He said it pulled you towards him. In my case, it pulled me towards him and down. There was no way, meeting E.J. Whitten, that I wasn't going to look up to the man.

Teams

In Round 8, Footscray defeated Carlton at Princes Park by 28 points, but the game had a strange, traumatic opening. Big Scottie was knocked out in the first few minutes, accidentally kneed in the head by Justin Madden. Medical staff clustered around him; his body could be seen convulsing on the ground. In the bunker, Ian Corlett said, 'They're giving him CPR [cardio-pulminary resuscitation].' There was a genuine anxiety in his voice. He'd seen a similar accident at the racetrack, and the victim had died. Players from both sides milled around in the centre of the ground, seemingly uncertain as to what they should do. Finally, the player was carried from the field, neck in a brace, and taken into the Footscray changerooms.

I followed them down and glanced inside the medical room. The player was sitting up, back against the wall, responding to questions. He was okay. Outside, a middle-aged woman was holding her hands to her face. 'It's his mother,' someone said. Fifteen minutes later, he slowly appeared at the mouth of the race in a dressing gown; with him was a younger woman. She was trembling. His face was pink and crinkled like a baby which has just been woken from a deep sleep. For the next week, he had to eat ice cream because of the lacerations to the inside of his mouth.

Axe said later that the incident alarmed him in a way that no other football accident – like Libber's in the opening match – had. During the ten-minute period when the game wasn't happening, he and Super called the Footscray team together. They started making noise. Even TC was shouting. When play resumed, it was Footscray who took the advantage. Upset by the seriousness of the injury he had inadvertently caused, Justin Madden dropped out of the game. Footscray's makeshift ruckman, Barry Standfield, began marking around the ground, casually almost. And Footscray stayed close. No one was alone at fall of the ball. Instead of having three or four good players, they had fifteen or sixteen. Super was fierce and adept across half-back. After the North loss, Wheeler had introduced a brother system; every player was personally responsible for one of his team-mates. He was trying to reinforce the team from within. Super's 'brother' was Scottie West whose form had been shaky since Perth. I thought back to arriving at our hotel in Perth on the Friday night, Super in the seat behind me, ever so quietly singing James Taylor: 'They'll steal your soul if you let them, Oh, don't you let them, You just call out my name …'

Twice, super tossed Williams, the Carlton centreman, in what the commentators called a show of strength. Wheeler also tagged Williams, Carlton's best ball-winner, with Libber. It was a shrewd tactic because it didn't require Libber to depart too far from his natural game. Williams had the edge in finesse, but no one surpassed Libber for desire. By stationing himself beside Williams and playing from him, he halved the effectiveness of the Carlton centreman. Leon Cameron was untouchable (Shane Ellen's word). He loped from one end of the ground to the other, gathering the ball, carrying it, distributing it with long accurate kicks off either foot. He twice goaled from outside the 50-metre line. At the age of twenty, there was a natural authority about his game. Kenny Hunter was again among Footscray's best. Kenny was shrewd and hard-headed. It was Kenny who told me how to appreciate Scott Wynd. 'He's a champion,' he said. 'Look at the little things he does.' Kenny was the blur diving across the front of the pack to knock the ball out of Stephen Kernahan's path and over the boundary line. He seldom made mistakes and didn't appreciate it when others – umpires or team-mates – made them on his own behalf. I liked him coming forward, too; he sought to be part of a larger picture. When Footscray lost in Perth, alone among his team-mates, he'd played like a winner. The way I scored Footscray's best and fairest, it had to be between Kenny and Leon with Crackers as the outsider. The boy from Werribee kept jumping and seizing the ball out of the air, and if the goal was on, he kicked that too. Crackers' game was simple but strong, and he played it with feeling.

It was Axe's 100th game. He was generally subdued, but he had one lovely moment: a lob handball in the second quarter that cleared Justin Madden's 209-centimetre frame and found a running Nigel Kellett. Kellett attacked the goal but miskicked slightly; the ball wobbled through the air, eventually dropping in the goal square, where it was marked by Choco. It was Choco's first game back. In the final quarter, when Carlton mounted its best challenge of the match, two chances fell Choco's way. In soccer language, they were half-chances – narrow angle on goal, Carlton players closing. He slotted the both, like an old craftsman.

It was Footscray's best team performance of the year, and suddenly 'team' seemed the critical word. Each week, the twenty players had to create something between themselves. As twenty individuals, they had no hope of withstanding the force directed against them.

The following week at the Western Oval, Footscray played St Kilda. With their uneven blend of brilliance and dogged triers, the Saints had been one of the character teams in the competition over the past few years. The elimination final they played against Geelong in 1991 is one of my fondest footy memories. The Saints were reduced to eighteen men by quarter time, but they continued to play bold, inspired footy. I thought they showed more in defeat than most winning final teams I have seen show in victory.

I had also been intrigued by St Kilda's home ground, Moorabbin. It was inhabited by mad, wild, anarchic spirits. Its flag was the rebel flag of the Confederate states and one section of the ground was known, appropriately, as the Animal Cage. Something always seemed to be happening at Moorabbin. When Plugger was kicking bags of goals, a group of St Kilda supporters would stand behind the goal at the grandstand end and chant, 'How big's your dick?' as the ball passed through the uprights. The goal umpire would duly raise two finger 30 centimetres or so apart and be roundly abused for boastful behaviour. The year

Plugger had won his Brownlow, Moorabbin had tipped and swayed with emotion like and overfull cup. Matches were like Wimbledon finals; after each goal, Plugger would return to the goal square and wait to receive service from a team-mate upfield. Half the opposition side would then try and stop him.

At the start of 1993, however, at the urging of the AFL, the Saints had relocated to the bland expanses of Waverley Park. An artist I knew named Eamonn Scott, a dedicated St Kilda Supporter who paints red Australian interiors with the small figure of Nicky Winmar letting a torp go on the horizon, feared they'd never be the same again. But four weeks before coming to the Western Oval, St Kilda had defeated Collingwood at Victoria Park. Then had come the protracted and glaringly public dispute with Nicky Winmar over money. Footscray was his first game back. He played mostly in defence, generating nothing of consequence. Plugger got one kick. Occasionally, he crashed into a pack, as if in the belief that by knocking people over (his team-mates among them) he'd make an impression on the game. Four weeks earlier, they'd been men on a missing. Now they were a ghost team. Footscray thrashed them by 64 points.

At the time, I thought St Kilda was the saddest side I had ever seen, but Footscray's day of truth was only one week away. In Round 11, exactly one week from the halfway mark of the season, Hawthorn beat Footscray by ten goals at the Western Oval and, had the match gone another quarter, I suspect the winning margin would have been twice as great. The architect of Footscray's defeat, many suspected, was its former player Darren Baxter.

Hawthorn played the Western Oval perfectly. In the first quarter, they successfully overcame all Footscray's attempts to confine the game to the eastern (downwind) side of the ground. Dougie had tormented St Kilda, playing a loose man in defence. Hawthorn put a quick, skilful player in Ben Allan on him and sought him out; Dougie couldn't contain him. To add insult to injury, Leon Cameron missed the match with appendicitis. Not only was Wheeler unable to display the talents of Baxter's replacement, he was unable to shield Atkins from Baxter's rigorous tagging.

It was a total defeat. North had exposed Footscray's lack of class. Hawthorn exposed an even more fundamental deficiency. A lack of pride, the old-timers said. I thought it was more a lack of belief. By the end of the match, a black hole had appeared at their centre. The team had been reduced to a collection of individuals without cohesion or unity, without collective will-power or a sense of purpose. Crimmo, the seconds runner, said it was the worth loss he'd seen in seven years at the club.

'I was angry after the North loss,' said Wheeler, 'but after this, I feel sick.'

The players were told they were required to stay in the social club and talk with supporters until 7pm.

'I don't care what you think of what they say,' said the coach, 'you're going to stay and face them.'

The following weekend was reserved for interstate matches. In Tasmania, Super was carried from the field after rupturing a medial ligament in his knee. Same injury as Steve Wallis. Winter had arrived.

Crimmo

Crimmo, the runner for the seconds, was Peter Crimmins' brother, and Peter Crimmins, who died in 1976, ravaged by cancer, is remembered as the Spirit of Hawthorn. He was small and blond, with a funny jerky little run which made his hair flop up and down. And brave. Hawthorn said he was brave, and Hawthorn believed the reward lay in serving the cause, not in being recognised or decorated for it. Crimmins had roved to Don Scott. They were one of football's odd couples. Scott had curly black hair, fleshy lips and shoulders as broad as a broomstick. He looked like a young Roman poet who'd spent too long in the gymnasium.

Crimmins and Scott were part of a Hawthorn team which was about as basic as a football team can get. In a rare interview, on the subject of the Catholic Church, Hawthorn's coach, John Kennedy, said religion wasn't meant to be easy. Nor, it followed, was football. Kennedy didn't much care how his players went about the game, so long as they abandoned all thoughts of fear and personal gain. This admirably simple formula meant he was open on matters of style which, in turn, goes some of the way towards explaining Huddo.

Peter Hudson was from the Derwent Valley in Tasmania, a broad river flanked by dark, silent hills. Huddo kicking for goal was a young bank clerk huddled over the ball, bum in the air; a few stuttering paces, then he would straighten, lean back and off on its unerring path would go a wobbly flat punt. Huddo broke all the rules. There was almost something feminine about him. His hips swayed when he walked. His lips were usually puffy because full-backs belted him, but he kicked goals on them all. One of the recurring sounds of my youth was a voice on the radio interrupting the broadcast match of the day to say, 'And Hudson's just kicked his eleventh at Glenferrie.' When he went back to Tassie, he got hefty but he was still worth watching. One year, he kicked 200 goals. He kicked 18 in one game and still only got two votes in the competition best and fairest.

Crimmo drove me home after training now and then. He was taller than his brother, with a thin friendly face and a fine crooked nose. You could see he loved having a kick, following the ball's flight through the air after it left his boot. His style was more laidback than Peter's, but you could tell he would have been a hard man on the field. Crimmo said footy was a simple game. He could only remember his brother talking about it a couple of times. One of them was saying how sore he was after the semi-final against St Kilda in 1971.

The grand final of that year was one of the most brutal in the history of the game. It was played in the wet which minimised the evasive action players could take. That was the year Cowboy Neale knocked Huddo senseless in the first quarter. Huddo played out the match with double vision and still kicked three, to equal Bob Pratt's record of 150 goals in a season. Ironically, St Kilda's coach that day was Allan Jeans. After Kennedy, Jeans was the next great influence in Hawthorn's evolution. He retained Kennedy's ethic of selflessness, but blended it into a system which he manned with highly skilled players. The 1988 grand final between Hawthorn and Melbourne was a no-contest, but, even so, Hawthorn's last quarter was about as good as footy gets. A marriage of force and finesse creating something immeasurably greater than the twenty individuals involved.

Crimmo never liked to think I had to catch a couple of trains to get home. The truth was the trains would probably have been quicker. He'd bot a smoke as we left the Western Oval and stop in at the TAB bar at the Rising Sun Hotel on the other side of Geelong Road to check the form. Crimmo worked as a cleaner for Bones McGhie. Bones's arms were livid with tattoos, and his black eyes quivered with a light that was both fierce and sensitive. He looked like a pirate king, but Crimmo said he was a good bloke. 'Good heart,' he said.

One night, crossing the Westgate Bridge, Crimmo told me about the worst toilets he'd cleaned, some of them early in the morning with a hangover. 'Fair dinkum,' he said, 'you'd have to hate humanity to do what some of these bastards do.' He also told me a sad story about a bloke who got into so much debt gambling, he took his life by jumping from the top of the bridge. On the city side of the bridge, Crimmo pulled into the Shell service station and put some petrol in his old Corolla. Coming back to the car after paying, he flipped me a Mars bar. He wanted to run me all the way home; he just had to go to North Balwyn first. I got out in the city and caught a train.

If I ever asked Crimmo how Footscray were going to go next Saturday, he'd grin and say, 'We'll shit it in.' He always said it as if he believed it. One night at training, I asked him how he did it, how did he keep finding the positive? After the loss to Hawthorn, there wasn't a lot of optimism around the club. He shrugged, as if it was something which couldn't be expressed. Then he looked at the smoky red sunset to the west. 'Ever lost a member of your family?' he said.

Winter

For Round 11, the Crows in Adelaide, Wheeler set up the forward line to suit Danny Del-Re. Danny, after all, had kicked 70 goals the previous year. He reinstated Glenn Coleman at centre-half-forward. Coleman tended to lead up the ground, not back towards the goal square which gave Danny more room. Wheeler also placed both his forward flankers – Grant and Rohan Smith – on the one side of the ground so that there was nothing between Crackers, in the forward pocket, and wingman Nigel Kellett. This gave Crackers his own space to run into and minimised the possibility of him getting in Danny's way.

The keys to Adelaide were McGuinness, McDermott and Modra. Kenny Hunter took McGuinness, TC Modra, Libber McDermott. The plan almost worked. Danny found space; he met the ball on the lead; he held his marks. But he couldn't kick straight. Footscray finished the quarter with a score of 2.7. Had it been 7.2, Footscray might have found the confidence and authority they showed at Football Park the previous year when they thumped Adelaide in the opening round of the season. Instead, Adelaide worked itself back into the game.

When Libber entered the rooms at half-time, he flung his tracksuit top across the room and shouted. Dougie entered hands on hips, red-faced and puffing, swearing silently. He'd got into a wrestling match with Andrew Jarman leaving the field. Kenny Hunter kicked the wall. Even TC was muttering. The older players knew they'd had their chance and blown it. Wheeler tried to persuade them the match was still winnable, but Adelaide were away and, in 1993, Adelaide was Tony Modra. Modra had English good looks and a certain aristocratic detachment from the cruder aspects of the game. He was an aerialist. In the course of a single season, he had become Adelaide's matinée idol, the most famous South Australian sportsman since Bradman. By the end of the match, with Footscray offering an abject lack of resistance in the mid-field and the ball rushing into the Adelaide forward line, TC had no hope of curtailing his leads. Modra kicked a casual seven and Adelaide won, comprehensively, by 45 points. Libber had tears in his eyes at the airport after the game. Before half-time, he'd shouted at one of the younger Footscray players for not chasing, saying he was cheating on himself and his team-mates. He'd played under Pagan at North Melbourne in the Under-19s. Under Pagan, he said, losses weren't acceptable.

Suddenly, everyone was talking about Denis Pagan. North Melbourne had defeated the reigning premiers at home, in Perth. The North players were now taking it in turns to step forward and receive the plaudits of the commentators and the crowd: Schwass one week, Blakey and Dean Laidley the next, but always, behind them, was the inescapable figure of Wayne Carey, buoyant, chesty, and as light as an old waltzing king on his feet. He played with a slight frown, like he was thinking about what to do next. The fans called him Duck.

Before the Perth game, Pagan had asked the North players to write a letter outlining their aims in the match. Preparing for Adelaide, Wheeler had employed a similar technique. He'd asked his players to draw a box and list in it the four or five ingredients which they considered to be basic to their game. Then he'd got them to draw a second box within the first; in it, they wrote the factors they considered essential to their game less one. By a process of reduction and elimination, the players ended up identifying the single most important aspect of their football. Wheeler tried to avoid influencing the choices his players made. A good team is a self-regulating mechanism; it has to know itself. The ingredients were: Nigel Kellett – smart running; Crackers – hit the ball; Dougie – concentration; Kolyniuk – concentration; Grant – good hands; Rohan Smith – kick goals; Leon Cameron – concentration; Axe – disposal; Libber – McDermott; Kenny Hunter – concentration; Danny Del-Re – confidence; Scott West – head over the ball; Scott Wynd – good jumping at the centre bounces; Peter Foster – desperation; Bernard Toohey – one on one; Glenn Coleman – work up the ground; Shane Ellen – know the game; Tony Campbell – last lunge; Barry Standfield – spoil; Anthony Darcy – attack. Wheeler had done his own square and the rest was entirely predictable – to be positive. But it hadn't worked for Wheeler. 'Who is there to coach the coaches?' he lamented.

The following Saturday, it briefly appeared as if Footscray might be about to lose to the Swans at the Western Oval, thereby giving the Sydney team its first victory in 26 matches. Press reports before the game had suggested signs of recovery in the Sydneysiders under new coach and former miracle man Ron Barassi, but in the first term they played like a scratch XVIII. Their kick-ins seemed to be an exercise of inventing new ways to imperil their team-mates.

At three-quarter time, Footscray led by the suitably emphatic scoreline of 10.13 (73) to 4.7 (31). Wheeler asked his players for an eight-goal win which seemed like par, particularly as they were kicking with the wind. As the quarter developed, however, it was the Swans who played the better football, attacking through the middle of the ground, running and kicking long. After 15 minutes, Sydney had halved Footscray's lead. The home side appeared demoralised, and it took a newcomer, Luke Beveridge, to save them. Whether or not Beveridge had a place in Footscray's best twenty remained to be seen, but for the moment he played with a self-possession which was lacking in his team-mates. He didn't just grab the ball and go; he insisted on exercising his right to choose what use he made of it. He kicked the steadying goal and the Dogs limped across the line, victors by 25 points. In the rooms, no one suggested singing the club song. Case, the skills coach, yelled out, 'Cheer up, it's not all doom and gloom! Sides play well and lose. Why can't you play badly and win?'

Peter Gordon was in the corner, leaning against a locker, 'It's so disappointing,' he said. 'We thought we had everything right this year, the right structure, the right players. We'd made a profit.' He shook his head dispiritedly. I was suddenly reminded of the enormous labour entailed in running a football club. Wayne Connor, Footscray's statistician, drove to and from the Peninsula suburb of Rye for every game, including the practice matches. Bob Krause, one of the recruiting scouts, had taken two weeks annual leave and gone to Adelaide for a fortnight with his wife to watch the Teal Cup. Cec Sargent ran the Bulldog Shop in Footscray Mall with a roster of 48 volunteers. It was their club, too.

The match committee was meeting in the coach's room. Wheeler let me in with a nod of the head. Case had been detailed to watch a young player in the reserves. 'What do you think?' Wheeler asked him.

'He only goes for the ball if he's 100 per cent certain of getting it,' said the skills coach. Wheeler drew breath. It was like hearing that a brand new sports car has only got two gears, third and fourth. He looked back at the whiteboard. Each of the players were represented by a small magnetic bar bearing his name. Wheeler leant across and picked up A T K I N S.

'Which brings me to the next matter,' he said. 'What are we going to do with Axe?'

Axe

Axe didn't hear the Bronx cheers, not until the last quarter of the Swans game. 'You don't,' said Wheeler, when I asked him. 'You don't hear anything when you're out there.' Late in the match, Big Scottie tapped down the ball at a centre bounce, Axe caught it and, virtually in the same stride, landed a booming torpedo punt in the goal square. At first, he thought the cheering was applause for good play. Then, a moment later, he got another possession in the forward pocket and heard it again. They were mocking him.

Ten months earlier, they had delighted in his skills. I'd watched a game on video from 1992, Round 13, Footscray versus Melbourne at the Western Oval. My first observation was that Footscray was a different team: for one reason or another, Baxter, Wallis, Macpherson, Del-Re, Smith and Coleman were no longer in the side. I now saw the difference Coleman had made. Nominally positioned at centre-half-forward, he roamed the forward half of the field, marking at will, kicking long and straight.

The connection between Coleman's contribution at centre-half-forward and Grant's on the flank was inescapable. Grant was so much more forceful than I had seen him. His attack on the ball was fierce. He was matched against a talented opponent, David Schwarz, and his winning edge was not great, but he maintained it for the whole of the afternoon. The game was Footscray's from start to finish; the ball was always eager to be bobbing their way. It wasn't until the second half that I began to perceive Wheeler's problem. There was no doubting his team's unity and conviction, but against a side which was not overwhelmed by these qualities they could be seen as lacking subtlety and variation. Basically, it was Axe who supplied them with their cleverness. He was the inventor, the one who constantly changed the pattern of play, who switched the ball about, who prevented the team from lapsing into predictability, who kept the opposition guessing. It was obvious. In fact, it was obvious to everyone, including the other fourteen AFL coaches.

Axe embodied Wheeler's Footscray, its potential and its vulnerability. He was a very good player, but he wasn't a great player. He wasn't Brereton or Carey or Ablett. He couldn't make his own space. Before the first game, I'd asked him what he thought a cheat was in footy. 'I reckon tags are cheats,' he said sourly. The old blokes said tagging was nothing new. They said it was the way football was played in their day: close and hard. Pig's arse, said Axe. Some boundary throw-ins, his opponents stood facing him, eye to eye. Their object wasn't the ball. It was him; they lived off his judgment and intuitions. After the Swans game, Ron Barassi appeared to express reservations about the tactic.

'Atkins has had a lot of that this year and it must be driving him nuts. I feel for him actually.'

How long do you need with the ball Axe? A quarter of a second. But he did need that long. For Axe to play well, he needed his team-mates playing well, disturbing the opposition. He miss Wally coming off the wing at centre bounce, hitting the packs, breaking them apart, creating gaps for him to work in. the fact that the team as a whole was down only made it easier for opposition sides to fix on him. Wheeler's critics said he wasn't hard enough on his centreman. They said he should either move him out of the centre or instruct him to sacrifice his own game and blanket an opponent. In Adelaide, the Crows had swept the ball through the centre of the field meeting no resistance. But the coach continued to allow him to try and play the game his way.

'Axe worries too much,' said Wheeler. 'He gives too much of himself to the team. I've asked him to be more selfish, to be less all-encompassing in his view of the game.' I'd seen the extent to which he worried. Coming home on the plane from Perth, he'd been saying, 'I couldn't think what to do, I couldn't think what to do.' He was referring to the period in the game when West Coast got their run on. How could he reverse the pattern of the match? There were voices in the club who said Axe should be dropped. 'Axe worked with me to get the team this far,' said Wheeler. Their rapport was largely unspoken, but the coach believed no one better understood what he was attempting at Footscray than his centreman.

The crown roared at Axe to go in and get the ball. Against Hawthorn, he tried to tear a path to the centre of the action but was immediately penalised for grabbing a player who wasn't in possession of the ball. It hadn't worked, but it didn't look natural anyway. Despite his bulky appearance, Axe wasn't a physically assertive player. His was a touch game, built on skill and vision. He felt for the ball the way that people feel for keys in the dark, and, having located it, he disposed of it in an instant, usually to someone no one else had spotted. There was a special sensitivity about Axe's football – to the bodies around him, to the position of the ball, to the unique possibilities of the moment – which, when his game wasn't working for him, when the ball was bobbing away from his hand, the crowd interpreted as weakness. Why didn't he just grab the bloody thing? They shouted at him to change his ways. He wouldn't surrender his belief in himself, so they shouted louder. He was walking from the ground after the Sydney game, red head held high, when two Footscray supporters came rushing towards him, their faces contorted with rage. Axe was about to respond when Billy Kolyniuk stopped and gave them a mouthful. The crowd rode Billy, too. But the look on the men's faces stayed with Axe. It was as if they wanted to hurt him. He stopped going to the social club after games, and went for a long walk with Ian, the chaplain.

Never Forget Where You Come From

The Brisbane game, Round 13, was Doug Hawkins's 300th. In a sense, I'd gone to Footscray to see Doug Hawkins. People said he was a great player, one of the four or five best to have represented the club. This year, he'd produced one moment of greatness, the mark in the dying moments against Fitzroy, but that had been all. One of the trainers told me Dougie was a better player when he drank. 'If he had a bad game in the old days, he'd go out and have a dozen beers and forget about it. Now, he worries.'

The new Dougie was a family man. He had responsibilities, a sports store in the Altona Gate Shopping Complex, two infant daughters. After the Fitzroy game, I'd seen him muttering to himself, fists clenched, 'I can come back. I've got character, I can come back.' He played well against Carlton, but everyone did. He tormented St Kilda playing loose in defence, but the same tactic had come horribly unstuck against Hawthorn. The Hawks matched him with Ben Allan, a skilful player who was faster than Dougie, and then played through him. Dougie was no longer as supple as he had once been. In his prime, he had been able to run, bent over the ball, guiding it with his hands through stampeding feet. Now he was more upright in his play. Nor was he as quick. 'They say you lose a yard,' said Charlie Sutton, holding up a chunky thumb and forefinger. 'All you lose is this' – his fingers were a few centimetres apart – 'but that's enough.'

One night at training, I had watched Dougie, Leon and Archie Selleck practise kicking goals on the run from the forward pocket. Leon was developing a banana kick delivered on the run. It was working too; he was averaging one goal out of every two or so shots.

'Taught him everything he knows,' said Archie humorously. Archie was still employing the old-fashioned method of cutting back towards the centre and pinging them over his shoulder.

Dougie smiled; a sad smile, but generous with it. 'Taught him everything I used to know,' he said.

Dougie hadn't touched the ball in the second half against Adelaide. That same week, he had gone to see Jeff Fenech's last fight. Fenech got beaten, literally, blood exploding from his mouth as he lurched backwards to the canvas, but Dougie said it wasn't the punch which put the former world champion down. 'He didn't want to be there,' he said. 'You could tell.'

For his 300th game, Wheeler played Dougie on the wing. The Doug Hawkins Wing. The crowd cheered when he ran to the side of the ground he'd made his own. Wheeler also played Choco and Peter Foster. I thought of them as a road crew – Choco the jackhammer, Fossie the backhoe and Dougie the bloke who'd gone to the shop and was due back any time.

The coach's critics said he was being emotional again – Choco was carrying injuries, Foster wasn't getting enough of the ball to play centre-half-back, Dougie couldn't cover a pacy opponent on the wing – but Wheeler believed it was an important day for the club. And it was. The Brisbane team joined their Footscray opponents in a guard of honour. The Hyde Street Band played. Dougie ran into the huge banner erected by the cheer squad and bounced off it. In the end, he had to engage in a tug-of-war to break through the multiple straps of cellophane. At the toss of the coin, he and the Brisbane captain, Roger Merrett, laughed and embraced. They knew a lot about each other, simply through both having played the game for so long. Then Dougie took up his position on the wing and Magic McLean ran from the back pocket to pay him a visit. Magic was small with strong, silent skills. He'd played for Footscray in '85 and been one of the players to stand by the club during the Fight back, but he was from Darwin. That's why he'd joined Brisbane; closer to home. Dougie and Magic shook hands the Aboriginal way, thumbs interlocked. Later in the match, when tempers flared, they briefly shaped up to one another. Dougie and his mates played his 300th game for real.

I spent the first half of the match on the Doug Hawkins Wing watching Doug Hawkins. Three things I recall, a kick, a mark and an attempt to win the ball. The kick was a chip shot which found its target. Clever. The mark was a strong grab over the back of a pack. Solid, but not spectacular. The attempt to win the ball was the one which set me thinking. He ran from a distance of about twenty metres and was in the air when he hit the pack, low and turning, like a cat. If the manoeuvre had worked, he would have landed over the ball; for an instant, he would have been stationary, then he would have been ready to exit in the direction from which he had come. He slightly overshot the mark, but it was like watching a gymnast. That's what Axe said about Dougie: every match he did two things you'd never seen before.

Wheeler gave Axe the job of tagging Nathan Buckley, the boy from the bush who had conquered the South Australian Football League by the time he was 20 and then headed for the Big Time. Axe and Buckley quickly came to a gentlemen's agreement, each playing his own game, Axe collecting 33 possessions to Buckley's 31. Axe was back, buoyant and abundant.

Nathan Buckley was a pleasure to watch, too. In the first quarter, he kicked a goal from an impossibly long distance at the Barkly Street end. I was watching the second half from the other side of the ground, on the boundary line in front of the E.J. Whitten Stand, when Gary Dempsey stood in front of me. Demps won the Brownlow Medal in 1975. He gave you the impression he thought he could win it again, if they'd only let him have a go. I was looking at the back of Demps's enormous overcoat which blacked out most of the ground when Nathan Buckley appeared to leap out of his pocket, knee raised like a Russian dancer. Having speared through the pack and taken the ball out of the air, he dropped to the ground and fired a 50-metre pass across the field to a leading forward. Then jogged away, crouched and contained. Demps turned, head nodding, brown eyes faintly amused. 'The boy can play,' he croaked.

Axe goaled, and was given another Bronx cheer. Brutus, the match manager for the reserves, shook his head. 'Some things here haven't changed in 25 years,' he muttered.

'They're not down on people who perform consistently each week,' replied Demps, over his shoulder.

But it was Dougie's day. The team won by 28 points, and the players chaired him off the ground on their shoulders at the end of the match. Then his official duties began. He spoke to the supporters. After he had showered, he spoke to the Footscray past players. Then he was taken on a tour of the various coteries and supporter groups. The following day was a family day at the club in his honour. Danny Del-Re took a group of little kids for warm-up exercises in the centre of the oval. They stood in a circle around him, swaying in time, like little pixies in a dance. Upstairs, in the social club, was a Doug Hawkins memorabilia collection. On a television in the corner, Dougie was talking about his knee injury in 1986, how in the wake of it he went on a long binge, eventually waking up to the knowledge that his fiancé was gone and he missed playing footy. When Dougie finally arrived in person, it was as the centre of a slow-moving crowd, like a politician on election day. But Dougie wasn't a politician; he was a local hero. If the Dogs went under, he might be the western suburbs' last.

I caught his fourth or fifth appearance on Saturday night in the Footscray social club. There was a presentation by one of the coterie groups and then Dougie had to speak. 'I look around and see a lot of old faces and that's a real thrill.' He spotted one in particular. 'Look at Magic over there. How are you, brother?' Magic McLean's round face beamed back from a corner of the bar. Dougie got on easily with the

Aboriginal players. He had told me about the day Jimmy Krakouer attacked him at the Western Oval after Jimmy thought one of Dougie's shepherds was too high. Jimmy was reported, but Dougie ran past him and said, 'Don't worry, brother, I'll get you off.' Dougie told the tribunal it was a show of strength, nothing in it. The umpire was real dirty with him afterwards. Dougie had laughed at the memory.

'Yeah,' said Dougie, 'the old Magic …' The thought lingered or a moment, then he said, 'I'm from Braybrook, I dunno what to say. Someone ask me a question, will ya?' People laughed, and Dougie saw someone else in the crowd he knew, Robbie Groenewegen, the 'Wagon'. He'd flown in from Tasmania for the occasion. 'Look at him,' said Dougie. 'He's a businessman now.' Then he tried a more serious line. 'There's something special about Footscray Football Club and Footscray people.' He thought about that, and added, 'It's all changed a bit since I turned up here with long hair and blokes hanging out the back of my panel van.' People laughed and, again, he paused. 'Footy's about people, that's all. You treat people as they treat you, and you never forget where you come from.'

Supporters

Jack McGovern, the assistant property steward, was saying that he came to Footscray with the first load of bricks. He pointed to the grandstand behind him. That was 1926, the year after the Bulldogs joined the VFL. Jack remembered when the Western Oval was a base for American soldiers during World War II. It had sentries around the ground. That was one of Jack's sayings: 'The only people who ever made Footscray leave the Western Oval was the American Army.' Another one was: 'I'm too old to tell lies.'

Jack, of course, remembered the '54 premiership. He pronounced it *preemyership*, like Charlie Sutton did. It was a big word, the way they said it, rising in the middle like a mountain. 'There are great times and there are tough times,' declared Jack, 'and the great ones make up for the tough ones.' The big change in footy, he reckoned, was that people only followed teams nowadays if they were winning. In the old days, you followed the team because it was yours. 'Winning was a bonus,' he said. One of Jack's friends took him to the

1970 grand final between Carlton and Collingwood. 'Great game,' said his friend after the match. 'Yes,' replied Jack, 'it wasn't a bad game, but one thing was wrong. The red, white and blue weren't playing.'

Old Jack was leaning on the boundary fence talking to two women who came each week to watch training, a mother and a daughter named Pat and Jenny Hodgson. The mother was originally from Queensland; she hadn't seen a game of football until her husband brought her to the Western Oval shortly after the war. Footscray won and her husband threw his Air Force cap into the air and she said to him, 'Don't you ever bring me to this place again!' It was the middle of July and she didn't have a coat on. Now, nearly fifty years later, she and her daughter were sitting at the Western Oval in the middle of July after nightfall with a tartan rug across their knees. 'Coming to training,' said the mother, 'is the best way of getting to know the players.' When training ended, she stood and clapped them as they left the field. 'Good on you, Glenn,' she called out to Galaxy. 'Well done, Fossie. Good on you, Dougie.' Dougie winked back. 'When you get to my age you can say these things because they know you're not romantically inclined. I'm just their grandmother.'

Her daughter looked like a music teacher, pale blue eyes, prominent, sensitive mouth. I ask her where she worked. She bent away from my question, as if the words had been spoken with too great a force. 'I work at Forges,' she said, nodding to see that I understood. 'In Footscray.' The daughter said Footscray was a club which didn't have a lot of luck. I'd been talking about luck with Super, and the crowd's treatment of Axe. He said there were a lot of negatives in the local culture, a lot of blame. Super was one of the mother's favourites. 'He's been here so long,' she said. 'But then I have a lot of favourites.' I asked the mother the question I asked everyone: what makes Footscray different? 'That's a silly question,' she said. 'They aren't different. They're ours, that's all.' Each week, she barracked, by which she meant she stood up and shouted for her team. 'No swearing, though.' She didn't mind what supporters from other clubs said, so long as they didn't run down Footscray players. That's what being a supporter meant, she said: not running down your own.

Above where we were sitting were the bright yellow lights of the social club. Last week, when the Big H's radio show, 'Selectors' Table', was being broadcast from the social club, one of the supporters had said Justin Charles was a joke. The supporter obviously hadn't seen Justin Charles after the Brisbane match. His big beaming face looked like an electric light with the globe taken out. It had been his first senior game for the year, his first chance. He'd been so keen to get the ball it kept bouncing off his big hands before he could close his fingers around it. No one had more feeling for Footscray than Justin Charles. He'd played in the first final of '92 and played well, following Wheeler's instructions to the letter. But one player had to be dropped from the side the following week because, at the last, Scott Wynd was declared fit to play. Justin missed. Wheeler told him after he arrived at the ground, eager and ready. 'Okay,' he had said, gulping for air, 'you're the coach.' Wheeler had felt his hurt. Big Justin came round to Wheeler's house and played with his kids.

The two women and Jack started talking about the

Fightback. Jack made a sweeping gesture at the sky. He was talking about the day of the rally. 'It looked like rain. I thought, hello, we're gone. I said to Bill Wood, 'We're not going to survive. The weather's against us and there's no one here.' Then the sky cleared and people poured into the ground. The day we won, the day the league surrendered to us, we drove through Footscray right up to the Mall. Held up traffic one and a half hours. People came out of their houses to applaud us.' Jack paused. 'And if they tried to take it off us again, we'd do it all again.' The two women agreed.

That night, after training, I talked to the players about Weary Dunlop. Weary had died that week. Wheeler introduced me quietly, saying my father had been on the Burma Railway with Weary, and that he had invited me to speak because he considered education to be one of the functions of the Footscray Football Club.

Geelong

Geelong Football Club went into the 1992 AFL grand final carrying the pride of Victoria. It was a big weight. Victoria was the site of the Eureka Stockade, the driving force behind Federation, the so-called jewel in the Liberal crown. It was the launching pad of the loony Burke and Wills expedition, scene of the Kelly outbreak and home of arch-monarchist Bob Menzies. As a history, it was sufficiently erratic to command the sympathies of just about everyone in the state. And it was where the game began.

The famous letter suggesting the formation of a 'foot-ball club' and a 'committee of three or more to draw up a code of laws', penned by T.W. Wills (no relation to the explorer), had appeared in a Melbourne magazine in July 1858 during a wildly optimistic and expansionary period in Victorian history. The Eureka Stockade had occurred four years earlier. Burke and Wills – ostensibly engaged in an act of exploration, in fact representing Victoria in a race for colonial pride with South Australia – marched off to their doom in

1860. All sorts of new words were entering the language. Shepherding was the practice of taking token occupation of a gold-mining claim to keep out rivals. A dummy was a claim for land lodged on behalf of prohibited persons. Larrikins were the new generation of native-born youths who were not cowed by authority, unlike their parents, many of whom were convicts. Ned Kelly was a larrikin. Ned had been born in 1854, the year of the Eureka Stockade. In his words, he was bold, fearless and free. Lawless, too. The Greta mob, with whom he rode, wore their hatbands under their noses and delighted in their skill and daring as horsemen. When the Kelly outbreak occurred, nothing like it had happened in New South Wales for two decades and Tasmania for five. The game reflects the place and time from which it comes. And, in nineteenth-century Australia, the word 'game' had an added edge. 'Tell 'em I died game' had been the proud last cry of many a young bushranger, usually escaped Irish-born convicts whose only choice in life was the manner in which they faced their deaths. To be game was to have spirit.

The exact origins of Australian football are in dispute. Some say it's rugby union without the off-side rule. Those of this belief rely on the fact that T.W. Wills was educated at Rugby and brought a knowledge of that school's famous game back from England with him. Certainly, the early organisation of the sport was private-school in character. Others say Australian football is Irish football with an odd-shaped ball. There are obvious parallels with the Irish games, not only in rules but in temper. Cúchulainn, the legendary Irish hero, was famous for his prowess as a hurly player and the manner in which he prepared for battle. It was called his warp spasm or battle fury and, from descriptions of it by Celtic bards, it seems to have been the original pre-match address: his body quivered, his face distorted – one eye protruding, the other disappearing into his face – and his mouth twisted until it met his ears…That's what Charlie Sutton said about Australian football: it had all the ingredients to fire you up.

There is evidence that a sport corresponding to football was played by Aboriginal people in Victoria in the early nineteenth century. A possum skin stuffed with pounded charcoal was used as a ball. The teams were organised on the basis of tribal totems. The White Cockatoo met the Black Cockatoo, or maybe the great rivalry of the Eagle and the Crow was played out. It seems to have been a game like keepings-off, special honour going to the man who leapt highest into the air to catch the ball. The game had a name: *marngrook*. Melbourne writer Jim Poulter says the last great gathering at which marngrook was played on an inter-tribal basis was at Warrandyte in 1854 where it was observed by gold miners. What Europeans added to the game, he believes, was the idea of goals. If this is correct, Australian football can be seen as an Aboriginal game with British goals played in the temper of Iris heroic endeavour. Poulter contends that the young T.W. Wills may have witnessed marngrook being played in the Western districts in the 1840s.

Wills' life is ripe for speculation. At Rugby, in addition to being captain of the school XI, he was dux of his class. In 1861, he survived the largest massacre of whites by Aborigines in Australian history on the Nogoa River in the Maryborough district of Queensland. Nineteen people were killed, including his father. Five years later, he was coaching the Edenhope Aboriginal team which made the historic tour of England in 1867. On Boxing Day 1866, he played for the Australian Natives against a Rest-of-the-World XI at the MCG; a team photograph shows a man of medium height with bushy (one imagines ginger) sideburns and a set, sombre face. T.W. Wills drank too much. In 1881, he died 'in tragic circumstances'; he committed suicide.

Victoria has been Australian football's imperial power. For one hundred years, the Big V, as it chose to be known, thought nothing of swallowing the best young talent from around the country and then sending them home for interstate matches in Victorian guernseys. In Tasmania, these ritual drubbings were taken in good humour, the great lesson of Tasmanian history being that it is folly to resist imperial powers. Tasmania and Victoria have a complex relationship. Victoria was founded from Tasmania (then Van Diemen's Land), but, in the wake of its new-found wealth from the goldfields, Marvellous Melbourne became ashamed of its island parent with the dark, ugly past. In the more genuinely independent states of South and Western Australia, however, the annual thumpings administered by the Big V were less well-received. In fact, they were bitterly resented and, by September 1992, Western Australia, through the agency of the West Coast Eagles, was poised to take its revenge. It was going to take the Australian Football League Cup, previously the Victorian Football League Cup, out of Victoria.

There was irony – but also justice – in the fact that Victoria's champion in the 1992 grand final was the Geelong Football Club. Geelong was where the 1980s recession started getting personal for many Victorians with the collapse of the Pyramid Building Society. In the wake of the Pyramid disaster, the city of Geelong looked as poor as it must have felt. Even so, people felt the Geelong team was capable of beating West Coast. Geelong were capable of doing this, it was felt, because Geelong were capable of doing anything.

If any team was close to the carefree spirit of Australian football as it must originally have been played across the breadth of Victoria, it was Malcolm Blight's Geelong. In 1989, they kicked 16 goals before half-time against the reigning premier, Hawthorn, and still lost the match (but only narrowly). Some said it was the greatest game ever played: the boys from the bush, all riding their own race, against one of the most disciplined and capable teams the game had seen. They met again in that year's grand final. That was the day Ablett withstood an early blow from Ayres which would have dented a car, got up, smote Dipierdomenico with a bump, kicked nine goals and, at the end of the match, publicly thanked God for his providence.

It was also the day that Dermott Brereton was taken out at the first bounce by Geelong's Mark Yeates. By this stage of his career, Brereton had taken the shirtfront – the hip and shoulder bump into the body of a man over the ball – to a terrifying new level of efficiency, delivering it at such speed and with such impact that at least one of his unsuspecting targets was left with whiplash and injuries consistent with a minor car crash. Two weeks earlier, in the second semi-final, he had used it to single-handedly destroy Essendon, thereby sparking a major controversy. Were his actions in the spirit of the game? The rule-makers hesitated. In the grand final, Geelong dealt with the matter in a predictable manner, by launching a pre-emptory strike and collecting Brereton off the ball at the first bounce. I didn't see it. I heart it, a voice rushing through the crowd: 'Brereton's down!' I was watching Ayres run at Ablett who was bent over the ball.

The '89 final was like something out of a storybook; by midway through the second term, it was apparent that the hero – Ablett – was invincible. The '92 final had a far more familiar plot. Geelong stole the early initiative, Ablett knocking Pyke senseless with another of his lethal bumps. The Eagles defender lay stretched out on the ground and a disconcerting stillness descended over the huge stadium. But this was the Eagles' second grand final; the previous year, they had been unable to match Hawthorn's intensity. In '92, they kept their nerve. They held on in the first term and gradually began working the ball forward in the second. In the third, Heady went into the centre and the tempo and frequency of the visitors' forward moves increased. Suddenly, cracks appeared in the Geelong defence; Peter Matera was through them and gone. His long goal early in the third term put the Eagles ahead for the first time in the match but almost immediately one sensed the game was over. Geelong had put on a bold front, but behind it was only a handful of highly talented individuals. The Eagles were the more evenly skilled team and they possessed a uniformly hard edge. Their full-forward, Peter Sumich, followed Matera's devastating act by kicking goals which defied belief, and grand finals are so much about belief. Suddenly, the Cats were three or four goals down, transparently lacking the physical and mental wherewithal to launch the sort of counter-attack needed to stop a young, talented, highly disciplined team with the march of history pounding in its ears. Geelong needed a miracle and Gary Ablett couldn't supply one.

The Geelong player who paid the highest price for the defeat was Billy Brownless. The reason Billy was made to suffer was because the preceding week in the preliminary final, and in the qualifying final a fortnight before that, he had killed Footscray. In both matches, he had rockets in his thighs. He leapt from standing starts and was half a body above his nearest rival when the ball came within reach. The crowd was hoarse with exhilaration. Footscray had no answer to him but, unfortunately for Billy, West Coast did – the white shadow, Ashley McIntosh. Billy still kicked three in the final – and God knows how hard he had to work for them – but there were no big marks, nothing to give Geelong supporters a wild explosion of hope to take home at the end of the day as a sort of consolation prize.

The Geelong rooms after the match were a black hole. The players moved about like shadows in a bad dream. I watched Billy leave. Two women were waiting for him, one old and one young – a mother and a girlfriend perhaps – their faces red and tearful. 'We lost,' he said, throwing his arms in the air and turning away. It seemed wrong that one so young had been made to carry such a weight of history. Victoria had been losing for years – its manufacturing sector had been blitzed by the flat earth economic policies of the '80s, its population was drifting north and west, it was steadily losing its battle with Sydney to be the nation's de facto capital. Billy was just the blond-haired boy who could out-leap his mates kicking end-to-end in the schoolyard. I said as much in the paper the following

Monday and was startled by a Geelong supporter who apprehended me, eyes bulging. 'Don't you see?' he said. 'While you keep writing things like that, he'll never grow up!'

But, in 1992, Geelong had succeeded in ending Wheeler's dream. The Doggies had considered themselves a chance against West Coast – they'd thrashed them in the mud and rain at the Western Oval two weeks before the finals – but to get at the Eagles they had to get past Geelong and twice they tried, and twice they failed. What they did win was the first half of the first encounter. There was nothing fancy about Footscray's play, but they were fast, synchronised and resolute. However, once Geelong's major players – Ablett, Hocking, Bairstow, Stoneham, Couch, Brownless – entered the drama, Footscray had no answer although Dougie attempted one. Positioning himself on the defensive side of the centre square after a revivalist goal by Geelong late in the second quarter, he took on the field. Against the run of play, he squeezed the ball forward and Danny Del-Re goaled. It was an inspired act of leadership. Unfortunately, it required a support act and none was forthcoming. Footscray lost the first final by 61 points and the second by 64.

By the time Footscray and Geelong met at Kardinia Park in July 1993, the passion and drama of the '92 finals series was a long way distant. Geelong were in a dormant phase; by the end of the season, they would have torn out West Coast's throat in Perth, thereby establishing themselves in the opinion of many as the best team in the competition, and missed the finals. For the moment, however, Ablett was basically doing it on his own. Three times, he'd kicked ten goals or more in losing sides. Footscray were in Perth when he kicked fourteen against Essendon. This was the day Kevin Sheedy sent out his runner with the historic message, 'Just tell them [the Essendon team] that all they have to do is outscore him.' News of his fourteen goals came over the radio in Footscray's team bus. Everyone laughed. Crazily. Ablett wasn't like other people. He was an inscrutable phenomenon, a muscular package of athleticism and detachment which no one, not even those who knew him, seemed to understand.

I watched the Geelong match from the coach's box. I'd never seen Footscray look fainter or smaller. If I'd been watching on television, I would have leant forward and turned up the volume, sharpened the contrast, anything to add life. Maybe they were haunted by their memory of the previous year's two finals, but Footscray have never done well at Kardinia Park. Each year, E.J. Whitten had driven to Geelong, jaw set, intent on victory; the best result he had managed in twenty years was a single draw.

Initially, Geelong didn't bury them in an avalanche of goals, largely because TC was doing relatively well on Ablett. Each week, my respect for TC grew. His opponents were some of the biggest names in the game – Lockett, Dunstall, Ablett – and if it was true that he was a purely professional footballer, it was also the case that he took a professional pride in his work. TC stayed in the contest until the last.

For three quarters, Wheeler shuffled his side like a gambler shuffling a pack, trying to conjure a winning hand, but the best quality Footscray could summon was perseverance. Barry Stoneham collected Leon Cameron at an early centre bounce and, for the rest of the day, the Footscray ruck-rover trailed the play. Mark Hunter strained his hamstring and had to leave the ground. In the third quarter, the Dogs willed their way to within 12 points of the lead. It was a desperate enterprise, one requiring enormous effort and concentration. Then Footscray made a simple error; Geelong arrowed the ball downfield, Garry Hocking angled from a pack, leant on to his left foot and goaled. He made it look as simple as posting a letter.

'These blokes know how to kick a goal,' said Ferret. Ferret was Ted Whitten Junior. He had the same pale eyes as his father and had achieved football honours in his own right, representing the State and playing more than one hundred games for the club. But Ferret was aptly named: his thoughts stayed down the burrow until they were good and ready to appear. Then they were expressed plainly, but with conviction.

In the last quarter, Bairstow and Hocking combined to execute a classy move which resulted in another Geelong goal. The margin had now stretched to sixty points. 'They're just too smart for our blokes,' said Ferret. Wheeler turned in his chair and stared at his old acquaintance. 'Don't say that to me, Ferret,' said the coach. 'That sets off all sorts of alarm bells in me.'

Personality

The day after Footscray lost to Geelong at Kardinia Park, Carlton defeated West Coast in Perth by one point. The reigning premiers played without verve, but they were their usual grimly determined selves and Carlton had to keep rising to the occasion to win. Such a collective effort requires inspiration, and Carlton centreman Greg Williams provided it, on one occasion goaling after a tumbling mark where he literally threw himself beneath an oncoming pack to catch the ball inches above the ground. Footscray lacked that sort of inspiration. Axe collected 31 possessions at Geelong, but it hardly seemed to matter; the sense of adventure which enabled his team-mates to take advantage of his unique skills and vision one year earlier had gone. In the absence of a player who could ignite them as a team, Footscray also lacked a player who could ignite the crowd – someone like Melbourne's Allen Jakovich.

Allen Jakovich is the Liberace of the game. Against Collingwood earlier in the year, the plump forward had run along the members' wing of the MCG, blowing kisses to the crowd, inviting them to share in his triumphs. Perhaps I should repeat myself. Melbourne was playing Collingwood. The Collingwood crowd is like no other. When Collingwood is on the march, the air hums. The ball comes forward as a rush of sound. Jakovich's performance would have had them leaning out of their seats, baying like hounds from hell. 'Most supporters are pretty okay,' Jakovich once remarked innocently enough, 'but there is definitely something wrong with Collingwood supporters. They're not normal people.' When Melbourne plays Collingwood, Allen Jakovich plays the Collingwood crowd.

The Perth match ended with Eagles wingman Chris Mainwaring hitting the post with the last kick of the day. He knelt, head in hands, for an extended period thereafter. The crowd responded with a long sigh. That's the problem when you have 40,000 people all barracking for one side: the game is constantly teetering on the edge of melodrama. It takes two voices to make a footy crowd, two opposing voices. That's why Allen Jakovich is one of the game's personalities. He gets them both yelling.

A Very Good Game

Wheeler benched Dougie for the Richmond game (Round 15). The commentators said it was a sensation. In the crowd, they said a lot worse. 'Resign, Wheeler!' shouted a plump man with a red face and small black eyes. 'Resign now!' Footscray were 23 points down by quarter-time. Enraged, the man with the red face and small black eyes broadcast a monologue of loathing: 'They're trash. Look at them. This has to be the worst side I've ever seen in the red, white and blue.' Turning to one of his companions, he added, 'And I never thought I'd hear myself say that two weeks in a row.' Then he got personal. 'Why don't you retire, Foster, you've just fallen over again,' and, 'Jeez, you're a top rover, West. Jeez, I'm a liar.'

Scottie West was back in the seniors. The eighteen-year-old's first game of league football had been the opening match of the season, against Collingwood under lights at the MCG in front of 60,000 people. He didn't know if it was a dream or a nightmare. In his fourth game, against Essendon, he had kicked six goals.

In his fifth game, in Perth, he had been shaken, physically and mentally. His form had deteriorated after that and he had eventually been dropped to the reserves after the Adelaide game. He found himself hearing the voice of doubt and derision on the other side of the fence. He even wondered how anyone enjoyed playing the game. Then he remembered the parachute jump. That had been about confronting fear. Spider Welsh, Wheeler's confidant, said the thing you had to understand about fear on the football field was that everyone felt it. The first competition was with yourself.

Wheeler didn't bring Dougie on until midway through the second term. Dougie was wild – real wild, he said later, at not having got on earlier. Positioning himself on the defensive side of the centre square, he started gathering possessions and distributing the ball, not giving it to his team-mates but placing it in front of them, making them stretch. 'I didn't care if it didn't go to anyone,' he said; 'I was going to make them run. You've got to take risks to win in footy.' I didn't notice the risks. What I noticed was that the ball started flowing through him, with the result that Footscray established a steady supply line, its first of the match. And no one panicked.

During the week, Wheeler had played games with them – innocent games. At training, he selected four teams and gave them silly names like the Maggots, drew up a rugby league field and told them to kick-off. Everyone laughed at Fossie because he couldn't learn the rules and kept getting off-side. At half-time, Wheeler told them to play like the Maggots, and Billy Kolyniuk did. Billy's Goal of the Year, against Collingwood at the MCG in 1991, had made him famous. The problem with fame is that it creates the expectation of repeat performances. Basically, the goal stood alone in Billy's career, like Phil Manassa's run with the ball in the '77 grand final. The Footscray crowd had come to doubt him, and they expressed that doubt cruelly, but you always sensed that Billy was watching the game out the corner of his eye, wondering if this was the moment when it would happen for him again. At the start of the final quarter, Billy went for it, torpedoing through the centre square at the first bounce from the right wing and collecting the ball. Centrifugal force was against him. It was carrying him, at best, towards the left forward pocket. He had to curve back, bounce the ball and evade a succession of increasingly desperate defenders. He had just taken his fourth bounce when he was stubbed into the earth by a Richmond player who collected him like a heat-seeking missile. The ball was left spinning beside their bodies. It was a failed attempt, but it was a great attempt.

Not for the first time, I also found myself noticing Peter Quill. Quill was in his first year at Footscray, having played in South Fremantle's WAFL 1992 premiership team under former Hawthorn player Ken Judge. There was a feeling that he was a fraction slow for AFL football, but he was brave, unselfish and artful. He was a commerce graduate and had an accountant's reserved, thoughtful manner, but after the loss to West Coast in Perth I had seen the passion in his eyes and sensed his deeper self. When Footscray was clawing its way back into the Richmond match and the ball simply could not be allowed to leave its forward line, Quill slapped an overcoat of a tackle on a Richmond defender in the goal square. He took him head-on, falling backwards with the body. Billy Kolyniuk had provided one sign; Peter Quill another. As an exhibition of skill and technique, the Richmond game was highly imperfect; but Footscray found enough belief to overcome their opponents. Down ten points at three-quarter time, Footscray finished with a 16-point victory.

Before the match, Wheeler had instructed his team to play one-on-one. All idea of the structure with which they had begun the season was gone; they were back to survival footy. 'Stand your opponent, respect him and then beat him,' he told the players. 'You're professional footballers. Don't create something false in your minds – control is a hard edge which is there to be got.' When they had gone and we were briefly alone, he said, 'If we lose today, all our work over the past three and a half years will probably have been for nothing.' He was wiping the whiteboard as he spoke. The school he had laboured so hard to build was at risk of being closed.

Afterward, it occurred to me that the Richmond game was possibly Wheeler's best for the year. The win came at a time when the team was depressed and going from bad to worse. Instead of burdening his players with the knowledge of the full consequences of the game, he had deliberately lightened their load. Once the match was over, however, the praise he gave them was highly qualified. 'Quillie,' he said, 'you're developing as an AFL player. You're always looking to do something with the ball. Sometimes, at this level, you don't have time to do that. You've got to put that knowledge into your back of tricks.' Scottie West had been among Footscray's best. He had taken on his opponents, and run past them. Wheeler acknowledged that he had also been good in close, where there was most danger. Grant's form had again been moderate, but in the final quarter he had broken a tackle and delivered the pass to Jon Ballantyne which eventually put Footscray ahead. Bernard Toohey was the source of much good football sense, and Wheeler now repeated one of his sayings: 'It's not always your day, but it can always be your moment.' Crackers was watching disconsolately from a corner, arm in a sling. He'd collected a high-speed bump in the act of clearing a path to the ball. 'If ever a player got injured doing what his coach wanted,' said Wheeler, 'it was Crackers.' Finally, reaching his captain, he said, 'And Doug Hawkins – that was a very good game.'

Voices in the Train

Travelling to the Western Oval, I sit beside two kids in school uniform. They're both chewing gum, mouths open. One's Indian. He talks about visiting relatives in Fiji. His mate has recently had cousins over from Vietnam. He wanted to show them something Australian so he took them to the footy.

'What'd they say?' asked the friend.

'They said, "How fucken fast is this!"'

Victoria Park

I was thirteen when I first went to Victoria Park. First time away from Tassie, too. Melbourne was vast and grey, with wide streets and overhanging wires and clattering trams. Its brightest attraction was a pinball machine with silver balls and flashing yellow lights in a small café opposite the Spencer Street railway station. On the Saturday, we went to Victoria Park. The famous ground appeared, out the open doorway of the old blue rattler, as a curving black and white wall; then, just inside the gate, I saw Peter McKenna. He was wearing a club blazer and talking to an old bloke in an animated way about nothing in particular, signing autographs as he did. Collingwood's star full-forward was much taller than I imagined.

I glimpsed the match from behind a row of heads, but nothing came between me and the deep roar when Collingwood took the field; it was savage but intimate, like an old promise renewed. The man standing beside me was in his forties with neat, oiled, curly hair and a beer can in his hand. I'd never heard anyone like him.

He broadcast from the start of the match until the end, but even at the age of thirteen I knew that he was basically talking about himself. No one had ever given him a fair go. No one ever gave McKenna a fair go either, but McKenna triumphed regardless. 'Good on ya, Macca,' he shouted. My first foray into the outside world and I'd met a Collingwood supporter.

Collingwood Football Club is larger than life in the way that Don Bradman, Les Darcy and Phar Lap are larger than life; it is the only Australian football club of which this can be said. Born during the depression of the 1890s, the club was forged from a knowledge of acute deprivation and a fierce, vengeful pride. At the time, Collingwood was regarded as the worst, smelliest and most rat-infested suburb in Melbourne. For two hours each Saturday, however, the residents of Collingwood met their tormentors on equal terms. No club ever had truer colours; there were no shades of grey in the Collingwood world view, only black and white, and, by the end of the '30s, the formative decade in Australian sporting history, the Magpies had established themselves as football's standard of excellence. The portrait of Jock McHale which hangs in the foyer of the social club at Victoria Park bears the inscription, 'Coach 1911-50 (World Record).' By the 1960s, however, Collingwood's legendary iron discipline was starting to lose its grip and a period of waywardness ensued. Collingwood famously lost a succession of finals, most notably in 1970, when a team considered to be one of the best in the history of the club led by seven goals at half-time. When Carlton changed the game – for ever, some said – by handballing at every opportunity, Collingwood went blank. The greater the suffering inflicted on Collingwood, the greater the mirth and delight among supporters of other clubs because the one lesson Collingwood refused to learn, no matter what fate befell it, was humility.

Crackers was standing at the mouth of the race when I arrived at the ground, arm in a sling. He was restless, unable to conceal his disappointment. Crackers always looked forward to playing at Victoria Park. 'I love it,' he said. 'They hate me and I hate them.' Crackers had been interested in what I had to say about Weary Dunlop. I wasn't altogether surprised. In the course of the year, I'd seen a play about Australian prisoners of war in World War II which had begun with the line, 'We shouldna surrendered.' That was Crackers. At Geelong, he had burnt like a solitary furnace, trying to ignite some feeling among them, but even Crackers admitted he didn't like playing at Kardinia Park. Somehow, you felt diminished down there. 'But not here,' he said. Whatever else was said about the Collingwood crowd, they didn't make you feel small. Everything about the game was bigger when Collingwood was involved. Crackers said Dougie liked playing at Victoria Park, too.

Dougie was a treat to watch that day. He started on the bench again. The Collingwood crowd hooted him for it and he grinned back at them. By the time Dougie came on, Collingwood had kicked six goals to Footscray's one behind. Collingwood's season hadn't been the same since their president earned them the Aboriginal curse, and they attacked with revivalist fervour. Kelly, their captain, was charging through the early centre bounces like a runaway bus. After 15 minutes, Collingwood had 56 possessions to Footscray's 23 and were in total control of the most vital area on the ground – the corridor between the goals. The ball was rushing through the centre of the ground unimpeded. Dougie slowed the pace of the game. Like a waltz, it was. He ran across the Collingwood goal bouncing the ball with his left hand, one eye on the players up the field. Thereafter, when he released the ball, it went where Dougie kicked it and at least one kick beyond. Simultaneously, the game opened, broadened. Footscray kicked four goals to trail by only 12 points at quarter time. Something was happening here.

The second quarter began with Grant goaling from the boundary. Then Axe tricked his tag into running across a mark and conceding a 50-metre penalty. That created another goal. Then Choco goaled, after marking and being dumped by Gary Pert, and Footscray was ahead. It was now a game of real consequence. After the most disappointing of seasons, Footscray finally looked as if they were being reborn, as if they had at least discovered the ingredients that would enable them to play with some sense of command. The next five minutes were the most decisive of the match, possibly of Footscray's season. It was a battle which glowed with its own white light. Either Footscray lost it, or Collingwood won it, because the home side slipped away to a four goal lead. For Footscray to have any chance an individual had to emerge as Dougie had done earlier, had to rise above the pattern of events and recast them in a new mould.

In the final minute of the term, Grant ran from his forward flank, vaulted the back of a pack and marked on the goal line, carrying the ball to the ground with him. It was a superb mark, brave and skilful. Was this the moment? Was this the man? By the time the umpires had placed him on what they considered to be the correct angle, he was virtually parallel with the goal line. His face, as always, was earnest and intent. He opted for the banana kick; it curved marginally too early and went through for a point. Somehow, it epitomised his season.

Before the match, Wheeler had told them there was no other day. 'Collingwood at Collingwood,' he said. 'That's an historic challenge. It'll go all the way. You expect nothing less here.' He'd told them to go with their reactions. 'If the play's on, give the ball. The quicker we move it, the more likely we are to catch them out. Make decisions. The worst thing you can do is not make decisions. Manage your team-mate's mistakes like you manage his successes; be at this side, encourage him.' Then, returning to his central theme, he said, 'There is no other day, no other group of players.' He named them individually. 'There's no other back pocket Darc, no other centre-half-back Ben, no other ruckman Scottie. This is it.' His tone then had been firm and commanding. At half-time, it was hoarser; pleading, almost. 'When you had the intensity, you took control of the game. You strung seven goals together. You could hear the silence through the whole stadium. They were thinking, "This side's too quick, too strong, too purposeful".' If Footscray's 1993 season were a three-act play, act one had ended with the Hawthorn match. That was when the team had been exposed. The closing scene of act two was half-time at Collingwood, the central character now alone with his first and last believe. 'Can't you see?' he implored them. 'You can do whatever you fucking want to do! You can be whatever you want to be!'

In the Back

Footscray continued to score throughout the second half, but Collingwood scored more easily and more often, Rocca kicking ten. Saverio Rocca was a big, strong boy who was suddenly sure of himself. The Collingwood supporters called him Saveloy. Craig Starcevich they called Starkers. As I recalled, an earlier Collingwood player, Paul Rissoti, was Rissole. Football in general, and Collingwood in particular, is a good place to observe the Australianisation of foreign-sounding names (poor Gary 'Franger' Frangalis, ex-Richmond and the Swans, never had a chance).

In fact, Collingwood is a good place to observe all manner of things. One cold, wet Thursday night in 1987, I sat in the grandstand at Victoria Park and watched training with a born-again Christian whose ambition in life was to go to California and rearrange the giant word HOLLYWOOD, above the suburb of that name, to read COLLINGWOOD. He was watching training before attending a meeting of the Goon Society which has access to Victoria Park because the uncle of one of its members played for Collingwood. 'That's how things work at Victoria Park,' said the young born-again Christian Magpie Goon.

I wandered around to the area in front of the Ryder Stand. From there, I had witnessed Billy Picken's homecoming in the opening match of the 1986 season. Billy was my favourite player in those brave Collingwood teams that made five tilts at the flag between '77 and '81. There was something irresistibly boyish about his football: the floppy fringe, the wobbly torps, the socks around his ankles. Billy was always falling over, but he was always getting up again. There is a photograph on the wall at Victoria Park from one of those great doomed finals campaigns, two layers of bodies and Billy above them, hands open, a look of anticipation on his face. Billy was the Boy Who Could Fly. Somehow, after the Hafey era at Collingwood had ended, Billy was lured north for a season or two with the Swans. He started his return match at Victoria Park on the bench; the roar which met his introduction to the game was like a Rottweiler's love bite, 30,000 of them. But the spring had gone from Billy's legs. He shuffled and fell on the ball. The only Collingwood player who held his own that day against the reigning premiers was Darren Millane.

At the first bounce, players from both sides had thrown themselves at the ball. The whistle had blown. An Essendon player was awarded a free. The man beside me spun towards me, eyes bulging, beer can in hand, shirt open to the middle of his chest. He looked like an off-duty butcher. 'Oh no,' he cried. 'Not another year like last year!' I glanced at his companion, a woman I judged to be in her early forties. Like many

Collingwood fans, she was dressed exclusively in black and white. She was poodle-like; her small thin face rested beneath an elaborate crescendo of curls. Noticing my attention, she smiled; a diamond glittered from her left front tooth.

I had wandered around in front of the Ryder Stand thinking my Collingwood tooth-fairy might still be there, but she was nowhere to be seen. What happened to Footscray, I wondered. Failure of nerve? I imagined that was what Wheeler thought. Failure of courage? I was sure the old players thought so. I met Harvey Stevens, ruckman in the '54 side, walking past the Ryder Stand. His face was dark and angry. 'Football's played from in here,' he said, punching his chest. 'You've got to have heart'. (Later, Super said the effort in coming back from six goals down was too great; they were exhausted.)

For a time, I listened to the Collingwood crowd delighting in Footscray's humiliation. 'Bring on EJ!' they cried. 'Bring on Charlie Sutton!' A young man with a grin on his face and a beer can in his hand was leaning against the steps of the old wooden stand, teasing the crowd. Collingwood's McGuane missed a goal from a set shot. 'Never liked him,' called out the young man. Heads in front of him nodded and murmured their assent. Rocca had a set shot and converted. 'Always liked him,' said the young man. More nods and murmurs of assent. The young man was a poet; he was playing with language.

I watched the game out behind the grandstand goal with Crimmo and a young ground attendant. Crimmo was fuming. He'd gone for a bet at the TAB in his Footscray blazer and attracted the attention of some

Collingwood supporters who told him Footscray was shit. The young attendance was a Collingwood supporter, but even he found Collingwood people alarming. He pointed to a moustache in the grandstand behind us. Collingwood was 62 points up and the moustache was still abusing the umpire. When Adelaide played Collingwood at Victoria Park in Round 7, Tony Modra had taken what many people considered to be the mark of the year in front of where we were standing. He had vaulted one opponent, ridden a second and taken the ball out of the air as the platform of bodies collapsed beneath him. Even the Collingwood crowd had momentarily been hushed by the sheer athletic virtuosity of his feat. The moustache had been one of the first to recover his composure. 'In the back,' he cried.

The Worst Result of the Year

The Melbourne game (Round 17) was Libber's 100th. The banner called him OUR LITTLE CHAMPION. His mother, holding anxiously to the fence, had tears in her eyes. 'It is not always easy being a mother,' she said. Wheeler invited his twin brother, Fred, into the rooms before the game. He looked like a larger, fuller version of Libber. 'I've known him for 27 years,' said Fred Liberatore quietly, 'and I'm very proud of what he's achieved.' The brothers shook hands.

Before the Footscray players left the rooms, Wheeler read them a small homily on winners: 'Winners believe in the path they have chosen even when others can't see where they are going. Winners are positive thinkers who see good in all things, from the ordinary they make the extraordinary ...' He didn't say so, but everyone knew he was talking about Libber. 'I just love that shit,' said Crackers, shaking his head and smiling, as we walked down the race. His arm was still in the sling.

Footscray had now lost its entire backline from the previous year's finals team through injury (TC and

Matthew Mansfield had been added to the list at Collingwood). I was beginning to wonder about injuries. I didn't doubt that people would continue wanting to watch Australian football, but I was beginning to wonder whether anyone would want to play it. The absence of an off-side rule meant players could be collected from any angle. Crackers had bared one eyeball and shown me where he had thirty stitches and what he called 'a bit of plastic' inserted after a football collision detached his retina and turned one half of his world the colour of port wine. 'This is what the old blokes don't understand,' said Terry Wallace, when I raised the subject with him. 'Players today hit so much harder.' The damage to Crackers' shoulder – the bump had been perfectly fair – was consistent with a motorcycle accident. Peter Foster wondered whether players would be physically capable of playing 200 games in the future. The youngest player in the club, sixteen-year-old Tyson Lane, had started the season on crutches after a knee operation and ended it with stress fractures in his shin. The number of games, and in consequence the amount of training, had also increased dramatically. Choco Royal saw young players like Steve Kretiuk suffering the sort of hamstring injuries he didn't begin to experience until he was twenty-seven and had played 100-odd games. Wally wondered whether the general public had any idea of what league footballers endured just to play the game. He had been taking anti-inflammatories for the past four years. He always remembered Carlton's Wayne Johnston saying that by the end of his career he was almost addicted to pain-killers.

Wheeler had invited all the injured players into the root before the Melbourne game. He assigned each of them to a member of the team; his role was to watch his team-mate and give him feedback at the breaks. It had been Wally's idea to begin with. He had rung Wheeler and said, 'Is there any way the injured players can help?' Wally was always looking to emphasise the positive. It was his philosophy in business – he was a qualified accountant with a Mazda dealership in Essendon – as well as sport.

But Footscray couldn't do it for Libber. After the match, he sat alone, his face a black emptiness that no one could enter or dispel. 'These blokes don't know what Libber's been through,' said Dougie. Neither did I, but I was beginning to guess. Libber's critics were never silent for long. They said he kicked too short, that speedsters like McGuinness and Francis were always going to run away from him. The said Footscray would never win a premiership while he was first rover. But I liked watching him. I could write a myth based on Tony Liberatore. It would be the story of an infant who discovers that he can make the sound of thunder by clapping his hands together. The sound is so awesome, so wonderful, that he spends the rest of his life trying to repeat the feat, but, as an adult, he finds that he has eighteen men fastened to each of his arms.

What Libber brought to the game was sheer naked endeavour. Nor was his game without finesse. Libber played football like a Greco-Roman wrestler. He couldn't be grounded – he squirmed, twisted, turned, wrenching enough of his body free to release the ball – and he was always in the heat of the action. That's where Dougie found him the previous week at Victoria Park. I'd seen Libber look up and spot him – it was like an infantryman seeing the cavalry come over the hill. Libber had been waiting all year for someone like Dougie to appear and prise open the game just enough for him to see the gaps between the legs and find some space to work in.

But that was last week when the sky was blue and the sun was shining. There was no sun in the Footscray rooms after the loss to Melbourne. Melbourne won because it played better into the wind. The Melbourne coach, Neil Balme, kept his forward line intact for the whole four quarters with Lyon, his captain, staying at centre-half-forward throughout. Footscray, on the other hand, dropped Wynd into defence against the wind. In the third quarter, they pulled their forward flankers back towards the centre to allow the forwards and mid-fielders space to run into. The tactic didn't work. Whereas Melbourne had a player at every contest when they kicked into the wind, Footscray's attacks kept failing for the lack of someone to carry the ball and, on each occasion, Melbourne then had the time to set up the game, to plot and plan from deep within their defensive half.

Footscray had been beaten at its own game, on its own ground, by a team going nowhere in particular. In every respect, it was the worst result of the year. It was now virtually impossible for Footscray to make the finals, but somehow making the finals had always seemed like a sub-plot. The season had begun with a much grander dream: winning a premiership.

Wheeler announced training for every night the following week. The air in the coach's room was hot and angry when he said it. The punishment would hurt him as much as it hurt the players – he wasn't that sort of teacher. Crackers said it was a pity I hadn't done the book in 1992. 'Last year, everything about this place was exciting,' he said. 'It was magic. At the end of games, you didn't want to come off the ground. What you're looking at now isn't the Footscray Football Club. It's just a collection of individuals.' I told Steve Wallis what Crackers had said. 'They're the feelings of a senior player,' he replied.

Wally

Steve Wallis had blond curls and blue eyes and a smile that appeared at the start or end of every sentence, but his boyish looks were deceptive. He had played 200 games for Footscray and, in the process, broken a leg (1982) and a wrist (1991), snapped a cruciate ligament (1987), acquired four stress fractures in his back and torn the medial ligament in his left knee (1993). He was slightly bow-legged and because of the damage he had done to his knees through playing league football, both legs would have to be broken and re-set when he finished to save him from acute arthritis. Wally said there was a transition from being a social footballer 'to being fair dinkum about your sport, to becoming a man in your football'. Wally was fair dinkum about his football.

He had begun his career as a centreman who spirited through packs, collecting clever possessions. He had played more than 100 games and twice represented Victoria when Malthouse approached him during pre-season training in 1987 and said that if he didn't change his game he was no longer required at the club. The truth, which Wally had been reluctant to acknowledge, was that he was being tagged and had found no solution to the problem. Malthouse had one. He could tag the tagger. He could learn to play in a wholly defensive way. For two years, Wally did a job he didn't want to do. He noticed that people's view of him changed. In fact, it dropped. He went from being one of the team's attractive players to another of its dour serviceable ones, but, at the same time, his view of the game and the people in it changed. Malthouse was delighted. In 1989, at the age of 24, Wally was appointed club captain.

Wally and Malthouse once undertook the same psychological test and were classified as total opposites. Wally was an optimist. What he loved about playing foot was 'its feel, touch and smell – the same as a new car or a new house. Before the night match against Collingwood at the MCG, I'd seen him rubbing his hands together and saying gleefully, 'This is why I do it.' He loved the adrenalin before a big game, and the eruption of energy at the first bound when everything that had been stored inside the crown and the forty players spilled free. As a kid, he had played cricket with the local team (he thought cricket was a 'magnificent game' because of the range of ages which played it). The old blokes in the side said Wally was like a pup, always getting in the way trying to help. Some nights, along with Super, Wally would be on the training track with his knee in a brace, lending encouragement to his team-mates. Wally believed in his club. When I asked him about some of the stories from Footscray's wild old days, he replied, 'Footscray's no different to any other football club. It's just more susceptible to speculation and bad publicity.'

It was Wally who always greeted newcomers to the club, but at the same time he was direct with them. When Crackers arrived, he told him, 'At this club, you get points by playing good footy and putting in for the next bloke. And if you burn me on the field, I'll tell you.' At the start of the 1990 season, Wheeler had taken the captaincy off Wally and given it to Dougie. 'It was hard for me personally,' said Wally, 'but it was right for the club. Doug was ideal at the time.' Before the first practice match, I'd heard Wally call out, 'Lead us out for another year, Hawk.' Wally was like a chrome metal bar, bright and hard. Wheeler said he was Footscray's biggest loss for the year.

Spring

It was Archie Selleck who noted the return of spring, 'Beautiful day, wasn't it?' he said to me one night after training. 'You could smell the grass, smell the people preparing to drink beer. It was real finals weather. You can't explain that to anyone who's not from Melbourne.'

The Saturday following the Melbourne game was beautiful, too. The moon was a pale stone in the blue air above the city. A one-armed trumpeter led the Hyde Street Band and added frills to 'Sons of the Scray'. The sun was a blazing ball of brilliance which watched the last half of the match from the shoulder of the E.J. Whitten Stand, reaching across the Western Oval, gilding the awning on the Doug Hawkins Wing. That's all the Doug Hawkins Wing is – a roof over your head. What a fitting monument to the man. That's why Dougie liked the Aboriginal players – they were so casual. 'Look at Lolly Bamblett,' he said. Lolly was plump and quick. He played in the '85 side; the ball would no sooner have been knocked from Simon Beasley's hands than Lolly would have snared it and gone. 'He kicked 60 goals that year, and he was two stone overweight.' The worry of his 300th behind him, Dougie was laughing again.

Halfway down the Doug Hawkins Wing is a metal tower which looks like the bridge off an old merchant navy vessel. This is for the opposition coach. Standing beneath it, you can sometimes hear the directions they should to their players. I wanted to hear Fitzroy's Robert Shaw; he was said to be tactically innovative. Wally respected him because he once said that for a period of three weeks in his career as a coach he was out of form. Then, walking around the Doug Hawkins Wing, I met two blokes from work. One was in a wheelchair. He talked rapidly, humorously, about the travails of barracking for Fitzroy. I had only spoken to him once before. That was the day I was called in by the newspaper to write an obituary for someone who wasn't dead. I'd run the hospital to confirm the bereavement and been put through to the deceased. At the time, I wasn't amused, but the man in the wheelchair was. 'You'll see the joke eventually,' he said, bright-eyed, almost as if there was a joke in the fact that I was refusing to see it already. His companion I knew slightly better. He had a kind face, like Tasmanian conservationist Bob Brown, only with a flasher hair-do. Every night for a year or so when he sat down to work, he had placed beside him a silver tin with a slit in the top and a Save the Lions sticker on it. All donations were welcome. Carn the Roys.

Fitzroy had been under threat for as long as I'd been in Melbourne. In '86, when David Parkin coached them, they'd got to within sight of the grand final. Their bodies gave way in the end, but they provided the game with one of its great romantic causes. They were an odd, uneven collection then; they had an old champion with creaking ankles in Bernie Quinlan, an acrobat at full-back in Gary Pert, an unguided missile on the half-forward flank named Micky Conlan and, at centre-half-back, the incomparable Paul Roos. The crowd did him the compliment of breathing his name, a lot whistling *ROOOOoooooos*! every time he touched the ball. He played with dash and flair, long black hair flowing behind him. He out-marked all comers one-on-one and scaled their backs if he was late arriving. That year, Paul Roos was Australian football at its fairest and best but the Brownlow Medal eluded him.

Mid-season '86, Fitzroy defeated Hawthorn, the eventual premiers, at Princes Park, but after the match I saw how spent the Fitzroy players were. They lacked the reserves available to the big clubs; they had only themselves. Rover Leon Harris had sealed the match, finding the energy in the last minute to sidestep two opponents in the forward pocket and lot a late goal. 'You threaded it!' shouted an excited supporter to him afterwards in the rooms. 'Yeah,' said Harris, quietly, 'I threaded it,' but it was as if he knew there weren't too many more where that one had come from.

Even David Parkin, it seemed, hadn't budgeted on the win. Parkin is what David Attenborough called a compulsive communicator. As he was leaving the post-match press conference, he declared, 'I'll never work this game out!' He walked through the door, clip-board under arm, then stopped, turned and came back. Another thought had occurred to him. 'But if I did – it wouldn't be a game!' Too true.

And all the time, off the field, the Fitzroy Football

club was fighting for survival. A crudely scrawled cardboard sign on a building site in Lonsdale Street declared, 'The Builders Laborers Federation Support Fitzroy Football Club and the People of the Philippines in their Struggle against Ferdinand Marcos'. That year, in the course of writing a story about Fitzroy, I visited one of the club's former greats, Butch Gale. We watched a Swans game together on television. 'There's a lot of athletes playing today,' said Butch, 'but that Greg Williams is a footballer.' I asked him what playing for Fitzroy meant when he was growing up in the suburb. 'It meant being a god in your street,' he replied. But the fate of the Fitzroy Football Club was little more than an occasional topic of conversation at dinner parties in present-day Fitzroy. The nineteenth-century city of Melbourne had exploded into hundreds and thousands of fragments. If Fitzroy Football Club had a home now, it was in the comfortable outer suburbs where the children of its former residents lived or perhaps in parts of the inner-city where the events of '86 had won it a certain fashionable support among younger people. But the greater truth was that Fitzroy had no home. In the early '80s, they played at the Junction Oval in St Kilda. In 1986, they were based at Victoria Park which Butch Gale's wife said was like living with your mother-in-law. After Victoria Park, Princes Park, and, after Princes Park, the Western Oval. The deal was announced midway through the 1993 season. Peter Gordon and the president of the Fitzroy Football Club had signed the agreement on air during 'Selectors' Table'. (The previous week, Chris Grant had signed his new contract on air – Harry called it 'live colour radio'.)

Before the match, the Footscray banner read:

FOOTSCRAY WELCOME FITZROY TO THE WESTERN OVAL, and, on the other side, THE HOME OF VICTORIAN FOOTBALL. Peter Gordon had said on 'Selectors' Table' that the most was mutually beneficial. The day after Footscray's wholesale loss to Collingwood at Victoria Park an article had appeared in a Sunday newspaper arguing for the creation of a Victorian super club to match West Coast and Adelaide, which are effectively State sides. The writer argued that the new super club could be created by merging two or possibly three of the existing Melbourne clubs. And the nominations for the merger were – Fitzroy, Richmond, North Melbourne and Footscray. For the first time since the Fightback, or the first time I had seen, Footscray had again been listed on death row. The president, characteristically, had counter-attacked, using Fitzroy's move to the Western Oval as a pretext to challenge Princes Park's status as a preferred AFL venue on the basis that it was now only a one-club facility. What other reason, he asked me when we met, was there for Princes Park receiving preferential treatment over the Western Oval?

How could I explain? Princes Park is not windy most days. It is pleasing to the eye. You can sit in the Robert Heatley Stand and look out across green parklands and see huge, still spring and autumn skies. It was the people who drew you back to the Western Oval, not the facility. I tried to begin by stating an obvious difference.

'Seating.'

'We'll get seating,' he said. The reply was faster than a return of service, and as firmly hit.

Before the Fitzroy game, I had stood in the race with

Peter Foster who had also been injured in the Richmond match. Fossie had started his career with Fitzroy but was part of the furniture at Footscray. He was one of the Scraggers. He remembered the day there was a power failure at the Western Oval. They'd stopped and started the game by ringing a bell on the boundary line. At half-time, the Footscray team had to huddle round the bath because it was the only part of the rooms with natural lighting. Fossie pointed to the crowd. 'It's not big,' he said. That was one of the question marks hanging over the move – would Fitzroy attract a crowd to the Western Oval?

Dougie played the Fitzroy game like a man on a piano. By half-time, he was playing requests. Wheeler had to tell him to stop passing the ball to Bernard Toohey. 'I'm not going to drop him,' he said. 'You can give the ball to someone else.' Dougie was dancing again. Going with his first thought, Dougie liked getting the ball when it was hot. 'It makes you think,' he said. 'That's what being a footballer means.' Being good enough to improvise.

The coach's rooms at the Western Oval had three rows of tiered seating. It was like a classroom, particularly given the way Wheeler coached. Axe sat on his own in the back right-hand corner. Big Scottie and Kenny Hunter sat together in the middle of the back row. Occasionally, you'd see Kenny's eyes gleaming with humour and Big Scottie would nod and grin and mutter a reply. Libber sat where the earnest pupils always sit, in the middle of the front row. Dougie sat in the front on the far right-hand side. Sometimes, before a match, you'd see him pumping himself up, taking in air, eyes alight. Other times, particularly at Friday night meetings, he'd be looking away, like he actively didn't want to hear. 'Too much thinking before a game can confuse you.' He said. Dougie said that was the problem with young players today – they thought too much about the game off the field and not enough on it. In the third quarter, Dougie held out an opponent, marked with one hand and held the ball up like a head on a plate for the crowd to see. Afterwards, in the rooms, he blushed and said, 'Shouldn't have done that.' But perhaps he should have. E.J. Whitten would have.

The Fitzroy game was when Ilija Grgic made his name. Originally, the other players couldn't say Ilija. At first, they opted for the aristocratic 'Hillier before transferring to the vaguely American 'Gilliga'. But the crowd got it right quickly enough. 'Ilija!' they cried. That was because he excited them. Ilija Grgic was a 203-centimetre mechanical engineering student at Melbourne University who also happened to be skilful at sport. Before adopting football, he had excelled at cricket and soccer. Sometimes, at training, he'd play with the football as if it were a soccer ball, tapping it from one instep to the other. In cricket, he had been a fast bowler. I imagined he had just the temperament for that pursuit; there was a red-faced intensity about him on the sportsfield. And he was ambitious. It was hard to get ahead in cricket, he said.

Ilija had played a handful of games in the course of the year, but it was against Fitzroy that he suddenly emerged as a force to be reckoned with. Perhaps he was responding to the plea Wheeler had made after the Melbourne game. 'Where's the person who says, "I'm going to stand up for something"?' the coach had cried. 'You're all waiting for someone else.

In league football, there is no one else!' First, Ilija demonstrated that he could out-wrestle opponents in the goal square. Then he attacked a couple of packs on the half-forward line, shattering them with the impact of his arrival and marking the ball. Then he came at packs from the side and took the ball off the top like a giant fruitpicker. For the first time for the whole year, there was a sense of danger and anticipation about the Footscray forward line.

Footscray won by ten goals. The previous evening, Essendon and Collingwood had played at the MCG before 85,000 people. The match had glowed with the heat of two teams meeting with total force and conviction; significantly, Essendon emerged triumphant. The match at the Western Oval, by comparison, was like a foxtrot or a waltz. Footscray won because it was lighter and brighter. Fitzroy, by contrast, played like strangers trying to persuade themselves to feel at home.

The Final

Every team's season has a final, a game which spells the end of its dreams or their fulfilment. To have any chance of participating in the final series, Footscray had to defeat Essendon at the MCG in Round 20. Wheeler summoned the piper.

I told Wheeler about the bagpipes. I had coached teams in the bottom grades of the Tasmanian amateurs, possibly the lowest level at which the adult game is played. Fun footy, but you still get to see a few things. One year, my second ruckman injured himself at training the Thursday night before the preliminary final by sliding into the concrete drain running around the rim of the oval and gashing his knee. He still wanted to be part of the team so we arranged for him to lead the side out playing the bagpipes. He played, too, after they'd won. Then in the rooms the following week, before the grant final, he played again. With one wheezing gulp of air, he recalled the previous match from start to finish – the anticipation, the deeply personal nature of the struggle, the eventual reward.

The music contained the memory.

On the day of the Jump, Wheeler had arranged for a piper to stand on the airfield and play as each plane departed. The previous day, some of the players had seen a parachutist seriously hurt. He'd attempted a fancy landing. At first, the boys responded with nervous laughter, but the instructors didn't. They ran to where the man was lying. Then an ambulance appeared and news helicopters came chopping through the sky. After the injured man had been loaded into the ambulance and taken away, some of the players walked over and had a look at the scene of the accident. There was blood and a dent in the ground. Axe led his group in a prayer before they boarded the plane.

The piper's reappearance before the Essendon game was meant to be a secret, but Axe saw him in the corner of the rooms. 'I know he's here,' he told Wheeler. 'The hair's standing on the back of my neck.' The players were seated in the coach's room when the first notes sounded. 'Listen to him, boys,' shouted Leon Cameron, 'he's playing for us.' Wheeler began speaking. 'We're sitting on the edge of a plane. We're about to step out into who knows what, but you know there's nothing to be afraid of. I don't care about the scoreboard, I don't care about the stats sheet, I care about how you stand individually.' During the warm-up, the piper continued to walk among them, tartan bag beneath his arm, black pipes across his shoulder. The players circled him, lifting the tempo, handpassing quickly and in close. When they began moving, half-jogging, half-walking, the piper went with them. Super followed the group, dumbly shaking his head. It was his song the man was playing, the old fierce cry of the Celts, and he was watching the match from the 3WRB commentary box with Harry and the team. The long broad ascent from the rooms first leads away from the ground; then you turn and glimpse the sky and the tall peering walls of the stadium and hear the crowd – a sound like the crashing of a huge sea. Footscray were back at the MCG.

Their opponents were Sheedy's new Essendon team. The great Essendon side of the mid-1980s had seemed to age prematurely. In its prime, it played football like Boris Becker played tennis – with power, precision and unashamed gusto. But, after '86, they seemed to lose their zest and become mechanical. They had the mannerisms of a great side without the inner driver. Then Sheedy began experimenting. I remember a day at Windy Hill when he had obviously told the full-back to run the ball at every kick-in. everyone in the ground knew what was going to happen. The element of surprise was zero, but the poor bastard kept trying to swerve past the opposition forwards who were arranged like a row of arresting officers ten metres from the square. At times, it seemed that Sheedy would try anything. The Bombers made the grand final in 1990 but that was basically the old team with a few spare parts; Collingwood paralysed them with grim resolve, and by keeping the ball at ankle level where Tony Shaw could get it.

Sheedy went back to the drawing board. He had already started recruiting Aboriginal players, but now he got a group of them. His 1993 team was new; it had a different chemistry. It had eight players under the age of twenty-two (and Wanganeen and Hird were absent). This Essendon team was built around youth with a sprinkling of experience and the novel, diverse talents of three Aboriginal players – Michael Long, Derek Kickett and Gavin Wanganeen. Essendon were currently leading the competition, but I was uncertain as to how good they were. They'd won the night final, but that's not the real thing. They'd stumbled early in the year and looked positively forlorn when the Dogs whipped them by 46 points at the Western Oval in Round 5. They were finishing the season on an even plain, but North had beaten them under lights at the MCG in Round 15. It had been like a tennis match between the game's two outstanding juniors, each pushing the other to find new dimensions in their talent. As I scored it, North had won in four sets: 6-4 6-4 2-6 6-2.

At Footscray's Friday night meeting, Wheeler had asked his players for one quarter, one quarter that was true to the high aspirations with which they had begun the season. If they could do that, perhaps they could begin anew. 'I don't care how tired or sore you are. I'm asking you for the best 30 minutes of footy that Footscray supporters have seen this year.' Essendon took the early lead, three goals to one. Ilija was the hope for Footscray, but the first time the ball lobbed into the forward line Essendon's Wallis played him with ease, bumping him with his hips like a samba dancer just as the ball was about to reach the big forward's outstretched hands. At that stage, Wallis probably thought Ilija was nothing more than a set of long arms, but moments later Dougie took the ball, pirouetted and handpassed in the opposite direction to which he was moving, thereby putting the ball into the path of Ilija who had foreseen a possibility and was running at goal.

It was a classic soccer move, one striker laying it off for the other. Ilija's shot went wide, but, a minute later, Grant's didn't. For the first time, I noticed that Grant had elastic limbs; he could kneel on one leg and goal with the other. Despite his height and bulk, it was as a ground player he excelled.

In defence, Toohey was having trouble combating Derek Kickett's pace and liveliness, and the spirit of Footscray's resistance was a kid in only his third game, Brad Nicholson. On the boundary, Peter Forster said not everyone was entitled to play with their socks down, but Nicko was. He was a skinny eighteen-year-old with a mop of thick hair. Off the field, he was unstoppable, diving under, over, in between, going on funny, bent runs through the middle of the ground.

Dougie got Footscray even. He didn't look, he didn't have time. The Essendon defence was only half a step away. The kick slewed backwards, high into the air, a parabola that eventually found its way between the goal posts. Scottie West kicked another and Footscray led by one goal at quarter-time. Wheeler was smiling.

He swapped Toohey for Nicholson. Sheedy swapped David Calthorpe, who had begun the match minding Libber, and Michael Long. Libber had won a sequence of important clearances from the centre.

Dougie kicked another at the start of the second. Grant marked on the half-forward line and he called for it to be brought in with a windmill wave of his arm. When the ball arrived, Dougie was dancing. His opponent, Mark Thompson, couldn't find a body to lean on and Dougie outmarked him. Footscray by twelve points. Then, just as the Dogs were beginning to take hold of the match, Derek Kickett kicked five goals.

In the first quarter, he had taken the ball out of the sky by patting it with one hand. In the second, he jumped into a crowded goalmouth, lifted the wet ball from a chorus of hands and hugged it to his chest. Later in the term, he finished a lead like a man in a long jump, both legs extended, catching the ball in the middle of his leap almost as an afterthought.

Part of the reason Kickett was so prominent was that Michael Long had become the game's dominant mid-field player. Wheeler swung Libber to the forward pocket, in the hope that Long would go with him, thereby taking himself out of the play. Libber promptly goaled from a free kick after making it look as if Long was impeding him. Long was furious. He ricocheted off a number of Footscray players while the ball was being returned to the centre of the ground, eventually cannoning into Grant's back. Players from both sides gathered angrily. A minute later, Ilija's long arm caught Long in the pocket. It came through like a pendulum and carried the Essendon player from half-past six until twenty to four. Ilija and Grant were close.

Kickett's fifth for the quarter (and sixth for the match so far), minutes before half-time, seemed to establish a secure 15-point lead for his team. It was Ace who put the match back into the balance. His minder, Sean Denham, had a face like a featherweight boxer, and was allowing him only splinters of time to work in. earlier, the Footscray centreman had gathered the ball, flung his body and dispensed a handball in one flowing motion, like a rugby fly-half. His goal was a glimpse from the back of a pack near the 50-metre line. He dropped the ball lengthwise across his boot, leant back and bent it ever so slightly. Wheeler said Axe's goals looked as if they were hit with a three-iron.

The match was evenly poised at the break with Essendon leading by seven points. The television camera followed Kickett as he walked from the field and then flashed back to show Choco Royal on crutches. Choco's season, and probably his career, was over after 199 games and 299 goals; he had torn his achilles tendon.

Kickett kicked another at the start of the third. Nicholson was first to the ball, but Kickett leapt backwards. Nicholson held his ground; Kickett spun around Nicholson's upper body like a hoopla but when he landed he had the ball in his arms. He had now kicked seven of Essendon's ten goals. Every one of them had been different, and at least four of them, notwithstanding the heavy conditions, were as good as you'd see. The television camera lingered on him. A commentator said he was worth the price of the admission on his own and recalled that he once won the Sandover Medal in Western Australia by 16 votes but had to forfeit it because he had been suspended during the season.

Footscray continued to work away. Before the match, Wheeler had told them, 'No score-line is going to tell you whether you've given what I'm asking for today.' Leon Cameron shot at goal. Dougie, his body locked in a wrestle, touched the ball as it passed him. When the full-back kicked into play, three men vied for the mark. It was Leon Cameron, the smallest of them, who plucked it from the air. For a spell in the middle of the season, he had appeared tired, but the young man had it all now: touch, confidence, authority. Salmon knocked the ball from his hands, incurring a 50-metre penalty. Cameron goaled from the square. For a period thereafter, every moment seemed to pulse with its own significance, as it should in a final. Danny Del-Re was fumbling, unable to hold his marks, but he nearly broke an arm trying to smother a boot in the square. Olarenshaw did the same for Essendon, only he risked his neck. Denham goaled for Essendon with what looked to be ominous ease. Salmon kicked another and one sensed the match might have slipped from Footscray's grasp. Next goal would tell. Next goal was Ilija's. He did what very few ruckman can do; he took the ball out of the ruck in the forward pocket, slid it down the left side of his body, and goaled. Essendon by eight points. The ball shot forward again for Footscray, and Fletcher, Essendon's schoolboy full-back, demonstrated his talents by out-marking Ilija. At the other end of the ground, Toohey ran at Kickett. He got there just as the Essendon player was falling and slid over the top of him. Kickett got up laughing, as if the attempt to silence him was laughably clumsy. Again the match was poised. One more goal and Footscray would have been as good as level. Just before the break, Dougie attempted the epic. He shrugged one tackle, shook another, swayed past a third defender but slightly hooked his shot. Essendon by eight points at the final change.

The Bombers struck what should have been a killer blow at the start of the fourth quarter. Bewick took the ball on the defensive side of the centre square and made one of his low, blurringly fast runs through the middle of the ground, bouncing the ball like a card-sharp shuffling a pack. Passing the 50-metre line like a sprinter crossing a finishing line, he scored. Leon Cameron did what he had to do. He ran with the ball.

He beat two Essendon players and went for a bounce, but the heavy ball hit the wet grass and slid away. It was desperate stuff now. Manton, an Essendon player I had hardly noticed, was sitting on the ground, panting, indicating to trainers that he couldn't walk. Anthony Darcy goaled from a Chris Grant handpass to bring the margin back to eight points.

All that Footscray had now was the blunt, aching force of the year's disappointments. They lacked Essendon's strike-power, but their young players like Scott West and Shannon Corcoran kept accumulating possessions. They forced Essendon to go backwards to move forwards, but it was also apparent that Sheedy's team knew how to vary the tempo of the game to their advantage. They strung together a series of short passes, giving their players a chance to slow down, settle, catch their breath. Then Kickett kicked his eighth. Nicholson had beaten him to the ball several times in succession. He beat him this time too, only he slipped. Kickett scooped up the ball and banged at goal from the right-forward flank; it bounced and nodded through.

Nothing changed after that, neither the intensity of the contest nor the scoreline. Footscray had displayed all the virtues which the British Navy prizes: fortitude, resolution, endeavour. What they didn't have was someone like Derek Kickett who could respond to the game, at vital moments in its evolution as a drama, in dazzlingly original ways. Later, at the post-match press conference, Wheeler complimented Kickett on his game, describing his skills as magnificent, but in the immediate aftermath of the game he couldn't speak. He had been ill during the week; now that the match and all that it represented had passed, he was spent.

Reserves coach Terry Wallace addressed the team. 'I thought our effort and commitment were as good today as I've seen all year,' he said. 'Our execution in a few areas could have been better, but a player in the other team has probably just played the game of his life. We've got two weeks to go. Our form's reasonable. We can either pack up our bags or we can have a real crack at the rest of the season. If we don't have a go, we could finish as low as eleventh.' He paused. 'This is an emotional game. You blokes are going to have to drag something out of yourselves for your own sakes and for the sakes of the other people around the club.'

For what seemed a long time after he had finished speaking, the players sat on the tiered seating facing the long whiteboard, exhausted and unmoving. Big Ilija was the first to leave the scene of the defeat. He got up and clomped off to the changing area, an enormously tall man with a pair of boots in his hand.

The Farewell

The following Saturday, Round 21, Footscray beat West Coast by 42 points at the Western Oval. It was the Eagles' second drubbing at the Western Oval in two years. Peter Matera was lively, but he didn't slice them apart like he had in Perth. It had been a long year for Matera. His brilliance in the 1992 final series had won him both national prominence and national attention. Twelve months later, you could see his nerve ends poking through – he'd been living on them all season, listening for the player who would hurt him if he could. In his fourth game of league football, Brad Nicholson handled Peter Sumich, and Ilija had the better of Glen Jakovich, West Coast's gun defender. Footscray were in control from the outset, Peter Quill leading the charge, crashing through an early centre bounce like a standard-bearer. Quill had played in a premiership team in Western Australia, and it showed. No matter how hectic the game, he never became lost.

In the ruck, Big Scottie administered a sound thrashing to Paul Harding, the West Coast player who had received a standing ovation in Perth for his winning performance on the reigning Brownlow medallist. Big Scottie had been like a semi-submerged island most of the year. No one knew how much the accident at Princes Park, which had left him convulsing on the ground, had taken out of him. His form had been consistently good, but he had only started emerging as a major force around the same time as Axe – the Brisbane game (Round 13). We had only had one conversation, after the Melbourne game when Wheeler imposed a week of training. 'If he was going to kick arse, he should have done it after North and Hawthorn,' said Big Scottie. 'They were the vital games.' He was a reserved young man, but he knew his own mind.

West Coast was to have been Choco's 200th game. The previous week, he had limped out to the huddle at three-quarter-time on crutches. Everyone knew then it was over for him. After 1999 games and 299 career goals. The figures seemed symbolic. As Jenny Hodgson, one of the women who regularly attended training, had said to me, 'Footscray's not a team that has a lot of luck', and if any one player deserved to be nudged over the line to a few minor honours it was Choco. For the past two years, he had been stationed in the forward pocket. He'd done the job, holding marks as packs crashed down on him and running big curves to squeeze in a shot at goal, but it was only a fraction of what he had been in his prime. Off the field, he was friendly and genial, but when he went out to play his mouth set in hard straight lines. By trade, he was a builder and, as a player, he seemed to be erecting constructions everywhere. His work was busy, thorough, with intent.

And honest. The second Collingwood game had exhausted Wheeler's optimism. At the end of the match, he had made his players stand and demanded they forget the match. Choco had approached him before he left. He couldn't forget a defeat. Didn't believe you should.

Dougie said Choco was the best player he had seen at Footscray other than Templeton, which meant he rated him ahead of three Brownlow medallists. Choco had won the club best and fairest in his first season, 1983. His twelfth game in the big time had been for Victoria. In '85, Footscray's preliminary final year, Dougie had won the club best and fairest and Hardie the Brownlow, but my most vivid memories were of Choco. He was like a turbo-charged lawnmower. In the course of an afternoon, he'd mow a big ground like Waverley a dozen times. Throughout the 1980s, he was a regular State representative and both Carlton and Collingwood had sought to woo him. Both clubs had legitimate premiership aspirations, but in the end Choco couldn't leave Footscray. He'd rung Leigh Matthews on the day of the Collingwood meeting and called it off. When the merger was announced, the players were warned to distance themselves from the Fightback campaign. Choco told an interviewer the merger made you wonder what football was about. Along with Rick Kennedy, Peter Foster and Super, he helped organise the meeting of players which resolved to support Peter Gordon at the Fightback rally. At the start of 1993, Wheeler had suggested he retire and met the full force of the player's conviction. He hadn't won a Brownlow, although he'd twice finished among the leaders. He hadn't played in a premiership team, although he almost certainly would have crossed to either Collingwood or Carlton. His last goal had been to play 200 games with the Footscray Football Club.

The Footscray banner before the match was inscribed in his honour. I didn't note the words because I saw standing beside him in the race. Dougie was beckoning to him to join the players, but he didn't want to go out on the ground. Fossie said he ought to go too, but Choco shook his head. This was the Footscray way, it seemed. Don't look at the crowd. Don't see how big you are in their eyes, because if you ever saw yourself in that way you'd no longer be one of them. Greenie added his voice, a touch impatiently so that it hinted at an order. 'Come on, Choco,' he said. 'They want to see you.' Finally, reluctantly, he swung forward on his crutches and limped out on to the field. He went about twenty metres, stopped and turned. Facing the crowd, he raised his right crutch into the air. The roar was a deep surge of sound that rushed to meet him like a wave. The force of it struck him like a blow. The people had spoken. Choco hobbled back to the race, lips trembling.

I missed the cocktail party held by the club that night in his honour. I had to attend the launch of a collection of poems by an Irish-language poet who also happens to be a keen Footscray supporter. The service was performed by Phil Cleary, and I drank anything I was handed. The Dogs had finally won a big one. On Thursday night, I went to the 'Selectors' Table'. Harry had Choco on the show and made a bigger production of it than *The Ten Commandments*. To cite one of the great clichés in Australian sporting history, women wept and brave men turned away, and Harry still managed to end every sentence with a plug for the sponsor, Paisley

Wilkinson, spectacle makers of Paisley Street, Footscray.

For the whole of that week, Choco kept saying, 'You don't realise what people think of you until something like this happens.' It was as if his bad luck had suddenly opened the club to expressions of feeling. In fact, four players were finishing up (or being finished up) – Choco, Glenn Coleman, Bernard Toohey and Peter Foster. The only one of the old blokes playing on was Dancing Doug Hawkins. Wheeler called a special meeting and invited each of the four players to speak. I was sitting with Choco in a corner. 'Wheels is good at these things,' he said. He meant ceremonies, acknowledging beginnings and ends. I gathered it hadn't been a feature of the Malthouse years.

Galaxy Coleman went first. Gal was stylish in a casual, slightly off-beat way. He'd begun his career with Fitzroy and spent his middle years with Sydney. A lot of people had laughed at him over the years, but he had been an important part of Footscray in '92. When Gal shone at centre-half-forward, Grant made hay on the flank. 'It would have been a real shame if I'd finished my footy in Sydney,' he said. Galaxy said he'd come back next year and chuck a beer can over the fence at them. Bernard Toohey was next. He told a funny story about Galaxy running him aground in a speedboat in Sydney Harbour, then thanked Footscray Football Club. 'There's a lot of potential at Footscray and if anyone ever wants my help, all they have to do is ring.' When it came Choco's turn to speak, he tried to give them a message. 'Footscray has to be more arrogant,' he said. 'I don't mean you have to be snobs. I mean you've got to stand up and believe you're as good as anyone else.' Fossie was last. Before the first Fitzroy game, Fossie told me that what distinguished footballers over time was their ability to overcome injury. This was the final injury. None of them wanted to go, except maybe Choco who had set his mind on a coaching career. Fossie, too, was on crutches. He thanked Ronnie Johns and the medical staff, the people who'd kept him functioning over the past few years. 'It's pretty hard,' he began, 'it's pretty hard after you're spent eleven years in a place.' When the coach told Fossie it was time to go, his mind came up with a hundred reasons as to why it wasn't so, why he was still needed, but in the end he had to accept it was final. 'I reckon the car will drive itself to pre-season training,' he said. 'When you've been at a place so long, it grows into you system ...' And that was about as far as he got before words failed him.

It was only a game, but the game had life. They'd felt it, and there weren't many feelings stronger. The folly of youth had been to think it would last forever, but now it was over and they faced a life much like everyone else's, with a mortgage and a car and a job if they were lucky. From their team-mate's point of view, 800 games of league football were walking out the door. From the club's point of view, four people who had seemed as much a part of the place as the furniture were not going to be there next year. The responsibility was with those who remained.

A Promise

Footscray beat North Melbourne at the MCG by twelve points in the last game of the season. There was a perverse justice in the result. North had fatally wounded Footscray – or, rather, the Footscray team which had begun the season – at the Western Oval in Round 7. Hawthorn had extinguished all life three weeks later and Melbourne had buried the corpse unceremoniously in Round 17. The new Footscray, I thought, had made its first fleeting appearance at Victoria Park. Two weeks later, it had won its first match against Fitzroy. It had then lost bravely to Essendon and started to work up some real momentum with its victory over West Coast.

The Dogs now had a volcano in the forward pocket named Mount Ilija. 'The big man can leap,' said a commentator early in the North game. That was before he did his soccer goalie's catch, flinging all 203 centimetres of his body plus the reach of his extended arms parallel to the ground to accept a low, sharp chance from Peter Quill. And when he didn't mark, he smashed defensive walls and in the chaos and disarray he created, Grant prospered.

The North match had begun with Libber shrugging his tag like a man ridding himself of an overcoat in hot weather. Libber had been deeply affected by Choco's departure and Fossie's speech. 'I just hope some of the young blokes realise what Fossie tried to tell them,' he said. Even the thought of being tagged seemed unbearable to him. Footscray's work at the centre bounces was copybook. Big Scottie palmed the ball – right hand, left hand, hard or soft – to the place designated by Axe and someone, usually Leon, collected it at pace. When it worked this well, the centre four were really the centre two: Big Scottie and a player with Axe's brain, Libber's heart and Leon's long, striding legs. Footscray had 100 points on the scoreboard by half-time.

In the third term, North rallied. Blakey, the former Fitzroy player, led them, but you sensed they were relying on some grim bedrock of resolve. At the Western Oval, they had played like men for whom doubt and fear were words from an old discredited language. It was St Kilda who had brought North back to earth. What a bunch of crazies the Saints were. They had played North under lights at the MCG in Round 17. Nicky Winmar had taken the field, black skin glistening with oil, and I thought then that the Saints might have decided to give this one a real go. North had lost other matches in the course of the season, but they had always been magnificent in defeat. That night, for the first time, they were beaten. One month later, the charm which had given North's season such lustre had disappeared. Full-forward John Longmire twisted his knee in the first quarter, thereby bringing his season to a premature conclusion. Carey missed the goals that earlier in the season he was kicking, the ones that would have tipped the momentum of the match North's way. It was Carey's first game back after injury; the great player of 1993 had backed into one too many packs and appeared wooden and restricted in his movements.

North had edged to within 18 points and restored a sense that the result of the match was still undecided when Martyn, North's feisty full-back, attempted to gather the ball on Footscray's forward flank. Ilija reached him with one hand, grabbed the collar of his Guernsey and swung. In mid-air, Martyn performed the considerable feat of attempting a handpass to a team-mate. Grant intercepted. He held the ball in the flat of his left hand, like a large egg on a plate. Having balanced it, he dropped it on to his left book, a North player diving across his foot momentarily too late. Goal of the Year, from Footscray's viewpoint at least. North stuck to its task and, with two minutes of the match remaining, there was some chance of a draw, but when a North player shot for goal from the forward pocket he kicked into the man on the mark. Luck had deserted them. Scott West, who was having another bountiful game, kicked Footscray's last goal for 1993 and the ball was in Peter Quill's hands when the siren sounded. Footscray by twelve points. The season had ended on a promise.

'Next year,' shouted an excited voice as players and supporters surged into the rooms.

'Next year,' echoed a second voice. It was older than the first and had a mildly humorous undertone. 'Always next year.'

III

The Return

I was at the Australian Tennis Open when I started my year with the Dogs. I had mixed feelings about the tennis. It had players from all over the world, but most of them seemed to live in Florida. Except for those who lived in London and Monaco. It was an airport sport. The press room at the National Tennis Centre was like an airport lounge. The woman with the microphone in the glass booth said, 'Monica Seles will be available in Interview Room number one in five minutes', and the press rushed to be there in case she said something you could write about.

What could you say about her games? They were the figures 6-2, 6-1 endlessly repeated. I like watching Seles. She imposed herself on the game, furiously, bashing the ball of either side of her body like a table tennis player. Her principal opponent, Graf, was interesting too, both strong and fragile. She quivered in flight. But that was about it. I saw one of Seles's opponents applauded late in the second set because she actually hit a winner.

The most interesting character in the men's was Boris Becker. He tramped the baseline like the mad painter Vincent van Gogh, shouting anguished soliloquies at the fierce mid-summer sky, but he was also outed in the first round. The final was between Courier and Edberg. For a period in the third set, the match toyed with the possibility of becoming a great game, but then retreated back into predictability. It sounds rude, but I thought the best moment of the 1993 Australian Open was watching the last day of the Adelaide Test between Australia and the West Indies on television in the press room. Slowly, inevitably, five days' labour, the drama of a whole summer, the history of thirty years' competition between two countries built to a climax which no writer of fiction would dare to try to get away with. Test cricket, that great creature of the sporting deep, had finally chosen to surface and reveal itself in all its glory. Having done so, it flicked its tail and was gone. Australia had lost by one run. I saw an American journalist collar one of his colleagues. 'Did you see the cricket?' he shouted, pointing to the television. 'Did you understand it?'

Tennis, we are told, is a sport of the future, a game for a shrinking planet. It is also a cross between the entertainment and leisure industries which delivers global exposure and fantastic wealth to its elite who are treated like famous actors and actresses. When the audience – mostly young and brown and expensively casual – are asked to be quiet, they oblige. So what did I notice going from a sport of the future to the Western Oval? At the Western Oval, there was always someone to talk to. Maybe it was Robbie, the trainer with the hare-lip scar and good heart who spoke almost exclusively in obscenities. Or maybe it was Gio, the football manager. When Gio was a kid, he found a flat dusty ball in the back of its grandfather's real-estate office in Bunyip. His grandfather said he'd give it to him the next day; when he did, it was shiny and taut with air. Gio took it to school and was given entry to all the games. 'I never thought I'd have the opportunity to be involved in footy at this level,' he'd say.

Or maybe I talked to Ian, the chaplain. Wally said you could trust Ian, and he was right. Words went in and never came out, not unless you wanted to see them. Ian and his wife had five kids, two of their own, three they'd 'picked up along the way'. His youngest adopted child was a three-year-old girl with Down's Syndrome. Another had been Aboriginal Youth of the Year. Ian believed Christ could be the bloke coming in the gate for training.

Or maybe I had a joke with Hillie. Hillie had a bald head and pale green eyes that bulged with laughter and the Pink Panther tattooed on his arm. On match day, he kicked the balls back to the players when they were shooting for goal during the warm-up. Opposition supporters called him Home Simpson or shouted, 'Look at the bald-headed bastard for Footscray, will ya! He can't fucken kick!' Hillie did security work part-time, escorting American wrestlers into the ring at Festival Hall. He'd walked Jake the Snake. Jake put a hessian bag in his corner. It kept rising and falling during the bout. Hillie thought it was a wind-up toy until Jake lost the fight and flung a live python across the ring at his opponent. One night I was sitting with Ian on the boundary line when Hillie came up and he wasn't laughing. 'You never get used to it,' he said.

His face was flushed, his voice louder than usual. 'You never get used to it,' he said again. Hillie worked as a fireman; the day before, he'd bashed down a door and walked through a smoke-filled flat to find an old man. He got him outside, then saw the head had been burned away. That, ultimately, was what I felt about the Western Oval: it was human.

I didn't talk that much to the players, at least not initially. The truth is I wasn't one of them. Tim Harrington, Wheeler's assistant, told me you play footy as a kid because you love it. Because you're good at it you go places, then one day you find yourself surrounded by people to whom the game means things you've never thought about. 'It kid of mesmerises you,' he said. H, as he was called, was tall, gentle, receptive; like Wheeler, a former teacher. He said the players had no escape, not even from their families because everyone wants to talk footy. 'You turn up for work on Monday and someone says, 'Gee, you didn't play too well on Saturday – six kicks and two handballs.' He said footballers nowadays had to be able to escape football. 'Some choose straight-out solitude. JB (Jon Ballantyne) goes home and plays his guitar. Away from football, TC's a businessman. It's hard to engage him in a conversation about football.'

So what were the players like that I did get to know? They were like ordinary people. 'You want stories,' said Greenie, 'you ought to go on the end-of-year trip.' Greenie said the boys thought they were pretty tough until they met a rugby league team on the Gold Coast who drank as much as they did and bit the sides out of their glasses. I didn't go; I'd always been ambivalent about footy trips, even when I was eighteen. But when I was eighteen, footy was fun. The footy field was a place where people were larger, sillier, grander. I didn't see much fun at all in what league footballers did. For the most part, it seemed to me to be a dull, aching struggle, like hanging suspended form a rock-face for a year, climbing, slipping, losing ground, beginning again. Maybe I'd seen it in a bad year – Crackers said I had – but by the end of the season I was beginning to wonder why they did it. What was the return on their physical and emotional investment? I didn't really see one, not until Choco turned and faced the E.J. Whitten Stand and a sea of feeling rushed out and claimed him. Choco was a champion, their champion. That was his rewards.

The Grand Final

Essendon won the grand final. Veteran commentator Jack Dyer said it was over after ten minutes, and some people thought that was a late call. In the second minute, Michael Long parted the glittering air, bounded through two lines of the Carlton defence and goaled. Stephen Silvagni protested passionately with the goal umpire, saying he'd touched the ball on the line, but Long was already running back to the centre of the ground for the restart. It was his game, and the Carlton players knew it. Blues forward Earl Spalding said later it was like a spell. Twice, Long held up play on the Members wing, waiting for the game to arrange itself to his satisfaction, and it did. In the third quarter, he staged a free kick on the far flank, diving after a push in the back. Someone asked him afterwards what he was doing lying face-down on the MCG in the middle of a grand final. 'Looking for worms,' he replied. The day before the grand final Long was best known for his shyness. The day after the grand final he was a personality, even answering questions on racism.

Education was the answer, he said.

Midway through the year, at the height of the hysteria surrounding the High Court's decision in the Mabo case, the *Herald Sun* issued a newspaper banner which read: MCG LAND CLAIM. That's about as serious as life gets in Victoria, a signal to the Premier, Mr Jeff Kennett, to raise himself to his full height and deliver a speech along the lines of 'We shall fight them in the Members, we shall fight them in the committee room …' But he didn't, and by half-time in the grand final it was probably too late. The Rainbow Serpent had taken possession of the ground. A man with a didge was standing on the roof of the scoreboard, the tall buildings of Melbourne behind him, making the huge stadium throb and hum with the ancient resonance of this land. Yothu Yindi sang 'Treaty', Koori kids around the oval jigged and swayed to the tune and the great Archie Roach sat on the earth, waiting his turn to sing. At the conclusion of the dancing, the Koori kids carried three flags onto the centre of the ground – Aboriginal, Torres Strait and the Southern Cross with the Union Jack. The crowd cheered, not wildly perhaps, but enough for you to know they appreciated the performance.

The previous day, Juan Antonio Samaranch had opened an envelope on behalf of the International Olympic Committee, famously hesitated and said, 'And the winner is Sinney,' Sydney had the games, and good luck to them, but we had the game. Footy would appear somewhere on the Olympic program because it was the only game which is wholly and uniquely Australian. You speak sport and you want to understand Australia? Watch Gavin Wanganeen, an Aborigine with blue eyes and funny little legs which seemed unequal to the feats they performed. He shot up packs like kids shoot up trees, appearing among the branches to steal the ball. He made reverse dives, landing beneath the feet of oncoming packs. He had no fear because God was with him.

I was glad Wanganeen won the 1993 Brownlow Medal. Football is weighted towards the hard men. One of the game's unwritten rules is that there are no rules in grand finals, and the history of Australian football is littered with examples of important matches turned by acts of violence. The Brownlow Medal stands apart from all that. It is an award for the fairest and best player. It honours those who most honour football as a sport; Gavin Wanganeen is such a player.

The day before the grand final I went into town, intending to visit the National Gallery and see some Australian art. The old woman I sat next to on the train had picked Wanganeen to win the Brownlow. She told her husband, 'Wonganeen'll win the Brownlow Medal', but he didn't follow football so she wrote it on a piece of cardboard – WONGANEEN – and placed it on the top of the TV so that her son would see it when he visited at the weekend. The old woman said Essendon would beat Carlton by 38 points. 'You can't win a grand final with two players,' she said, referring to Carlton's Greg Williams and Stephen Kernahan.

I did see some Australian art when I reached the city. I saw the grand final parade. The cheer squads came first. Richmond's had a Vietnamese girl in it so I cheered her. Supporters of Australian footy regularly declare that it is one of the world's great games; the only evidence for that proposition is that succeeding waves of migrants to this country have adopted the sport as their own. I cheered Brisbane for coming all the way from Queensland (they'd probably come all the way from a flat in St Kilda). I cheered the Bulldogs because I knew the two players, Shannon Corcoran and Steve Kretiuk. Shannon was a former private-schoolboy from Adelaide. He was light and fine, a natural wingman. Kretiuk was a 21-year old Pole from St Albans with a stiff, muscular gait. He was bold and eager. But both of them had had seriously interrupted seasons with injury. I yelled out to them. Shannon turned and grinned.

The stars of the show were waiting in front of the Arts Centre. Nathan Buckley was first. He had polled the highest vote in the Brownlow Medal of any first-year player; he looked as sleek as the sports car in which he was sitting. Then I saw Long. His head, followed by his long arms, was flicking from one autograph book to the next. An Essendon official was sitting in the car beside him. At Footscray, that person would have been Ian. I was beginning to understand how league clubs worked. The player who looked alone was Wanganeen. He seemed startled by the adulation, by the closeness of the faces. His eyes were slewing from side to side as if he feared what might happen next. Even in his moment of Brownlow victory, he hadn't lost his self-possession (or was it self-consciousness?). People slapped his back and he bounced back to the perpendicular like a rubber toy. But that was why I thought he was a good chance to play well in the final, even though he was only twenty years old. On the football field, he didn't have to look at other people. Gavin Wanganeen was a religious footballer. He had eyes only for the ball.

A few cars back were Williams and Kernahan,

probably the two best professional footballers in Australia. Kernahan's six goals had sunk a depleted Essendon in the second semi-final, but only just. In the final quarter, Wanganeen stationed himself at the centre-half-back and played like a kid with a pinball machine. The ball kept striking his body and ricocheting back. Williams was known as Diesel. Centremen nowadays had names like Diesel, Plough (Terry Wallace) and Axe. In my youth, the centre was a place for dancing feet. Now it was a place for heavy industry. Williams was slow in every respect but one, hand and eye. Axe thought he was great. He had spent one whole practice match at Barooga watching Williams, observing how he decided what to do with the ball before he got it. Williams already had one Brownlow Medal to his credit, and he strongly believed he should have added the '93 award to his collection. In one match, he'd had 44 possessions and not polled a single vote. But Derek Kickett hadn't polled three votes for his performance against Footscray. In fact, after playing every match of the season, Kickett had been dropped for the grand final. That, I thought, was Sheedy's gamble. Even if Kickett's form was down, I knew Essendon supporters who aid it was, he seemed to be such an important part of their team. In a low period in the club's fortunes, he'd given them spirit and a welcome element of wild unpredictability. He had been the only Essendon player to fire after half-time in the 1990 grand final. In 1992, I'd seen a match in which he took the mark of the day, kicked the goal of the day and led the cavalry charge when he deemed a young team-mate had been subjected to unduly rough treatment by his Geelong opponent. He was a leader, an inspiration, a potential match-winner. How would they be without him?

Watching the grand final parade, it seemed to me that I understood the climax to the '93 season better than I had understood any previous VFL or AFL final and that I had Footscray to thank for it. Essendon was the outer-suburb club with the reputation, until Sheedy, for conservatism. Its great centre-half-forward of the '60s, Ken Fraser, had been a lay preacher, and the bulk of its '65 premiership team had subsequently served the club as either coaches or administrators.

Carlton, by comparison, was an exotic. Carlton was the inner-city suburb with a difference. Unlike Fitzroy and particularly Collingwood, it had been designed by a town-planner (Collingwood had been built by speculators) who had sought to create a 'Bloomsbury in the bush'. However, the introduction of electric trams in the 1890s enabled the more affluent to live further from the city in suburbs like Hawthorn. At the same time, the depression of that decade decimated the middle class. Thus it was that when the first wave of migrants began arriving in Melbourne in the early years of the century, many of Carlton's large, elegant houses were available for rent. The first wave of migrants were mostly Jews, fleeing the pogroms of Eastern Europe and, later, the madness of Adolf Hitler. After World War II, the Italians came. Carlton enjoyed a large following among the Jewish and Italian communities. It had also been influenced by its proximity to Melbourne University. Generations of students had wandered across Princes Park in their leisure time to watch the footy. In the process, Carlton Football Club acquired the support of a professional class and a close and continuing connection with the Liberal Party. Two of its number-one ticket holders, R.G. Menzies and Malcolm Fraser, have been Liberal prime ministers.

Carlton attracts almost as much animosity as Collingwood. Collingwood supporters are offensive by nature. They can't help themselves and probably wouldn't if they could. Carlton offends people with the vulgarity of its wealth and power – for example, the bluff assertions of its president, John Elliott, as to who should and should not be in the AFL – but, in one respect, Carlton's taste cannot be faulted. The Blues have always liked players with style and flair, and their great sides have always played great footy. The 1982 grand final is one of my favourites, in part, because it was retribution for 1973 when Carlton's wonderful full-back Geoff Southby was knocked senseless and it seemed that the game had degenerated into a display of brute force. In '82, Carlton withstood the prolonged fury of Richmond's assault, gained the edge with skill and held it. Similarly, the '86 second semi-final between Carlton and Hawthorn is one of the best games I have seen. That was a meeting of two different philosophies as much as two different clubs. Hawthorn were the Team, highly motivated and intensely disciplined. Carlton were individuals – Dean, Motley, Doull and Harmes in defence, Rhys-Jones and Johnston across the centre. The Blues won. But in the 1993 grand final, Carlton only had Stephen Kernahan. Essendon had too many bright young faces in too many places and two cool, assured heads in Thompson and O'Donnell.

After the match, Essendon's rooms were a celebration. Gavin Wanganeen and his fiancé, who is even smaller than he is, stood in the shower area. 'Got to get away from all the people,' he said shyly. Even so, people found him. An Aboriginal family, the wife and four kids all in 'Gavin Wanganeen Brownlow Medal' T-shirts, came and stood beside him for a photograph. In the next room, the Essendon vice-captain Gary O'Donnell was holding a magnum of champagne in one hand, the premiership cup in the other, and bellowing, 'It was fate.' That, indeed, was how it seemed. But Essendon had paid a price for their victory. However great the occasion, there was a sense that someone was missing. At his press conference, Sheedy said he had been ringing Derek Kickett to try and discuss his omission but there had been no answer.

Carlton's rooms were desolate. I watched Williams leave alone. Denham had tagged him and got the better of him early, playing in front of him and beating him to the ball. In the third quarter, the Essendon player was suddenly seen lying on the ground behind the play with a bloody face. For five minutes or so thereafter, Williams worked feverishly to arrest Essendon's momentum and swing the match Carlton's way, but Sheedy replaced Denham with Chris Daniher, the fourth most famous freckled face to leave the tiny Riverina town of Ungarie. Williams broke one tag, but he was unable to break two. Kernahan was talking to a swarm of reporters when I arrived, perhaps because he could. He'd kicked most of Carlton's score. Behind him on a bench, saying nothing, saw a row of a dozen Carlton players. They were in their club uniform: blue blazer, cream trousers, white shirt and tie. They looked like school kids waiting for a bus which they now feared might never come.

The Business of Football

Nominally, the season was over, but football was no longer seasonal. There was no rest, no fallow period, no awakening to a new year. Football, said Wheeler, was now one long continuum. First came the November draft, by which time the clubs had to reduce their lists from 52 players to 42. Essendon cut Derek Kickett; a sad story kept getting sadder. It was said in the press that Kickett hadn't endeared himself to the club by boycotting their premiership celebrations. That made it sound like a punishment, but if Footscray's experience were anything to go by, the decision wouldn't have been that easy.

Wheeler admitted three or four players can be cut from a list of 52 without great difficulty, but by the time you got to number ten you were hacking into the body of the club. Among those to be told their services were no longer required at Footscray were Jon Ballantyne and Justin Charles. JB had begun the year as an integral part of Wheeler's structure. Justin Charles was the person I always heard singing around the club. Wheeler had to defend another of his selections, bulky wingman Michael Frost, at Footscray's best and fairest night, just as he had to defend clearing Darren Baxter to make way for Leon Cameron twelve months earlier. As it happened, Frost was redrafted by St Kilda, but he was one of only four discarded players to find another AFL club. Everyone was looking to youth. Sheedy had changed the game – again. Even so, Wheeler's nomination for coach of the year was Carlton's David Parkin. 'Look at the players he had,' he said softly. 'Look how far he got them.'

Leon Cameron one Footscray's best and fairest. It was a popular win. When Leon was good, he was very good. He had also polled 14 votes in the Brownlow, only four less than Wanganeen. Having begun the season at one crossroad – establishing himself as a pivotal player – he had finished at another – establishing himself as a player in Brownlow Medal class. That's what Terry Wallace said footy was about – overcoming the next hurdle. Libber was runner-up, having polled 220 votes to Leon's 222 (Footscray rated each player out of ten in each game). Big Scottie was third on 219 and Axe, after all the criticism levelled at him, finished fourth on 213. Axe had still collected 500 possessions for the season, the most of any Footscray player and the 15th highest tally in the league. He had watched the grand final at home, on his own. 'We beat Essendon at the Western Oval, and we could've beaten them twice,' he said, when I asked him what he thought of the game. 'And we thumped Carlton.' Axe had kept faith. He still believed Footscray could have won the premiership. Other Footscray awards: Most Consistent, Mark Hunter; Most Determined, Peter Quill; Best First-

Year Player, Scott West; Best Junior Prospect, Brad Nicholson; Best Clubman, Scott Wynd; Leading goalkicker, Danny Del-Re (36 goals). Charlie Sutton Medal for the club champion, Leon Cameron.

In the lead-up to the draft, Footscray made the fateful decision to invest in former Fitzroy and Swans forward Richard Osborne (ahead of Hawthorn's Dermott Brereton). It was their major signing for the coming season and, at the time, seemed and astute purchase; even so, I couldn't help sparing a thought for Ben Sexton who had played promisingly at full-forward in the last two games. Clearly, Osborne now stood between the 20-year-old and the position. Before the season began, Mark Hunter had told me you needed luck to make it in league footy, and it was true. With selection, with injuries, with team plans. At one of the first team meetings I attended. Galaxy Coleman told his team-mates they'd have to improve 20 per cent to finish in the same position they had in 1992. That is, they'd have to run 20 per cent faster to stay on the same spot. That was true, too. The competition at the top was withering. That's why so many footballers admired Hawthorn's Jason Dunstall. He kept doing it, season in, season out. He was like Uluru, the great red rock in the desert. Permanent, lasting.

Wheeler said that each year in league football you have to find a little bit more. That was why he had invited me to write the book. He had told the players I was part of his commitment to them winning the 1993 AFL premiership. But instead of finding a little bit more, Footscray had found themselves with a little bit less. What the Dogs lacked in '93 was energy. Maybe '92 had been too draining, maybe getting to that level had taken everything they had. Crackers described '92 as the thrill of the kill. But he also admitted that when the magic stopped, it was 'a huge anticlimax'. I was shocked by the deep weariness in Big Scottie's eye after the last game. He seemed less than happy. He spoke to me pointedly about the media and the extent to which it shapes public perceptions. A ruckman, he said, jumps, and gets jumped into, one hundred times per game. In the fortnight after the last roster match, he also had operations on both knees. The players called it 'having a clean-out'. The club doctor said only two or three players on the Footscray list had finished the season without an injury of some sort. 'It's starting to get depressing being involved in footy,' he said.

Injuries hadn't helped Footscray, although I felt they ended the year a better team than they started it – quicker, more youthful, less predictable. Their two biggest losses had been Wally and Super; when combined with Axe's loss of form, it had meant Footscray lacked leaders. If the club gave an award for its outstanding entertainer in 1993, the winner would be Doug Hawkins (again; Libber runner-up). Watching Dougie at Collingwood, I understood how television, which always stays with the ball, can never convey a sense of the spell that one player can cast over a game. But Dougie could only sustain that influence for relatively brief spells. Footscray had no Carey, no Long, no Kernahan, no individual who could arrest a game and send it off in another direction. To claim a match, Footscray needed to have the bulk of its players – George Bissett said fourteen – winning their individual positions. For most of the season, particularly during the long dark spell between the Hawthorn and Fitzroy games, they hadn't. But, at the end of a disappointing year, the Dogs had finished only one game out of the six and only two games behind first-placed Essendon. That's how unrelentingly even the competition had become.

I wished the Dogs well in '94 – I wished them noise – but if this were a report, I would make only one recommendation. Don't tamper with the club song. Originally, it went:

> Sons of the Scray,
> Red, white and blue,
> We'll come out snarling,
> Bulldogs through and through.
> Bulldogs bite and bulldogs roar,
> Remember '54
> 'Cause you can't beat the boys of the Bulldog breed
> Who made old Footscray's name.

Then '54 got changed to '89. That was fair enough; one Footscray supporter told me the Fightback was worth four premierships. Then it was changed to '92, and ultimately the Dogs didn't win anything in '92. So, in '93, it had to be changed again, and so on, and with each amendment the team gets further trapped within itself, within its own venture, within its own small time zone.

It was Crackers, after the Geelong game, who said, 'You've got to get excited by what other blokes do on the football field!' And have done. In 1924, VFA club Footscray defeated VFA club Essendon and were proclaimed champions of Victoria. Some newspapers said champions of Australia. The '54 premiership had been the triumph of the workingmen of the west, the vindication of a history and a tradition. The Fightback in '89 deserved to be even more famous than it was. It had been a victory for the principle of community at a time when politicians were actively in pursuit of what, in Thatcher's Britain, was called the atom state: every particle on its own, every working man and woman for him or herself. It had also been a victory for a community which represents the multi-racial and multi-coloured Australia that is coming. Footscray Football Club had fought for its place, and that of the game, in the twenty-first century.

An old bloke who had been with Melbourne in its prime told me that what Footscray lacked was ruthlessness. He led me to believe that successful football clubs are dictatorships and, sure enough, in grand final week, a Carlton director, Richard Pratt, said that his club was one which didn't tolerate dissent. Footscray would always be open to dissent. That was Peter Gordon's curious weakness. His opponents couldn't hurt him – for example, when they said that he was only using the club to launch himself into politics – because they were the enemy. The people to whom he was vulnerable were his supporters because the president was truly a Footscray man and, at Footscray, all men (and women) are equal. That was the great irony in the character of the club, its weakness was its strength.

You couldn't become involved with Footscray and not feel for them. There was a basic warmth about the place. If I rang anyone after the season ended – Gio, Hillie, Super – the conversation always ended with the same question: 'When are you coming out again?' Even Greenie said it, and Greenie said I was the worst-dressed bastard on earth. It was Shane Ellen who said that at Footscray you felt like you were part of something.

Throughout '93, the club continued to work at integrating with the local community. They transported 30 bus-loads of kids to the second Essendon game. For many, it was their first sight of the MCG. The club also cajoled most of its senior players into donating blood tissue to the Bone Marrow registry. The club newspaper had a wonderful photo of Dougie in his Footscray guernsey, bare arm proffered to a nurse with a needle. From the look of terror on his face, it seemed the thought he was about to be harpooned.

Footscray had one win in '93. Harry and Tommy were named football's Media Personalities of the Year at the North Melbourne grand final breakfast. They had quadrupled 3WRB's audience. I'd seen Harry from behind during one of the reserves finals. He wasn't calling the match, he was conducting it, directing the panel's tempo with a biro as if they were a showband. But he looked terribly tired. There was a story that tensions at the community radio station had resulted in Harry being left without the talk-back facility during the Footscray Football Club talk-back program he had pioneered. Apparently, the Big H and his companion had to go it alone, improvising on the theme of Footscray and the team for the Big Game for a whole three hours. I imagined it as a great Australian play: *Waiting for Godot at the Western Oval.*

Footscray's reserves made it to the preliminary final and then died mysteriously. All the reserves finals were like that – it was as if the power of what the teams were attempting, the quality of football they were trying to play, was too great for their abilities and the sides could only manage to produce it one at a time. I felt for Terry Wallace. A reserves premiership might have secured him the coaching job at Hawthorn. As a player, he had been brave and prolific. As a coach, his comments were simple, clear and direct. It was Wheeler who created the opportunity for Leon Cameron to excel. It was Terry Wallace who told Leon at the end of 1992 that his football was going nowhere. After the reserves' losing final, I found Super with Harry and the team in the 3WRB commentary box. Super was shaking his head. 'They didn't want it,' he said. Super and Cúchulainn would have got on fine had they ever met, provided it wasn't on the field of battle. Super believed you had to want it so much you didn't know if you were playing badly or well. He said that when you could no longer hear the voices, any voices, you knew you had become part of the game.

Super said thinking didn't always help. That, he suspected, was Chris Grant's trouble. After the Melbourne game, Wheeler had named two or three individuals who hadn't 'stood up': Grant was one of them. at half-time the following week, Wheeler talked about Jason Dunstall, about the number of times the Hawthorn full-forward won the ball with his last effort. He drew one of Dunstall's diving chest marks on the whiteboard behind him. Ten minutes later, Grant attempted a diving Jason Dunstall chest mark; the ball slipped away. It was the right lesson wrongly learned. Chris Grant wasn't Jason Dunstall. The February edition of the club newspaper had a beautiful colour photograph of Grant marking in one of the practice matches at Skinner Reserve. It was classical – body above the pack, eyes fixed on the ball, fingers spread.

Of the four players pictured, he was the only one balanced. He lacked neither courage nor strength – he broke tackles and maintained his momentum in bumps – but there was still a question as to whether he was a centre-half-forward. Centre-half-forwards are trees that people climb over. They need a special deep-rooted strength. Grant and Mil Hanna had played a wonderful duet when Footscray played Carlton at Princes Park, but that was an old-fashioned contest. They both played on their skills. Most weeks, Grant wasn't allowed that liberty. He might break free for the odd quarter, but rarely for a whole match. Until, that is, Ilija arrived.

Footscray's first public post-season drama was when Richmond pursued Ilija in the way that Richmond pursued talent in the days of old. With gusto. This was the Footscray nightmare revisited, its talent being looted by wealthier clubs. But Ilija chose to stay. He was one of a group – Peter Quill and Chris Grant among them – which had formed in the course of the season. It was the basis of a new side. Time was also with Ilija. No one – including, probably himself – yet knew how good he was. So Ilija stayed; but TC went.

Wheeler interviewed each of the 52 players on the list individually after the last match, personally advising those who had been cut of his decision. It was not part of the job he enjoyed. TC, who had survived the cut, began his meeting with Wheeler by saying (with, I imagined, a slightly embarrassed grin), 'I've got a bit of a bombshell.'

TC was going to America to try his luck at grid-iron. More money. The photograph the *Age* ran with the story had TC hugging a ball to his chest in a Footscray guernsey and reflecting sun-glasses. It looked as if he had just taken a mark somewhere high in the French Alps.

'Were you angry with him?' I asked Wheeler.

If Footscray had known TC were going, they would have been unlikely to release Bernard Toohey. They now faced the prospect of starting 1994 with two 19-year-olds – Nicko and Western Australian recruit Danny Southern – in their key defensive positions.

'How could I be?' replied Wheeler. He was the coach who quoted *Jonathan Livingston Seagull*. TC had flown all right. Over the seas and far away.

It had been announced at the best-and-fairest night that Dougie was stepping down as captain. Then, renegotiating his contract, he found his base rate had been cut. It wasn't Dougie's first contract wrangle, but it threatened to be his last. There was even talk of him going to another club. The dispute escalated when Dougie went public; the club was bombarded with phone-calls from angry supporters. Gio, as official spokesman for the club, copped most of the abuse. 'I suppose I can say I'm a real football administrator now,' he said soberly. But eventually Dougie and the club came to an agreement. No one wanted him to go. Dougie was part of Footscray in the way that blue is part of the sky.

The worst news of '93 was that the club made a loss, its first since the Fightback. The president began his report at the annual general meeting with the words, 'It is with some embarrassment that I stand before you tonight.' The amount, $386,455, could be covered by the club's accumulated profits from the previous three years but another year like it and Footscray would be back on the road to a crisis like '89. The AFL's projected dividend for 1993 had been $1.5 million, the president said. The actual sum paid to the club had been $280,000 less. Nor had the pokies proved to be the financial bonanza Footscray and other league clubs had hoped. But there was also an expenditure problem – the football budget had leapt by $1 million since 1991, largely through a $650,000 increase in the salary cap, but also because of the $350,000 paid to support staff. There were going to have to be major cutbacks. The old tension between the president and the coach was re-activated. Super's hours on the Care for Kids program would also have to be reduced.

While Peter Gordon was urging Footscray supporters to sell more raffle tickets in 1991, and figures were being released which showed that Footscray had the highest rate of urban unemployment (23.8 per cent) in mainland Australia, West Coast and Adelaide were declaring profits of $2 million and $1.12 million respectively.

West Coast had looked jaded in '93, as reigning premiers often do, but Adelaide had almost made the final. Against Carlton, in the second semi, they showed their inexperience, rushing their shots, trying to play too quickly, so that the ball bounced off their boots and went out of bounds or missed Modra on the lead. But against Essendon, in the preliminary, they found touch; their first and second quarters were scintillating, a perfect co-ordination and blinding speed, faultless skills and inter-linking. But once their game dropped a fraction in quality, as sooner or later it had to, the match entered a second, more combative phase. Essendon's captain and vice-captain, Mark Thompson and Gary O'Donnell, had done relatively little against Footscray. Perhaps they were resting, because in the preliminary final they led their young team-mates on the long, hard, grinding journey back into a game which had initially sped past them. Forty-four points down at half-time, Essendon caught Adelaide with minutes to go. It was an historic victory, but few doubted that the Crows were, at most, two years away from an AFL final. Everyone in South Australia – barring, it seemed, Port Adelaide players – wanted to be part of the Crows.

The AFL was drifting towards an elite competition. Footscray's costs were escalating, but its revenue was static. The club had succeeded in activating its traditional supporters, but I saw no evidence that it was attracting significant numbers of new ones. In fact, in 1993, its match attendances dropped 11 per cent. Footscray stubbornly clung to the conviction that it could still participate in finals, still be a force in the competition, still win a premiership. The club remained committed to paying the full salary cap, but the need for success was becoming greater, not lesser. Ten short months earlier, Peter Gordon had told me, 'We're secure now, but things can change.' They had. Footscray was not as yet playing for its survival, but that scenario existed and could no longer be dismissed as pessimistic brooding.

The boys, as Greenie called the players, went to Cairns for their end-of-season trip. Wheeler and I took an end-of-season trip of our own. We went to Warburton – the place, he said, his football came from.

Warby

We drove in his car, a maroon Ford station-wagon. Wheeler reckoned I didn't trust him because I kept stabbing my foot for a non-existent brake pedal. He also couldn't believe I didn't know where we were going. Wheeler always knew where he was going; his training schedule for the entire year (with all its constituent parts expressed in percentage terms) had been published before the season began. 'Warby's only 50 Ks from Melbourne,' he said incredulously. But it had taken me the best part of ten years to get to know Melbourne. It had taken me a season with Footscray Football Club to begin to get to know Footscray and the western suburbs. The state of Victoria was something else again. I knew where Geelong was and the approximate locations of Bendigo and Ballarat, and I had once spent a couple of bumpy hours in a light aeroplane flying to Ararat to see the then Minister for Health, Tom Roper, an open extension to the blue-stone prison which at the time housed Victoria's criminally insane. The minister and a row of dark-suited officials stood in one semi-circle, the inmates gathered in another. I could almost see Jack Nicholson leaning against the far wall, quizzically eyeing the performance. As soon as the circle was completed, an Aboriginal bloke stepped into the middle of it and started reciting verses about Australia. The warder beside me watched him with narrowed eyes. 'He went eight rounds with Tony Mundine,' he whispered. But that had been my only visit to Ararat. Australia was a big, silent, mysterious land; like most Australians, I only knew part of it.

Wheeler and I were the same age. He had started playing in the Yarra Valley and Mountain District Football League in 1971, when he was 16. He gave me a description of Alan Walker, a Marysville player of that period – arms tanned to the elbow, faded green and gold guernsey (number 17), baggy black shorts with silver buckles on the side, pot belly, Elvis Presley hair-do. He sounded like Chalky Barwick, captain of Bridgewater reserves. Bridgewater was in my old competition. The convicts had built a stone breakwater across the Derwent River at Bridgewater; black swans gathered in the calm waters beside it. Bridgewater played in the WA state guernsey with the black swan as its emblem. A few kilometres to the south, on the western side of the river, was Claremont. They were a working-class club. They wore Collingwood colours and hated our guts because we were university students with long hair and rings in our ears. To the north-east was Sorell, another old convict town. They didn't like us much either. I think they saw us as the team from the officers' quarters. Sorell reserves had a mad Maori in the back pocket known to his team-mates as Jungle. With team-mates like that, who needs opponents?

Wheeler and I had grown up in different parts of Australia, but we had played the same game at the same time. The difference between us was that I played social footy. Wheeler didn't drink alcohol until he was twenty-two. 'Terry was always going somewhere,' said Robin Fisher. Robin, who played footy with Wheeler's father, had been born in Warby, but had wed a Millgrove girl – in local terms, a mixed marriage. For a few years, they lived on the boundary of the two towns, before eventually choosing to settle in Millgrove a few kilometres back down the highway. Robin and I went for a walk to the Millgrove footy ground. There are some pretty football grounds in Tasmania – looking west from Launceston's York Park, past the poplars in their autumn glory and the old railway yards, towards the rough blue outline of Mount Barrow, or sitting in the press box at Devonport watching the white yachts lean and slide through the water at the mouth of the Mersey – but I haven't seen one prettier than Millgrove. Sunlight was flashing off pools of water in the lumpy green paddock behind the far goal. On one wing, a clump of apple trees were in blossom; spikes of yellow broom rose from beneath an old wooden fence and, a kilometre or so away, like a giant backdrop, was a high blue wall of mountain. Robin said Millgrove always had trouble getting a team but still managed to win lots of premierships. It made him grin and shake his head to recall the fact; Warburton, I gathered, had the players but not the winning knack.

Millgrove was at the mouth of the Yarra Valley. There was a moment on the drive into Warburton when the valley narrowed until its two sides were only the width of the road and the river apart; the hill on the right at that moment was called Little Joe. 'This,' said Wheeler emphatically, 'is Warburton's Maribyrnong. This is what you have to pass through to enter Warby.' When the Hallets, a large family of potato farmers, left Millgrove, the Millgrove Football Club finally folded and merged with Warburton. The Warburton-Millgrove Football Club had its rooms at the Warburton ground.

Inside the club house, I saw Dick Treloar, the trainer Wheeler had told me about. There was a painting of him on the Dick Treloar Award Board: hat back, lean, quizzical face, white overalls. He looked remarkably like Footscray's Jack McGovern. Wheeler, I noticed from reading the board, had won the club best and fairest in his second season, at the age of only seventeen. A strong player, Robin Fisher said.

'What about his father,' I asked, 'what sort of a player was he?'

'Alan was a kick-and-mark man,' said Robin. Not like Terry, I gathered. Then he added, 'Did you meet Terry's mother?'

I hadn't.

'You ought to,' he said. 'She's very strong, Terry's mother.'

The Warburton-Millgrove Football Club was conscious of its history. In addition to the normal team photographs, it had a display of newspaper clippings and old programs. Warburton Football Club even had its own writer, Len Stratford. Wheeler found a box with some of his notebooks in the secretary's office. I recognised the method; scores on one side of the page, scribbled notes on the other. Also on display was an article about Ralph Story. Ralph Story was a football legend in the Yarra Valley. Wheeler described him as a gentle man. He had played on the MCG in the '30s when it was still used for private school matches. Angling was his other sport. When Wheeler was trapped on the boundary by a bigger opponent in his first season and cruelly dumped, Ralph Story waited until after the game. Then he handed him a ball and invited him to get past. The boy couldn't. They reversed roles. The coach poked the ball into Wheeler's face. He blinked and the coach pushed past. The game, Wheeler realised, could be taught. He'd gone to Footscray at eighteen, the same year he undertook his Higher School Certificate. As a player, he had modelled himself on Charlie Sutton. But, as a coach, he had modelled himself on Ralph Story.

The Warburton-Millgrove rooms are a spacious grey-brick building of recent design and construction. Wheeler wanted to show me Warby's old rooms, the weatherboard ones built on the opposite side of the ground beside the Yarra River and beneath the brow of Mount Donna Buang. We walked across the oval. It was a very different ground from Millgrove, uneven, rising in the middle and dropping to one end. It looked as if a creature with a long spine was trying to prise itself out of the earth. You could imagine drop kicks casually spinning past the sun at Millgrove, but not here. Warby was made for robust play. As we had to wait for a second key, I went for a walk and listened to the rushing sound of the river and noted the muscular girth of the gums around the oval. Millgrove was a farming community. This was timber country. Wheeler and Robin were talking quietly, leaning on the wooden stands where Wheeler's mother had once served tea and scones using white china at half-time. When night fell, his father would park the car by the back door of the clubrooms so that the light angled through the car window when the time came for the three kids to go to sleep. The key finally arrived, the old rooms were opened. 'Home,' said Wheeler.

It was like a large living-room – varnished wood as high as your eye, white ceiling, twisting wooden staircase leading to the time-keeper's box. Wheeler wanted me to see he hearth which was blackened with use. The women sat around the fire. After the players had showered and changed, and the fire had been lit, his father would open the wooden partition that divided the home team's rooms from the visitors'. The area would double to the size of a small hall and the two communities would mingle – men, women and children. 'Imagine this with all the photographs from the other rooms' said Wheeler. Photographs of Warburton people and Warburton teams, and every Warburton team photographs in the same way, at the same end of the ground, with the hill known as Little Joe behind them on their right, as if they were defending the pass which signalled you were entering their territory.

And in the End...

In the end, Warburton Football Club's greatest enemy hadn't been Millgrove. Or Marysville or Yarra Junction. It was the city. It was television and motor cars. It was everything which made the world smaller and, in so doing, meant that placed likes Warburton were no longer communities with attitudes and beliefs that distinguished them from the people who lived 10 kilometres down the road. Warburton was now a picturesque destination one hour from the outskirts of Melbourne, ideal for weekenders and craft shops and day trips. And as the city was no Warburton, so was global commercial culture to Australia. A poll of Year 10 students in Australia conducted in the course of 1993 revealed that their number one sporting idol was American basketballer Michael Jordan. Michael Jordan has never been to Australia. In this country, he is solely a product of the media.

After the success of the American basketball team at the Barcelona Olympics, Arthur Ashe said he thought basketball would replace soccer as the new world game.

This may well prove to be the case, but to watch Brazil and Germany play soccer is to see two different interpretations of the one sport. Basketball, it seems to me, is always basically American in character no matter who's playing. I watched precisely one half (that is, one and a half games) of the 1993 NBL play-off between the Melbourne Tigers and the Perth Wildcats. I liked Melbourne's Andrew Gaze. He was different – grey and bent with a young boy's smile – and he kept finding swerving paths to the basket where none seemed to exist. The Wildcats' Ricky Grace was good to watch too, smooth and subtle, but the rest of the players were young men of much the same physical type performing much the same physical function. There was no Libber, no Wanganeen, no Kickett. And there was no mid-field; it was a game played at the two ends and with immediate results. The famous insult, credited to journalist Bruce Wilson, was that if you started every basketball match at 99-all with one minute to go, not a lot would be lost. But in the space of a few short years American basketball has become part of Australian youth culture.

Will Australian football survive? Kevin Sheedy thinks so. Why, I asked him, 'Because it's a great game', he said. It is; but, from here on, it will have to be protected and nurtured. Watching Stephen Kernahan in the grand final parade, I felt I understood the precise advantage he carried into the following day's match. He knew that, as a sporting contest, the grand final would be relatively normal. It was the bank of eager faces on the other side of the boundary line, the people watching on televisions around Australia, who gave the day its aura, its sense that at stake was some ultimate crowning glory. That excitement was a product of thousands of interactions over a period of more than one hundred years, around kitchen tables, at workplaces, within families, with strangers on public transport. Football is a part of the fabric of people's lives. But fabrics can unravel.

During the finals, there had been a furore over the AFL's decision to permit McDonald's, the American fast-food chain, to advertise its logo on the balls used in the finals. Phil Cleary had best expressed the danger to Australian football. 'You keep changing things,' he said, 'and then one day you find you've changed one thing too many and the magic's gone.' Because the game is magic, and business isn't. Business is business.

My end-of-season trip ended at five o'clock on a Friday night in Punt Road, near Richmond station. 'From now on,' I said to Wheeler, getting out of his car, 'you'll have to remember to push the brake pedal yourself.'

He enjoyed jokes like that, mind games. On a football field, it was called bluff. As a player, he told me, he had always kept an eye out for Crosswell, probably because Crosswell played the game even better than he did. Wheeler said you never knew what Crosswell might do. But beneath their masks both were serious men. Crosswell's belief was of the solitary kind possessed by artists and writers. Wheeler's was communal, and I had benefited from it. From the time the season began, he had treated me with extraordinary respect. Not once had he declined to answer a question or deny me access to a meeting or seek in any way to influence the book. That was what Wheeler called coaching: creating the conditions which enable others to do what they do best. On Monday, he and his wife Lynn were leaving on a one-week holiday without their kids: they had no idea where they were going and intended keeping it that way. Tonight, they were off for a drink in a Williamstown pub where the locals did him the favour of talking to him about anything but football. The light changed to green and he drew away in a gleaming caterpillar of traffic.

On the other side of Punt Road, surrounded by its giant light towers, was the MCG. The great stadium was empty. It needed people; we all did. Directly opposite was the Punt Road oval, former home of the Richmond Football Club, another grand old Melbourne institution which refused to die. I'd gone to Footscray to learn about the game. I had. I'd seen a great player (Dougie), a great passion (Libber), and a man acclaimed as a champion (Choco). I'd learned about the character of teams and the demands of the game, but, as much as anything, I had learned about clubs. Australian football is not American professional sport; it doesn't rest on a platform of college sport. The clubs are the hub of our game and, from what I could see, they were irreplaceable. Australian football is a product of the nineteenth century. The modern world is too transient, too individual, to create new clubs, great clubs, clubs that will live for one hundred years. And thus, with every club that ceases to exist in the country or the city, the game is diminished.

The first item of graffiti I saw entering Richmond station said that all journalists were liars. I didn't believe that, but I did wonder how free many of them were. That was something else about the footy; it was a place where, for better or worse, people said what they thought. I was about to enter the dark noisy tunnel beneath Richmond station when the second item of graffiti caught my eye, a silhouette of a Sherrin football. It was poster size and neatly done in black ink. Inside the football, Ronald McDonald, symbol of the McDonald's fast food chain, was standing with his trousers around his ankles gleefully humping the kangaroo which is the Sherrin trade-mark. Above it were two words: STOP IT.

Postscript

Wheeler rang me at home on the night of Tuesday April 5.

'What's happening then?' he said, in his slow, mildly humorous way. It was a joke: the man everybody's talking about asking a bystander what's going on. The newspaper had rung me an hour earlier asking if I could confirm the rumour: had Wheeler been sacked? Reporters and photographers were being detailed to stake out the Western Oval. No doubt film crews were rushing there, too. The sacking of a coach is like the death of a king. Wheeler said it was true; they'd finished him up. He was ringing because he wanted to talk about the press conference the following day. He knew the manner in which he wanted to depart; he just wanted to check on a couple of the words he was going to use.

It was over for Wheeler, or at least this part of the story. There was sadness in his laugh, but it was still a big, easy sound. Ultimately, Wheeler believed football was a game. He loved its nuances, its romance and richness, but he also knew there were losses far greater than any incurred on the sports field. His father had been digging in his vegie garden when he collapsed and died. Eventually, Wheeler had decided he wanted to go back and visit the spot, but when he did he took his nine-year-old daughter with him, thereby allowing her to see what his father had meant to him. That's what Libber said about Wheeler: he taught you there was a strength in being open.

Wheeler's dismissal was initiated by Peter Gordon, the man with whom he once dreamed such grand dreams. The romance of the Fightback was over in more ways than one. Footscray had lost to the Swans in the first round of the Foster's Cup. Coming in the middle of the club's annual membership drive, it was a disastrous result. The way the team played had been ominous, too; the lowly Swans had blasted Footscray off the ball. In the first roster match, the Dogs withstood Richmond's youthful exuberance and won by two points at the Western Oval, but the following week, at Kardinia Park, Geelong clobbered them by 88 points; Footscray were never in the game. The match against Geelong – the team which denied Wheeler a grand final appearance in 1992 was the only side Footscray failed to defeat during his time as coach – was Wheeler's last.

Footscray's preparation for the season had been unsettled. Only weeks before the season began, prize recruit Richard Osborne announced he was going to the United States to try out with an American football team. In the wake of the loss to the Swans, the tension between Gordon and Wheeler escalated into a full-scale dispute over the captaincy. Wheeler wanted Axe. The captain, he argued, had to be an extension of the coach.

Given Axe's form in 1993, however, it was a high-risk strategy. In the end, Big Scottie was appointed but the decision angered Super. He had been overlooked on the basis of his physical breakdowns, but, like everyone else in the club, he knew that Big Scottie's knee injuries were threatening to become chronic. Super was also critical of the human development course Wheeler had incorporated into the pre-season program. He said it was okay for players at his age and stage, but he thought it was seriously misleading for the younger ones. Football knowledge, Super believed, had to be gained through experience.

In 1992, Terry Wheeler had taken his team to the mountain. He'd got them high enough to see the view from the top, then urged them to take the next step. The prize was a permanent place in the history of the game; all that was stopping them, he said, was themselves. Wheeler's belief in his players verged on reverence. He was a natural orator, but his addresses were delivered either at the Friday night team meeting or 90 minutes before the game. That was so the players could prepare themselves, individually. Wheeler believed the game would eventually evolve to the point where players had individual coaches, like tennis players. It was, he said, the players' game.

Wheeler's vision was uncommonly generous. He didn't seek to create teams in his own image. He delighted in human difference, embracing people utterly unlike himself, but, in the end, had his Achilles' heel been one of the oldest in the game: had he made the mistake of thinking his players could do what had come naturally to himself? In the end, had Wheeler's teams lacked intensity – the one quality, which as a player, had never been absent from his game? Dougie was the man with the long view. He'd had nine different coaches at Footscray. The two who stood out, he said, were Malthouse and Wheeler. He couldn't compare them; they were too unalike. 'Mick was hard and ruthless, Wheels was a communicator.' Dougie thought the board had made a mistake. Crackers was writing Wheeler a letter. 'He had the highest expectations for his players,' said Crackers, 'but I didn't think they were unrealistic.'

Most people didn't question the decision so much as its timing. 'Is there ever a right time?' said Peter Gordon. Yes, said the traditionalists. This was too bloody, too public. On the radio, David 'Swan' MacKay said it was the sort of thing Carlton – supposedly the ruthless corporate club – would do. Gordon defended himself by saying that hard decisions were a fact of public life, and those who didn't make them dropped out of the race of history. The Melbourne clubs' battle to survive was getting harder and meaner. Mighty Hawthorn was talking of mergers. The president of St Kilda was refusing to discuss the future of his club in terms of more than one year. Peter Gordon embodied Footscray's will to survive, but survival would come at a price and, in this case, Wheeler had paid it. The fact was that Footscray's most traumatic loss in 1993 had occurred not on the field, but in its accounts. That was the coach's argument: his dismissal was for reasons of business, not football. He was one of the most successful coaches in the club's history. He had won four of his last six games. He was innovative (he was the man who asked, 'Any coaching for the coach?'). It wasn't fair, but Super said football wasn't. What had happened to

Wheeler had also happened to Darren Baxter and Jon Ballantyne and Justin Charles. Players (and coaches were players) were people implored to give everything. They did; then, one day, their right to appear in the place where they had committed so much of themselves was abruptly taken from them. 'That's football,' said Super. 'That's what you have to write about.'

The new coach, Alan Joyce, had won two premierships with Hawthorn and had a reputation as a strict disciplinarian. The older players quickly recognised a man in Malthouse's mold, but even for them the change was unnerving. Libber said new coaches put the fear of God into you. Wally said it was like arriving home and seeing all your belongings piled up on the pavement. He'd been captain when the last new coach arrived. On Wednesday, at Joyce's first training session, there were no witches' hats on the field, fewer balls in the air, nothing sophisticated about the routines, and one rule for all. Required to train with everyone else, Matthew Croft, painstakingly restored to fitness by Wheeler using a special rehabilitation program, tore a hamstring. But Libber also said it was one of the most intense training sessions he had attended. At a team meeting, the players decided to support the new coach. On Thursday night, Axe, on the recommendation of the match committee, was dropped. On Friday, Terry Wheeler rang Alan Joyce and wished him all the best.

The next chapter in the history of the Footscray Football Club had begun.

APPENDIX

Senior Player Statistics 1993

	FIRST PLAYED	GAMES		GOALS	
		1993	Total	1993	Total
Atkins, Simon	1987	20	113	12	67
Ballantyne, Jon	1990	6	20	13	46
Barrow, Gary	1992	4	6	1	1
Beveridge, Luke	1989	8	50	9	50
Cameron, Leon	1990	19	61	8	26
Campbell, Tony	1986	10	110	0	63
Charles, Justin	1989	3	36	2	24
Coleman, Glenn	1980	4	194	0	113
Corcoran, Shannon	1990	5	21	0	2
Croft, Matthew	1991	2	8	3	6
Darcy, Anthony	1992	12	13	2	2
Del-Re, Danny	1990	14	59	36	138
Ellen, Shane	1993	4	4	0	0
Foster, Peter	1980	9	169	2	58
Frost, Michael	1992	6	13	1	3
Grant, Chris	1990	17	76	34	153
Grgic, Ilija	1993	9	9	19	19
Hawkins, Doug	1978	20	308	6	209
Hunter, Mark	1988	16	90	0	2
Kellett, Nigel	1989	19	56	7	21
Kolyniuk, Steven	1987	14	77	12	92
Kretiuk, Steven	1992	5	17	0	3

	FIRST PLAYED	GAMES		GOALS	
		1993	Total	1993	Total
Liberatore, Tony	1986	20	104	12	59
Macpherson, Stephen	1982	9	171	2	150
Mansfield, Matthew	1991	14	56	19	24
Nicholson, Brad	1993	10	199	21	299
Quill, Peter	1993	8	20	13	23
Reynolds, Keenan	1990	6	20	6	16
Royal, Brian	1983	20	52	11	20
Sexton, Ben	1991	4	7	4	9
Smith, Rohan	1992	17	263	2	115
Standfield, Barry	1989	4	205	0	52
Thorpe, Alan	1992	17	17	21	21
Toohey, Bernard	1981	19	98	2	13
Wallis, Steven	1983	8	32	1	5
West, Scott	1993	5	5	1	1
Wynd, Scott	1988	13	13	5	5

Match Details 1993

DATE	OPPONENT	VENUE	FFC	SCORE	AGAINST RESULT
March 26	Collingwood	MCG	13.17.95	17.13.115	lost
April 3	Melbourne	Princes Park	15.13.103	13.17.95	won
April 10	Fitzroy	Princes Park	14.17.101	14.14.98	won
April 17	bye				
April 24	Essendon	Western Oval	20.7.127	11.15.81	won
May 2	West Coast	Subiaco Oval	13.6.84	19.11.125	lost
May 8	Nth Melb.	Western Oval	17.8.110	22.9.141	lost
May 15	Carlton	Princes Park	15.16.106	11.12.78	won
May 22	St Kilda	Western Oval	22.11.143	11.13.79	won
May 29	Hawthorn	Western Oval	9.8.62	20.13.132	lost
June 13	Adelaide	Football Park	8.14.62	15.17.107	lost
June 19	Sydney	Western Oval	13.16.94	10.9.69	won
June 26	Brisbane	Western Oval	17.19.121	14.9.93	won
July 3	Geelong	Kardinia Park	8.6.54	15.20.110	lost
July 11	Richmond	MCG	10.18.78	8.14.62	won
July 17	Collingwood	Victoria Park	11.15.81	21.19.145	lost
July 24	Melbourne	Western Oval	14.13.97	16.14.110	lost
July 31	Fitzroy	Western Oval	22.14.146	13.6.84	won
August 7	bye				
August 14	Essendon	MCG	12.13.85	14.14.98	lost
August 21	West Coast	Western Oval	14.10.94	7.10.52	won
August 28	Nth Melb.	MCG	20.15.135	18.15.123	won
					W11/L9

AFL 1993 League Ladder

	W	L	D	FOR	AGST.	P.C.	PTS
Essendon	13	6	1	2333	1959	119.1	54
Carlton	13	6	1	2315	1969	117.6	54
North Melbourne	13	7	-	2597	2150	120.8	52
Hawthorn	13	7	-	2166	1858	116.6	52
Adelaide	12	8	-	2168	1840	117.8	48
West Coast	12	8	-	1912	1651	115.8	48
Geelong	12	8	-	2354	2109	111.6	48
Collingwood	11	9		2086	2060	101.3	44
Footscray	11	9	-	1978	1997	99.0	44
Melbourne	10	10	-	2101	1873	112.2	40
Fitzroy	10	10	-	2001	2011	99.5	40
St Kilda	10	10	-	2040	2166	94.2	40
Brisbane	4	16	-	1886	2504	75.3	16
Richmond	4	16	-	1753	2480	70.7	16
Sydney	1	19	-	1837	2901	63.3	4

Brownlow Medal Voting

G. Wanganeen (Ess.)	- 1st
G. Williams (Carl.)	- equal 2nd
G. Hocking (Geel.)	- equal 2nd

Leading Goalkickers

A. Modra (Adelaide)	129
G. Ablett (Geelong)	124
J. Dunstall (Hawthorn)	123
P. Sumich (West Coast)	76
J. Longmire (North Melbourne)	75

THE GAME IN TIME OF WAR

15 September 2001

Walking towards the G with a head like a bass drum that's been beaten for four days and nights. Within, a sense of emptiness and foreboding; something has begun—where and how will it end? I don't feel like going to the game. Why? Because it is—so transparently—a game. Someone's flown planes into the Pentagon and the World Trade Center. Over 3000 people have died and the most powerful nation on earth insulted and shown to be vulnerable. Ego, politics and religion have met at one murderous intersection, and more is sure to follow. A friend, Shane Howard, rang me about an hour after the attack occurred, around midnight our time, and said, so gently that he almost whispered the words, that I was going to wake up to a new world in the morning. He was right.

I've taken the exit from Richmond station and am walking towards the Punt Road oval when I see the Richmond Social Club is open to the public and decide to go in for a beer.The truth is, I don't want to stand alone in the crowd, waiting for the game. There's no loneliness like the one that descends upon you in a crowd. I walk in and immediately find myself in a gallery of old-style Richmond supporters; men with worn faces and wispy remnants of seventies hairdos, women with equally lined faces and names like Jim Jess and Kevin Bartlett sewn onto the sleeves of their duffle coats. I stand on the edge of a circle. No-one seems to mind, probably thinking I'm another Richmond supporter. Not much is being said, then someone mentions what happened in New York and the bloke beside me lowers the beer can from his lips, shakes his head, and says, 'That's fucked.' Millions of words have already been spent on September 11 but that is one of the two most eloquent statements I've observed. The other is a headline in a French newspaper, above a photo of an airliner exploding through the World Trade Center: LA NOUVELLE GUERRE.

Having finished our beers we move by unspoken consensus towards the ground, passing another Richmond supporter who holds an infant of perhaps eighteen months in the air while a woman kicks a football in their direction; child, with assistance of man, attempts to catch it. It's called teaching them young. As we approach the ground it occurs to me that if I wanted to create deep panic in this country, if I wanted to do it serious psychic harm, I'd fly a plane into a sports stadium during a big game, a Test match or an AFL final. I look around. A slight hill and buildings provide some sort of cover to the north but it's open to the south. It's a strange thought, one I try to put back.

Inside the ground, we wordlessly go our different ways and I find a foothold on the terrace directly behind the goals at the city end, standing with a group of younger and particularly manic Richmond supporters known as the Tiger Army. The Tigers, in the finals for the first time since 1995, are matched against Carlton, their great foe from the sixties and seventies when Richmond were a power in the game. For serious Richmond supporters, the situation could hardly be more charged. Some Olympians lap the ground, waving and smiling blandly to the crowd.The Tiger Army tell them to fuck off. 'Get over it,' one of them yells. 'The Olympics was a year ago.'

When Richmond finally take the field, there is thunder in the stands above and around me which is accompanied by the Tigers' bold, brassy club song. At the appointed place, the music breaks for a phrase, and the entire Richmond crowd, from the bottom of their lungs, bellow: 'Yellow and Black!' The Richmond players run first towards the end where the bulk of their supporters are camped and are met with rapturous applause, the sort that lets them know that their fans are passionately and indissolubly with them—for the moment, at least. Then, almost ceremonially, they turn and face the Carlton goal. It's like a cavalry charge. As the players pass out of the shadow at the Richmond end and into the golden slash of green that is the rest of the playing field, I see the pride in their style, their dash. A wave of something liberating passes through me and I find myself laughing out loud.They're taking the game seriously! They have to be joking! What's more, in an absurd way, I love them for it.That's one of the reasons people go to the footy—it's a place where you're allowed to be absurd.

Carlton come to the Richmond end for the warm-up. Why, I wonder. Does their coach want to harden them to the sort of abuse they can expect before the match begins? The Tiger Army have been singing for some time but suddenly I am conscious of what they're saying. Putting it politely, something I am loath to do, they're alleging two of the Carlton players are practising homosexuals. A lot of their invective is aimed, predictably enough, at Carlton's best player, Anthony Koutoufides, who started playing football as an athlete with a magnificent physique and, for a long time, had no idea how good a footballer he was. His problems began when he did get an idea, simultaneously saw how much Carlton relied on him, and started playing like a worried man. But unlike many athletes who take up football late, Kouta had actually learned the game and is now at the height of his powers. Early in the match he is strong, graceful and clear about what he is doing. In the second term, however, he goes down in front of us clutching his knee. The likelihood is that he will miss a whole year with the injury. I should feel shocked and concerned, but I don't. It may be the drink I had before the match at the Richmond Social Club, the moment of comfort I derived from the philosopher with the beer can, or it may be the crazy spirit the Tigers displayed in taking the field, but somehow, for this match at least, I have become passionately committed to their cause. The deeper truth is I've taken leave of my senses and entered the sublime unreality of the game.

Richo, Richmond's centre half-forward, arouses deep feelings in the Tiger Army, and with reason. At six foot four inches, he can leap like a gazelle. I don't wish to swamp the reader with visual images but with Richo it's hard to avoid. He rides packs of bodies like surfers ride waves. It's the type of thing a certain sort of kid did in the schoolyard when I was a boy, the sort who was so talented that he invented his own way of doing things to keep himself from getting bored. In so doing, he taught himself a lot of bad habits along with the good. Most players have their bad habits knocked out of them by coaches as they get older but Richo, depending on your point of view, is either a slow learner or forever young. In Tasmania, where he comes from, it is said you can have four seasons of weather on the one day. Richo can have four seasons of football in a single match, and in this game summer comes early. Mobile, sure in his marking, he makes Carlton look defenceless. To win, Carlton need to close the game down, control it in the clinches, and gradually they succeed. By half-time, notwithstanding the loss of Kouta, Richo is looking autumnal, and the Blues are back in it.

For the entire half-time break, the Tiger Army chant:'Tiger Ar-mee! (clap, clap, clap) Tiger Arm-ee! (clap, clap, clap).' I look at them.Young, mostly but not exclusively male, one Asian, plastic beer cups in hand. There's a huge body of Richmond supporters around them but the Army are the most vocal, the most extreme.

By the third term, the game is increasingly being played on Carlton's terms. The Tigers bring on reserve Nick Daffy. Once a crowd pleaser, his career is on the edge. His forte has been unlikely acts of skill, goals kicked when only a splinter of light was showing between the posts and he only had an instant with the ball. Daffy needs an open game to demonstrate his wares, to prove again to the selectors that he is needed. Instead he gets a high ball falling out of the sky on top of him. The Duck, as he is known, does the team thing, stands his ground. It's like watching a car hit a guide post, with the oncoming pack being the vehicle and the Duck the stationary object. The Duck is hurried from the field by trainers, nursing a broken shoulder. The Tiger Army applauds. After the match Richmond coach Danny 'Spud' Frawley will refer in emotional terms to Daffy's courageous contribution, but the crude reality is that his career at the Richmond Football Club is over. If he'd played on his intuition as he normally did, he would have artfully avoided the collision. Had he then gone on to kick a couple of goals, his fate would almost certainly have been different. But, in the maelstrom of the day, that is not what happened.

Midway through the final quarter, it's the Tigers by six points but Carlton are willing themselves to win. Richo's now in the winter of his discontent and it's not a pretty sight. He's tossing his head about and getting petulant with team-mates. Desperately needing a goal, Spud Frawley gambles and puts Rory Hilton to full-forward. Rory's not a great player, never going to be one. He's too short to play full-forward but he's brave in a way I've been admiring all my life. Let me paint Rory Hilton as I see him at that moment: socks down, hands on hips, weight taken on right leg, golden fringe worn a fraction too long so that he is obliged to carry his head thrown back ever so slightly. Like so much of the old Australian aesthetic, it's one of those styles that exists up until the moment it's identified as one. As I say, not a great player, but if the ball comes Rory's way two things are sure: one, he will throw his left arm back so that it collects his opponent in the midriff, thereby supplying him with a disincentive to accompany him to the ball; and two, when he gets to the action he'll have what is known in the language of the game as a crack or a red-hot go.

Alert to the high drama of the moment and anxious to be of assistance in any way they can, the Tiger Army begin a chant. Delivered in a tone of serious respect, they utter: 'Rory Hilton—he's a tough cunt. Rory Hilton—he's a tough cunt.' The chant continues, the ball swerves forward. In the climactic confusion it falls off hands and lands loose in the goalsquare. Rory swings a boot, connects, goals! The MCG bounces before my eyes—not the grass, the other bit, the dark one filled with heads. The Tigers have it won! It's an orgy of noise now, ariotous wave of naked energy with a fond glow about it, and I'm sucking it in, gulping it down, getting as much of it as I can. In ten minutes, this will all be over. I'll be on a train bumping through the suburbs, being reacquainted with the real world and its epic uncertainties. I'll know what I saw was only a game, one that recedes in my mind's eye by the moment.

But here's the funny thing—when I get onto the train, it's not like that, not quite. I still feel empty in my core, like I did before the match, but with this difference: every particle around that central emptiness is vibrating. Like a didj that's just been played.

1915

War manifests in the game. Always has. The 1915 season began the day before the Gallipoli landing, although news about that bloody slaughter didn't reach Melbourne for several weeks. Initially, it had been thought the war would be over in a week and numerous gleeful metaphors were spun from sporting parlance to describe the war and attract young men to its service.Typical of the patriotic fervour of the day was St Kilda's decision to change its colours from the red, white and black used on German military insignia to red, yellow and black, the colours of the Belgian flag. War was 'the greater game', but ill feeling was soon being expressed by the president of the amateur football association that players from his ranks were 'answering the call' more readily than those from the professional or working class clubs. The early casualty lists caused people to sober up a little and by 1915 there were voices in the press saying that with young men away fighting for 'the great cause' it was improper to be playing football, and eventually a vote was taken among the clubs about discontinuing the season. Resistance to the motion was led by the working class inner-city clubs—Collingwood, Carlton, Richmond and Fitzroy. The following year, they would be the only teams in the competition but in 1915 the season was played out as normal, the grand final being between Collingwood and Carlton.

Collingwood's ruck division that year was led by Paddy Rowan and Doc Seddon. Paddy, the taller of the pair, took the tap at the centre bounces and boundary throw-ins; Doc cleared the space for him to operate in. A cartoon of Seddon after the war shows him sharpening his elbows before a match. This can be taken to mean that he wasn't frightened of employing them in collisions with opponents' heads. Rowan's real name was Percy Rowe but he fought as a boxer as Paddy Rowan so his mother wouldn't find out, then took the name with him to Collingwood when he joined the Pies in 1911 because he was still bound to the South Bendigo club. Later, during his short time in the army, Rowan fought for and won his battalion title, leaving his opponent with what he would describe in a letter home from Egypt as 'a sore I suppose' (rhyming slang for nose). Rowan subsequently fought a twenty-rounder representing the battalion, and finished up in hospital. But he won. Winning was what Collingwood was about.

Rowan and Seddon worked together and played cricket together. Midway through 1915, they also enlisted together. Seddon had previously introduced Rowan to Louisa Newby, a young woman from Liverpool Street, Collingwood, whom Seddon had known since childhood. In 1915, Rowan and Louisa were married with Seddon as best man and, by the time the First AIF boys went overseas, Louisa was pregnant. Before then, however, there was a grand final to be played against an old foe, Carlton.

On the morning of the grand final, the Collingwood secretary, E.W. Copeland, motored out to the army training camp at Broadmeadows to collect Rowan and Seddon. He arrived to find his two players had been ordered on a twelve-mile route march that morning by an officer, reputed in Collingwood folklore to have been a Carlton supporter. Of such stories was the Collingwood legend made. Having risen from Melbourne's worst slum, Collingwood Football Club represented people who believed the world cheated them at every turn. The football field was a place they could get even and their emotion, even when they won, was not always a pretty sight. Little Smith of Collingwood, one of the characters in C.J. Dennis's phenomonally successful colloquial verse accounts of Gallipoli, has fags stuck in his hat and a string of dirty insults on his tongue. It goes without saying he's a Collingwood supporter.

In 1915, the Magpies also had one of the glamour players of the era, full-forward Dick Lee. It is no exaggeration to say Dick Lee flew through the skies of Melbourne before aeroplanes did. A photo of one of his high marks has him appearing like a kid reaching from a branch at the top of a tree. One of the players spilling free from the trunk of bodies beneath him is Doc Seddon.

The grand final was played before 39,000 people. Down at half-time, Collingwood made its move in the third term with Rowan and Seddon putting in a desperate effort and lifting in the ruck. I have seen a photo of Big Paddy Rowan contesting a boundary throw-in during that match. In fact, he's not that big, probably not much above average height nowadays. He's either got there late or been out-jumped because his Carlton opponent is above him, but every sinew in Paddy's body is stretched as taut as wire as he seeks to extract maximum effort from his failing body. The fierce light in his eyes that seeks to take him beyond the darkness of defeat is what is known as the Collingwood spirit.

Early in the last quarter, a Dick Lee goal put the Magpies' nose in front for the first time in the match, but then a free kick—as always, in Colling-wood's eyes, an unfair free kick, but one which the press also expressed doubts about—gave Carlton the goal that steadied their ship. That was the end of it, really, the Blues cruising home by four goals. One of the pressmen gracelessly noted in his report of the game that Seddon and Rowan had 'slowed down' since enlisting.

Paddy Rowan was killed in France the following year. The 27-year-old plumber never saw his son. Doc Seddon came home and married his widow. If you'd asked Paddy and Doc to describe their relationship, they would no doubt have said 'best mates', two words that went as deep as any in the culture. Beyond that, nothing would have been said. It would be expressed in action or not at all. This was the culture of old Australia and something I understood from an early age.

I became acquainted with the story of Paddy Rowan and Doc Seddon in the lead-up to the 2000 Anzac Day blockbuster at the MCG when Essendon was, as usual, playing Collingwood. In 1915, Essendon had been one of the clubs that had voted to disband the competition.

They were a lower middle class club with a conscious air of Protestant respectability. Playing for them that season, mostly in the back pocket, was a 22-year-old Scotch College old boy named Fred McIntosh. His father had been killed when he was thrown from a horse near Omeo in north-eastern Victoria. His mother remarried then died, leaving him to be raised by his stepfather, a minister in the Presbyterian church, who sent him to Scotch. Having played two seasons for the University club before its closure in 1914, McIntosh now represented Essendon as an amateur.

At the time of the 2000 Anzac Day game, a sports historian named David Allen was operating from one of the MCG's many nooks and crannies, a crowded Nissen hut at the back of the Olympic Stand. Allen, a large bespectacled man with a vaguely professorial air, had spent years researching the stories of footballers killed in war. He told me working class players like Paddy Rowan were a lot easier to track than upper class footballers like Fred McIntosh because the latter were shrouded in 'the mythology of the day'. McIntosh became a lieutenant in the 59th Battalion and saw some of the worst fighting on the Western Front. He died two days after being wounded at Polygon Wood in Belgium in September 1916; the story is that he stood above the trenches to lead a charge and was hit by his own artillery.The only known photograph of him is a cameo that subsequently appeared in a Scotch College magazine, along with a number of other old boys, all officers, who had been killed. Above the portraits a short verse says they died like kings fighting treacherous hate; it is titled 'Pro Patria'. The great poet of World War I, Wilfred Owen, described the Latin maxim 'Dulce et Decorum Est Pro Patria Mori' ('It is Sweet and Seemly to Die for One's Country') as 'the old lie'. Wilfred Owen was twenty-four when he was killed; so was Fred McIntosh.

At the time I was researching my story on McIntosh and Rowan, a Melbourne artist named Eamonn Scott held an exhibition of graphite drawings titled 'Wasteland' at the Counihan Gallery in the old Brunswick Town Hall. One of them was of a football grandstand built in the aftermath of the 1914–18 war with the words 'Lest We Forget' sombrely inscribed on one arch. Instead of being surrounded by a neat fence and trees and pleasant green grass, the artist has placed the grandstand in the shell-pocked muddy expanse of a World War I battlefield. Relying on photographs from the archives of the Australasian College of Surgeons, Scott had also drawn portraits of returned soldiers with noses and jaws missing and, in one case, a large fragment of skull gone.This was a time before plastic surgery. They were like faces made from bits of plasticine crudely lumped together. Alf Baud, Carlton's winning captain in the 1915 grand final and the youngest in the history of the game, was hit by a fragment of exploding shell at Anzac Ridge in France and left with no vision on his left side and an inability to look downwards. That reminded me of another Wilfred Owen poem, 'Disabled', about a former footballer returning from World War I without his legs. 'Some cheered him home, but not as crowds cheer Goal.'

Carlton's second-best player in the 1915 grand final, wingman George Challis, came from the tiny town of Cleveland in central Tasmania. So does my father, and George Challis was one of the footy stories I grew up with. In Tasmania, he played for Launceston Club and was one of Tassie's best at the 1913 interstate carnival. On his last leave, he came home and visited Cleveland's tiny school. Uncles and aunts of mine were among the twenty or so children in the room. He told the boys he'd return after the war and give them some pointers on the game, but he never did.A lot of the Cleveland footy stories I grew up with were about the difficulty of getting a team together in the years after World War I; George Challis was one of a generation who didn't return from the War to End All Wars.

Cleveland has only one church, the size of a chapel. A local landowner built it which meant it was Protestant, but Dad had been taken there as a kid for a slide night by his mother who was determinedly open-minded on matters of religion, having had an Irish Catholic mother and an English nonconformist father. The cemetery in the Cleveland churchyard has maybe a dozen gravestones—the biggest, among the first as you enter on the left, is for George Challis, killed in action in France. David Allen showed me the following mention of Challis's death which he had found in the diary of a lieutenant with the 60th Battalion: '16 July. First real glimpse of war. Much impressed with gruesome sights. Aerial torpedoes. Men on fatigue in communication trench while stretchers went past. Various expressions on their faces. Capt Mair and Sgt Challis blown to bits.' Learning there was nothing beneath the gravestone bearing George Challis's name in the Cleveland cemetery was like feeling the aftershock of a long distant explosion.

Each year now, I dread Anzac Day with its muddle of meanings. The Anzac myth was vigorously manipulated from the start, the most obvious example of this being the story of Simpson and the donkey. The Simpson I was told about at school in the 1960s bore little resemblance to John Simpson Fitzpatrick, the big Geordie who worked with donkeys as a kid and knew a disaster when he saw one, having grown up on the edge of the Newcastle coalfields. Over 1200 coal miners perished underground each year in England before World War I. Among miners it was understood that, if trapped underground, a man might whistle and make jokes but he didn't spread his fear. Simpson whistled, made jokes and didn't show his fear as he went about collecting the wounded at Gallipoli, loading them on his donkeys and carting them back to the beach. The Allied commanders had budgeted for 3000 casualties for the whole campaign. There were 2000 among the Australians and New Zealanders on the first day. From my reading, the opening scenes of the film *Saving Private Ryan* give some sense of the onslaught our soldiers faced landing at Anzac Cove.

Conventional battlefields have a front, a support zone and a rear.At Gallipoli, there was only a front. That meant no latrines, unburied dead, flies, stench, and medical stations under constant threat of enemy fire.The injuries from machine guns fired over ranges as short as ten or fifteen metres were fearful. On the first day, Simpson worked alone, reportedly carrying men on his shoulders.Then, on the second morning, he spied a donkey in the cove and had the idea that posthumously made him famous. It was said he had a charmed life, lasting as long as he did. He lasted twenty-four days.

Six months after he was killed, an article in the *Sun*

newspaper described the man with the donkey as a 'six foot Australian' with 'a woman's hands'. John Simpson Fitzpatrick, who had joined up under his middle name to avoid arrest, having jumped ship to enlist, was five foot eight and a half inches and had hands like the coal stoker he had been. He also spoke in the Geordie dialect. Seeing the donkey for the first time, Simpson of the Anzac legend was said to have remarked in good British Australian: 'I'll take this chap with me next trip.'

Simpson's first biographer, the Reverend Irving Benson, was an admirer of Liberal Prime Minister Sir Robert Menzies, a devout believer in empire and a collector of Winston Churchill's writings. Benson's biography, which was published in the sixties, cut out most of John Simpson Fitzpatrick's rude parts and all of his politics. In letters home to his mother and younger sister, Fitzpatrick called Australia the workingman's paradise, belittled the House of Lords and praised our arbitration system. The Reverend Benson's Simpson embodied the British heroic virtues of duty, sacrifice and restraint. John Simpson Fitzpatrick carried a possum in his jacket, didn't mind a fight and drank more than his share of beer. Once, en route to the Middle East when the beer ration was being served, a cry came from the upper deck that the German battleship *Emden* had been sighted on the horizon. Men scampered to get their first sight of the enemy. Simpson stayed below, emptying every available glass.

Paddy Rowan would have recognised Simpson at a glance. So would have George Challis. These are the sort of young men who died in their thousands at Gallipoli, invading a country with whom we had no difference beyond the alignments of empire.

The Bloodbath

World War II ended six weeks before the 1945 grand final was played. In Melbourne, people celebrated by dancing deliriously in the streets, office workers tearing up the papers on their desks and flinging them from windows, showering the city in homemade confetti. There was mass exhilaration yet at the same time a terrible new consciousness was being born: a weapon had been invented that could eliminate humanity, the war in the Pacific having been ended by the dropping of atom bombs on two Japanese cities. Street interviews conducted by newspapers showed people were already thinking about the bomb's implications. Some said Japan should be flattened, others that atomic energy would prove a great boon to industry, but everyone was adamant control of the bomb had to remain with the United States and Britain.

It was not a settled time.The White Horse in the outer Melbourne suburb of Bulleen had stripes painted on it to look like a zebra, the word 'Peace' written on its hide, the word 'Atom' at its base. Already, with men yet to come home from the war that had just been fought, there was concern about a new enemy, communism, and the name B.A. Santamaria was appearing in print. There was an upsurge in vandalism. On Victory in the Pacific Day, some of the shop owners in the city boarded over their fronts, fearful of the mood the celebrations would take. The *Age* reporter who covered the event wrote: 'It was a celebration of strange, confusing, violent, emotional import that will long be remembered. Nothing like it in sheer exultation had ever been seen in Melbourne before. It was a social eruption that may—we hope and pray—never again be witnessed. It was tempest after storm.' Six weeks later, the most violent grand final in the history of Australian football was played.

Remembered simply as the Bloodbath, the game was played between Carlton and South Melbourne and it was the death of Jack 'Basher'Williams, one of the South names associated with the match, that alerted me to the fact that if I didn't find out soon what happened on that day it would be too late. In the event, when I started looking in 1999, I found only four South players still alive. One of them, Don Grossman, told me it had been a bastard of a day, wind gusting from the north-west, rain from halftime. As the MCG was being used as a base for military personnel, the game was played at Carlton's old home ground, Princes Park.The crowd began arriving at seven am. At 2.45, when they finally closed the gates, the 63,000 spectators were so crammed many were unable to move arms or feet. South's Jack Dempsey spent the morning of the game working as a clerk in the shunting yards at Spencer Street station. When knock-off time came, he went for a steak at the cafe round the corner then caught a tram to Elizabeth Street and a second tram along King Street to Sydney Road, arriving at the ground an hour or so before the match. He couldn't believe the number of people, the strange excitement.

The Carlton supporters stood where they always stood, behind the goal at the Sydney Road end. Richmond captain-coach Jack Dyer, one of the legends of the era, said Carlton supporters were even more fanatical than Collingwood's.The South supporters, not nearly so numerous, were on the northern wing. International visitors from Britain and the United States had also come to see what was billed as the 'Victory' grand final. The rest of the crowd were recently returned soldiers. The stage was set.

Football had changed during the war. Match payments had been halved and the closure of the MCG meant the game went back to the suburban venues and the fierce parochial loyalties from whence it had come. Rule changes at the end of the 1930s, particularly to do with dropping the ball, also played a part. Suddenly, the game sped up. Simultaneously, there was a radical reinterpretation—or corruption—of the rule permitting a player to bump an opponent within five yards of the ball. Intended to cover the situation where players were running side by side, it was suddenly used to condone running at players from the opposite direction and collecting them, at speed, head-on. Don Grossman said the word 'shirtfront' wasn't heard in Australian football before the 1940s. My father, when I asked him, thought this was correct.

Thus, while a war was being fought away from home, the local game acquired a new and potentially dangerous dimension, one that could break bones and knock men unconscious. In popular memory, the player most associated with this innovation is Richmond's Jack 'Captain Blood' Dyer, but among its other principal exponents was Carlton's Bob Chitty. If Chitty is not as well-known as Dyer now, he certainly was back then. One difference between the pair was that Chitty was only five feet eight inches in height. He mostly played on the half-back flank but had played full-back, outmarking Collingwood's high-flying forward, Ron Todd. Along with E.J. 'Ted' Whitten, who attended the 1945 grand final as a 12 year old and declared it was the best game he ever saw, it was said Chitty could have won a Brownlow Medal had he played by the rules. Instead, like Whitten, he played by his own rules, on and off the field, and, again like Whitten, he was popular with team-mates and a natural leader.

Of the seven members of the Carlton team that I tracked down, a number were quick to mount the traditional defence for players of Chitty's ilk: he copped plenty back, don't worry about that, and he never complained. Part of the legend of the Bloodbath is that Chitty lost the top of one finger in an industrial accident during grand final week and played regardless. The accident actually occurred three weeks earlier, before Carlton played North Melbourne in the first semi-final, but the rest of the story is true: he played regardless, at half-time abandoning a protective metal guard made for his finger because it was interfering with his ballhandling. One of thirteen kids, Chitty was quick and physically powerful; he trained as he played which meant team-mates had to be wary of him on the training track.

These were the days when there was only one field umpire and no video surveillance; every team had a 'protector'. South's was centre half-back Jack 'Basher' Williams. 'No friend of Jack Williams ever called him Basher,'Don Grossman said to me. Grossman claimed the name was an insult flung over the fence by Collingwood supporters, but in later life Williams cheerfully ascribed it to some paper boys in South Melbourne. Williams' life illustrates the fact that this was a generation of men who had grown up during the Great Depression, many of them having known hunger. One story has Basher Williams working in a mine near Maryborough at the age of thirteen and coming to Melbourne in his late teens to be a pro fighter. More than once I have been told that Depression footy, when men played for the the family income, thirty shillings a win, ten a loss, was the toughest footy of all.

Many of the players in the 1945 grand final had fought in the ring. The police and the fire brigade had their own titles, while during the war years there had been regular bouts between different battalions and branches of the armed services. Basher Williams had standards—to the end of his life, he would physically enforce his rule of no swearing in front of ladies (the one charge he would plead not guilty to after the Bloodbath was obscene language)—but, like Chitty, he trained as he played, and any team-mate who humiliated him in a practice match could expect to be harshly dealt with. In the context of the 1945 grand final, another material fact about Basher is that he had money on the outcome, having wagered his match payments for the season with the Carlton president, J.G. Luke. In the aftermath of the match, the large amount of money wagered by supporters on both sides would give rise to wild rumours about the result.

South were a team with a reputation. They had been the glamour side of the 1930s and South's two big names in the 1945 grand final—centreman Herbie Matthews and full-forward Laurie Nash—had played in that era. Matthews, South's captain, had tied for the 1940 Brownlow Medal with Collingwood's Des Fothergill and won five club best and fairests. Like all sides with a reputation for style and flair, however, there was a countering belief that South didn't like what is euphemistically known as physical pressure. The previous year, Matthews' leg had been broken in a match against Carlton at the Junction Oval; blame for the incident had fallen on Carlton ruckman Ron Savage. In the same game, Chitty had knocked out a South player and a dozen supporters jumped the fence. After the game, a police escort had been necessary to get Savage past the mob of angry South supporters to the St Kilda railway station. In the opinion of Grossman, Matthews was never the same player again.

This was to be both Matthews' and Nash's last match. Laurie Nash has a far greater claim to sporting memory than his part in the Bloodbath. He was the young man who said he could do anything on the sports field—and did. In Basher Williams' words, he was a truthful skite. He would invite his opponent to nominate which foot he should use when kicking for goal. In his prime, Nash could, and did, play centre half-back against the wind and centre half-forward with it. He also played two Test matches for Australia as a fast bowler and, in the opinion of himself as well as others, would have played a lot more had he been given a fair go. Having volunteered to bowl Bodyline back at the Englishmen in 1932–33, Nash found himself used as a pawn in the backroom manoeuvering whereby the tactic was eliminated from the game.

But in 1945, Nash was no longer the young man who had held the sporting world in awe in the 1930s. He was thirty-six, having been enticed back to South Melbourne for one last year after an absence of seven years from league football. Never a big man (five feet nine inches), he now tipped the scales at fourteen stone three (eighty-nine kilograms). When I briefly met him in Launceston in the early 1980s and asked him about the Bloodbath, he dismissed the day with a shrug saying he was 'old and fat by then'. When I put this to Billy Williams, South's rover in 1945, he said,'Yeah—old and fat and good.' Playing full-forward, relying on skill and anticipation, Nash still kicked more than fifty goals to be South's leading scorer for the season.

With the exception of Chitty, the Carlton team of 1945 had no big names. The club best and fairest would eventually be won by Ron Savage, a 25-year-old ruckman with Nordic good looks and an enigmatic personality. One aspect of wartime football was the availability of players who were in the armed forces. It was not unknown for players to be dispatched to northern Australia by well-placed supporters of other clubs, hence the absence of South full-forward Bob Pratt, who unexpectedly found himself sent to Darwin. Equally, servicemen transferred into south-eastern Australia could be recruited by Victorian teams. Carlton proved highly adept at this aspect of the game. Having lost three of its first four games—around which time the decision was made to play the grand final at

Carlton, since the Blues seemed to have no prospect of being involved—they built a team that won six games in a row to make the finals in fourth spot. By grand final day, Carlton had won twelve of their last thirteen matches. Nevertheless, with sixteen wins and four losses, South finished top of the ladder.

As violent as the Bloodbath proved to be, the preliminary final the previous week between Carlton and Collingwood was said to have been more violent—at least by the Carlton players. Collingwood had taken a player called Len Hustler, listed in *The Encyclopedia of AFL Footballers* as 'a vigorous ruckman', into the game and planted him in the forward pocket. Jim Clark says Hustler 'antagonised' the young Carlton defence, enabling Collingwood to build a lead. Meanwhile, Des Fothergill, Collingwood's most talented player and leading goalscorer, was shirtfronted by Chitty. The press reports describe the tactic as 'crashing' or 'deliberately attacking an opponent'. It happened twice, once after Fothergill had taken a mark and had his eyes on the ball. At a time when there was virtually no coverage of injuries, it was reported on the Wednesday after the match that Fothergill had four cracked teeth, several chipped teeth and six others badly jarred, and that he would be off work for two weeks.

The Magpies were five goals up midway through the final term when the Carlton full-back, an intensely introverted young man named Vinnie Brown, was dropped behind play. Len Hustler was deemed the culprit by Brown's team-mates. What followed was described by one journalist as 'a fierce melee in which boots and fists were used with abandon', but—significantly for later events—there was only one report. Carlton wingman Freddie Fitzgibbon, undersized but highly spirited, ran half the length of the ground and launched himself over the milling throng to land a right on Hustler's jaw. Although Fitzgibbon received a three week suspension for the act, half-back flanker Jim Clark believes it revived Carlton's spirit. The Blues kicked seven goals in ten minutes to win by ten points. After the game, various commentators expressed concern that the game had reached a point where the best and fairest players were being routinely eliminated by brutal tactics. Much was also made of the fact that only one report had come from the preliminary final. For the grand final, a new umpire, Frank Spokes, was appointed.

South was coached by a Tasmanian, Bull Adams, who had critics among his senior players. Carlton, on the other hand, were united behind Perc Bentley. 'Being part of Perc Bentley's team was like being part of a family,' Jim Clark told me. In 1945, Clark was a 20-year-old back flanker.'When we won, he'd stand at the top of the race with a smile on his face. When we lost, we'd walk past him and say, "Sorry, Perc." ' In the Bloodbath, Clark wore number 26, the guernsey previously belonging to Jim Park, a Carlton player who had been killed in the war in the Pacific two years earlier. Both clubs had players killed in action. Perc Bentley let his players listen to the running of the AJC Derby on a wireless in the rooms before the game. In the South rooms, beneath what is now the Heroes stand, Bull Adams told his players to expect trouble but warned them not to get taken in.

Carlton kicked with the wind in the first quarter of the 1945 grand final. South held them to two goals and at quarter time Basher Williams was heard to say, 'We've got them.'The South captain, Herbie Matthews, told him to keep his mind on his opponent, Carlton's 18-year-old centre half-forward Ken Hands. With the wind at their backs, it was South's moment to take hold of the match.The South team contained two talented teenagers, 18-year-old rover Billy Williams and 17-year-old centre half-forward Ron Clegg. Between them, they would win South's next six best and fairests. Clegg would also win a Brownlow Medal. In the second quarter, Chitty collected both, knocking them senseless. Williams he hit with an elbow to the head, putting him into the picket fence. As the teams had only nineteen men and both sides had replaced injured players in the first term, there were no reserves. The two youths played on.

At the other end of the ground, Ken Hands made one goal and kicked another. He was then observed lying on the ground unconscious with Basher Williams, hands on hips, beside him. Carlton players ran to where Hands lay, and for the first of four times, umpire Spokes stopped the game to restore order. At this point, memories of the match diverge. South say the Bloodbath started when Williams and Clegg, their two youngest players, were felled and question whether Chitty was acting with Perc Bentley's foreknowledge. Carlton say the Bloodbath began with Williams dropping Hands. Hands, too, played on, although the Carlton club doctor later testified that he was 'quite stupid' at half-time.

What pressmen agreed on was that the felling of the two young players, particularly Clegg, caused South to lose their way. Their captain, Herbie Mathews, was reported for the highly undisciplined act of throwing the ball away after a free kick was given against him. South wingman Des Whitfield, a more erratic character, was reported for kicking the ball away after a free kick was given against him. Basher Williams was reported twice, once for 'adopting a fighting attitude' towards Carlton ruckman Rod McLean, also a hard man of renown. McLean declined the invitation, which Jim Clark said was seen by his team-mates as a victory—their discipline was holding. Basher was reported a second time for abusing the umpire leaving the ground during the half-time break as the Carlton fans howled at him over the incident with Hands. On the scoreboard, South trailed by only two points but, afterwards, pressmen would write that the 1945 grand final was over by half-time.

A lot of those who were in the Bloodbath insist good football was also played on the day.The Movietone clip, one minute in length, doesn't show a single punch. Most of the players have long sleeves, the ball is moved forward with sweet precision using drop kicks and stab passes. In the ruck, Carlton's youthful quartet and the wind combined to negate the skilful Jack Graham. South's other perceived advantage, across the centreline, was reduced by centreman Clinton Wines' fine performance and the Blues' tactic of going long from half-back to half-forward. Even so, South's centre-line of King, Matthews and Whitfield got enough of the ball to create attacks, but they fell down at centre half-forward, where Clegg was groggy, and at full-forward, where Nash was humiliated.

Nash was the man who routinely replied when asked the greatest player he had seen, 'I look at him every morning in the mirror when I shave.' At a function in the city for the two teams during grand final week, Nash had told some of the younger Carlton players like Clark and Hands to watch out for themselves on Saturday. It was interpreted as a threat, but was probably gamesmanship. Nash was all but gone and must have known it. He had arthritis in both knees and a leather guard over a broken bone in his hand. He had little or no speed left. His opponent, Carlton full-back Vinnie Brown, would run in the final of the 1946 Stawell Gift. Nash was one of those sportsmen who see no reason to deny their talent. His brazen confidence had been a source of joy to South for a decade, but in this, his final match, Percy Beames, the *Age* correspondent, pronounced him 'the weakest link' in South's side. Reduced to gathering the scraps that fell his way, Nash managed to score two of South's ten goals.

Sport is seldom kind to old champions in decline. A lot of money had been bet on the game and one Carlton story is that South initiated the violence because of the sums wagered on the game by their supporters. The South story was that a member or members of their team had been 'got at' by Carlton supporters with money on the result. Given his importance to their side, Nash's performance was one of those to come in for withering scrutiny. Perhaps the real story of the two teams was summed up by Herb Coates from the *Truth* after their one previous meeting for the year which Carlton won by a goal. South struck him as a team 'in a lag', with experienced but slow players combined with juniors who weren't yet quite good enough. Carlton, on the other hand, was 'a fine young team with a wonderful future'.

In the event, Nash's final appearance in league football would be memorable for another reason. In the last quarter, he ran to mark a ball in South's forward pocket. It was precisely the opportunity Chitty had taken the previous week to shirtfront Fothergill and now, with Nash in his sights, he began one of his low, lethal charges. Nash's legs might have gone but his reflexes hadn't; with the special awareness that is the province of great players, he saw Chitty coming. Some accounts have him forgetting the ball altogether, others say he took the mark. Whatever, employing a short chopping blow to the temple taught to soldiers for use in unarmed combat, Nash knocked Chitty out.

Few in the Carlton ground had ever seen Chitty fall. Trainers rushed and raised him to his feet. He motioned them away, then fell again. Carlton coach Perc Bentley transferred his swaying form from defence to a half-forward flank where, minutes later, he positioned himself in front of a pack, won a free kick and goaled. 'I can still see him,' Jim Clark said.'The rain spitting down, him wiping his boot on the back of his left sock.'The roar that met his goal was the loudest of the day and made the air blur. Among the players from the Carlton 1945 side still alive, Chitty's goal was their most common memory of the game, although some of them located it in different quarters. It was the symbolic moment of victory.

What follows reads like farce. South's Des Whitfield was reported for attempting to strike goal umpire L. Whyte. When Whyte moved to take his number, Whitfield pulled his jumper up over his head and ran up the field with the goal umpire in hot pursuit. With ten minutes to go, an interaction between

Don Grossman and Carlton rover Jim Mooring saw Mooring go to the ground. Fifty-five years later, Grossman was still insisting that he had been attempting to shepherd and that Carlton ruckman Ron Savage then jumped into him from behind, throwing a roundhouse right. Players ran in and a brawl ensued.'There were some pretty handy fellas among them,' Jim Clark recalled in his laconic way, 'and they were really throwing them.' He was watching from the opposite end of the ground. When his opponent made to move towards the fray, Clark touched his arm and said,'Don't you think it's a bit quieter down here?'

At the climax of the brawl, a small figure in an overcoat was seen to launch himself from the Carlton bench, run across the ground and enter the fray. It was Freddie Fitzgibbon, suspended for having made a similar run the previous week and striking Collingwood's Len Hustler. 'Freddie got another four,' Jim Clark told me drily, 'but the spirit was appreciated.'The final siren found Carlton ahead by twenty-eight points. Leaving the ground, agroggy Chitty asked Clinton Wines, 'Is it over? Did we win?'

It took the umpires until 6.30 to finish their reports which eventually ran to nine players, not including Freddie Fitzgibbon, and fifteen charges. The tribunal was held in Australia House on the following Tuesday night, also the evening of the South Melbourne Football Club ball. Whitfield declared that as he had already bought his ticket to the ball, he wouldn't bother going to the tribunal. In his absence, he was suspended for a season. Up on four charges, Basher Williams pleaded not guilty to only one—obscene language—and received thirteen weeks.

While the tribunal deliberated, the Carlton players were kept in one room, the South players in another. Nevertheless, Basher Williams strode into the Carlton room and invited Chitty outside 'to finish it'. Chitty said nothing. If a film is ever made of the Bloodbath, this is the key moment for the actor playing Chitty. Does he smile, ever so lightly? It seems to me that one of the two 'protectors' in the 1945 grand final used violence a lot more effectively than the other. More strategically, if you like.

On grand final night, in the Carlton clubrooms, Jim Clark had said to Chitty,'You copped one, Bob.' 'Yeah,' Chitty replied in his husky voice, 'but we won.' Chitty got eight weeks for elbowing Billy Williams; the same penalty was awarded to Grossman, Ron Savage and Gentleman Jim Cleary, the South full-back, who later remarked he'd been suspended for defending himself.

From a distance of more than fifty years, what is most remarkable about the Bloodbath is the lack of comment it aroused at the time. On grand final day, the *Age* ran a single story of ten lines on the game with the headline 'Big Crowd Likely'. The newspaper didn't deign to cover the tribunal hearing, preferring to give space to events such as the lecture by the headmaster of Wesley College on the topic that Australia was a nation of philistines, which he defined to mean addicted to the second-rate. His first item of evidence in support of this proposition was the Australian accent which he described not as a dialect but a corruption. Australia was still a class society in 1945, but the game somehow existed outside that. The violence of the 1945 grand final did not elicit a single editorial and the only letter to a newspaper I found was in the *Sun News Pictorial* four days after the event, a brief six-liner signed 'One of the Dads' saying what an inglorious exhibition the 'Victory' grand final had been.

Instead, the papers were dominated by world figures like Stalin and Churchill and, each day, there were fresh reports of Japanese atrocities and lists of prisoners of war found alive in places like Thailand and Japan. In the sports pages, the Saturday after the Bloodbath, it was reported that Jim Baird had been included in the Carlton cricket team for the opening round of the Victorian Cricket Association season. No mention was made of the fact he'd played football for Carlton the previous week. And that's what they said, these old footballers, when I tracked them down and asked them if much was said about the Bloodbath afterwards, if the players sat around and discussed it among themselves. No, they said, no, it was just another game of footy.

So what was the connection between the Bloodbath and the war? Initially, I had assumed that the players were returned soldiers giving vent to their horror. In fact, perhaps as few as two, South's Laurie Nash and Carlton's Clinton Wines, had seen action.

Nash I met in Launceston in the early 1980s. In twenty minutes in his company, I sensed a man who would happily tell the world of his sporting exploits in a blustery spirit of humour, but beneath that was another much more private being. He had been in New Guinea with the 2/2 Pioneers, having foregone the opportunity offered to other leading sportsmen like Don Bradman to spend the war in a physical training unit. Nash, who boasted so outrageously about games, was remarkably reticent and modest about his war experiences. Perhaps he knew war wasn't a game.

The other player in the game who had certainly been to war was Carlton centreman Clinton Wines; he'd been at the battle of El Alamein. In later life he became a teacher of history and geography. Asked about the connection between the war and the match, he replied shortly, 'There isn't one. In football, you have to protect your body. In war, you have to protect your life. War is a far grimmer business.' He meant there was no comparison between playing in a football match and fighting in a battle.

Wines was the one Carlton player I spoke to who didn't seem fond of Chitty. Basically, he said, Chitty 'either beat you or he belted you'. Wines saw the Bloodbath as being a particularly violent game, but what had made for the violence? Was it the unsettled mood of the time? And what did it mean that young men who hadn't been to war played a game seen as a measure of their masculinity before a huge crowd that included young men who had? Was the crowd involved in what occurred? I asked Wines. 'The crowd is always involved,' he replied with classical precision.

In terms of those who played in the 1945 grand final, genial Jim Clark was a lot closer than Clinton Wines to the norm. He'd tried to join the army on three occasions, once even forging his mother's name on a form, but had been knocked back each time. As an apprentice fitter and turner at the Newport railyards, he was a worker in a required industry. What Clark treasured from the 1945 grand final was a remark made by one of the many returned soldiers who was at the game.The soldier told Clark it brought tears to his eyes, watching that match, seeing the spirit of Australians at war.

Peter Schwab

On Saturday evening, 15 September 2001, Hawthorn played Port Adelaide in an elimination final in Adelaide. An American brother-in-law of one of the Hawthorn players, Daniel Chick, had died in the World Trade Center attack four days earlier. The Hawks had made erratic progress towards the finals, their form all over the place. Port Adelaide, on the other hand, were the measure of consistency, a team which played to the same level and in much the same way, week in and week out. Writing in the paper, however, I sided with the Hawks. I did so because I thought their coach, Peter Schwab, would be able to better explain the significance of the game in light of the world event.

I first met Peter Schwab, known to all as Schwabbie, in 1986 through his Hawthorn team-mate Rodney 'Rocket' Eade at a function at Waverley Park after a match in which the Hawks had defeated premiership rivals Carlton by a point. Rocket had seen me across the bar and shouted, 'There's a bloke over here who likes your sportswriting.' I knew Rocket from the Tasmanian

University Football Club where his old man, Brian Eade, forged a series of wonderful amateur sides out of a generation of students otherwise seen as long-haired, dope-smoking radicals. I was not a member of those sides, but I did write the club newsletter and play in the Fourth XVIII under a poet coach named Peter Hay, two lines of whose appear as the epigraph at the start of this book.

The night we met, Schwabbie was standing by the bar in a jovial mood; he may even have been drinking. It had been the last meeting of the year's two contenders and the Hawks believed their victory, however minimal the margin, gave them the edge going into the finals. Almost immediately, we were sharing our appreciation of former ABC sportscaster Doug Heywood, which in Schwabbie's case meant doing an impersonation of Heywood's wonderful throaty voice breathing his fervent appreciation of the game's great performers. The conversation turned to sportswriting. His favourite book was Arthur Hopcraft's *The Football Man*.

He quoted parts of a passage Hopcraft had written about Duncan Edwards, Manchester United's 21-year-old centre-forward who was killed in the Munich air disaster in 1958. It said: 'Edwards represented the kind of self-respecting modesty which is not nurtured in the ferocity of the modern game. He represented thousands in their wish for courage, acclaim and talent, and he had all three without swagger. The hero is the creature other people would like to be . . . Edwards was such a man, and he enabled people to respect themselves more.'You know a lot about a man once he confides in you his heroes.

In 1989, Peter came to work for the *Age* and was

seated beside a woman writing for 'Accent', the women's page. Feminism in the late eighties still had a lot of journalistic clout and the women who ran 'Accent' were committed people. After Schwabbie had been at the newspaper about six months, his office neighbour met me in the corridor. 'He's not your stereotypical footballer, is he?' she said.Well, of course, none of them are stereotypical footballers, but perhaps he was more different than most. That year, he missed the grand final through suspension after he crashed late into the back of an Essendon player taking a mark during the second semi-final. The tribunal suspended him for three weeks and suddenly I saw the difference between being one of the crowd and being out there, in that green space with the white line around it where everything is intensified come the finals.

I'd been out there once myself. Three years earlier, Geoff Slattery, a great sportswriter and total maverick, had deemed it necessary for my education to push me into the train of Hawthorn officials as they accompanied Allan Jeans on his way from the coach's box to the boundary line to claim victory with five minutes of the 1986 grand final to go. As a result, I saw and felt and heard the game from inside the fence. The match was over as a contest but what seemed like an electric sheet of sound and light still accompanied the ball wherever it went. It was a hyper reality. Schwabbie and I met for the second time after that game. As Hawthorn came back into the rooms, he saw me and nodded. 'Martin, isn't it?' he said. Later, he wrote a piece for the *Age* saying that for ten minutes or so after you've won a grand final you feel your total self. There is nothing you want or wish for. Briefly, you are.

He was suspended on the Monday night before the 1989 grand final. On Tuesday, he came to work, we went for breakfast and I saw how upset he was. To provide him with some consolation, I gave him a copy of W.B.Yeats' poem 'An Irish Airman Foresees His Death'. To my mind, the poem says that each excitement ('the lonely impulse of delight' the pilot feels above the clouds) comes at a price, a price some of us are prepared to pay. As he was reading it, he was rung by a journo at the *Herald-Sun* anxious for the standard identikit story on the tragedy of the footballer who misses the grand final, accompanied by the photograph of the glum-looking player, child on either knee, with his wife on the couch, beneath a headline like: GRAND FINAL AGONY! 'What are you doing?,' asked the reporter. 'Reading W.B. Yeats' "An Irish Airman Foresees His Death",' said Schwabbie. He thought the reporter sounded surprised and noted that the fact did not subsequently appear in his story.

He wrote a piece about that year's grand final, about watching one of the great games, the sort that comes along once a decade if you're lucky, him knowing exactly how mighty it was and trying to be fair to those whose immense good fortune it was to play, but also knowing the scale of the opportunity that had passed him by, knowing it like a pain in his guts. I understood because, for me, being a player is like being a writer. In the end, I'm not a writer because anyone thinks I am particularly good at it. I'm a writer like some people are footballers and others are boxers, because it's my way and no other form of self-expression offers me nearly the same release. Schwabbie and I talked a lot about football and writing.

He wrote some good pieces for the *Age*. They were solitary in mood with a hint of poetry at their edges. One was about being hailed by an old Russian woman one afternoon when he was driving through St Kilda with his wife.They ran the old woman home who then invited them in. Gradually, it became apparent that no-one ever visited her and she was anxious they come again.The story ended with him leaving knowing he'd probably never return. Another was about returning to his old high school after it was closed. It was the sort of writing I'd like to see more of in newspapers, about the character of ordinary moments, and, usually, his companion in his stories was the warm, generous girl he met at high school and later married. Her name is Jenny. I didn't know it then but she's as brave as he is.

Over the years, we swapped books, records, movies. One of his favourite films is *On the Waterfront*. He does a good impersonation of Marlon Brando as the young boxer whose chance of a shot at a title has been spoilt by the mob, saying:'I coulda been a contender.'We watched footy games together and he taught me to look for little things. Good players, he said, don't go to ground. Watching the 1970 grand final, he hit the rewind button to show an incident where the great Alex Jesaulenko is over the ball, running, and is twice bumped at full speed by opponents. He rides both blows, not even breaking stride. Another time, he put on a video for my benefit and said, 'Look at this mark of Carey's.' The North Melbourne captain was heading backwards into a pack when his legs were taken from beneath him. He was doing a catherine-wheel backwards. 'Watch his eyes,' said Schwabbie. 'They never leave the ball.'

In his playing days, Schwabbie was a robust

half-back flanker, although he had played in the centre in the 1986 grand final. He was a tough player in a team that was both tough and skilful, but, to be frank, he wasn't the sort of player who caught my eye, which is ironic given that I have since benefited from seeing the game through his eyes. He was a polite and considerate man—my kids liked him because he always engaged with them—but he had limits. Once when I was at a game with him, a mouth in the crowd near us kept yelling 'Kill him, kill him' when a certain Essendon player went near the ball. He said it like he wanted the person hurt and wanted someone else to do it. In the end, Schwabbie turned and told him to shut up in a way that made it clear he meant it. Another match we watched together was the 1994 preliminary final between North Melbourne (now the Kangaroos) and Geelong. Carey was supreme that day. Bluey McGrath pursued him like a blue heeler, but he couldn't subdue him. Geelong coach Malcolm Blight left McGrath on Carey because he didn't have anyone else who'd do any better. Someone near us in the crowd was sledging Carey for the whole of the game. Again, the tone of what was being said was mean and nasty. Schwabbie told the sledger he was an idiot. 'Carey's a champion, mate. You're privileged to see him play.'

That was something else we shared: we both loved sport in a pure way, for its own sake, regardless of everything that went on around it. We also shared an interest in boxing which, it hardly needs to be said, is widely condemned for being violent. I'm not so sure about that. I've seen violence—it's unjust and unfair. That's what hurts most. And if you employ it on any large scale it's horribly random in who it hurts, which breeds a near irresistible logic that the only answer to violence is violence. In boxing, that force is controlled, regulated, made to confront its equal. I once met a teenager in a boxing gym in the western suburbs of Melbourne who had previously been in street fights with broken bottles and knives. I asked him what boxing had taught him. Respect, he replied.

It has always mattered to me what Schwabbie thought of my footy writing. His thinking about the game is so clear, so logical, but he likes sportswriting that goes beyond the obvious. He has a way of transferring belief, of making me feel like a writer who should be confident of his perceptions, which is is why I always thought he'd be good at coaching. Then, in 1997, his 7-year-old daughter Emily died of a brain tumor. I will always remember her, desperately ill, being asked how she felt.

'Fantastic,' she replied.That same visit she sat on my wife's knee like an injured butterfly, running her fingers over my wife's face, saying, 'You're so beautiful,' and all we could see was the beauty of this small child. I never learned more from Peter than I did through that time. He and his wife proceeded in the belief that, however awful the looming reality, each moment had to be lived for its own sake.

The Hawks defeated Port Adelaide in the 2001 second elimination final. I thought they might. Port had been conditioned by a long triumphantly successful history in South Australian football to take the field each week with a shield of psychic armour around them. If a doubt ever got inside, it could do an awful lot of damage. Port basically only had one way of playing the game. Hawthorn, on the other hand, sometimes looked to be making it up as they went along. I thought they were better equipped to find their way at a most unusual time to be playing a game. I also knew they had a coach who had thought deeply about the relationship between sport and issues of life and death, and believed in sport nonetheless.

Preliminary Final Week, 2001

The Thursday after the Hawks won in Adelaide, I went to watch them at training. I went because the shadow of *la nouvelle guerre* was growing and I wanted to get away from it for a while. I like going to training during the finals. Ever so briefly, for the follower of a successful team and those weird types like myself who follow no single team but the game itself, there is a simple moment of joy to be had. The shouting will begin again the following Saturday, or whenever the next final is played, but for the moment the angst is put on hold, the last victory is victory enough, and the world seems briefly like a place of promise. Nature helps, spring and autumn in Melbourne bringing days that are like still pools of golden light.

Glenferrie is the oddest of all the old grounds, red-brick grandstand of the plainest design behind one goal and trains passing so close to one narrow-hipped wing you can see the faces of the passengers. At the opposite end to the grandstand, a school of thin and wavy gums have broken through the narrow cement terraces where the less affluent supporters once stood.

However peculiar the ground, it is not without its legends, notably a conservative Catholic high school principal named John Kennedy who had no regard whatsoever for the aesthetics of the game and saw it simply as a test of the human spirit in which the strong prevailed and the weak perished. I was present at a post-match press conference when he quoted Karl Marx. That was in his later incarnation as coach of North Melbourne. The Krakouers, two Aboriginal brothers from Western Australia and among the smallest men on the field, had just sliced an opposition side apart. Kennedy was asked how he assessed their game.'Ah, well,' he replied. 'As Marx said, "From each according to his ability." '. Kennedy always looked mildly amused by the press, watching them with bright eyes from beneath a half-lowered head. My impression was that journalists never surprised him. I suspect he saw them as creatures who did their job by day and returned to purgatory each night. Kennedy ritually declined to be interviewed, but I did see him once remark that the Catholic faith became too easy after Vatican 2. His football philosophy is summed up by a famous address he made at half-time during one grand final.'At least do something,' he bellowed to his players. 'Don't think, don't hope. Do.'

How Kennedy had ever played the game was a mystery to me as he didn't appear to have the body for it. Tall and scrawny and pale, he looked like some large old bird that had been plucked, but he had played in the ruck for Hawthorn with ferocious spirit and a canny brain. He then returned to the club as coach. Hawthorn's colours in his day were dull yellow and mud brown, nothing to excite the eye or distract anyone from what the game was really about. The Hawthorn tradition as I understand it begins with him in the 1960s. When Allan Jeans arrived as coach in the eighties, he refined the style, deliberately cultivating skilful players while keeping the flame of Kennedy's belief alive. Jeans' great sides had a class lacking in Kennedy's teams, but were no less stoical.

Then, as happens, a generation of great players passed into retirement almost as one, and the Hawks had to start building all over again. As I understood it, at a time when the game was becoming more planned and pre-programmed, with more and more of the thinking being done by men in glass boxes and not the players on the ground, Schwabbie was trying to develop a side in which the players made the decisions themselves. His team had proved erratic, one observer describing them as 'a collection of unhinged athletes'. Others questioned their hardness at the ball, the principal virtue of the old Hawthorn teams, but now, having won two finals, the crowd was there at the training session, supporters old and new, unanimous in their applause. Hawthorn had targeted the Asian community as potential supporters, and there were quite a few Asian faces in the crowd. Sausages were being cooked, there was a lot of quiet but excited chatter. I stood among them, letting the current pass through me, causing the odd light to flicker.

After training finished, the players stood signing autographs. I particularly sought out Daniel Chick for a closer look. Chick was Hawthorn's hard man, although that term no longer meant what it did in the days of Chitty and Basher Williams. Chick wasn't that big but he had a way of bullocking to the centre of a pack, getting over the ball and either winning it or stopping anyone else from doing so. When he was in or near the game, his young team-mates seemed to steady. Chick's resolve was fundamental to the Hawks and he had played in Adelaide, despite the death of his brother-in-law in the World Trade Center. His performance had been subdued but the team had benefited from his presence. Chick was one of the last to finish signing autographs, then the players disappeared up the saggy wire race which protected the players from abusive supporters in the old days, passed through a battered set of dark brown doors and were gone. The session was over.

Walking away from the ground, I had one last look at the white gums standing like the ghosts of supporters past at the other end of the ground to the grandstand and headed for my daughter's car, which I had borrowed and left in a car park on the other side of Glenferrie Road. Passing through a small arcade, I saw a bookshop and, without thinking, went in. The world of books was another comforting place to be in the aftermath of September 11, connected as it was to other times, other minds. In my pocket, I had five dollars. What could I get for that? What I found, or perhaps what found me, was not so much a book as a pamphlet, sixty-odd pages containing four lectures and a sermon given by Martin Luther King in the last year of his life and titled *The Trumpet of Conscience*. I took it home and over a period of weeks, possibly a month, read it with great care, starting with 'A Christmas Sermon for Peace'. King described a time in which 'we have neither peace within nor peace without...everywhere we see the ominous possibilities of war'. That sounded familiar.

Later, when I mentioned what I was reading to Neil Murray, a friend with a reputation for plain speaking, he replied, 'Does it still stand up?' It was a good question. Did Martin Luther King still speak to our time? He quoted God a lot and spoke with revolutionary fervour. Did that make him a fanatic? No. A fanatic's vision always excludes part of humankind, invariably the greater part. King excluded no-one, but he made the necessary point that he didn't like everyone. He didn't like those who threatened to kill him 'day in and day out', who bombed people's homes, who oppressed others to sustain their economic advantage. He didn't like them, but he refused to be drawn into hating them.

What I admired about his writing was that he acknowledged the negative aspects of the reality he was addressing, even when they were disadvantageous to his cause. He also pre-dated New Age notions of cost-free spirituality. Among those then called hippies, he observed a remarkable contradiction and predicted correctly that as 'a mass group' they would not last long.'He [the hippie] uses drugs to turn inward, away from reality, to find peace and security.Yet he advocates love as the highest human value—love, which can exist only in communication between people, and not in the total isolation of the individual.' King also observed among the youth of his day what he called 'a growing alienation', a building awareness that ordinary people have no say in the important decisions of the day; this development, he said, was emptying the content of American democracy and contributing to a vulgarisation of American culture. In the decades since

King's death, American democracy has moved further towards plutocracy while Hollywood has pumped out ever more violent and wantonly reckless fantasies.

Basic to his view was the belief that peace, no less than war, has social causes.'The developed nations of the world cannot remain secure islands of prosperity in a seething sea of poverty. The storm is rising against the privileged minority of the earth, from which there is no shelter in isolation and armament.' He also said, 'If there is to be peace on earth . . . we must finally believe in the ultimate morality of the universe.'That was certainly a question for our time—did people believe in 'the ultimate morality of the universe' any more? Did they believe in God or did they merely believe in their own particular gods which they called God? In 1993, I interviewed Jonathan Sachs, Chief Rabbi of the Commonwealth. He impressed me as a man of humility, which is surely an essential ingredient of a genuinely religious sensibility, and had just delivered the BBC Reith lectures in which he had expressed the fear that we were on the verge of seeing medieval wars re-fought with twenty-first century technological wizardry. As we say in sport, it was starting to look as if the Chief Rabbi had made a pretty good call. Sachs argued the answer lay not in liberal thinking, which ultimately negated religious belief, but in the proper understanding of religious tradition.

The final decades of the twentieth century had been characterised by an upsurge in fundamentalism, not only in the related creeds of Islam, Judaism and Christianity, but also in capitalism. Lacking on all sides was any widespread belief in humanity. Of peace, Martin Luther King wrote: 'It really boils down to this, all life is interrelated.We are caught in an inescapable network of mutuality, tied into a single garment of destiny. What affects one directly, affects all indirectly.' In the weeks and months following September 11, the thought that crystallised in my head before any other was that peace, like love, has to be made if it is to hold its place in the withering reality of the world. Meanwhile, the game went on.

The Saturday after I discovered Martin Luther King in the small bookshop off Glenferrie Road, Peter Schwab's young Hawthorn team went within one kick of dethroning the reigning premiers, Essendon, and playing in the 2001 grand final. Down six goals at half-time, I rang my wife who was listening at home on radio and declared the Hawks were 'gone'. They weren't. As the game evolved, it became apparent that Hawthorn's belief was still intact. Furthermore, the longer they hung in, the more uncertain Essendon, previously confident and given to flourishes that pleased their fans, became. By the final minutes, it was anyone's game. The climax of the match came when Trent Croad, the most precocious and wayward of Hawthorn's young talents, had a chance to level from a long way out. He made the distance with ease but the kick brushed the goal post in passing. The Hawks lost.

In the moment that follows a close final, when you sense the result could have gone either way with a train of consequences in both directions, I heard Marlon Brando say, I coulda been a contender.

11 September 2001

The Tuesday before Rory Hilton's goal eliminated Carlton from the finals—that is, on 11 September 2001—I went to watch Richmond train at their old home ground, Punt Road Oval. It was different from watching training at Hawthorn, less obviously social, less bright chatter.A couple of decades ago, the Tigers were in the finals as a matter of course.They believed they belonged there. They still half-believed it and the excitement was a low, intensely responsive hum to what was occurring on the track, so that you could hear the players' exertions as they trained, hear them calling one another's names in blunt, sharp voices. This was like watching racehorses work out a couple of mornings before the big race is run.

One of the attractions of the Richmond Football Club is the cross-section of people it gathers. They come in different sizes, shapes and colours, but there is, for all that, something common about them, perhaps because Richmond is a common club. Traditionally, Richmond, like Collingwood, Carlton and Fitzroy, gave voice to the marginal. Carlton had gone up-market, Fitzroy had gone to Brisbane and Collingwood was in the process of being transformed by new president Eddie McGuire; Richmond was somehow constant in what it represented within the game. Even so, I was surprised to see a woman wearing a Muslim shawl sitting on the boundary line with two little kids. Standing beside them, watching the players in a measured way, was a young man with brown skin and a black beard wearing a Richmond guernsey. His name was Waleed Aly. Around eleven o'clock that night, he was at home watching *Talking Footy* when his father rushed into the room with the news that America had been attacked.

Waleed was then a law-engineering student at the University of Melbourne with an interest in journalism. Having identified himself in something I wrote, he began sending me examples of his work. Of rare intellectual precision, his articles were to do with Western perceptions of Islam. Over the months, as we talked more often, I tried to change his focus—instead of writing about Western perceptions of Islam, why not write about Islam? Waleed's religion, as he explained it to me, was like a deep pool of knowledge, a place of endless contemplation built around a great reverence for scholarship. At that time, I was doing a series called 'Faces in the Street', a phrase I pinched from Henry Lawson, and Waleed agreed to let me do one on him.

We met by mutual agreement at Punt Road. I was standing at the back of the grandstand when he came over the hill, past the grey skeleton of the old scarred tree, towards the ground. It was his smile I saw first, then his easy walking style. He was wearing a white collarless shirt and open jacket with jeans. As we entered the old ground, Waleed looked around and wondered aloud what it must have been like to see Captain Blood (Jack Dyer) play there.

It is difficult to imagine a humble Richmond supporter. Waleed was one but that is not to say he was without his resentments. His older brother Ahmad had been a 'huge cricket and footy head' who followed Richmond, and Waleed was duly handed the faith. 'No-one my age chooses to barrack for Richmond,' he said, a touch remorsefully. His brother also had him playing football and cricket from an early age. This competition gave Waleed a flying start when he first got to school but eventually, as a footballer, his slight frame told against him. Cricket he stuck with longer and, at the age of fourteen, he made a representative team which played at Punt Road. He still shuddered with awe at the memory of playing, as a boy, on the same ground his heroes did.

That day, as we sat in the Jack Dyer grandstand, Waleed Aly and I had the first of our many conversations on the world, religion and the future of Australia. Waleed's words came out of silence, but that was because they were thought through before he uttered them. As a conversationalist, he reminded me of Paul Kelly and the more we talked the more I thought about some lines from one of Paul's song, 'To Her Door'. A Queensland cane cutter is riding through Melbourne in a silver cab on his way to try and fix his marriage so that he can be with his kids. The various people in his life are like pieces of a picture. He's approaching the door of his estranged wife, his nerves shaking at the task that awaits him:'Could he make a picture/And get them all to fit?' That was the theme of our discussions about Australia. Could we make a picture, could we get all the different parts of this country to fit, especially given the ever increasing stresses upon the unhappy trinity of Islam, Judaism and Christianity? Waleed said the time had come when all the parties to the deepening global crisis needed to pause and look within. I was with Waleed.

His studies had impressed upon him how subjective the world is.'Basically, technical disciplines like economics and law come down to ways of looking at the world,' he said. 'It's not so much that they disagree; they have different frames of reference.' This perception was consistent with his religion.'Muslims understand the truth is not known to anyone but God. It is an arrogance to think we have all the answers.'At this point in his religious life, Waleed was into what he called 'substance over form'. He said five different people reading the Koran literally can arrive at five different interpretations. What was crucial, he said, was 'depth of understanding'. Waleed Aly's view of history, which extended back to the European Dark Ages when much of the intellectual heritage identified with Western culture was kept alive by Islamic scholars, saw Islam as now being in a period of 'intellectual challenge'.The more I got to know Waleed the more I admired his quiet intellectual candour.

The woman I first saw Waleed with was his sister-in-law. By the time we met at Punt Road oval, he was married. His wife, Susan, a convert to Islam, is descended from a First Fleeter. Most of Waleed's education had been in the state system and he saw himself as Australian. In the late nineties, he had gone to Egypt, the country his parents emigrated from, and been charmed by the chaotic energy of the place and the humanity of its ordinary people. But he confused them—how could he be Australian? He wasn't white. But by birth he was Australian and there were key ingredients of Australian culture we shared.When we first met,Waleed was disturbed by the government's anti-terrorism laws. He wondered if he would come home and find ASIO on the doorstep. 'Some racial stereotyping is inevitable,' he said. A year later came the ASIO raids.Waleed could see Australia polarising, with himself in a disappearing middle ground. He sensed the attitudes of other Australians changing. He was even worried about going to the footy.

The Game and I

How does it happen? How does a grown man of nearly fifty come to invest so much meaning in a game? It begins when you're a child. A window is opened onto this other world that is called sport. Later, you realise some people look down on it and see it as being common, but your first impression is that it's a place where uncommon things occur, particularly when compared to church and school. On the sports field, people are larger, freer, more open, than they are off it. Sometimes they're comic, giving vent to aspects of their personalities otherwise kept locked away and out of sight, but something about skill executed in the presence of danger takes your breath away from the start. And you get to see all this close up. For a time in my early teens, there was an intimacy associated with being on the sports field that I knew nowhere else.

At thirteen, I saw a team called East Devonport win its first premiership in twenty years. East were led by Graeme 'Gypsy' Lee. Thirty years later, I learned that Gypsy included among his forebears Dolly Dalrymple, a famous Tasmanian Aboriginal matriarch. Does this matter? It may do, because Gypsy changed how I saw the game, and later the game changed how I saw Australia. The local team, Cooee, had a Collingwood coach who preached the usual harsh male creed. What it produced to my eye was dull uniformity. Gypsy's team were different. Instead of one personality they had twenty. Following them was like following a serial on radio or TV. I squeezed into the rooms and listened to Gypsy's half-time addresses. He didn't rant and rave. He spoke to his players as if they were agreed on a common purpose. If each was the best he could be in an unselfish way, they could make something larger appear.

As a player, Gypsy had long lean legs and black hair oiled flat on either side of his head; he wore number 1 and attacked direct from centre half-back with drop kicks that travelled scarcely above head height, which made them so much quicker through the air. The grand final was played at Burnie on a bright blue day with no wind, which was in itself a miracle as the ground edged Bass Strait. The other team, Ulverstone, had a Victorian coach and Victorian coaches were mythical. I remember watching the opposition coach standing in the forward pocket, oiled and impotent, as Gypsy's creature of many parts took flight like a giant bird and flew off with the flag. It was the single most creative act I had seen up to that moment in my life.

What sort of a player was I? Scared, mostly. Originally, playing footy meant the joy of green grass zipping past beneath my feet, the heightened excitement as the ball came near. I was eleven or twelve when a boy from the toughest school in town with a name like Gerard MacCarthy swerved up to me as a match was about to start, poked his lean, pale face into mine and said if I went near the ball he'd smash me. His words numbed my being. I suspect the ghost of Gerard MacCarthy was somewhere on the ground every time I played thereafter. I did master my fear for one game, my last, a grand final, and learned too late that with concentration and application I might have gone at least some of the way towards living with my shadow. John Kennedy, one of the toughest coaches in the history of the game, is said to have told his players that everyone feels fear. As I heard the story, he told his players you either grip it and hold it in place or let it float around outside you, which means it can take you by surprise, inducing panicked reactions.

Most of my football was played in the southern Tasmanian B division amateurs, possibly the lowest level at which the adult game is played. Early on, my most distinctive features as a footballer were that I had hair down to my arse and a crimson headband, liked to train with bare feet and could kick the ball as far without boots as with them. By my fifth year, I had improved a bit and that season I was runner-up in the association best and fairest. I think what I loved most about footy was being part of a team. Once, in far western Victoria, I was shown a football ground that used to be an Aboriginal dancing ground.Walking around it, I was reminded of all the mad bastards I had played with and against. I first found forgiveness on a footy field surrounded by other fools laughing at their folly.

I was a better coach than player.We never forgot, in my teams, that sport is about play.We grew in the act of coming together, revelling in our differences but finding common belief.The last match I played in, the grand final, I was captain-coach. The other team had been training seriously since January.We'd been training seriously since the Tuesday night, but we had some fine players who decided to turn up and give their best. We lost by nine points. Part of the reason we lost was because I didn't believe we could win. I had no vision. There's an old saying about grand finals—you've got to lose one to win one—which isn't much consolation if you only get there once.

I stopped playing and coaching at the age of twenty-four when I left Australia to go wandering around the globe. I did play half a game after my return, but it was a nightmare. Having people crashing in upon you and trying to knock you off your feet from every conceivable angle requires a robust and highly flexible sense of self. I'd lost that in the course of consciously losing myself generally over the previous two years. After that, I went back to watching the game, which was probably what I'd done best all along.

The game had always been part of my family. In the years before the war, Dad played senior football with North Hobart and Devonport. He also captain-coached a combined country side against a Victorian team. We had one of his guernseys at home when I was a kid, blue and gold, the wool all loose, Number 1 on the back which meant he was the leader. In the 1990s, after his eyes had gone, I took him to see a game at New Norfolk in the statewide league. The day before, the local newspaper ran a back-page story in which one captain-coach had provocative things to say about the other. 'They always do that,' said Dad. He meant they'd been doing it for the eighty years he'd been following Tasmanian football. He still listened to the radio each

Saturday and peered at the back page of the newspapers to keep up with what was going on. When we got to the game, I read the names from the program and described the action to him and he told me what he knew about each player, where he'd come from, whether or not he was any good, plus any other information that came to mind. He called the game blind.

How did I start writing about the game? By standing on tables wet with beer slops at Uni footy club dinners, borrowing John Arlott's gravelly Hampshire accent and making poetic observations about members of our first team of the sort Arlott habitually made about Test cricketers in his BBC radio commentaries. I went from there to writing the club newsletter and match reports for the university newspaper. I also wrote a novella about a megalomaniacal disc jockey who takes over a town through the medium of talkback radio. I meant it as a satire on Hobart in the aftermath of the dismissal of the Whitlam government. I now see that I sold myself short. It was actually a futuristic piece about Sydney at the start of the twenty-first century. One night, two of the older players, Rod Radford and Bernie Hoggett, offered to raise the money to publish the novella. They were probably no more sober than I was at the time, but you never forget the community that first recognises you as a writer.

When I joined the Launceston *Examiner* and started writing about northern Tasmanian football, I found that I communicated with a wide crosssection of people. At the *Age*, which I joined five years later, there was a culture that was receptive to my work. Without really seeking to do so, I became more immersed in the game, spending a year with the Footscray Football Club and writing a book, *Southern Sky, Western Oval*, based on that experience. That year changed how I saw Melbourne. I journeyed through Australia, attending events like the Yuendumu sports weekend, also known as the Black Olympics.That changed how I saw Australia and the place of the game in it. With time, the game became my quickest and most reliable way of seeing Australian culture from within.

At Yuendumu, I heard for the first time about the connection between football and dance and ritual in Aboriginal culture. That connection provided me with a central strand in my novel *The Call*, an informed imagining of the tragedy of Tom Wills, founder of the game. As a journalist, my secret joy in writing stories on players—people generally, in fact—has been in finding words just beyond their reach that give deep and sincere expression to what they want to say. Trust has followed from that, relationships have grown, so that today I believe I am part of what is called the footy world. An odd part, perhaps. Kevin Sheedy's first name for me was 'Deepness' which he later changed to 'Irishman', standing in front of me, rubbery Robin Williams face grinning, saying, 'Irishman, how are things in the land of dreams and visions?' To which I reply, 'You ought to know, Kevin.' Sheedy is an old clan chief with a dagger in his sock and an insatiable curiosity for the world.

People see footy as basic, but I trust its basic sense of values and seek to employ them in what I do. Respect is the hard currency in footy—love is too inflammable; fans who love you one week can hate you the next. Respect endures. The relationship between respect and honesty within the game is not simply stated—a person may be seen as honest in some areas and not in others—but it is a fact that the relationship exists and is central to endless debates and arguments.

So what is football to me? It's been a window, a game, a second language. Some years it has mattered more than others and some seasons have only come alive at finals time. My relationship with footy had never been severed, but nor had its power ever been tested. That's why, as the unthinkable slowly dawned on me—the war in Iraq was going to happen and Australia was going to be involved, regardless of the wishes of the Australian people—it came as a considerable relief to find I could go to a game and for a couple of hours escape what was happening in the world.

Michael Voss

Picasso said you have to see a lot of bullfights to see a great bullfight. This is also true of football matches and players. Late in the 2001 season, I went to Geelong and saw Brisbane play. I have a memory of Michael Voss from that day after he has taken the ball in the middle of a pack. Initially, he has swung right, ball in hand, right arm fully extended. The wall of players running towards him, mesmerised by the ball, have veered in that direction. Simultaneously, he is looking left, to the gap he has opened where one of the speedsters in his team like Akermanis or Lappin will shortly appear to take the possession he is providing. What do I see in that moment? Power, poise, presence of mind. Downfield, the Brisbane forwards will have read the movement better than their Geelong opponents, which means they will break a fraction earlier when Akermanis receives the ball.Voss is the axle, Akermanis is one of its spokes, and each week the Brisbane wheel is spinning faster and faster.

During the first week of the 2001 finals,

I interviewed Voss at the Lions' training ground at Cooparoo. Below medium height and ginger-haired, he has a boyish laugh and carries himself with an ease that is the opposite of machismo. When I asked him his history with injuries, he laughed and said, 'How long have you got?' Back in Melbourne I checked his file and prepared this shortlist. He injured his left ankle in September 1996, missing a preliminary final. He tore the posterior cruciate in his right knee in July 1997. He snapped his right leg June the next year, breaking both the tibia and fibula bones. He damaged his left ankle for the second time in September 1999, again missing a preliminary final. He then had an ankle reconstruction. He also played the 1999 season with a plate in his right leg. I asked to speak to the club medics about Voss but coach Leigh Matthews vetoed it. Medical knowledge about his star player was classified information.

When I asked Voss about his future, he laughed again and said,'A player lives for the here and now.' He left worrying to the doctors and physios. More and more though, he admitted, he had to play with his head. I asked him, given his injuries, if he had his time over again, would he play an individual sport like golf or tennis? His answer was an immediate no. 'The great unique thing about football are those moments when twenty-two other people know exactly how you feel.' He admitted he enjoyed the intensity of a close game, those last few minutes when his mind burned and he came more to life as a footballer than he would ever otherwise be. Did he like pressure? That question extracted another laugh from him. He shook his head and said, 'Pressure's humbled many a man.'

I'd rung up Collingwood captain Nathan Buckley,

a keen judge of the game, to see what he thought about Voss. Buckley's great to talk footy with—clear and deeply thought.When they played together at Brisbane in 1993, Voss had a shoulder injury and Buckley was unsure of how good he was. But he had no doubt now. 'To come through what he has, and do what he's done, is a magnificent effort.' Buckley said Voss was now the most respected player in the AFL.

I knew Voss was a great player when I went to Brisbane. What I didn't know was that he was a natural leader. 'Vossie's the man,' said team-mate Simon Black. He admired Voss not only for the range of his skills but also his ability to play with injuries.'You only find out after games what injuries Vossie's been carrying,' he said. 'Going in you wouldn't know he had any. 'Tall defender Matthew Kennedy compared Voss to John Eales, one of the all-time greats of Australian rugby union and a gentleman by nature.'It's the same sort of respect people have for Vossie,'said Kennedy.'He's the opposite of a big head when he's got every reason to be one. He actually plays down his influence.' Kennedy had been with Voss since they began with a club called the Brisbane Bears, which had something like a toy koala as their mascot. Even back then, when Voss was only seventeen, Kennedy remembered people listening to what he said. 'He always made sense.'

The week after Richmond's emotive win over Carlton in the 2001 first semi-final, the Tigers were flogged by so much in Brisbane that I didn't watch long enough to note the final score. Such aspirations as Richmond possessed were snuffed out within seconds of the match starting. Brisbane were too fast, too skilled and too knowing of what each other was doing, and in the middle of this non-stop galloping action was Voss, Voss, Voss. He set the mood and tempo of play with an attacking run straight into the heart of the Richmond defence that brought together momentum, balance and faultless delivery. It was like watching a conductor tune up an orchestra. Soon they were all playing in the manner he had suggested. The difference between the Richmond team and those of us at home was that the Richmond players got to see all this from a lot closer up.Waleed said he was not surprised. Richmond's final for the year was the week before, he told me. Against Carlton, the old enemy.

Michael Long

The big news of grand final week 2001 was that Michael Long had broken down at training and would not play. Long was said to be upset. Just how upset I would see for myself a few months later when I was rung by Beverly Knight, the Essendon director and Aboriginal art dealer described by Long as his 'friend/mentor/mother', and asked to write the article announcing his retirement. Long was so emotional he could hardly speak. It would be some time before I understood even in a vague way the depth of his feeling. I would need to learn more about the Stolen Generation and the dimensions football could assume in the life of a family whose parents had been uprooted as infants from their traditional cultures, as his had. I would also need to learn more about the grand and colourful story football is as it snakes around Aboriginal Australia and Michael Long's special place within it.

One year earlier, a football team from three traditional Aboriginal communities in central Australia had come to Melbourne to see him. Eight of them had Long in their name. Xavier College arranged billets for the players and that is where I encountered them. 'Where you live?' Gregory Long Akemarr asked me. I told him.'Where that?' he said. I pointed south-east—about eight kilometres away. 'Where the MCG?' he asked. I pointed towards the light towers protruding through the foliage of Yarra Park. Five kilometres that way. 'Colonial Stadium?' Gregory was getting his bearings, like he would in the desert.

Playing as Sandover, the team had a couple of scratch matches against Xavier and were taken on tours of football's sacred sites. At Arden Street they met Wayne Carey who promptly took off his training guernsey and gave it to one of their number, a young man called Calvest. Three days later he was still talking about it in a whisper I initially mistook for shyness but later realised was sound enough for a desert man. 'Wayne Carey, he give me his jumper.' Calvest's community plays in the Kangaroos' colours. Out Utopia way, there's a story that football has a kangaroo dreaming and Carey's jumper was a major prize. Glenn Archer, the Kangaroos' famously angry man, pulled off his, signed it and handed it over too.The boys from the centre were then invited in for a post-training mug of soup. They take football seriously up there, the coach of the team, a young whitefella named Simon Turner, told me. 'There's not much else for them to do.'

Mostly, though, the young men came to meet Michael Long. He would be one of them but for the fact that his father, Jack Long, was stolen from an Ammatyerre woman as a three year old under what is broadly known as the assimilation policy. The old

Ammatyerre people had been meeting in the desert to try and work out where Michael fitted in had Jack never been stolen, what stories and dreamings would have been his. Long's mother had been taken from Daly River at a similar age, being transported by boat to Bathurst Island. Long's parents had met in an orphanage on the island and were adopted into the Tiwi community. As a result, during the early years of Long's playing career, he was mistakenly thought to be a Tiwi.

I was present when Long and his kinsmen met. Beverly Knight said she had never seen him so nervous before, but even so he took the initiative, moving forward in his quietly fluid way, shaking each of their hands as they acknowledged him with a nod, ever so briefly exchanged glances and quickly looked away.Afterwards, they stood back in a corner and their coach, Simon Turner, roared: 'Say something to him. You talk about him all the time when he's not here.'

Turner and Knight had organised an exhibition of footy paintings by the team, together with four paintings of Michael Long's. They were an interesting collection. Stevie Loy Akemarr's Wayne Carey had fierce blue eyes and a near shaved head with a kiss curl at the front. He was in bright blue and white and behind him the crowd were in a sea of yellow. He looked like a figure at a beach carnival. When Kevin Sheedy saw his portrait by Roley Long Akemarr, he said,'Do I look that bad?' He meant red face scrunched up like a rubber ball. Each painting was accompanied by a small script detailing the qualities of the player portrayed. Sheedy particularly liked the one accompanying Blake Caracella: 'He has good eyes and always looks for the open man.' A good coach is always learning, said Sheedy.

I bought one of Michael Long's paintings. It's of his mother's country in the deep blue of evening—trees, a bark shelter, a fire, some small black figures and, the brightest object in the whole painting, a tiny red ball.The title? 'Family footy.' Beverly Knight had no idea Long had any ambition to paint, but her gallery had given him the opportunity to meet and get to know Ginger Riley and desert painters like Kathleen Petyarre and Barney Ellaga. Long said he could see the beauty of their spirits in their work and, from Ginger Riley, he said he learned about listening.

Knight deliberately withheld Long's early works from sale.They're of Melville Island.The colour that defeats him in some of his early attempts is white—big blinding blobs of it in the middle of the pieces. In the later works, he abandoned the world of his childhood places and went to ones he had never been—his mother's country near Daly River, his father's country at Ti-Tree—using the medium of football to transport him.The artist's statement with one of his works reads:'Camping with my cousins at Daly River—the Ti-Tree earth signifies the link between my mother from Daly River and my father from Ti-Tree. This is who I am.' The earth upon which the game is being played is the bluish-brown colour of a ti-tree leaf.

In another, he had rubbed dirt through the paint so that the earth was gravelly and red. On it were small black figures, some with red stripes on their torsos, some with yellow, some with red hoops on their legs, again some with yellow. Imagine, in one hundred years time, a person looking at a painting by the foremost Aboriginal footballer of his day and then reading this statement by him: 'These players are naked with ochre body paint designs. The red and black signifies my people, the yellow and black stripes are a visiting community. It is a sports gathering and the eventual winner will be regarded as the strongest clan of all'. It was Sheedy who pointed out that the colours of the two teams add up to the Aboriginal flag.

The reason Michael Long influences people is that he is capable of great sincerity. What he says is simple, heartfelt and clear. I might have once said unsophisticated but Knight put it another way. 'Maybe he's highly sophisticated,' she said. 'He keeps reducing information to simple propositions.' Long believed Aboriginal people have a gift for knowing who to trust. 'Nine times out of ten they're right,' he said. By working on the basis of trust, he also engendered it. Sheedy said Long was one of the best leaders he'd seen. In 2000, when I asked Long what captaincy was about, he paused before answering. Teams are like family, he said. Now, one year later, he was out of the team.

After thirteen seasons and three knee reconstructions, 2001 had been Long's toughest year. Tonsilitis combined with an operation on a floating bone in his knee to weaken him. What began as a two-week injury had stretched to three months, but he'd fought his way back, braving the cold waters of Port Phillip Bay at seven o'clock each winter morning to strengthen his injured knee. Two weeks earlier, playing in the VFL at Ballarat, he kept falling over, but against Hawthorn he had come on to a huge reception from the Essendon crowd and moved freely. Watching television that night, Long heard commentator Scott Palmer announce that he wouldn't be playing in the grand final and was about to retire. He had no thought of retiring.

Long believed football had given him inner strength, the knowledge he could meet any challenge. He'd met all the ones great players meet, plus a few others besides. His quietly resolute stands on issues of race had been responsible for transforming the culture of the game. Crowds weren't as racist as they had been, nor were players. David Wirrpunda, an Aboriginal player with the West Coast Eagles, said Long had 'made the next day a bit easier than the last one had been'. Now Long had met what looked to him like a minor obstacle and learned from the television there was thought of him retiring. Suddenly, instead of being able to fix his attention on the grand final, everyone was asking him if he was giving the game away. He thought he was still good enough to play. In the latter stage of his career, handicapped by the cumulative effect of major injuries, he had invented a new way of playing that involved smacking the ball to passing team-mates. It meant he didn't have to gather it. He dived into packs like a diver into a wave and smacked the ball behind him to a teammate three or four metres away. He'd got slower but he'd compensated by finding a way of playing quicker.

But Essendon clearly had doubts. On the Tuesday night, the club put him through a special fitness test. Already emotional, he thought, Why doubt me now? He passed the test. It was the next night at training, the last major training before the grand final, that his body failed him. In the end, it wasn't the knee that had given him so many problems, the damaged knee which he always suspected would come back one day to haunt him. It was the hamstring on his other leg. He went inside the medical room, shut the door and wept.

Before he left, Sheedy asked him to speak to the players the following morning.That night, Long tried to write something but could only manage three words; on Wednesday, he stood in front of the players and told them he loved them. It was after that team meeting he'd walked out on to the ground and been captured by a television news camera, embracing a teammate red-eyed, waving to the fans. For Michael Long, leaving Essendon Football Club would be like leaving his people, the ones in red and black.

The 2001 Grand Final Parade

Voss was in the leading car, behind the Scottish pipers, the brass band and the clowns on stilts. He had not, as expected, won the 2001 Brownlow Medal, losing to team-mate Jason Akermanis, who was a few cars behind looking like the urchin who could run faster than any other kid in the street. Alongside Voss, wearing dark glasses, sat an impassive Leigh Matthews. If, as they say, most of a grand final is played before the teams take the field, observers considered Matthews the winner in the early exchanges with his Essendon counterpart. Sheedy had sought to arouse local passion by branding Brisbane an interstate side. Sheedy never stopped playing those sorts of mind games. Matthews rarely, if ever, did—to an extent that was unnerving since it showed how undistracted he was in his view of the game—but on this occasion he responded by saying that Victorians didn't identify with Essendon, seeing them as arrogant. It was true. That was how a lot of people saw the Bombers, or rather their supporters, particularly after their record-breaking run in 2000.

But there was another factor at play.The Brisbane Lions represented the nominal merger of the Brisbane and Fitzroy football clubs at the end of 1996. About half of Fitzroy's members had joined the new club, the others leaving in disgust, but many were now sneaking back for a look. Popular sentiment in Melbourne, always close to Fitzroy, was now with the Lions.

Chris Johnson was in the second Brisbane car. Johnson has a special status in the game since, in the eyes of most Fitzroy people, he is the last Fitzroy player. Alastair Lynch played with the Roys but left the club when it was struggling; in fact, his departure contributed to its declining fortunes. Martin Pike, who had spent time with Fitzroy, had also been with three other clubs and was considered a man of loose footballing affections. But Johnson had started with the Roys and stayed with them until the bitter end. Back then, he was just a young Koori with a lot of talent; now he was a mature footballer, highly skilful and physically composed. He responded to the crowd's excitement like a rock star, building it up.

The night before the grand final parade, I'd gone back to Fitzroy's old home ground, the Brunswick Street Oval, looking for ghosts. Only the grandstand and a brick ticket box remained of the old ground. On the ticket box, in response to George Bush's grandiosely named 'Operation Infinite Justice', someone had sprayed the words,'Operation Infinite Hypocrisy'. Already the American rhetoric was disturbing; it was, literally, like something out of a Superman comic.

I'd gone back to Brunswick Street with Simon Turner, the coach of the Sandover team who had come to Melbourne the previous year to meet Michael Long. He said, 'They're still talking about you, Moneytop. 'The team had given me the name—Moneytop—after the old man on the top of the two dollar coin. 'What do they say?' I asked. 'They say you're an uncle for that place (Melbourne) and a keeper of the football story.'Simon didn't have much doubt about anything but he had none whatsoever about the Lions winning the grand final. They hadn't lost a second half in sixteen weeks, he said. I have to admit he persuaded me, particularly having seen how much Essendon struggled against the Hawks in the preliminary final.

Kevin Sheedy was in the first Essendon car of the 2001 grand final parade with two young women I took to be his daughters. One was wearing an Essendon jumper with Michael Long's number on it. The matter of Long's retirement would not be settled for some months, but in the end, Long would not be able to leave the club until Sheedy, whom he described as a 'coach or father figure', told him to do so. 'I had to hear it from him,' he told me. What Sheedy told him was that he had nothing to fear from the outside world.

The grand final parade, having travelled along Swanston Street, swung into Collins Street. At Treasury House, there was a long delay that looked suspiciously like it was for the convenience of the television broadcaster. Eventually the two teams appeared, led by their captains. In 1996, James Hird and Michael Voss shared the Brownlow Medal. Both were great players, both were the natural leaders of their teams, but now Hird, as everyone knew, was carrying an injury. His test would come not in the first quarter but the third.

The Lord Mayor said he hoped the best team would

win, which, of course, no supporter wanted to hear, and there was booing and shouting, a waving of flags. I will paint that moment as I recall it—bright blue sky (spring in Melbourne), a sun that is warm and friendly, a crowd that is noisily alive and threatening no-one. Club songs are being sung like that's a contest in itself. Brisbane took Fitzroy's song, which borrowed the tune from the French national anthem, 'La Marseillaise'. Essendon has the altogether more pedestrian 'When the Bombers Fly Up', but even so the thrust of the song is up, not down. The crowd was alive, there were toddlers on parents' shoulders being baptised into this strange ritual, the sunlight was shining through a maroon flag in front of my face and suddenly, strangely, I realised I was as happy as a child.What's more, in that moment, I had no wish to be otherwise. If football could give me relief, a break from the worry of a world building for who knew what, I would take it like a drug.

I wrote an article in which I suggested Brisbane might run away with the game in the second half, which they did. I also wrote that at the end of the parade—when, for the first time in three weeks, I felt the joy of being alive—the players were standing on the steps of the Victorian Parliament House. Alas, they were a block away on the steps of Treasury House, a building which bears little or no resemblance to the Victorian Parliament. A woman wrote to the editor and said if Martin Flanagan could get something that simple wrong, why should she believe a word he wrote?

Outside the Ground

Leaving a game between Essendon and Hawthorn at the MCG late in the 2001 season, I was on the edge of a conversation between my day's companions, a journalist with broad experience, including foreign postings, and a historian. It hadn't been a great game, the Hawks having failed to fire, with the result that eventually it had been a case of waiting for the siren to bring the dismal matter to an end.This may have influenced the tone of their discussion. The pair were speaking in the manner of old acquaintances so not everything they said was familiar to me, but one of them referred to a remark by a third party that Australia *as an idea* was dying. I recall that moment as being the opposite of an epiphany, a sort of thunderstruck fear.

The Cricket Tragic

The Australian cricketers of Mark Taylor's time called John Howard 'a cricket tragic'. It wasn't the nicest name to be called since it implied that, even by their standards, they thought his affection for the game was over the top. He once said he would sooner have been captain of the Australian Test cricket team than Prime Minister. His hero, predictably, was Sir Donald Bradman. I once saw John Howard bowl in a social match on television. He was a practitioner of cricket's least demanding skill, the slow off break. He was one of those people who puts the thought and concentration of a great player into what he does without appearing to know that he looks nothing like one. He was the sort of figure you laugh about on the sports field when you're young and then are sobered to learn, a lot later in life, that he's also the sort of person who becomes Prime Minister of Australia.

In the mid-1980s, during his first term as leader of the federal opposition, I sat beside Howard on a light aeroplane as he flew to the Victorian electorate of

Flinders, then being contested by the young Peter Reith who met us like a worldly prefect anxious to impress the new headmaster. In the course of the flight, Howard and I talked about a book he was reading which I had just finished, Geoffrey Serle's biography of General Sir John Monash. In the evolving story that is Australian identity, Monash is a figure of particular interest. Of German-Jewish extraction, he had no great love for imperial Britain as a young man and, while being conscious of his persona as an Australian, was one of the outstanding Allied generals—some say *the* outstanding Allied general—of World War I. His refusal to engage with the antidemocratic elements that emerged among the returned soldiers during the Great Depression contributed to Australia's stability during that period. We agreed that it was a fine book about a major Australian.

Ten years later, shortly before the election was called in which Howard finally became Prime Minister after a decade of climbing what Disraeli called the greasy pole, I sought a second interview. I had been told his office was refusing all journalists so I modified my request and asked to speak to him about two subjects—cricket and Sir John Monash. I knew I could learn a good deal about him by engaging him seriously about cricket, while Monash remained a promising door to open further. This request was also refused. His office said that, given his many years in public life, Howard felt the Australian people knew who he was and there was nothing to be gained from further personal exposure. In retrospect, I would vigorously contest that view. Furthermore, insofar as our non-meeting represented a tactical manoeuvre, it was a manoeuvre he won.

However hard I pressed him on the available evidence, where no evidence existed, perhaps because of my legal training, I believed I was obliged to give him the benefit of the doubt.The result, rather than being a portrait, was a largely blank outline.

In preparation for the interview, I had read Howard's entire file, a fat wad of clippings, and found only three articles that were seriously interesting. At the time, most people, myself included, thought he had no personality—in fact, he has a strong one—and he was commonly described as boring. It seemed a measure of the man that he was the only federal Liberal leader not to have had a biography written about him; even lightweights like Peacock and McMahon had scored that much. Mired as he then was in economic debates, no-one saw significance in Howard's story or the family culture from which he had come.The one article on his file that explored this in any depth was by a senior *Sydney Morning Herald* journalist, Milton Cockburn.

What Cockburn explained was the impact of World War I on Howard's family. Both his father and his grandfather enlisted. There is a story of them finding one another on the battlefield at Mont Saint Quentin a few hours before the fighting began; when it did, the grandfather was wounded in the stomach and the son gassed. Cockburn wrote: 'John's father, Lyall, was a proud patriot. There are family suspicions that he was a member of the New Guard, the unofficial militia which prospered between the wars.' That is speculation, but this is fact: Howard is John Winston Howard. What is more, he was born in July 1939—that is, before World War II began. Generally speaking,Winston Churchill only became a hero in this country after World War II;

before then, he was remembered as the author of Gallipoli. Lyall Howard died when John was sixteen. The legacy of memory must have been a large one.

Lyall Howard had a corner garage.The Howards are usually described as thrifty, hard-working and ambitious. In the 1940s, when Bob Menzies sought to assemble a new conservative force to combat the socialistic policies of Labor, he identified families like the Howards as Australia's 'forgotten people'. Denied an interview, I went for a look at the Howard family garage in the lower middle class Sydney suburb of Dulwich Hill. Snub, round and grey, it was rather Howard-looking.The garage was now owned by a Greek Macedonian called Arthur. Howard had visited him once and asked him a hundred times if he was glad he bought the business. Why one hundred times? I asked. 'He had to keep sayin' it for the cameras,' replied Arthur, who was more interested in talking about a feud he had running with the local council over waste collection. Howard was all right, but Arthur said he wasn't gunna marry him.'He's a politician,' he said.

John Howard is suburban man and I went for a wander round the suburb he had grown up in. The houses were small and made of brick, each with its own yard. In the eighties, when Australian politics were primarily about economics, houses like these, only a bit bigger and with a white picket fence, featured in Liberal Party campaigns.These were the years when Howard failed to capture the Australian imagination. Somewhere along the long road that was his political career he had uttered the fateful lines 'The times will suit me', and eventually they did.

When the Howards were in Dulwich Hill, the lower

middle class suburb was exclusively white. It was still predominantly so, but in nearby Marrickville it was hard to know what country you were in. The only constant in the faces you met in the street was the mix. As he built towards the prime ministership, Howard clearly determined to speak for those he now saw as being the forgotten people—those he had grown up among. Thus began grubby cultural war in which the frontline fighters were talkback radio hosts and tabloid newspaper columnists, who paraded short-sightedness and prejudice as robust common sense. Meanwhile, backstage, a furious battle was fought to bring key cultural institutions, most critically the Australian Broadcasting Corporation, to heel. Voices of opposition and dissent were ritually dismissed as elitist and politically correct. I challenge anyone to prove that I am either.

As an Australian monarchist, Howard belongs to a group that has seen the status of the British royal family reduced to the level of a tabloid cartoon but been determined nonetheless to fight for the space they once occupied in the national psyche. At the same time, they have championed an economic creed that ultimately means the only viable mythologies are those that survive in the marketplace. This, in turn, means mass consumption of American commercial culture. Extended over a sufficient period of time, this combination of factors will eventually reduce being Australian to a certain nostalgia and not much else.

Paul Keating was a Labor patrician in the tradition of Whitlam. Much was made of his ego; no-one saw Howard's. In defeating Keating and the vision of Australia he proposed, Howard presented himself as a plebian, telling Australians he would make them feel more comfortable and relaxed about themselves—that is, like they did in the Australia he grew up in, the one that protected its sense of self with measures like the White Australia Policy and assimilation. As a politician, Howard has a history of taking a stand on issues that can be given weighty names like security but that also happen to be about race—his opposition to boycotts against the apartheid regime and Asian immigration in the eighties, his refusal to apologise to Aboriginal people in the nineties, his response to predominantly Muslim refugees and asylum seekers in the 2000s. In his first term as Prime Minister, footage was released of a rare visit he made to an Aboriginal community. Flanked by minders, the man who encouraged others to feel relaxed and comfortable in their own country walked about with a frozen smile on his lips. If it was his own country he was in, he didn't look at home there.

On occasions, I must admit, I have supported his views. One was his move against guns in the wake of the Port Arthur massacre. I was grateful for the distinctly Australian character of his conservatism then, the gun lobby, mercifully, not being part of the Australian conservative tradition. And I also supported him in the role Australia played in the liberation of East Timor. It is still unclear as to exactly what that role was, but I was in no doubt that Australia had some debt of honour to the East Timorese stretching back to World War II. It wasn't an obligation between governments but between people, their civilians having helped our soldiers at great risk. Fairly or otherwise, Keating's insistence on engaging with the Suharto regime had made him appear complacent on the issue.

The argument over Howard's place in Australian history will ultimately come down to one question: to what extent did he speak to the Australian people, and to what extent did he speak to their fears? In 2001, he was trailing in the polls when the extraordinary national morality play known as the Tampa crisis occurred. The suspicion that the crisis was engineered by the government for the sake of the forthcoming election had the potential to shadow Howard in the way the Petrov affair follows Menzies, but then September 11 occurred. Howard immediately identified with the American response. As it got bigger, so did he, flying off to meet Bush and Blair like Churchill off to Yalta.A man of partial vision was now projecting Australia to the world.

In the aftermath of September 11, Osama Bin Laden said Australia's actions in helping to liberate East Timor were part of the crusade against Islam. I knew Muslims who didn't agree, but no doubt there would be those who did. My position on this war would not be a simple or automatic one. In times of deepest need, to paraphrase the English poet Stephen Spender, I think on those who were truly great. I returned to my first political hero, Abraham Lincoln, and began re-reading his speeches. Lincoln did not seek out the catastrophe of civil war. In his first inaugural address in 1861, he summarised the difference between the two sides to the debate, stating his opponents' case dispassionately in the manner of a trial judge, before making it clear that he believed he was bound by his oath of office to preserve the union. But he ended by foreseeing a time when Americans would again be touched,'as surely they would', by the better angels of their nature.

Four years later, when he gave his second inaugural address, the war was nearly won but the casualties had been horrendous. Lincoln pointed out an obvious but uncomfortable truth—both sides had prayed to the same God, and read the same Bible. 'The prayers of both could not be answered, that of neither has been answered fully.' His speech ended with a vision of his deeply wounded country moving forward in a spirit of reconciliation which he defined as walking 'with malice towards none, with charity for all'. In an article in the *Washington Post* in March 2002, Edwin M.Yoder Jr described Lincoln as 'a man of moral modesty' who successfully defined the national crisis of his age, and 'the deepest mind and spirit ever to ponder in high office the great issues of American destiny'.

Lincoln's presidency was consumed by a civil war, not a foreign engagement, but I don't believe he would have delivered George W. Bush's 'Axis of Evil' speech. All Lincoln's great speeches either address, or are inclusive of, the argument of the other side to the conflict. Bush's rhetoric appealed to only one side. Indeed, as an exercise in public language, the Axis of Evil speech was little different to Iranian mullahs calling America "The Great Satan". In both cases, for those who respond to its call, the effect of such language was that no more reasoning is required. No more questions need be asked. Twice, during the troubles in Northern Ireland, I was approached to write articles sympathetic to the IRA. I declined, not only because I believed the significant journalism on Northern Ireland—journalism that led to greater insight and understanding—could only come from Northern Ireland, but also because from where I stood, half a world away, some of the acts in that conflict looked like murder. But not for one moment did I think those acts existed independently of a social or historical context that would have to be addressed if a peaceful solution were to be found.

Lincoln had urged the people of the Confederate states not to be hurried into war.We were in the war against Iraq before we knew it.The intellectual subtext for the conflict, the clash of civilisations theory, holds that conflict between Islam and the West is inevitable. Like all prophecies of war, it had a self-fulfilling momentum and, although it was a fact that tensions between Islam and the West had heightened and had the potential to explode, when I thought of a civilised man, I thought of Nelson Mandela. Having been to the new South Africa, and seen the depth and complexity of the tensions within that society, I had a whole new appreciation of the savagery of the civil war Mandela had averted. The first person I had spoken to in South Africa was a businessman of Afrikaner descent.'Mandela isn't a saint,' he told me.'He's just a guy who kept on becoming.' Who or what were we becoming?

Here, as elsewhere, the issue of the war in Iraq was coloured by repeated references to Winston Churchill on the basis that the threat posed by Saddam Hussein was analagous to the 1930s when most British parliamentarians, with the conspicuous exception of Churchill, wanted to ignore the threat posed by Adolf Hitler. Even putting his part in the Gallipoli fiasco to one side, as prime minister of Britain in World War II, Churchill made it clear that the defence of Australia was not his priority, but the omen of Churchill went largely unremarked upon in the Australian press as it swung behind the war in Iraq. The steps by which the Australian public were brought onside could be summarised by a series of tabloid images. In rough order, these would be the World Trade Center crumpling, Osama Bin Laden, Afghanistan (no-one in particular, particularly not Osama), the Axis of Evil speech, Saddam Hussein. I wondered if Australians understood how few people around the world shared, or regarded as complete, this account of events. A dangerous gap was opening between the way Australians saw themselves and the way they were seen in the world.

In 2002, a journalist attributed to Howard—wrongly, it seems—the quote that he wanted to be the US's deputy sheriff in Asia. For a lot of people in our region, that was precisely how he was now seen and, with him, us.

The Shinboner Spirit

Wayne Carey was the player gifted by the gods to play Australian football. He was skilful and audacious. He was tall, physically powerful and blessed with the balance of a ballroom dancer. He was the player most admired by Michael Voss because, as a captain, he regularly won matches for his team. The media called him the King.

Some of his feats from what might be termed his early period are, to my mind, unforgettable. Here is but one, circa 1993. Hawthorn has peaked but is still a great team. North are with them midway through the final term. The ball is kicked into North's forward line. Four or five players run to meet it. Coming from the opposite direction, looking back over his shoulder, Carey leaps headlong among them, marking the ball as he does. This act has the obvious football virtues like courage and judgment but, at such a critical moment in a big game, it has something else: a confidence that beams like a lighthouse. The young North team rally around their captain and secure a magnificent victory.

Not only was Wayne Carey one of the great talents of the footballing age, he also commanded the most strategically important position on the field—centre half-forward—and the team plan designed by North coach Denis Pagan to accommodate him was as elementary as a Hills hoist: kick long out of defence, move the ball as quickly and directly as possible, look for Carey once you cross the centre-line. Pagan was one of the hardest coaches of the era, his teams being intensely drilled and remarkably close, but privately he made allowances for Carey; he was the one player who didn't necessarily respond to instructions from the coaching box. Even if Carey didn't get the ball, he drew extra defenders, leaving lesser team-mates free. Two premierships for the cash-strapped club followed, 1996 and 1999.

How great a player was Wayne Carey? As seems to happen to great players, serious injuries took their toll—in his case, to his hips and shoulders. His leap was gradually worn away and he had difficulty marking over his head. Even so, I often wondered why one of the few players to match him for bulk and mobility, West Coast's Glen Jakovich, not only had the better of him on most occasions they met but did so with relative ease. In boxing terms, the contests between them should have been fifteen-rounders but were usually over in two or three. Most incredibly, it seemed that Jakovich, with minimal difficulty, could get Carey to play his—that is, Jakovich's—game. No-one I have seen regularly beats Voss or Buckley or Hird in that way. Jakovich would draw Carey into wrestling contests, the one area he had an advantage in. It was as if this were a challenge Carey couldn't resist. At the very least, he didn't seem to be a player who thought a lot about what he did. Most great players never stop thinking.

There was also the strange case of the 1998 grand final when Carey was subdued by a much lesser player, Adelaide's Peter Caven. Carey missed an easy goal just before half-time that might have revived his team's confidence and then, along with most of his team-mates, played the second half as if paralysed. In fairness to him, he returned to be, in my opinion, best on ground in the 1999 grand final, but I suspected Carey was more of a confidence player than people thought. It was just that so few opponents were able to take the King outside his realm and into the shadowland where doubts begin to take grip.

North's teams during those years had two other characters of note, Anthony Stevens and Glenn Archer. Stevens had the sort of grin you see in photographs of First AIF soldiers standing in front of the pyramids in Egypt, shortly before being shipped to Gallipoli. With him in the photo would be Carey and Glenn Archer. The reason the three of them would be in the photo is because they were best mates, although, in retrospect, Carey is said to have been the leader.

Archer is known as the toughest man in the AFL, a misleading reputation in one respect since it belies the complexity of his nature. Shorter than Carey, he is squarely built and surprisingly skilful when you really watch him play. On the field, he burns with a fierce flame. Off the field, he's an altogether different human being, although your judgment of him would vary according to how close you got to him since he is deeply reserved. A woman working at the Kangaroos, a graduate from the University of Melbourne, described

Archer to me as a gentleman. After that, I watched him more closely, particularly at training. He gave time to each person who approached him, man, woman or child, and not in a false or matey way, but with an old-fashioned formality.

The drama that was to cast the three apart broke just as the 2002 season was about to begin: Carey resigned from the club. At the press conference, he said his leaving was a personal matter and he would not be answering questions, but the story travelled quicker than a bushfire in the high country. Carey had been having an affair with Kelli Stevens, Anthony Stevens' wife. The affair had been discovered during a party at Glenn Archer's house.

If ever a non-elected individual in this country has received saturation coverage of the sort endured by the British royal family, it was the King of football and those whose fates were haplessly entangled with his in the days, weeks and months that followed. The public appetite for details was insatiable. Meanwhile the club staggered like a boxer who's been hit. North had recorded trading losses totalling two million dollars over the previous two seasons and recently parted company with a newly appointed CEO. With the departure of Carey, it had lost not only its best player and captain but also its primary marketing tool.

North's an old Catholic club that dates back to 1869. The club never had a godfather like Collingwood's John Wren, never attracted powerful business interests like Carlton. A lot of the players in their early teams worked at the local abattoirs, hence their name—the Shinboners. Whole seasons passed with the Shinboners rarely winning a game, but it would be a great mistake to infer from their results that the Shinboners played without their own particular brand of passion and pride. Carlton's Ken Hands told me that in the year of the Bloodbath grand final neither Carlton nor South were the toughest team in the competition. The Shinboners were.

Arden Street, North's old home ground, has an oval with a first-class playing surface and a pleasant view of the city. It also has a condemned grandstand occupied by pigeons and a football department housed in Nissen huts in the car park. Denis Pagan, a former North Melbourne player, left the Kangaroos at the end of 2002 which I thought was sad. Pagan wasn't just the coach of the club; he was its storyteller. To quote the club historian, a Catholic priest named Father Gerald Dowling, he kept its ghosts alive. To walk around Arden Street with Pagan was to hear a story for every locker, every bench, every name on the honour boards. For years North had been called the Kangaroos, but when Pagan talked to me, and no doubt when he talked to the team, what he spoke about was the old Shinboner spirit.

In 2001, I received an e-mail from an American follower of the game. Having picked up Australian football on pay TV in the eighties and become an avid Carlton supporter, his wife had given him a return ticket to Melbourne.What he did was haunt the old grounds. He went to Arden Street. Max Stone, North's gentlemanly doorman, has been with the club since 1969. Most modern sporting clubs don't let you in. Max Stone can't remember turning anyone away. The American was taken in and shown around. He ran into Aboriginal player Byron Pickett who casually agreed to be photographed with him. 'Do Australians understand?' asked his e-mail. 'There is nothing like this in America!' As sport becomes more of a business, the fans' knowledge of the players is tailored to staged events. At North, to quote Glenn Archer, people just walk in off the street.

About half a dozen games into the 2002 season I spent a week at North and briefly met Archer. When I asked him what made North different as a club, he laughed and said, 'Jude,' a reference to Judy Francis. At the time, we were sitting in the tiny chamber adjacent to the players' change rooms where Francis, one of the club's women volunteers, prepares their training day meals. He said it jokingly, so she heard, but there was some truth in what he said. Judy Francis was the club mother. Players had wept on her broad bosom after losing grand finals.Years ago, a youth not long at the club confided in her that he had a strange rash on his genitals and was scared to show the doctor. 'Give me a look,' she said. 'Go on, I've got two sons. 'The young lad did as he was told. 'Go to the doctor,' she said. 'You've got nothing to worry about.' The club psychologist, a smart young woman, told me that when she started at the club she chose to work alongside Judy in the kitchen. That's how she got inside the club.

Judy Francis had felt the trauma of the Wayne Carey saga like a family blow-up. She had gone to Carey's wedding, although, like most people at North, she called him the Duck. She admitted she missed him and said in a slightly sad way that she still hoped to hear from him. 'He was an arrogant big bugger, but he had a good heart.' Given the depth of feeling people at North still had for Carey, I asked why the club rallied round Stevens to such an extent in the aftermath of the revelation. Her eyes narrowed as if she suddenly thought she may have misjudged me. 'Because he's such an honest little fella.'

Women have always been involved at North Melbourne. They had to be; everyone was needed. Judy Francis's offsider, Jean Burmister, used to go to the dances and soup nights under the grandstand. When the Kangaroos made their first grand final in 1950, Jean queued for a ticket. The result was the most painful loss of her football life until Wayne Carey's departure.'Sometimes I still wake up and think it's a nightmare, that it hasn't really happened.' She told me she still loved Carey, but hated what he had done.

Another of Jude's helpers, Greg Ryan, came from a third generation North Melbourne family. Basically, Carey was his idol; one room of his house was full of Carey memorabilia. 'Maybe people like me were part of the problem,' said Ryan. Maybe they were. For his whole adult life, there had been people who treated Carey as a footballing god.

In 2000, Greg Ryan had a nervous breakdown. He said coming down to Arden Street kept him sane.Anthony Stevens kept saying to him, 'Just keep smiling, mate. You'll get through it.' That's what Stevens did, kept on smiling. At that time, Stevens was battling dual misfortune, a gash to his neck from a pane of falling glass having severed muscles and nerves and caused him to think he was dying from loss of blood, plus a knee reconstruction. My favourite memory of Anthony Stevens as a footballer comes from a night preliminary final in, I think, 1996.A taller Carlton opponent, ball beneath his arm, has run straight at Stevens. The North player, who is not much bigger than a rover, takes him front on, around the waist, simultaneously flinging his feet upwards to clap a wrestling hold on the Carlton man's top half and bring him down like a horse whose legs suddenly buckle beneath him. It was an act of wild, uninhibited athleticism that went to the spirit of the team. If Carey was North's best player, Archer and Stevens were its two bravest.

Asked to explain the spirit of North, club medic Dr Con Mitripoulos summoned three stories. The first is about the wound to Stevens' neck. He was supposed to be out for twelve months. He was back in twelve weeks.The concern, given the damage to the muscles in his neck, was what would happen if he was in a head-on collision. He went out and immediately dived into a pack.The second is when Archer injured the joint in one shoulder, played on, injured the joint in his other shoulder, could hardly lift either arm and still didn't want to leave the field. The third story is about the injury to Anthony Stevens' ankle in the 1999 preliminary final which left it the size of his knee and caused the then club doctor to declare,'If you play with that in the grand final, I'll grow a cactus out my arse.' Stevens played. Archer and Stevens are Shinboners.

Anthony Stevens could be forgiven for never wanting to see another journalist in his life, but he saw me because Judy Francis asked him to. Significantly, he and Archer saw me together, in Jude's kitchen. Archer had been on the masseur's table and was wearing a towel, leaning forward in his seat. He glanced at me just the once, then looked away. Jude Francis told me he's a shy man, really, but no journalist was going to get close to him in a hurry. Stevens was leaning back, arms folded across his chest, still with his trademark grin, only now I was conscious of its bravery. I asked them about North's traditions and Archer recounted that when his mates from Noble Park Football Club asked him the difference between Noble Park and North Melbourne, he said (jokingly), 'Noble Park's got better facilities.' Stevens said that because North hasn't got what other AFL clubs have, it's closer to the country and suburban clubs, to the original spirit of the game. 'You can't get big-headed at North,' said Archer.

Next door in the medical room, I met Marenepe, a 22-year-old Maori in a wheelchair with cerebal palsy. A graduate in journalism who is working as a cleaner, Mare-nepe was more than happy to talk to me. The reason he likes North Melbourne Football Club, he said with some difficulty and great emphasis, is because 'here I'm treated as an equal'. The players had taken Marenepe, or Muzza, as they call him, to their functions. Archer usually organised that. Judy Francis told me Muzza also liked playing his version of football. She said Carey and Archer would get him out of his wheelchair, put him on the floor and throw balls to him for hours.

As was observed in pubs and workplaces around the nation, the drama that exploded at the Kangaroos at the start of 2002 is not unusual in the history of the game. What was unusual is that clubs have traditionally dealt with the problem of extramarital relations between players and other players' wives, firstly, by keeping the matter firmly under wraps, and, secondly, if it was too big a problem to be ignored, by getting rid of the lesser player. In this case, the better player—in the opinion of many, the best player of his generation—was made to see he had to go. To a large extent, he was led to this conclusion by his team-mates, principally Glenn Archer, saying they wouldn't play with him again.

Archer's fury would not become fully public for another fourteen months when the Kangaroos played Carey's new club, Adelaide, in a strange match that affected most who saw it. Archer and Stevens each had altercations with Carey which told anyone watching that the three of them were part of some terrible triangle from which they might never break free. On the scoreboard, Carey won, kicking four goals, but at the end of the match, apart from Leigh Colbert, his direct opponent, not one North player went to him and shook his hand. He walked from the field jauntily enough, as he always had, but alone in a way he hadn't thought he'd be. He had also managed to alienate a lot of the North crowd, many of whom had wanted to welcome him back. Carey had given the finger to the Kangaroos cheer squad after kicking the first goal of the match. Perhaps something was said to him, but if ever there was a game when he needed to show restraint, perhaps even humility, this was the one. A sporting king who loses his subjects isn't left with much at all when his playing days are over.

Throughout the drama Judy Francis referred to as 'the disaster' or 'the tragedy', Carey's high profile manager, Ricky Nixon, was constantly in the news. Carey had been one of the first generation of celebrity footballers. Meanwhile, Anthony Stevens' manager, Ron Joseph, wasn't seen in public. Joseph is a former North adminstrator; with Allen Aylett, he oversaw the revolution in North's fortunes during the 1970s.

With Glenn Archer and another senior player John Blakey, it was Joseph who drove to Shepparton to see Stevens after he retreated to the family home. I don't know what was said at that meeting, but as vice-captain, with Carey gone, Stevens was now the official team leader.

The story broke on a Monday. On the Thursday, Stevens re-entered the change rooms at Arden Street and walked to his locker. No-one knew where to look. What do you say to a man whose most private ache is known to the nation? Was there ever a football injury like this one? An hour or so later, with Glenn Archer behind him, eyes flashing lest any prying journalist try to get too close to his mate, the man he would remain true to before any other, Anthony Stevens displayed the Shinboner spirit one more time, leading the team out on to the field for training, running the gauntlet of television crews lined up and jostling for a glimpse of his inner hurt. Ask North people there that night to describe that moment and most are lost for words. One said it was like winning a premiership. Their club was alive again.

Exploring Australia

Midway through 2002, I drove from Melbourne to Darwin with Neil Murray.The journey began in the Corner Hotel, Richmond, on a Sunday night, with me listening to Neil sing 'Melbourne Town', my favourite Melbourne song. It's about a grey winter's day and a football crowd going home defeated 'once again', but the rain on the singer's shoes suits his solitary mood. Neil's a solitary man. His forebears migrated from the Scottish highlands to Lake Bolac, in western Victoria, and he was then dividing his time between Lake Bolac and Darwin, where he had a small daughter. A couple of times he'd asked me if I wanted to do the drive with him, sharing the long hours of driving and the costs.

We first met in 1987 at Yuendumu, on the Warlpiri tribal lands outside Alice Springs. A former farm boy, he had dark reddish hair and the sort of build commonly described as wiry. He'd just completed a tour through northern Australia with the Warumpis, the first Aboriginal rock band to sing in Aboriginal dialects, which he had co-founded. At the time he didn't think much of journalists and I understood why. The rock media had only the vaguest inkling of his world. We were standing backstage at a concert being put on for the community at the end of a day's play in the football carnival. Although not eager to engage me in conversation, he did say a lot of people from 'down south' who come to the centre never go back. Over the next decade I saw why.

In the late nineties, I went to the south of France, saw the Riviera and thought it no more beautiful than central Australia—rocky outcrops that glitter in the noonday glare, snow white gums in blood red sand, mountains that go pink then lavender as the sun falls from the desert sky. And that's only the scenery. Certain currents that exist as low murmurs in the national psyche when living in Melbourne are as grand as opera up there. If I were young and single, I'd go and live in central or northern Australia for a while. As it is, what I know about those parts of Australia would appear on a map as a mess of dots—the result of flying visits. By driving from Melbourne to Darwin I would at least see the land as one unbroken line. I'd be able to see changes in the landscape as they occurred and be reacquainted with the vastness and character of this land. Always, in Australia, we're in danger of thinking we're somewhere else.

We left the pub in Richmond around midnight and drove to Lake Bolac. The next day we crossed into South Australia, went from one side of Adelaide to the other in peak-hour traffic and spent a night in a cheap motel at Port Augusta.The following morning, a few k's north of Port Augusta, we saw a sign saying 'Welcome to the outback', and it was true—the landscape was quite unlike the silver wheatfields we'd driven through the previous evening. The red earth was either bare or covered in rough grey-green scrub. And the hills weren't smooth and conical like the ones bordering the wheatfields. They were nude, flat-topped, purple. We passed a sign pointing to Woomera, site of the detention centre for asylum seekers where inmates had sewn their lips together in protest at their treatment. I have an inkling that in one hundred years time, people will speak of Woomera as we now speak of places like Port Arthur.

We passed three wedge-tailed eagles beside the road, not ten metres from it. I slowed down to get a better look at the weight of their glistening wings, the thrust of their chests, their bright, acquisitive stares.They were watching for road kill. We stopped at Lake Hart, an expanse of glittering white salt. For the first time in my life I needed sunglasses, and was reminded of a farmer named Coulthard who died looking for water in these parts in the early nineteenth century. He scratched on his empty water bottle: 'The white is dassling [sic] and my tongue is stuck to the roof of my mouth.' I found that line in *The Dig Tree,* Sarah Murgatroyd's retelling of the Burke and Wills expedition. In that book also is a quote by C.E.W. Bean, the World War I historian, saying the desert plays the part in the Australian imagination that the sea does in the British.

People have disappeared out here and entered Australian legend.With this in mind, I tried to slow my gaze to the speed of a man aboard a faltering camel coming back from a doomed bid to traverse the continent north to south. Neil had a song about Burke and Wills on his *Dust* album with a line Shane Howard was fond of quoting:'Mr Burke, where did all the blackfellas go?' Burke's response to Aboriginal people was a blend of fear and contempt, when they were his only hope of survival. He died, pistol in hand, on the banks of Cooper's Creek; when he was younger, Neil had gone to the actual place and camped a night there. I tried to picture the last two of Burke's companions, Wills and King, stumbling through the saltbush, but the attempt was futile. Cars travel too swiftly for such imaginings.

One perspective the modern traveller does share with the early explorer in the desert is that the horizon soon swims before your eyes and, before long, all I was seeing was the long blue tongue of the road drinking us up.What Neil saw was fences. He'd been coming up here since the seventies when the road was dirt and fraught with corrugations; in those days, there were no fences and you drove off the road each night and camped where you liked. He doesn't feel like he's back in the desert until he's had a night or two sleeping out. At Coober Pedy, we visited the underground church, chiselled from stone like a grotto. At a cafe over the road, we were forced to listen to a loud young English backpacker who seemed to believe, yet again, she was discovering the land for the rest of us.

What fascinated Neil, the former farm boy, about Aboriginal people was their self-sufficiency. Look at what we need, he said—an army of people to make this road, build this car, erect that roadhouse. Past Coober Pedy, a sand goanna darted out in front of our left tyre and was killed. Neil stopped and grabbed him. Finding a stretch of road without a fence, we drove through the scrub and camped among a clump of mulga trees, making a fire from its fallen branches. We cooked the goanna in the coals, tearing away the charred leather of its skin to get at its dry white meat. Lying on plastic sheets, we looked up at the blackest sky I'd seen since Africa.

The stars were strident dots of white surrounded by smoky veils of light, the occasional thin streak of silver being a satellite. Cyclonic rains across the Top End had closed the highway north of Alice Springs around Katherine and, during the night, I heard only one truck. Next day, when we got up, I felt like I was on the road, like I'd left home.

We reached Alice Springs around noon and tracked down a friend of Neil's called Sweeney. They'd met years ago at Papunya. Sweeney was working at the community's art gallery and sharing a house with a young historian named James Warden who was working for the Central Land Council.We stayed with them a couple of nights while Neil got the car looked over, passing a hot noonday watching a replay of the 2001 grand final. Sweeney was a Swans man with strong views on footy.Voss hadn't won the Norm Smith Medal for best on ground in the final, but Sweeney was adamant he should have. Having watched the replay, I had to agree. Television lets you see what happens in close and no-one is better in close than Voss. Early on, I saw him collect Hird. The Essendon captain didn't see it coming which is saying something, given his vision.Voss met him front on and took the wind out of him.Voss was not only more skilful than most others. He was also harder.

On the wall of Sweeney's house, I saw a painting by

Pegleg Tjampitjinpa, an old Bindibi man of eighty then living at Nyirrpi north-east of Yuendumu. The painting was like a sand map—three sets of uneven concentric circles joined with rough black lines overlaid with a splashing of white dots. It described possum and western quoll dreamings from his country. Most of the Bindibi only came in or were brought in during the 1960s. Sweeney showed me a book written in the 1950s, Donald Thompson's *Bindibi Country*, which has a photograph of Pegleg as a young man—pencil thin, totally naked, one leg ending at the knee. He is looking into a camera for the first time.

In the 1980s, a Bindibi family who had continued living like Pegleg's mob walked into Kiwikurra, in the north of Western Australia. A few years later, I happened to be in that community. One of the family was pointed out to me, but I was told not to be seen looking as members of the media had made arseholes of themselves getting their story. I glimpsed a young man with the blackest skin and a magnificent upright carriage. Later that day, I saw him jump into one of the community's trucks and drive off and was struck by the paradox that while the knowledge necessary to make the truck had taken centuries to acquire, he'd probably learned to drive it in an afternoon. But I was also told his older brother, Pyirrti, had gone back out into the desert. Alone.

Now, a decade later, sitting around a table in Alice Springs, people were telling stories about Pyirrti. Not of seeing him—no-one, it seems, sees him—but of coming across his tracks or visiting remote parts of Bindibi country and lighting a fire, as required by custom to signal you were approaching, and seeing one lit in return. At a time when the rest of the world was moving towards global uniformity, Pyirrti was, quite literally, out there. Pyirrti is my nomination for the next legend of the Australian desert.

Perhaps because of Pyirrti, the second half of the journey seemed more crowded than the first. One hundred kilometres north of Alice, we passed the Coniston turn-off, site of the last mass shooting of black people on Australian soil in 1928. An inquiry the following year admitted thirty-one people had been shot, not eight as originally reported. The policeman in charge of the party, Constable Murray, said he shot to kill because it was too far to carry the wounded back to 'civilisation'. In Sweeney's gallery in Alice Springs, I met the Papunya artist Billy Stockman, a white-haired old man in a wheelchair. The story is that he was present as a baby at the massacre, that his mother saved his life by covering him with a coolamon. To travel through northern Australia is to be reminded that the memory of war exists within this land.

At Barrow Creek, near where English tourist Peter Falconio disappeared, we stopped for a beer. Walking to and from the car, the heat was like a heavy overcoat you couldn't slip out of. Inside, the pub was a grimy curiosity shop, a wall of autographed paper money ending with a crisp new euro five, items of once sexy female underwear layered with desert dust, local snakes preserved in tall glass jars, a collection of battered hats belonging to former locals with names like Tossa Reidy. Aboriginal people sat around outside the pub, probably by choice. A gravel car park away were the graves of two white linesmen speared by blacks in 1874.

The road was still closed at Katherine and we were

meeting no traffic. The road, the land, was empty but for us. A few hours down the road at Wycliff Well, in the middle of what most people would call nowhere, we came upon a roadhouse painted black with a lurid galaxy of stars and swirling planets on it. Wycliff Well, said the sign, the UFO capital of Australia. Statues of little green men were walking to and from the toilets. It was such an absurd sight you had to stop and get out of the car. And listen.The silence is radical, extending to the horizon and who knows how far beyond. In this immensity, you're as significant as the next insect. Meanwhile, your mouth is getting drier with every breath. It's one of those moments, so defining of the early Australian character, when you have no option but to push on through the emptiness.

Shortly afterwards, out of the desert appeared a topple of orange boulders balanced on one another. Whitefella name? The Devil's Marbles. Blackfella name? Don't know, but there is a women's fertility place here. The stones looked like giant snake eggs. Back down the road at Coober Pedy, where legendary quantities of multicoloured opals have been taken from the ground, the rainbow serpent is said to lie. Even when I was a kid, people talked about the dead centre of Australia. To the people who had lived here for thousands of years it was a hard place, no doubt, but it was also a story as large and spectacular as the land itself.

In the Aboriginal township of Elliott we saw a large purple bloom of the sort jazz singer Billy Holliday might have worn in her hair.The air was humid and fertile; you could smell growth happening. We were in the Top End now. In the Elliott pub, Neil was recognised from his Warumpi days—the first rock band to sing in Aboriginal languages will never be forgotten in these parts. When we asked whether the road to Darwin was open, no-one seemed to know, but the young man humbugging me for a six-pack of beer told me the last time Katherine flooded a saltwater crocodile found his way into the meat department at Woolworth's. He said the crocodile wasn't happy. Perhaps he didn't like the prices.

As we'd gone into the pub, Neil had said, 'Only take the money you want to spend.' We left with none in our pockets, having had a few beers and bought a few for others, and drove through the night. Neil was in a mellow mood, telling stories of the Warumpi days. Already, a lot of the Aboriginal people he knew from that time were dead. He'd seen a world few Australians knew about, he'd written about it better than any other contemporary whitefella I'd read, and in the larger mainstream of Australian culture he was a half-known figure on the edges. Everyone knew Michael Voss because he excelled at the Australian game, but if you pursued Australian culture just as fearlessly you ended up in the margins. Wasn't this why the writer Xavier Herbert, who had trod a roughly similar path to Neil a few decades earlier, had despaired so richly about Australians? We never looked into our own interior to find ourselves, or never for long enough or in enough numbers to make it really matter culturally or politically, instead slipping from one imported notion of self to the next when our own stories were so much more revealing. And did anyone really give a fuck anyway? Sometimes, I wasn't sure I did anymore, then I went out into the land, rediscovered it all over again and felt something deep within me come on like a light.We drove on, just us and a road that ran to the end of the continent and a night so deep and dark we might have been moving quickly or not at all.

We spent our last night at the Larrimah Hotel, a magnificent old Territory pub whose walls are open to the cool evening air. During World War II, it served as a base for American officers, although the building was then further south at Birdum. From Alice Springs north, there is an uninterrupted sequence of World War II landmarks—air-fields, storage depots, hospitals, staging camps. At Adelaide River, there's a war cemetery with a section for civilians; unlike the rest of Australia, this place has a memory of war.The Japanese bombing raids during World War II lasted eighteen months and fanned across northern Australia.

For forty dollars we got a room in the Larrimah pub with two beds, an old air-conditioner, a tree outside the window with leaves like dark green plates and a cane toad in the toilet. By the time we reached Katherine the following day, the flood had dropped. Vegetation was swept around in big muddy swirls and there were silvery lakes beside the road. We zoomed on towards Darwin, the green growing ever brighter and more luminous, rocky knolls sprouting foliage from every crack and pore. I drove the last leg. Entering Darwin, a downpour of tropical rain caused the station wagon to shift as it briefly lost tread. In Melbourne, it was mellow and autumnal. In the Top End, it was the Wet Season.

Our drive north coincided with the sixtieth commemoration of the first bombing of Darwin on 19 February 1942. News of the attack was strictly censored. Among the subjects not disclosed were the extent of civilian deaths and casualties and the allegations of looting and large-scale desertion by Australian military personnel. Australians have a proud history as fighters. So what explanation is there for what happened in Darwin? Could the answer be found in a quote attributed to a Lieutenant Dudley Vose in the commemoration's official literature? Arriving in Darwin from Sydney, he found it 'a very isolated, unreal sort of place. Some men couldn't believe they were still in Australia'.

In Darwin, on the Saturday night, I attended the fiftieth anniversary celebrations of the St Mary's Football Club. St Mary's has the record for the greatest number of successive wins by any team in the history of Australian football and has produced two Norm Smith medallists, Michael Long and Maurice Rioli. Its clubrooms are also the place in Darwin where most of the big Stolen Generation meetings are held, the club having been formed by the Catholic church partly for young men like Michael Long's father, Jack, taken from their mothers in other parts of Australia and sent to Catholic orphanages in the Top End.

I was beginning to understand why, when John Howard helped float the idea that the term Stolen Generation was a myth, an upset Michael Long had written him a letter. He had it in his pocket at Beverly Knight's gallery when he met *Age* journalist Robin Usher. Learning of the letter, Usher asked if the *Age* could have it and the following day it appeared on the newspaper's front page. Long called the Prime Minister a cold-hearted prick. The spin doctors in Howard's office went berserk, but Howard got what he deserved for making political play of deep and genuine suffering.

To be Aboriginal is to know intimately, and be known in, the place you are from. In lives all around

Australia, that connection had been severed or disastrously weakened as a result of the policy of taking children away. Encouraged by Beverly Knight, Michael and I had discussed the possibility of doing a book together; what interested him was going back to northern Australia and re-assembling the connections that had been severed with the removal of his parents from their families. He wanted to continue the process he had begun in his art and reclaim the whole of his history. But it was a book that would take a lot of time, something he didn't have.

At the St Mary's Football Club's fiftieth anniversary I met Jack Long, Michael's father. Jack Long was renowned as the toughest man in Darwin footy in his day. Michael told me he could scarcely remember a game where his father didn't knock someone out. An opposition player had once fractured his forearm breaking Jack's nose. Both players had to leave the field but it was Jack who walked unassisted as if in no pain; that story was St Mary's legend. But Jack Long had never been back to the community he was taken from as a child, instead choosing to live on Bathurst Island where he had been adopted by the Tiwi community. I didn't know why he hadn't gone back, but I did know that for some Stolen Generation people the prospect of going home and not being known is more fearful than never going back at all.

It was towards the end of the night when Jack beckoned me over for a talk. Having let him know I was there a few hours before, I had waited. In Aboriginal culture it's called showing respect. Now he was ready to talk. What was Michael's main quality? I asked. 'Determination,' was the quick reply. Where did he get that from? 'His father.' I thought he was joking. The set of his face, the dark passionate eyes, told me he wasn't. 'I could have gone to Melbourne too,' he said. His eyes were burning. Why didn't you? I asked. 'Because I loved Michael's mother.'The toughest man of his day in Darwin footy had tears in his eyes.

The day Jack's wife died, five of his sons turned up and played for St Mary's, as she had instructed. Michael, sitting in the grandstand, was then thirteen. He was particularly close to his mother and believes she accompanied him during the 1993 AFL grand final which he dominated as comprehensively as any player of the modern era. He believes it in the way that others on the field that day believe they were wearing boots. When she was brought to Darwin as a small child and shipped across to Bathurst Island, she had never seen the sea before.The sight terrified her.

Everyone remembered Michael as having been a quiet kid. Jack told me Sheedy had 'taught him to talk'. In his teens, Michael had briefly toyed with abandoning football for basketball after an Adelaide team offered him a contract. He arrived home to find all his belongings on the doorstep. That was Jack's law: leave football, leave the family. All Michael's early memories that he related to me revolved around football, the early games being family games. His mother, no less than his father, was central to that.There was actually debate within the St Mary's club as to who was the best footballer among the Longs, one school of thought having it that the honour belonged to the eldest brother, Steven. When I asked Michael the difference between him and his brothers, he said, 'Opportunity.' That related to what I had heard him say in a speech about Sheedy—that he had opened the door for Aboriginal players.

At the St Mary's Football Club, Australians of European, Aboriginal and Asian descent sat around as equals in an atmosphere of mutual respect. Patrick Dodson, the father of the reconciliation movement, played for St Mary's. When Howard effectively marginalised him by not reappointing him as chairman of the Council for Aboriginal Reconciliation, I sent him a message through his offsider, Paul Lane: 'Tell the big bloke he's still Joe Louis to me.' The day after the reunion, I attended a club singalong which started around noon and was led by a tall Tiwi schoolteacher with a crackling laugh and a guitar. When he started 'My Island Home', I rang Neil and said, 'Get over here, they're singing your song,' but he was too tired after a day in the heat looking for a new place to rent for him and his daughter. He was missing western Victoria, its grey skies and cold winds. Funny how Aboriginality, if you pursue it far enough, eventually leads you back to the place you're from.

On Tuesday, I attended the ceremony commemorating the bombing of Darwin. More than one hundred Americans, mostly sailors aboard the USS *Perry*, died in the initial attack on Darwin. I wasn't blind to their sacrifice in the defence of my country. Ten American Kittyhawks were arriving from the Philippines when the first wave of Japanese bombers appeared overhead.The five Americans who were in the air engaged the enemy, the five who had landed went back up. Only two of the ten aircraft made it back. The American ambassador spoke, making reference to terrorism and September 11. Later, he would publicly rebuke Opposition Leader Simon Crean, who opposed a war in Iraq without UN backing, for his attitude to the United States. What would have been the reaction if the Indonesian ambassador had entered into public debate with the Prime Minister? I understood the need for alliances and the nature of them, but the US ambassador's behaviour went to the character of our independence.

The official ceremony didn't include the dance by which the Tiwi people of Bathurst and Melville islands committed the bombing to the memory of their culture. I was surprised, having already seen an impromptu performance of the dance, one bloke with pretend binoculars scanning the air, another with a pretend machine-gun jumping about and firing into the heavens. They had seen the Japanese bombers approaching from the east. Yet another of the mysteries surrounding the disaster is that a warning radioed to Darwin from Bathurst Island twenty minutes before the attack wasn't acted on. Could it be, like Burke in the desert, they had no respect for black intelligence? The day after the commemoration of the Darwin bombing, I boarded a plane and crossed the continent in five hours, seeing and learning nothing.

Nathan Buckley

Nathan Buckley looks like one of Noel Counihan's footy cartoons from the 1930s—a thatch of light-coloured, springy hair, narrow slits for eyes, broad grin, strong jaw. Of average height and solidly built, he has a certain way of talking. If he were a tree, you'd say his voice comes from his trunk and not the upper branches. When we first met for an interview in 2001, before I could ask him a question he asked me a series of them. He followed my writing and was eager to know more about what I did. Half an hour went by and the interview still hadn't started. Buckley was not as I had expected. Like other people who become introduced to the public essentially through the tabloid media—including, ironically, Collingwood president Eddie McGuire—his identity had been reduced to a caricature.

To say Nathan Buckley's Bradmanesque is a slightly dangerous thing to do, but what I mean is that he is a man who fixed his considerable intelligence on a game and what he could do within it. Buckley has half a degree in applied science, having specialised in human movement, and a couple of years of a town planning degree that he started when he first left school. No-one at that stage, with the exception of his father, Ray, saw what he might become as a footballer. Around the age of fifteen, as a reaction to his father's unrelenting ambition for him within the game, he gave up football for tennis, enjoying a sport in which he was responsible to no-one but himself. 'We [father and son] still talk about it,' he said, with one of his grins, but I could tell it was a delicate topic. He added, 'At the time, I thought he was very hard on me,' but stressed that he wouldn't be where he was if not for his father's influence. Eventually, Buckley inherited his father's ambition and became, in his own words, 'very driven'. Asked how much thought he had given to life after footy, he replied, 'Not one second's.'

Buckley's father, a former Woodville ruckman, was a professional footballer, moving around Australia. As a result, his son went to thirteen different schools. It meant he didn't build the usual boyhood friendships. 'If I wanted friends, I played footy.' He saw his first AFL game in 1980. He can remember the scoreboard, the wooden seats, the backs of the people in front of him, but nothing of the game. The power of his concentration has an effect on his memory. He grinned at that thought, too.

In 1988, after he switched to tennis, his father, then living in Darwin, sent him to Salesian College in Victoria as a boarder, ostensibly to bolster his studies, but also to encourage him 'to absorb the passion of Victorian footy culture'. The following year, he saw the famous roster match between Malcolm Blight's Geelong and the Hawthorn side that would qualify as one of the teams of the century. The Cats led by sixty points at half-time; Hawthorn overhauled them. Sitting two rows from the fence, 16-year-old Buckley knew he was seeing the game being played as well as it could be.

Even so, he was undersized and the following year he only scraped into the Port Adelaide under 19 grand final side when a regular wingman withdrew through injury. His performance in that grand final was the first time he was conscious of having impressed the club. The following year, he was introduced to the Port seniors and the year after that he won the Magarey Medal. That part of his history is well-known. What is less well-known is that during those three years, he also played in the Darwin competition during the summer months with a team called Southern Districts. For the three years prior to his arrival in the AFL, he played football all year round.

Talking football with Nathan Buckley is a rare pleasure. For example, he told me of an early AFL match in which he was tagged by Carlton's Brett Ratten. Buckley liked to stand three metres off the play at stoppages. Ratten stood one metre off it. Buckley observed the Carlton player's skill at reading the ruckmen's hands in the air, his sense of the other players around him and the spaces available to him to operate in. To compete with Ratten, Buckley realised he had to get closer to the contest. In Buckley's view, being able to find new methods is the test of a player. It's why he sees longevity as being the key indicator of football success; to Buckley, a champion is 'the bloke no-one can quell'. His style of language is modern colloquial.

What he got from playing football in the Northern Territory, with its profound Aboriginal and Islander influence, was a bank of alternative ideas on how to play the game. 'If you can pick up twenty touches as a mid-fielder in Darwin it's a fair feat, because NT football's nearly unreadable. You don't kick to a tall centre half-forward and crumb, or you didn't back then. Anything goes. The ball can go backwards fifteen metres before it goes forwards forty. Little passes—zip, zip, zip.You'd be trying to hit targets round the corner twenty metres away. You'd get it maybe one out of ten times but players would play for the excitement of doing it just that once.' He was grinning as he spoke, like a jazzman remembering an old tune on a piano. 'The other nine times the ball would stay on the ground but it wasn't worth collecting unless you'd paddled it past another player, and picking it up after three paddles going flat chat was always better than just getting it clean. Footy in Darwin was about enjoyment, about being a bit of a lair.'

In the Darwin competition, he played as an 'undersized centre half-forward'. He was a good mark, better than he is now. 'I used to take plucks everywhere, used to love snapping the ball over my shoulder. I had a good sense around goals.' Ray Buckley laments that the highly structured nature of AFL football has caused some of the skills his son had in Darwin to drop away. (When I relayed this to Schwabbie he laughed weakly at the thought that he had only ever seen the lesser Buckley, the diminished version.) In 1992, Buckley won the Magarey Medal and played in a Port Adelaide premiership team, but it was two other happenings that combined to shape his cast-iron ambition.

In a back room of his grandmother's house, where he was living, he found a set of weights his uncle had left. He started doing dumbbell curves, incline flies, sit-ups. It was the first time he'd done something like that without being told to do so.

Having discovered his limits, he experienced a deep satisfaction in pushing beyond them. Later, he applied this principle to learning how to do things on the field like kicking goals from outside fifty. The experience persuaded him of the power of self-discipline. Even now, doing things in a game that are not natural to him gives him more satisfaction than doing things that are.'You're the one who does it,' he says, by way of explanation.'You had to make the decision to do it. It didn't come naturally.'

What also happened in 1992 was that, after playing in the Northern Territory, he found South Australian football predictable and easy to read. 'The ball'd go bang long from the back-line, then cross to centre half-forward where there'd be a contest and it'd either go forward or there'd be a quick kick out of the pack. If you sat yourself thirty-five or forty metres off centre half-forward, you'd get heaps of possessions from panic kicks that came out at forty-five degrees towards the wing.'

The following year, in the words of Paul Kelly's song 'Bradman', Nathan Buckley arrived in the AFL, 'just a kid in from the sticks, just a kid with a plan'. He played with Brisbane, won the Norwich Rising Star for the best first-year player in the AFL and, at season's end, transferred to Collingwood after a chorus of clubs came bidding for his services. People didn't know how to read the move from Brisbane. Irecall a commentator saying Buckley could be the new breed of football professional, the one who sells his services every couple of years. What they didn't see was his relentless appetite for self-improvement—he couldn't see

Brisbane improving. It was soon rumoured he had trouble getting on with his new team-mates. The word that began following Nathan Buckley around—or rather preceding him—was 'arrogant'. It became the habit for crowds to boo him as they booed Wayne Carey.

I had the idea he was a braggart, but that was not how I found him. In fact, he was the opposite. His judgments about other players we spoke about were uniformly generous. Like a certain sort of outstanding sportsman—George Best, Laurie Nash—he was candid about himself, but he was just as open about what he didn't know as what he did.The person he described as his best mate, a former flatmate he met after joining Collingwood, had spent the past four years travelling the world. The idea of an immense world beyond his own intrigued him, making him grin and shake his head like a kid outside the window of a shop he's never been in.

What this former student of human movement knew most about was the game of Australian football. He enjoyed watching soccer, but believed the Australian game was more complete and was strongly against further rule changes.The game, he said, always finds its way. He believed football was always evolving in one direction or another. The change of direction occurred when an individual appears who reads the play so brilliantly that he undoes all the systems of thought devised before him. He believed a player like Peter Daicos would have been able to undo the defensive tactic known as flooding. 'The ball's on the ground a lot and it wouldn't matter to him if there were one, two or six players around—he'd find a way.' Daicos, in Buckley's estimation, was wholly unpredictable and, for that reason, one of those who couldn't be quelled.

Nathan Buckley knew volumes more about football than I did. I suspected he knew more than the umpires who mysteriously failed to give him the Brownlow votes that have seemed his due over a series of years. His weakness had been his lack of patience with people who didn't understand the game as well as he did and, before the start of the 2001 season, Collingwood had sent Buckley to do a course to assist his captaining. There were stories that other Collingwood players, notably Chris Tarrant, found him overbearing. I suspected Buckley wasn't troubled by the fact his team-mates weren't as gifted as him; what he would find hard to accept was that they didn't have his ambition or application. They didn't choose to be better.

The question of the relationship of individuals to teams clearly vexed him when I raised it, causing him to pause and search for words.'I know in myself that all along my thought process was to benefit the team and prepare myself as best I possibly could for the benefit of the team. People miss out on the last six words. What I would say now is that my focus is to play the best I can to enable my team-mates to be better.' He says maybe he was abrasive in his methods when he began, but he clings to something Robert Walls, his coach at Brisbane, said: Nathan Buckley embarrasses other players with his commitment to the game.

I asked him if he wished he'd stuck to tennis. If he'd been anywhere near as good at that game as he is at football, he would have procured enormous wealth and world fame. His answer was a swift and unerring no. He preferred footy. Why? 'Because it's a team game.'

That is the paradox of Nathan Buckley: when he was young and forever the new kid in town, he played footy to make friends, but at the same time the transient nature of his upbringing led him to conceive of the game in a solitary and individual way.

We talked about great games. Buckley says great games—the ones people remember—always have something riding on them. They're usually finals. At that stage, he had played in only one final, in 1994, his first year at Collingwood, against West Coast in Perth; Collingwood lost narrowly. Each year since, the biggest game of Nathan Buckley's season had been the Anzac Day match which, as he says, is like a final but isn't one. Nevertheless, in 2001, the Anzac Day match was one of the best of the year. I put it to him that James Hird won the match for Essendon. 'Yeah,' he said ruefully, adding half-humorously, 'bastard.'

No-one is harder on Nathan Buckley than Nathan Buckley. 'In the last quarter,' he offered, 'I was on Hird at the stop plays.' In the final term of the 2001 Anzac Day match, Hird kicked a goal off one step around his body. He also handballed over a defender's head in such a way that the ball bounced up into the arms of a team-mate running towards goal. Mere moments in the execution, they were the game's killing blows. I suggested that when games are at the point of being decided, Hird knew how to win them. Again, Buckley agreed. 'It's something you learn from being in that position,' he said, adding quickly,'but you have to be good enough to execute it.'

He didn't say it, but clearly his team hadn't been in the position very often for him to master that dynamic to the same extent. Buckley wondered aloud about

Hird, where he got his flair from, where or how he learned the game. He has a photo of a school team he played for in Canberra, the Ainslie under-13s; the kid beside him is snowy-haired James Hird.What did he remember about him? 'Nothing,' he said flatly, in a way that suggested he had tried. The match Nathan Buckley nominated as his most memorable was one he was confident no-one would remember, a pre-season game in Western Australia in 2001. Collingwood beat West Coast in Perth for the first time in nearly a decade, but more to the point it was, in Buckley's estimation, the game in which Josh Fraser stood up, and a couple of other young players showed a bit. At last he sensed the Pies had a future.

With Collingwood in the Top End, 2002

Among those waiting to meet Collingwood when they arrived at Darwin's Marara Oval on their mid-season tour to the Top End was John Kelly Country, the man who sent a bad spirit to torment the Magpies in the early nineties.That was after then president Allan McAllister provoked a furore by saying blacks were welcome at the club so long as they behaved like whites. If you can imagine that being said without malice, with a strange sort of innocence that is also ignorance, you have not only a picture of the Collingwood president of that time but also an idea of the state of relations between the club and Aboriginal Australia. Kelly Country had blown up a curse.

Claiming he was now afflicted with a bad conscience as a result of Collingwood's subsequent lack of success, particularly as he had blown up a couple of flags for Adelaide, Kelly Country placed his lips to the painted wooden pipe and summoned up a good luck charm. He then sold the didjeridu to a club official and departed. Later, when the players were sitting around waiting for the bus, Leon 'Magic' Davis sat blowing some notes on the instrument. When I approached him and asked, he told me it was a skill he learned from his father. Ours was a brief exchange, but I sensed both his natural shyness and the confidence he took from those around him—his team-mates. Magic, or Maj, as he was more commonly known, was part of the club. You could tell by the pats he gave and received in passing from team-mates, the wordless communication he was constantly engaged in.

Davis is a Nyunga from the south of Western Australia and his career has been crucial to Collingwood. A few years after the incident with McAllister, an Aboriginal mate of mine invited to Victoria Park for a function asked me to go with him because he didn't want to go alone. Collingwood had a nasty reputation on the issue of race. By the end of 2002, that was no longer the case, a change I credit in good part to president Eddie McGuire. I have had a public difference with Eddie over the issue of conflict of interest, but I am not an Eddie basher. He's like a certain sort of American, a dynamic individual who sees no limit to what he can do (hence the problem with conflict of interest), but one who also supports a range of social initiatives in a spirit of what might be termed enlightened self-interest.

Racism was simply no good for Collingwood; all the young Aboriginal footballers dreamed of going to Essendon because that's where Michael Long played. Any club denied access to the footballing talent of Aboriginal Australia doesn't have much of a future. Eddie decreed there would be no racism at Collingwood and that meant none. Collingwood's other

Aboriginal player, Richard Cole, is a young Warumungu man from Tennant Creek. Cole had wanted to play for Essendon and he lived with Michael Long's friend and adviser Beverly Knight after coming to Melbourne. Eddie fixed that one too. Cole now wears Long's old number, 13, as a sign of respect for Long, but plays for Collingwood.

Eddie also contracted a coach, Mick Malthouse, who had credibility in Aboriginal Australia. During the years when his champion West Coast team was winning premierships, football trips by club representatives to remote Aboriginal communities in Western Australia commonly ended with Malthouse sitting in a circle with the elders. Naturally inquisitive, but also interested in how to better understand his Aboriginal players, Malthouse had learned a lot about Aboriginal culture.

Like most AFL coaches I had got to know, there was more to Mick Malthouse than met the eye. His playing career had begun at St Kilda, but his failure to impress at that club had led him to Richmond where he played in the 1980 premiership. I always thought Mick Malthouse played footy like an Apache, straight-backed and wild but with a hard, disciplined edge. In his first coaching appointment, at Footscray, he took an uneven team to a preliminary final. After that loss, the press grilled him as to the failure of one of his key players, a battler who had been out of his depth. Malthouse was seated; he looked like a young military officer under interrogation. 'We came together, we'll go home together,' he said. I knew from the year I spent at Footscray writing a book that he had left the club with the respect of the senior players. At West Coast, having been handed an awesome array of underachieving talent, he forged a meanly efficient unit which powered its way to two premierships. Mick's relations with the media led to him being dubbed Mick Shithouse by some in the press box, which changed to Mick Greenhouse when he took a stand on Western Australia's old-growth forests. He is a man with a strong empathy for the natural world. Early on, back in his Footscray days, I had written a profile on him and rung back to check his quotes. Thereafter, he had always talked to me if our paths crossed and, although this happened rarely, I learned that he came from a very tough background and had a flood of stories about it. He had a desire to teach what he called life skills. Meanwhile, his ideas about coaching were evolving along similar lines.

The entire Collingwood squad had been flown to Aboriginal communities throughout the territory in a project jointly sponsored by Collingwood, ATSIC, the AFL and the Pratt Foundation. Suffice it to say most of the players had seen nothing like it. They were in no way spared the reality of contemporary living in outlying Aboriginal communities (the previous year, twelve young men in one community south of Katherine attempted suicide in a week), but unlike most whitefellas visiting such places, who are ignored or apparently ignored, the Collingwood players were greeted like heroes.

At Milikapiti on Melville Island, where I went with Nathan Buckley and three other Collingwood players, the shouting began before the light aeroplane's single propeller had stopped. Standing with a line of kids behind the metal gate, as excited as any of them, was an old woman with white hair whose name, I learned, was Mary Elizabeth Moreen. She quickly informed us she was a traditional owner for Milikapiti and a Collingwood supporter. She described the occasion as 'first time welcome the players on our community. Really happy to see them, especially Buckley. His mother used to work with my sister in the hospital'.

We were driven to the community in four-wheel drives. A long banner outside the local primary school read 'Milikapiti is the Home of the Magpies'. Ray Fett, the local school teacher, was impressing upon anyone who would listen how important the visit was. Garden Point, where the Longs and Riolis are from, has had numerous visits from AFL personalities including Kevin Sheedy. The AFL premiership cup had even been there. But this was a first for Milikapiti. Fett was one of several white workers who also wanted to talk about the community's problems. Last year, the island had a spate of suicides. Fett hoped to get the players into the classrooms to talk to kids about attending school. Instead, in his words, there was bedlam. 'But that,' he said goodnaturedly, 'is what footy is out here.'

Mary made a speech welcoming the four Collingwood players to her country. They were joined by the Collingwood supporters in the community and dozens of kids singing the club song, 'Good Old Collingwood Forever'. It was something to witness: 'Side by side we'll stick together, to uphold the Magpie name. 'Then the dancing began, the excitement building all the time. In each case the dancers, embodying the spirit of an animal, came right up to the players as a sign of welcome. I had been told by some women accompanying the party, who had been out with the players in Darwin the previous night, that the two best dancers in the Collingwood team were Richard Cole and Brodie Holland. Halfway through the buffalo dance, Holland, who had been watching intently, suddenly joined in.That was the biggest, most joyful shout of the day.When a bag with footballs and Collingwood caps appeared, a Pratt Foundation worker made the mistake of bending over it, presumably to oversee an orderly distribution of the goods. She literally disappeared from sight beneath a swarm of small black bodies.

The players went into the school to leave handprints on a wall as mementoes of their visit. Coming out a kid passed Buckley a ball. He had clearly played Top End schoolyard footy before; leaning back, he aimed a banana kick to pass between two coconut trees a few metres apart. The ball bounced off the nearer tree. A small voice cried 'Hit the post!', and it was like a siren had sounded. Leather footballs began flying in all directions. In addition to his mother, Karen, training health workers on the island, Buckley's father Ray used to visit the Tiwis when he was director of coaching in the Northern Territory. Phillip Daniels, a senior player with the Milikapiti Magpies, told me Buckley plays 'the territory way—he got skills like a blackfella'.

Next item on the schedule was a fishing trip for the players.We travelled to Shark Bay in the back of four-wheel drives, the journalists discussing the issue of television screening rights, having been met with vigorous protests about the reduced number of games being beamed into Milikapiti this year. As we bounced through the bush, we passed a collection of weathered pukumani poles leaning out of the earth at odd angles, guarding the spirits of the dead.

Missionaries didn't reach the Tiwis until the 1940s; one of them, Brother John Pye, brought a footy with him.The best and fairest medal on Tiwi grand final day is called the John Pye Medal. The previous year, I had tracked him down in Darwin living in a home for elderly clerics. He was a crusty old fella in a thin, hard, physical frame. He told me that there were places in northern Australia in the 1940s where you could still be met with spears. 'The Tiwis met you with a smile,' he said.

After meeting Brother Pye, I'd gone to a match between the Tiwis and a central desert mob. A lot of pride was riding on the match. Pre-game, by prior arrangement, I snuck into the Tiwi rooms. I intended to behave as I would with a whitefella team, stand at the back, stay out of the way, look and listen. In the Tiwi rooms, the team preparation stopped while I was introduced. 'Everyone, this is Martin.' My name, accompanied by flashing smiles, came back to me from around the room. The Tiwi tactics, I learned, were to keep the ball on the ground because their players were smaller, and to speak in language so the other mob wouldn't know what they were thinking. The Tiwis won.

When we reached Shark Bay I asked Mary if it was safe to walk along the beach with crocodiles around. 'Yes,' she said,'safe to walk. They only come up at night, except sometimes at day.' While the players were out fishing, she cooked a couple of mud crabs, occasionally talking aloud to herself. She said her country was nearby, meaning the place of her ancestor spirits. I wondered if she was talking to them. Memory is an altogether different concept in places like this. Back at Milikapiti, I'd met a whitefella named Chris Aitken who played with Melbourne in the sixties. He wasn't surprised that I couldn't remember him as a footballer. What had surprised him when he came to the island was that there were Tiwis who did.

When the fishermen eventually returned, they were asked if they would like to visit the Milikapiti cultural centre, Jilamara. It had been a long day but Buckley said they would. In the back of the four-wheel drive, he said to the other players,'Let's do the right thing, boys.' And they did. At the cultural centre they were taken through the museum, shown some recent paintings, pukumani poles and tunga baskets. As we left, a kid aged three or four climbed aboard and sat on Damien Adkins' knee. Leaning forward, he whipped Adkins' sunglasses off his nose and put them on his own face. When we reached the airfield, I could see Adkins didn't know what to do. 'You better ask for them back,' I said.

By then the television cameramen had gone but the best image of the day was the last, old Mary as she embraced Buckley, the gratitude and affection in her face. This was something that would enter the memory of the place, the day Nathan Buckley brought the Collingwood Magpies to Milikapiti for the first time. On the way back to Darwin, in the confines of the noisily vibrating light aeroplane, Buckley confessed to me that he didn't understand racism. He shook his head. He didn't understand it like some people don't understand algebra. It was almost as if he wished he could understand it because then he would know better how to deal with it. Because of the game he had become fluent in two cultures without knowing he had bridged a gap most of his countrymen and women would never cross.

Next morning in the hotel, the players I spoke to seemed quietly touched by their experiences. Over breakfast, Malthouse described his players to me as 'a humble lot'. He'd actually like a few more of what he called scallywags in his squad, but what he didn't want was dickheads. 'Dickheads ruin a club.' A word like scallywag sounded odd coming from his mouth and I wondered exactly what it might mean. I had no doubt, however, about the fate that would befall any player aspiring to wear the Collingwood guernsey who fell into the second category.With Eddie McGuire's support, he had set about rebuilding Collingwood from the bottom up and, at the end of his first year with the Pies, Malt-house had cleared three of his best players. All had done well at their new homes, but for one reason or another they hadn't fitted his vision. Buckley told me it wasn't since his old Port Adelaide days that he had experienced such unity of thought at the top of a football club.

On the last morning, I was waiting for the team bus with one of the young players, Alan Didak. We were talking about the World Cup. Didak played footy like a soccer striker, always lingering within range of goal, spinning on a coin, hitting the ball with either foot. Among the mountain of luggage beside us was the didjeridu purchased by the club from John Kelly Country. Putting it to his lips, Didak eventually found a note, one that was young and earnest. He was blowing the spirit of the Pies in 2002.

The 2002 AFL Grand Final, Brisbane V. Collingwood

Sport is never more thrilling than when, on the basis of decades of thought and observation, you know something can't possibly happen—and it does! An example of this was Collingwood's victory over Port Adelaide in Adelaide during the first week of the 2002 finals. No team seemed more grimly deter-mined—or, it has to be said, pre-programmed—than Port. Assured of a place in the finals from relatively early in the season, they thereafter approached each game like a big powerful car going for a test drive each time it hit the track, tuning itself for the finals.

In fairness, the week before the finals Port played in the match of the year—in Adelaide, against Brisbane. That game was so good it burst open like a plant in seed and each seed was a game within the game. My favourite was played out between Port's Chad Cornes and Brisbane's Jonathan Brown, two young players on the rise, both on the verge of becoming major presences in the game, both sensing how much was up for grabs for themselves and their teams. For one half, their duel was a test of craft that was also uncompromisingly physical. Cornes' ability to out-leap Brown, no mean feat in itself, meant the crux of their contest was about getting front position when the ball was directed towards Brown on the Brisbane half-forward line. In only his second year, Brown was being seen as the heir to Carey as the next great centre half-forward. Before this match, Cornes' status was slightly undecided. After it, he had a reputation in his own right as he got the better of Brown.

Then, in the third quarter, Cornes was suddenly no longer there, having been swung from defence to attack. With the edge having been taken from Brown's vigour, Port coach Mark Williams could afford to bring the slower Darren Mead on to the field to secure him, thereby releasing Cornes to play forward. This sort of thing was going on all over the ground. With minutes to go, Brisbane appeared to have won the match. Port bucked one last time, ran the ball forward and goaled. I heard it described as the best game in twenty years. Collingwood, meantime, had limped into the finals like a dog with three legs. It was also without Buckley, who was injured. I imagined him watching from the sides and felt for him. The match would have been only his second chance to play in a final and, in the folklore of the game, the finals are where great players prove themselves.

Like most of Melbourne, I gave the Pies no chance. I didn't even bother to watch, instead meeting some Greek friends at the Bendigo Hotel in Collingwood to listen to some traditional Greek music.The band we had gone to see weren't there; in their place was a dance band. As fate would have it, however, above our table was a television tuned to the match in Adelaide.

There's a certain ingredient the best matches have, a sustained tension and excitement that is reflected in the crowd noise and the commentary. This one had it. Somehow, Collingwood, the rank underdogs, knew how to win and Port, the raging favourites, didn't. In the third term, polite conversation was abandoned; we bolted for the bar, abandoning the music. A late Leon Davis goal, celebrated with a twiddling of the fingers, secured the game for the Pies and the Port players left the field like men being escorted to a prison van. At the final siren, the camera flashed to Malthouse in the press box. If they ever replay it, check out the glint in the old eagle's eye. It was his victory, his belief that had sustained the Pies.

Among our number in the bar of the Bendigo Hotel that night was an avant-garde composer from New York. I would love to know what he made of the evening, particularly the toothless bloke with the tatts in the Collingwood guernsey who led the bar in a rendition of 'Good Old Collingwood Forever'. We were only a street or so away from where John Wren, Collingwood's godfather from the early 1900s, had his illegal tote. Who knows? We probably woke the dead.The following week, Collingwood disposed of Adelaide to make its first grand final in more than ten years. And Buckley was back from injury.

The 2002 grand final was widely considered the best since 1989, which meant we were either on or approaching the slopes of football's Mount Olympus. During the Sydney Olympics, the Greek government had provided a collection of arte-facts—frescoes, sculptures, hand-painted plates and vases—created in Greece at the time of the original Olympics. This was supplemented with visual displays recreating the amphitheatres where the games were held. Basically, the original Olympics were men's business conducted in the presence of the gods. The results were considered fate. The exhibition ended with the bust of a young boxer, face battered, sense of self as clear as when he had begun his bout. He was the dead spit of Gary 'Buddha' Hocking, one of those whose name will forever feature in accounts of the 1989 grand final. That game could be described in many ways, but at one level it was a contest between a champion team (Hawthorn) and a team with a champion player (Geelong). So, too, was the 2002 grand final.

I sat in the upper tier of the Ponsford Stand beside Barry Richardson, a surprisingly gentle man who played in Tom Hafey's terrifying Richmond teams of the late sixties and seventies. Early on it rained, so the players slid about and kicks didn't go far. Buckley's use of the wet ball was a revelation. He played on Brisbane captain Michael Voss and had the better of him simply by being more influential. In the third term, or what is known as the premiership quarter since it is when most grand finals are decided, Buckley rose to even greater heights, imposing his will on the game. Collingwood got ahead and the most unlikely victory looked possible. Those voting for the Norm Smith Medal for best on ground did so at the twenty-minute mark of the last quarter. Thereafter—that is, in the last ten minutes of the game—Michael Voss won it for Brisbane, kicking a goal from outside fifty metres, intercepting a Collingwood attack on the half-back line, ordering Brisbane's play. As Voss rose, Collingwood sank, thereby launching an argument that will never be settled about the Norm Smith Medal.

In the immediate aftermath of the game, as the sense descended upon the crowd that they had just witnessed something remarkable, a weeping Malthouse was seen with his arm around Paul Licuria. Much was made of this. Malthouse was the coach with the fixed demeanour, or so it seemed. In Darwin, Malthouse told me the biggest thing he had learned about coaching was to treat players as individuals. Licuria was an Essendon reject, his disposal of the ball was faulty, but he was wholehearted and brave and his blanketing of the highly rated Josh Francou in Adelaide two weeks earlier was a large part of the reason Collingwood had got to the grand final. Malthouse had made Licuria as a player and he wasn't the only one in the team of whom that could be said.There was the kid with the learning disability the coach shielded not only from the press but even his team-mates. I knew only a fraction of what had gone on behind the scenes at Collingwood, but what I did know was that a team that wasn't great had very nearly achieved a great result.

The Norm Smith Medal was awarded to Nathan Buckley. Coming down from the dais, Buckley halfpulled the medal from his neck, an act for which he was much criticised, but in an interview that night he described the game as a cruel twist of fate and I felt I knew what he meant. As determinedly as he had done anything in his football career, the loner had set out to become one who thought group, not self. It was part of his life's object. His team had reached the pinnacle of the sport and might have won. Instead, his opponent had held aloft the premiership cup while he had received something he no longer sought, yet another decoration for his individual self. In a photograph taken of him after the game, the great Collingwood champion of his era sat slumped in a corner of the rooms, staring into the absence that shadows all our driven selves.

Bali

The first I heard about the Bali bombing was when a close mate, a mad Hawthorn supporter named Michele M. Gierck, otherwise known as Gurkha, rang me from Queensland to say she'd just heard a story about a bomb exploding in a Bali tourist resort. Gurkha knows a bit about war, having been in the mountains of El Salvador during the closing stages of that country's appalling civil war. Players from two AFL sides were in the blast area, she'd been told—Melbourne and West Coast. I rang the *Age* news desk. They confirmed the fact of the blast, but knew nothing about West Coast and Melbourne. A suburban team from Perth was involved and there was concern for some footballers from the Victorian coastal town of Port Fairy.

A few days after the bombing, Amanda Smith from the ABC radio program 'The Sports Factor' rang and asked me to say something on her show about what had occurred. I said I didn't know what to say. It always takes me time to work out what I think. In a kind and polite way, she pressed and eventually I agreed.

But how do you write or speak about slaughter? With time, I recalled having asked that question of myself a few years earlier when writing a piece on the first anniversary of the Port Arthur shootings. That was a Tasmanian tragedy, in part because so many people in Tasmania were connected to it in some way. My sister Mary had taught the killer, Martin Bryant, at a special school. I'd worked with his uncle—an old sailor with a heart of gold—in my first job after uni. One of my brother Richard's kayaking mates was the first officer on the scene at the Black Arrow Cafe. Actually, he was a fisheries inspector, but he was the first man in a blue uniform with a pistol holster on his belt. People came running from everywhere, asking if they were safe. All he knew was that a young man with long white hair was loose in the area with a semi-automatic weapon and that there were already many casualties. Did he tell the truth and frighten them further or did he calm them? He said they were safe. Two of my best mates from university were involved in the immediate battery of responses from state government departments. When I went to Hobart a year later to talk to them, I couldn't believe how much they had been affected. One of my friends said Bryant was more frightening than a torturer because a torturer knows he's inflicting pain. And this was just the start of my inquiries.

When I came back to Melbourne and tried writing the piece, I couldn't. At some point I remembered Wilfred Owen, one of two poets I was struck by at school. He'd died at the age of twenty-four, one week before World War I ended, but by then he'd seen the lot—death, maiming, mass random destruction. One of his poems is about being home on leave, hearing people complain about petty things and expressing loud, uninformed opinions about the war. Owen, who achieved a deep compassion in his short life, saw such people as cursed, barred from 'whatever mourns in man . . . when many leave these shores/Whatever shares the eternal reciprocity of tears'.That was the only spirit with which I could approach events like Port Arthur and Bali, but I began my talk on 'The Sports Factor' with another poem, Peter Porter's 'Phar Lap in the Melbourne Museum'. It concludes with my favourite lines from Australian sports literature:

> It is Australian innocence to love
> The naturally excessive and be proud
> Of a big-boned chestnut gelding who ran fast.

Someone had likened the Bali massacre to the murder of the eleven Israeli athletes at the Munich Olympics, but I saw differences. The Israeli team were consciously representing their nation. Our people weren't; they were on holiday. The Israeli team were elite athletes who had disciplined themselves to climb a pinnacle of world sport. The Australians, mostly from local teams on end of season trips, played their sport a long way from the high theatre of the Olympics. In fact, chances were they resembled the sportsmen and women I'd known in my youth, but that also made them representative of Australian culture as I understood it. Critics of sport mock it, saying that it's childish, that it's adult make-believe. They're probably right, but that doesn't make it any less real for those who do the believing. That's why the surviving members of the Kingsley footy team had stayed behind in Bali, sorting through the wreckage of the two nightclubs, trying to find the remains of their team-mates.

Eight months later when Jason McCartney, the Kangaroos player injured in Bali, made it back for a single match, playing in a body stocking, I went to watch. After the bombing, McCartney had given up his seat on the plane back to Australia to someone he thought more injured than himself; later, his condition sank to critical. In part due to two of McCartney's efforts in the last quarter, the Kangaroos defeated Richmond by a few points.

McCartney's from Nhill in western Victoria—hard, dry country. Last I'd heard, water reserves in that region were down to six per cent. In that culture, the surest way to invite ridicule is to make unwarranted assertions about self. That's why, after the match when he said he was spent, you knew he meant it. He also said he'd been as excited during the game as he was the first time he got a kick in the Nhill Little League. You knew he meant that, too. The young Jason McCartney thought footy was as big as the universe, and hence a game for heroes.

Footy tells stories you don't otherwise hear much anymore. Reality TV shows like *Big Brother* tell us what people do when they're doing nothing. Most television programs are American while in video stores violent, fear-ridden fantasies masquerade as entertainment. In the final minute of the McCartney game, the Kangaroos trapped the ball in their defence. McCartney said he knew they weren't going to lose because Stevo and Arch were in there—Stevo and Arch, Stevens and Archer, the two great Shinboners of their time. After the match, standing in the circle with the players belting out the club song, round face beaming, was Judy Francis. Most people watching that night felt something. It's Australian innocence for a young man injured in a bomb blast to want to play one last game.

The 2002 Boxing Day Test, England V. Australia

In the build-up to the 2002 Boxing Day Test at the Melbourne Cricket Ground, two features of the famous landmark changed. Outside the ground, maybe 100 paces from the original boundary line of the MCG, the living top of one of the two old scarred trees had finally broken and fallen. Its scar was the result of bark having been stripped from its trunk by Wurundjeri people before white settlement for the making of a canoe or a shelter. That meant the tree had been there when the Melbourne Cricket Club first chose the place among the trees as the site for its playing field in the 1840s. It was there when the first English team visited in 1861 and fifteen thousand people, or one in twenty of the Melbourne population, came to see them play. The old tree probably had urchins in its branches that day. It heard the rumble of outrage as Larwood ran in to bowl at Bradman during the Bodyline series, and it was part of the backdrop when the MCG was used as a military base during World War II, thereby requiring the Bloodbath to be played at Carlton. The hot winds of the 2002–3 summer had brought an end to its stand, but until the last it had continued to sprout a few green leaves from its withered head. I scooped my hand into the rubble at its base and collected a piece of the rotten wood with its ancient bark to give to Joy Murphy Wandin, the Wurundjeri elder. Like most of Melbourne, the MCG is on Wurundjeri land.

The second change was to the stadium itself. The Ponsford Stand had gone. The MCG looked like a face with the front teeth knocked out. A few days before the Boxing Day Test, I went to the MCG to meet Megan Ponsford, granddaughter of Australian cricketer Bill Ponsford, after whom the stand was named. Megan Ponsford is a passionate supporter of the Melbourne Football Club and two years ago, while attending a game at the MCG and standing in an upper room of the Members' Stand, she suddenly realised how much she was going to miss the place when it was gone. Her grandfather, with whom she had come to both the cricket and footy, had played here.There was a large oil painting in the Members' of him taking the field with Bradman at the Oval in 1934. In the infamous Adelaide Test during the Bodyline series, it was Ponsford who stood up to Larwood, then at his most lethal, having hit one Australian batsman in the heart, another in the head. Ponsford top-scored with eighty-three, sustaining numerous blows to the body. The great West Indian sportswriter C.L.R. James claimed the tactic of Bodyline was a logical expression of a world moving towards global conflict.

Megan Ponsford recorded the parts of the MCG about to disappear. Unlike most sports photography, her images are about neither action nor crowds.

They're about a grand dame of a sporting theatre. Megan mostly came at dawn. Her sense was that she was aboard a ship, and to walk with her through the place was to have your eye awakened to small features that are quaintly out of time, like the heavy glass door on the top tier of the Members' Stand with the hint of art deco in its metal work. She even found parts of the stadium no-one knew existed any more, like an old squash court and bar beneath the Ponsford Stand.

As a person, I liked her unashamedly colloquial manner. As an artist, I liked the way she revived the ordinary. Her photo of the red brick turrets at the entrance to the Members' Stand has them pointing into the clear blue air like old-fashioned spaceships.

Inside the Members' pavilion, she captured the 1920s interior, the porcelain urinals, the dark, lushly wooded bars which looked like they belonged on an Irish racecourse; but she was true to the whole, having also taken photos of the drab concrete upper tiers of the Olympic Stand looking back towards the city on a wet day. She wasn't unduly sad about the proposed redevelopment that would eventually knock out half of what had been there a few months before. 'This place has always been changing,' she said, which is true. But, equally, she started taking the photos because she wanted her two small sons, Edoardo and Alessandro, to have some sense of the place when a whole grandstand bore their great grandfather's name. 'I've got the memories' she said, patting her portfiolio. She told me she was trying to get them published as a book, to be titled 'Home Ground', and I encouraged her to do so. The G is everyone's home ground.

I went to the first day of the 2002 Boxing Day Test.

In the first over, Matthew Hayden contemptuously swiped the English opening bowler back over mid-wicket. Initially, the ball looked to be sailing for six; in fact, it went for four, but much of the tension in the five-day match went with it. This was not Larwood bowling to Ponsford, the air crackling with every pace of Larwood's magnificent charge to the wicket, a blend of speed, menace and beauty. As a kid, I loved cricket as much as football, but my view of the summer game had shifted. I still think it's a great game, but, like a lot of Australians, I find my response to it becoming increasingly complex. As a game, it has an acknowledged aesthetic and the potential to create towering moments of sporting drama. It also demands from its practitioners a purely physical courage of a sort not known to players of that other summer game, tennis. Cricketers are helmeted for a reason.This is a game for hard men with an overlay of nineteenth century Victorian gentility.

Cricket literature insists on the importance of the manner in which the game is played and here's the rub, or rather one of them. As the Australian team has soared to ever greater heights in recent years, the perception had grown, both at home and abroad, that they play the game in a mean-spirited way and with acts of needless aggression. Each summer, it seems, the marriage between the Australian cricketers and the Australian public is tested anew. It may be that cricketers are no worse or better behaved than other Australian sportsmen, but the questions their behaviour poses assume larger proportions in the national conversation because the Australian cricket team is, or has been up until now, *the* Australian team.There was now a permanent chorus of derision aimed at the most notorious of the cricketers, leg spinner Shane Warne. Warnie's charms were not altogether lost on me, but it was sobering to think that he was probably the best known Australian in the world, given his profile on the Indian subcontinent. With his departure from the World Cup for taking a prohibited substance and his subsequent shock and bemusement at the ban he received, I also saw a man who was somehow both street smart and unworldly, and, as such, perhaps truly representative of my country.

Another question for the sport was whether the Australian cricketers were climbing ever higher or were some of the mountains getting pretty low? In the two countries that had provided Australia with its greatest rivalries, England and the West Indies, cricket was on the wane. The last time England brought a good team to Australia, I once heard Ian Chappell say in his magnificently blunt way, was in 1970–71. That being pretty much the case, a lot of people at the 2002 Boxing Day Test went for entertainment rather than a serious sporting spectacle. Just how many of them were English is hard to say, but it felt like most of them. For a start they were so colourful, wearing the playing strips of English soccer clubs and draped in the white flag of St George with its blood-red cross. And they were noisier, singing and chanting.

Meanwhile, out on the field, Matthew Hayden played what could be termed his favourite hits, making mighty parabolas in the sky to the left and right of the wicket.At times during this, his summer of plenty, Hayden reminded me of certain kids you saw at school, the ones who were monstrously big and had whiskers at thirteen, playing with kids their own age who are otherwise children. Sometimes, he didn't even wait for the bowler to release the ball before deciding to amble down the crease and meet it on the bounce. At the other end, Langer played like a miser about to get his hands on his first million.

Notwithstanding the treatment their team was receiving, or perhaps because of it, the English fans continued chanting and singing. Wanting to get down the detail of what they were saying, I went to one of my favourite haunts behind the goals at the city end. On a railing was a Barmy Army t-shirt, written upon which were the lyrics of some of their songs. It was damp and dirty to touch but I turned it over and began transcribing their version of 'Yellow Submarine': 'In the town where I was born lived a man who was a thief, and he told me of his life, robbing banks and shagging sheep. (Pointing to Australians) You all live in a convict colony, a convict colony . . .' I had about one verse down in my pad when a bloke tapped me on the shoulder. He was Australian. 'I wouldn't touch that if I were you, mate,' he said, pointing to the t-shirt. 'We all pissed on it and one bloke wiped his arse on it.'A few bays around, another group of English lads were getting their excitement from chanting: 'Get your shit stars, get your shit stars, get your shit stars off our flag!' In another place, there were songs about the exchange rate. ('We got three dollars, for every pound we got three dollars in our hand.')

Totally unused to such insults, the Australian crowd didn't know how to respond. The Poms taunted them for that, too. 'Did I hear the Ozzies sing? (Hands to ears) I didn't hear a fuckin thing.' The songs and chants would grow from one to another, then recede like waves heading back to the deep sea of malicious glee from which they had come. In the end, an Australian voice shouted, 'If our team were as bad as yours, we'd be too embarrassed to speak.' It was true. Australians go to see their teams win.The English had come—happily, it seemed—to see their team lose. For them, the sport was incorporating what happened on the field into the action around them. It was also true that if the Australians in the stands behaved as the English did, there would have been fist fights and brawls. I was half-embarrassed by our lack of words, half-impressed by our tolerance.

Eventually, I did get talking to a member of the Barmy Army, a young Man United supporter. The conversation soon turned to the war in Iraq. At that stage, I knew no-one who was for it. My companion said no-one he knew back in England was for the war either. (Two weeks later, in mid-January 2003, an *Age* poll revealed six per cent of people supported a war without UN backing). Standing in the outer at the MCG that day, I realised this war hadn't started with us. It hadn't started with the Man United supporter. It hadn't started with me. It hadn't started with anyone I knew but, at the same time, no-one I knew was doing anything about it. My father had asked me, 'Why are people so apathetic?', and I hadn't been able to answer him. It was as if the issue had triggered some deep absence of belief within us. I left the Boxing Day Test with Australia ahead on the scoreboard and the oddest feeling in my guts, like something had been taken off us we might never get back.

Birrarung

Maybe it was me. I'd just finished a book. Bound to leave you feeling empty, people said—enjoy the break from writing. But there was no joy in the world I was seeing. In January, a man recently arrived in this country wrote a letter to the *Age*, ridiculing the United Nations as an ideal. It seemed that the real world meant living in a state of permanent insecurity. Part of me wondered if the letter writer was right. Another part wanted to dispute the notion but I could find no words. I still had the habit of my craft, but what I didn't have were words born of inspiration, the ones that run on ahead, showing you which direction to go in next. Late in January, I went to see the Wurundjeri elder Joy Murphy Wandin, in part to give her the piece of bark from the old tree her forebears had marked at the MCG.

Joy Murphy Wandin lives in Healesville, place of tall trees and birdsong, about an hour from Melbourne by car. As soon as you open the car door, you hear bellbirds, their high calls clear as water. You hear other birds too, magpies and kookaburras; maybe, also, the mimic call of the lyrebird. Occasionally, you might even see an eagle overhead. This is also Wurundjeri country and the ancestral spirit of the Wurundjeri is Bunjil the eagle.

Now in her fifties, Joy Murphy Wandin is womanly in a youthful way but an elder in her reflections. I see beauty in what she does; she says the beauty is in her culture. She had no Christian influence in her life and her family never left Wurundjeri land. She is a mother, a grandmother and a passionate St Kilda supporter, her brother Juby having played for the Saints as James Wandin in the 1950s. She also stands, in the tradition of the Wurundjeri elder William Barak, as an inspired leader of her people.At a time when others profit from poisoning the well of race relations, she sweetens its waters again and again, albeit in a way that brings recognition to her people.

For this reason, some years ago, she agreed to welcome John Howard to Wurundjeri land when he gave a talk at the Healesville RSL. She wanted him to hear the story of her father, Jarlo Wandoon, who appears on the Healesville RSL's World War I roll of honour as James Wandin. Jarlo tried to join the First AIF as an Aboriginal man proud to fight for his country but was refused on the grounds of his race. Family legend has it that he was admitted under a subclause covering American negroes. She finished her talk by offering Howard her most precious gift—a feather belonging to the Wurundjeri creator spirit, the eagle. She doesn't care for Howard's politics but noted that he received the gift with respect and, three years later when they met again, he remembered her. He ended up holding her hands as they spoke. My guess is it's the first Aboriginal story Howard has ever connected with. In central Australia, there's a story of an elder referring to Howard as a boy after meeting him during his time as leader of the opposition because the old man found him so lacking in knowledge. But the story of Jarlo Wandoon is a World War I story, and World War I is a drama that goes to John Howard's essence. Is part of his dreaming, if you wish.

In 2001, New York composer Philip Glass wrote a major concert piece called 'Voices' using a text written by Joy Murphy Wandin, which was then performed at the Melbourne Town Hall and New York's Lincoln Center with accompaniment by New South Wales didjeridu player Mark Atkins. Glass said Joy's words, which she delivered in four parts, put the listener 'within easy reach of the music' by permitting them to accompany her as she walked through Wurundjeri land, listening to and interpreting its story. Glass surrounded words with an ocean of organic sound counterpointed with the bare, hard resonance of the didj, and Joy told of the creator spirit who became an eagle, the singing and dancing in his name, the effect of white occupation which had almost broken her people and, with that, her. She finished with Birrarung, the river wrongly named Yarra by the first whites. For Joy Murphy Wandin, it is a symbol of endless flow.

In the treaty they signed with explorer John Batman, the Wurundjeri were promised a yearly tithe. Needless to say, it never appeared. Subsequently, in return for handing in their native weapons, they were promised an area of land. The property, called Coranderrk and originally measured in thousands of acres, was eventually squeezed to half an acre that is now a sacred Wurundjeri burial place. Two of Joy's siblings, a sister and a brother, are there, as are her grandparents. Barak, who saw the first whites arrive as a child and lived until 1903, is also buried there. Barak is said to have walked to Melbourne to hand deliver a letter of protest to Government House. Paintings he did, recording the customs of his people before white arrival, can be seen in the Australian gallery at Melbourne's Federation Square. Barak outlived his three children; Joy is directly descended from his sister.

Coranderrk is only fifteen minutes from where Joy lives. We drove there by car, sat and talked. We had thought of driving further and going to sit by Birrarung but she looked exhausted from her public duties. She does them out of a sense of duty to her ancestors. 'If we don't keep up, our story will get lost,' was how she put it. At her house she had showed me some of her writing, which she had sent to a publisher and had returned.The publisher misunderstood the simplicity of her language, thinking it suited a children's story. What she did was treat words as spirit beings, not as a wall of text, but the story was adult, all right. It was about someone who continues to see a creative purpose in the world after all the injuries and insults their culture has received, who continues to sing the spirit of a place into being after a city of four million has appeared in its midst.

She showed me where her grannie's house was. There were about 300 Aboriginal people here then, she said, many brought from other places.We didn't get out of the car or enter the cemetery. She was too tired. Part of what drives her, precisely because she believes she is her culture, is a feeling of loss. At times you sense it passing through her like a big wind through a tree. Instead, she spoke some Wurundjeri for me, a sort of small song, and we resolved to write something together. That night, I imagined setting her words in a book that created an ambience as Philip Glass's music had done, and got exuberantly drunk doing so. I was replanted in the landscape of my language.

The Richmond Mascot

All through that strange summer as nature went into revolt and fires began burning, Waleed and I kept talking. One day, going for a walk by Port Phillip Bay, we had a discussion in which I outlined my problem with formal religion. Like all our discussions, it was gentle and full of ease. It seemed to me that as most people weren't capable of the feat of inner balance whereby religion remains a force for good, it inevitably degenerates into ideology, with ideologues in its positions of power. Waleed could see the logic of what I was saying but explained that he came from a tradition resting upon the belief that once upon a time power resided in a man worthy of handling it.

We were driving back to my house in sombre mood, me thinking that perhaps there are gaps between cultures that cannot be bridged, when Waleed made a startling disclosure. On two occasions, at the MCG, he had been the man inside the Tiger suit, running around waving to the fans before the start of a Richmond game. A friend of his from high school, an actor called Jeff, had the contract for being the Richmond mascot but twice, when he was unavailable, had asked if Waleed could help out. From within the Tiger suit, Waleed had beheld the strange sight of people thrusting babies into his arms to be photographed and wondered, in his quiet way, how these same people would feel if they knew he was a Muslim. On one of his appearances, Waleed had been wrestled to the ground by the Bulldog mascot. Feeling he owed it to the Richmond fans to put up a fight, he had responded with a grip of his own and accidentally torn the Bulldog's mask off, thereby violating the first rule of AFL mascotry. But the Tiger Army had loved him. It was in the aftermath of this shock disclosure about the extent to which Waleed had penetrated Australian culture that I rang to interview him more rigorously upon the subject of football. The following extracts could be titled 'Talking Footy with Waleed Aly'.

Who was his favourite Richmond player of all time? 'Royce Hart.'Why? He paused for thought, as he customarily did. 'For the mystique. For the fact I never saw him play. I like the way people talk about him. It conjures up images of a player who may never have existed but it's nice to think that he did.' Who was your first Richmond hero? (Laugh) 'Michael Roach. I sent him a letter in grade 2 [at primary school] and he replied.'He quoted two lines from the letter.'Thanks for being one of my fans. It's nice to know I have some left after the way I've been playing recently.' In response, I told Waleed that Michael Roach is from Longford in northern Tasmania, where I spent my childhood, and my father taught Michael Roach's mother at Longford Primary School. I also told him that when I worked for the Edinburgh council in the eighties, driving a mini-van and scouring the Lothian region of Scotland for broken bollards and stolen road signs, I had a big picture of Michael Roach's mark above my desk. 'That mark,' said Waleed, and I could hear his smile down the phone. For the benefit of the uneducated I will describe what had appeared in both our mind's eyes: a pack of Hawthorn and Richmond bodies beneath the ball reaching up, Roach having arrived late and hurtling across at the height of their hands to take the ball on his waist. In the picture, he's looking down as if he can't quite believe where he is and what's landed in his lap.

Waleed loved David Rodan but said everyone did. Rodan was a pocket-sized Fijian destined for rugby union when his father shifted to southern Australia and the boy started playing footy for his local surburban club. Mix flair, exuberance and speed and you had Rodan. But, as Waleed pointed out, a Richmond supporter saying he loved Rodan was stating the obvious. 'I like someone who performs within his limitations, who gets the maximum out of himself, someone with Duncan Kellaway's virtues.' Kellaway was the sort of officer who stood above the trenches. Extremely courageous and modest was how Waleed put it. 'He's not a big personality. He just gets on with it.'

And, now, the inevitable Richmond question. What did he think of Richo? This brought the closest thing to a speech I had ever heard from Waleed Aly. 'I've got a mate, a graduate from the Victorian College of the Arts, who is extremely theatrical.' This was Jeff, the Richmond mascot. 'His favourite player by a mile is Richo.'This might be taken to mean Richo was merely a performer, but after a pause Waleed elaborated. 'He [Richo] is not quite co-ordinated. He doesn't look like a footballer yet he's capable of doing things no other footballer can do. He's got no emotional control. He's like a 6-year-old kid with freakish talent. If it doesn't go exactly his way, he spits the dummy. You can't help loving him and you can't help being totally exasperated by him. He's everything a filmmaker would want.'

I asked him about the Richmond captain, Wayne Campbell. 'A good leader,' said Waleed. My elder daughter is a Richmond supporter. At the age of fifteen, she got chronic fatigue; a lot of the joy dropped out of her life, but she continued going to Richmond training when she could. Wayne Campbell learned of her condition. He never saw her that he didn't give her time.

And, finally, Rory Hilton? Remember him? Golden-haired, undersized, socks around his ankles, waiting for the ball in the goal square during the last minutes of the post–September 11 final, the Tigers' destiny in his hands? 'Not a lot to say. He does everything within his power. You genuinely see a true footballer's spirit within him.'Waleed said, and I agreed, there was something archetypally Australian about Rory Hilton.

The Fires

On Saturday 30 January 2003, the temperature in Melbourne topped forty-four degrees with a strong northerly blowing. Canberra had exploded the previous weekend in what the Prime Minister had described as an act of summer terrorism. With the combination of wind and resurgent high temperatures, another outbreak of fires throughout south-eastern Australia was expected. Around eleven in the morning, I drove down to the bay and went for a walk by the water, knowing that elsewhere people were losing their houses. The air was smudged from fires just to the north of the city and the water was fretful and nervous. I sat on a retaining wall, the smooth black boulders beneath me warming to the wanton heat of the sun.

The fires were being blamed in part on the drought. But what part had global warming played in making the drought, and was it any coincidence that just as Australia was following the United States into war with oil-rich Iraq, Australia had also followed the United States in refusing to endorse the Kyoto Protocol on global warming arising from the burning of fossil fuels? Regardless of the issue of war, there was an issue of global vision. A few months before, I had gone to the Wimmera in western Victoria and been shocked to learn the region was down to ten per cent of its water reserve. I'd sat with Brigitte Muir, the first Australian woman to climb Mount Everest, on a rock shelf near Mount Arapiles looking out across the drought-parched plains with the great white blisters that once had been lakes. 'The expedition is here now,' she said. She meant the great challenge, the great task, was before us, in our own land. Back in the metropolis, not one person I asked had a clear or accurate idea of the water crisis in an area that represented one sixth of the state. As I sat beside the waters of Port Phillip Bay thinking these thoughts, the small mountain township of Omeo, and the district around it, burned with a ferocity even old-timers could not recall having seen.

One month later, I drove up to Omeo and saw paddock after paddock, hill after hill, not so much charcoal black as dark brown, the trees not burned but scorched, such was the speed with which the fire had moved. Omeo itself was like a chessboard and on each white square was a house.You realised a battle had been fought hereabouts and our side, the human side, had won. The fires got more than halfway to Swifts Creek where Peter White lives. He's the president of the Swifts Creek Cricket Club.The day I visited, the wind was blowing from the south-west, which is preferable to the north, but the sky was white and acrid with smoke. Roads were closed all around and the town football and cricket ground was covered in tents housing firefighters from as far away as New Zealand, one of the Kiwis having shinned his way up a goalpost to leave an orange hard hat perched on its top.

Peter White's home is in a heavily wooded gully further up the same road as the oval. He has a small spring, a natural water supply being used by the CFA (Country Fire Authority) trucks. The saplings beside it, ten to twenty metres high, were bent nearly to the ground in the screaming winds of 30 January. The sky that day was a wild orange glow. All the windows in White's home were covered with corrugated iron, as was the latticework around the foundations. This was to fight what's called ember attack. For nearly three weeks now, they'd been waiting for the fire to come roaring through their valley with flames twice as high as the gums. 'You end up wishing that if it's going to come, it would come now,' said White. He was in his early forties, solidly built with a deeply creased face that could still break into a grin. In the city, the bushfire story had led the news while life and houses were threatened. But there was no story in the fire once that threat had passed. In fact, the fire was still burning on a front of several hundred kilometres, one edge of which was only seven k's away. I'd gone up to write a column on the place of sport at such a time and now felt the absurdity of doing so. Nonetheless, he and his wife Marijs invited me inside for a cup of tea.

We sat in the kitchen, beside a freshly cut hole in the kitchen floor from which a hose protruded. The kids were in Melbourne, the valuables, the paintings and photos, were in an underground cave they'd dug. They were planning to stay. You fought the embers for as long as you could, he told me, retreating into the house or the cave when the heat became too intense.

He estimated the fire would take between five and fifteen minutes to pass over them during which time, I imagined, they'd pray.

An older bloke, a local who owned trucks and happened to stop in, joined the conversation. He remembered the terrible bushfires of 1939, the year World War II began, when seventy-one people died. Along with his mother and brother, he'd been sent south to Haylesford.The smoke cloud was so heavy that the sky began to darken around four o'clock.

He and his brother had been sent down to the local river to play. There they saw a group of people, later identified as Seventh Day Adventists, calling out to God and saying they knew the world was coming to an end.When he went back and told his mother, she said, don't worry about them—they're just silly. Decades later, on her deathbed, she confessed that she hadn't been so sure at the time.

Peter White was a shearer from New Zealand who had come to the area in 1987 and promptly been cajoled into playing football for Swifts Creek. The first time he got the ball he was pinged for throwing it in the rugby manner. He subsequently moved a couple of hills away and was cajoled into playing for Ensay. He played in a side that lost by forty-seven goals one week and fifty-two the next. When they finally won a game, they got in a circle and no-one could remember the club song. It was that long since Ensay had won a game. His wife, Marijs, told that story. After three and a half weeks of living with the possibility of fire, she still had a quiet humour and a remarkable sense of calm. She's the trainer for Swifts Creek Football Club. Sport's like that up here, she said. In the late nineties, Swifts

Creek's one mill closed. It had its own drought in addition to the one now ravaging the country, severe floods and an outbreak of disease among its sheep population. In 2001, when Swifts Creek won regional premierships in netball, cricket, football and tennis, the residents of the town, officially numbered at 450, held a ball under the banner 'Well Done, 2001'.

Peter had also been a trainer. Once, when he was shearing a mob of sheep with scabby mouth, he treated some of the local footballers to a vigorous rub with a special lotion learned in his youth for keeping warm in the mountains of New Zealand, adding cayenne pepper to the oil. When the young men of Swifts Creek came out in violent rashes, it was initially feared the team had contracted scabby mouth from the trainer with the shearer's hands. I got him talking about shearing and asked him if he could imagine the men who launched the shearers' strike of the 1890s, from which the Australian Labor Party was born. His eyes lit up at the thought. 'One thing that doesn't change about shearing,' he said,'is the character of shearers.' Strong, wilful men with a history of doing whatever is necessary to defend their interests. Peter White knew all about that, having sought work as a New Zealand shearer in Australian sheds during the eighties. But it was a measure of the original Labor Party's sense of purpose that it started as the shearers' party. It was an office party now, devoid of passion, bereft of any big imagining.

In the end, White had to remind himself to go and have another look at the fires. I said I'd go too but before I did Marijs gave me a copy of the Swifts Creek Nearly Nude Calendar, for which she had taken the photos. It was a gallery of recognisable Australian types.

There was Grant Mooney, the town's most talented cricketer, who made 294 with a hangover. He looked a bit like Les Darcy, only more mischievous. There was Adam Markich—the boy who could have played in the AFL, according to the locals.There was one of them in every country town. Markich was handsome and powerfully built, but even in a nude calendar which encouraged extrovert behaviour he was somehow reserved. It was said he didn't like cities. And there were the local CFA boys, Rory Hiltons every one of them, grinning and pointing a giant hose at a little barbecue. 'That's before it got serious,' murmured Marijs. The day I visited, half the Swifts Creek cricket team were on the line, fighting the fires.

By late afternoon the sun was a wild crimson eye dropping in a white sky to the west, but I left Swifts Creek glad I had come. What is the place of sport at such a time? It's a shared experience, a fount of humour and anecdote. Driving down through the Omeo valley, I stopped beside the winding Tambo River, which still happened to be in flow. Elsewhere in Victoria and Tasmania, I had seen lakes drying up and rivers that were dying and each time I felt something dry up and wither in me.The road being closed, no other vehicle was about. I switched off the engine and heard the deep silence of the valley, its only sound coming from the near side of the river where the clear brown water was toppling down a small descent of stones and, in that summer when nature raged and roared, that was sound enough for me.

Ned Kelly and thc Old Dark Navy Blues

So there we were, standing outside the State Library during Melbourne's big anti-war rally, people stretching into the distance in every direction as far as the eye could see. First media reports said the crowd was 100,000 people. Bullshit. That's a grand final crowd. There were at least two of those, probably more. So many people, in fact, it was slightly frightening. People were trapped inside Melbourne Central station, unable to get out the entrance and with more coming up the escalators pressing them from behind.The body of the crowd was in Swanston Street, but it had limbs extending both ways at every intersection. As with all protests I have ever attended, my feelings were mixed as the reason for being there is inevitably blurred. One sign, which I was to see a number of times during protests in other places, said, 'War is *SO* twentieth Century'. This struck me as dangerously naive. There will always be war and rumours of war. Most of the signs said it was a war for oil. I wasn't persuaded of that, although some would undoubtedly profit a lot more from the exercise than others, but in this case I inclined to the belief of the American monk, Thomas Merton, that the root of war was fear. (Not so much the fear men have of one another, wrote Merton, as the fear they have of *everything*.) Of the speakers, Bob Brown was best.'This is not Australia's war,' he said. 'This is John Howard's war.'Australians were now being told that the war in Iraq was a war of liberation; they were being told this by a government that had sent back to Iraq people prepared to risk their lives fleeing the regime.

Outside the State Library, a young bloke with a red flag climbed the statue of Sir Redmond Barry and grabbed him in comradely fashion. Being made of brass, Sir Redmond couldn't shake him off but I knew what was going on inside his head. He was shuddering with rage and shouting, 'I'd hang the damn lot of you!' Sir Redmond didn't crack a role in the latest Ned Kelly film, which was a pity because he was a big player in the saga. He sentenced Ned's mother to three years on the dubious evidence of Constable Alexander Fitzpatrick, a man later dismissed from the Victorian police force on the grounds that he was impossible to trust and never did his duty. Fitzpatrick had claimed Ned shot him in the wrist. Sir Redmond said he would have given Ned fifteen years had he been in the courtroom, notwithstanding the fact that Ned had neither been tried nor found guilty of the charge and denied being present when the incident occurred.

Sir Redmond was a Protestant Irishman. Ned was of Irish Catholic descent. Two years later, in a Melbourne courtroom after Sir Redmond sentenced Ned to be hanged, Ned told Sir Redmond he would meet him in that place to which he was going and, sure enough, twelve days later, in a way that did no harm whatsoever to Ned's booming posthumous reputation as a figure with supernatural powers, Sir Redmond died of a poisonous carbuncle on his neck.

In addition to being party to a feud of dubious legality against the Kellys, Sir Redmond was largely responsible for establishing such worthy institutions as the State Library and the University of Melbourne and a few years ago, when researching my novel *The Call,* I had pursued my suspicion that he was also involved in setting up the Carlton Football Club. I knew he was connected to the Carlton Cricket Club and I also knew that Carlton's original colours were not blue but blue and orange. Sir Redmond was an Orangeman. After a check of the football club's early committees failed to reveal his name, I abandoned the inquiry. Then in 2002, a journalist named Brian Hansen published his enormously detailed history of the Carlton Football Club, *The Blue Boys,* which revealed that in 1864, as benefactor of the Carlton Cricket Club, Sir Redmond ordered the creation of a football club as a winter pursuit for his cricketers, thus repeating the initiative that led to the birth of the Melbourne Football Club from the Melbourne Cricket Club the previous decade. Now I knew for certain: Carlton Football Club was started by the man who hanged Ned Kelly.

I've always been interested in Ned as a footballer and once heard a story that he had a run with Benalla. It's not impossible. By 1880, the year of Ned's execution, football was enjoying widespread popularity in the colony of Victoria. What's more, there are strong correlations between Ned's life and the spirit of the early game. Ned was born the year of the Eureka

Stockade. His early years were spent in that central corridor of Victoria which was awash with traffic to and from the goldfields. A spirit of optimism and revolt was in the air. Ned said he and his friends would ride bold, fearless and free through a land they regarded as theirs.That, on my reading of it, corresponds with the spirit in which much of the early football was played.

The new film on Ned, like the Mick Jagger version made in 1973, basically told the story as a re-run of the English versus the Irish, thereby obscuring and missing the Australian nuances of the story. In each film, the Kellys, and those around them, speak with Irish accents. I am not persuaded they did. (There are people who would know. Jim Kelly lived until 1948.Ten years ago at Greta, I met a woman who had known him as a child.) Ned's story may have been rooted in his parents' Irish Catholicism, but it also transcended his origins. When the police moved against Ned's Greta mob, it was specifically to take 'the flashness out of them'. No less than James Dean or the Beatles, Ned was of a generation. Known as 'larrikins', one of the places in the city where they regularly met and made trouble was at football matches. In the fortnight between being sentenced to death and executed, a petition for clemency circulating in Melbourne, which then had a population of about 300,000, obtained 32,000 signatures. The larrikins would continue to be seen as a social threat until World WarI when C.J. Dennis, a writer I admire, would take characters from their ranks and turn Ginger Mick and his mates into Gallipoli heroes.

I enjoyed Heath Ledger's portrayal of Ned as a serious young man poised between thought and action.The film was based on Robert Drewe's novel *Our*

Sunshine,a book distinguished by the zest and flair of its language. Drewe's Ned, however, was late twentieth century man, watching his fate descend around him with irony and humour. Nothing typified Drewe's book more than the fact that he had a circus present during the final climactic hours in the Glenrowan Hotel.The film made Ned a man of his people—the Irish selectors. To this end, they had him make his famous advance at night, walking iron-clad out of the hotel towards a small army of troopers, pistol in hand, in a bid to draw their fire from the terrified hostages trapped inside the hotel. This was one of the film's many historical distortions and omissions.

In fact, having been wounded three times in what is called 'the first volley', Ned rode off, supposedly to warn his supporters that their uprising in favour of a republic in north-eastern Victoria was botched, then spent the night bleeding in the bush. It was the following morning, just as dawn was breaking, that he stepped out of the mist, armour clanking, and lumbered towards the hotel where his brother Dan and Steve Hart were still trapped. On hand were the pressmen who had been in the train Ned had tried to de-rail, thereby making the Glenrowan siege the most electrifying press call in the history of Australian journalism. No-one knew who or what this thing clanking towards them was. One journalist said he felt like Hamlet seeing the ghost of his father. In the furious propaganda war that had accompanied the Kelly outbreak, Ned had been depicted by the authorities as a coward. After Glenrowan, and the manner in which he carried himself through his trial and execution, that view had no currency.The popular view was summed up by the phrase: as game as Ned Kelly.

The first film about Ned was made in 1906 and there've been plenty since. In *The Glenrowan Affair*, made in 1951, the man cast in the role of Ned was footballer Bob Chitty, Carlton hero of the Bloodbath. On hearing of his casting, Jack Dyer, his great adversary, is said to have muttered, 'Only time Chitty ever needed armour.'

Georgia Savage

Ron Savage, who featured in the Bloodbath grand final of 1945, also won Carlton's best and fairest that year. In 1946, he stunned the club by leaving, in what was considered his football prime, and going to Tasmania. Carlton refused to clear him and he 'stood out' of football for a year. One of his team-mates from the Bloodbath told me Savage was almost impossible to know, and in the island state he continued to confound. There are stories of him reading Shakespeare in the rooms before matches and he confided to Georgia, then in her teens, that what he really wanted to become was a poet. He had no interest in physical work and saw football merely as a way of making a living. With his tall, blond good looks and bohemian ways, he was immensely attractive to women. He and Georgia married in 1949.

Ron Savage has certain parallels with an intellectual Carlton eccentric of a later generation, Brent Crosswell. Both professed to have no real love or interest in football but remained deeply knowledgeable about it.

Both had an ambiguous relationship with the violence of the game which came, I suspect, from the belief that in a violent world the safest course is to hit first, or make people think you might. When my father saw Savage play, Dad thought he was better at the appearance of being a protector than the real thing.

Chitty also ended up in Tasmania, in a town called Scottsdale, where there are all sorts of stories about him. He was described to me as a rum cove, an old Tasmanian phrase, which implied he remained something of an outsider. But he was also remembered as a good storyteller which meant his stories stayed with his listeners.

Dad saw Chitty play for Scottsdale at Longford. An altercation occurred and Chitty settled it. Dad described his action as a blur of arms and legs. Chitty could fight; not everybody who throws a punch on the football field can. I suspect that was the difference between Savage and Chitty. My first newspaper editor, Michael Courtney of the Launceston *Exam-iner*,a man with a ferocious eye for the truth, saw Savage play in Hobart in 1947. He said he was a dopey-looking big bastard, but no-one was game to take him on because he had a reputation, having copped an eight-week suspension after the Bloodbath. Ron Savage became a professional footballer, playing his last game, a losing grand final, for Mooroopna against one of Grumpy Kenna's Shepparton United teams. He was then thirty-six, an old footballer but a young man. A few months later, he was involved in an industrial accident which lost him one of the frontal lobes in his brain.

Georgia Savage lives not far from me. She doesn't have a fortune but says she is rich in other ways, 'like

Anthony Koutoufides'. She still loves the Blues. Once a season we watch a game together on TV, usually when Carlton are playing. Georgia has some of the best football stories I've ever heard. She tosses them my way like scraps of paper and says I can have them, but they're as big as a novel and only she can write them. Ron Savage was an orphan with a deep sense of loss. The game gave him one means of expression but he longed for another. Most of his friends were in the arts. After the accident, his personality changed. He lost his love of books and became industrious, applying his mind to physical tasks. Companionless now in the landscape of literature, his young wife eventually started writing. Georgia Savage's best-known novel, *The House Tibet*, is about a young woman with both a deep hurt and an irrepressible zest for living.

When I asked Georgia Savage about Bob Chitty, she described him as a compelling figure.There was a magnetism about him, she said, an energy for life. Georgia told me Ron Savage loved Chitty 'to bits', her way of saying he liked him a lot and probably looked up to him.All the Carlton players I spoke to, with the exception of Clinton Wines, did. When Chitty and Savage met up in Melbourne after Ron's accident, Savage told Chitty the injury was to his brain. Chitty replied, 'Lucky you didn't lose something worth having,' and the two old footballers, the warrior and the intellectual poet, laughed, in Georgia's words, like drains.

David and the Magpies

My first memory of Doffan Paz is him sending me words of praise for my writing. The letters had lots of sunshine in them. My wife was then teaching at an Orthodox Jewish school, he was a parent and we met at a school athletics day. Doffan was in his running gear, about to go in the parents' race, looking a bit like a skun rabbit but with a grin as big as any I'd seen. Later, Doffan had us to his home. The meal was in good part ceremonial, Doffan sitting at the head of the table and reading at intervals to his family, the book from which he was reading being one of mine. In Doffan's house, I was the equal of any author found in his impressive library, in which at least half the books were Australian. Doffan approached Australian culture with the same seriousness he approached the culture of his forefathers.

Soon he invited me to a circumcision he was to perform in St Kilda one morning before work. I arrived early, for fear of causing offence, was briefly mistaken for a rabbi because I was bearded and hurried inside. Later, we met in cafes or he came round to my house for talks. I would ask him to tell Bible stories because he related them with such feeling and clarity. Once, in a cafe in Elizabeth Street, he gave me a version of Joseph and his coat of many colours. Doffan had been going for half an hour and the story showed no sign of ending when I twigged that to Doffan the stories of the Old Testament don't really have beginnings or ends but are part of a long, brilliant, technicolour history which he carries within him at all times.

Doffan grew up in a country town on the New South Wales–Victorian border. He left when he was nine and a half but says those years made him. His father, the town doctor, was 'a conspicuous Jew and an honoured one'.The result was that Doffan had no experience of racism as a child. His mother's family came to Australia in the 1840s; his grandfather was a pearl diver in Broome. He once told me how he had gone on a tourist bus in Broome. The tour guide, in Doffan's view, had been racist in the inferences he made about the local Aboriginal people. Doffan waited until the last tourist had left the bus and then approached the driver. As he told me the story, I could see it all happening. The tour guide would have looked up and seen this nervous, friendly, bearded face with words spilling from its lips. It would have taken him some minutes to realise this unusual looking man was actually deeply serious.

Doffan was Australian by generations on both sides, his father's family having arrived in the 1890s. When he went to Israel for the first time, he was particularly moved by the Negev, which translates as 'dried-up' (or, he says, outback), and the gum trees around Galilee. He felt like he was back in the town he grew up in. As a youth growing up in Australia, he worked out that 'being bright won you no kudos at all, being funny helped, but that if you wanted to make any serious inroads into the culture you had to be good at sport'. Doffan, who lists the three great Jewish sports as talking, eating and playing chess, was then captain of the Mount Scopus second XVIII. 'There was no way to be damned with fainter praise in the world of sport,' he says, 'than to be captain of the Mount Scopus second XVIII.' But he discovered there was one athletic quality he did possess—endurance. He could run and he could keep running. He had since run many marathons, including New York's three times, and the first examples of Doffan's writing that he sent me were about marathons, the places he went in his mind while his legs were working away beneath him. Doffan wanted to become a writer—that is, learn to tell his stories to the blank stare of the page rather than an audience of family and friends sitting around a table—and to that end had chosen the pen name Doffan Paz.

Doffan is a *cohen*, a hereditary title denoting descent from Aaron, the High Priest and brother of Moses, and one of his roles in the Jewish community has been that of *mohel*—the man who performs ritual circumcisions. He says it's the second most looked-down upon job in medicine, the first being female circumcision. Not a dogmatic man, he's open to a discussion on the issue. In his teens, when he was questioning the existence of God, Doffan continued to pray; he explained to me that the Aramaic word for prayer has the same root as the word for father. He would have continued praying, regardless of God, because his father had prayed before him and his father had before him. He says he was never the surgeon his father was—that required a degree of hand-eye co-ordination he lacked. His forte as a doctor was his bedside manner. Doffan has a grin the size of a banana.The light in his eyes says this is a man who wants to engage with the world and, in 1994, partly out of curiosity, he began taking locums in outback Aboriginal communities and, for the first time in his life, he encountered patients he couldn't talk to.

One of his stories,'Jonathan's Country', gives you an idea of what it's like to sit beside an old central desert man called Jonathan, who is spitting his lungs over you and the interior of the light aeroplane as you seek to rush him to a hospital in Alice Springs. Jonathan is of a generation who grew up with little or no knowledge of white culture and 'came in' from the desert in the 1950s and 1960s. What awaited him were diseases like measles which made him cough so hard he destroyed the elasticity in his right bronchial tube and eventually his right lung. There is no possibility of banter between doctor and patient; there's just the spectacle of this hopelessly ill old man and the bare red land passing beneath the aeroplane's wings. The doctor attends him as best he can, contemplating the possibility of having to give mouth-to-mouth resuscitation, all the time wanting to say something but being unable to do so. The story ends with the news that the old man has been released from hospital and been flown back to his country; the doctor, hearing this, has a feeling of relief. He must have done some good.

Doffan is a man who is strong and secure in his religious tradition. He's also a Collingwood man. The piece he wrote about Collingwood is one of the maddest, most wonderful voices I've ever heard from the outer. It begins with him trying to explain

Collingwood to a friend in Israel which means translating 'Carna Pies' into Hebrew. The best Doffan can arrive at is 'Let the ravens of the brook ascend'. Doffan's brother barracked for Melbourne, the establishment club and the great power in the game when Doffan was a boy. In his youthful imagination, Melbourne became Goliath which made Collingwood David. However, his son, brought up in Melbourne, had grafted directly to the model of the one-eyed Collingwood supporter with the result that, when they went to games, the son got irritated by the father always seeing the other side of everything. Doffan was like me, poor fool. He loved them all.

The Heart of the Game

In a bid to sign up new members after winning their second premiership, the Brisbane Lions took the coveted silver cup on a country tour. I planned to be there when it was brought to the Shepparton United Football Club, but as the Lions officials were late arriving I had a look at some of Shepparton United's memorabilia.The club's glory years were the 1950s when they were coached by a local legend, Kevin 'Grumpy' Kenna. One newspaper story pinned to the walls said Grumpy had been a front gunner on a bomber during World War II. When ammunition ran low, the story said, Grumpy attached a bayonet to one of his guns and told the pilot to 'go in low'. I'm old enough to remember those sort of stories being part of the game. At the time, I was young enough to believe them. I'd ask Dad if they were true and he'd shake his head, maybe grin slightly and say, 'No, I don't think so.' I must confess, I was always a bit disappointed.

Grumpy used words like 'jib' and 'mug lair'. I remembered them too—in fact, sometimes still heard them. A mug lair was someone who thought looking good mattered at the expense of reality. An international sportsman who took a prohibited substance so that he would look good in front of the television cameras would be at serious risk of being called a mug lair. A jib was someone who pulled out at decisive moments. It was not something you wanted to be known as. Mixed up in all this was a certain humour. Once, when United's rover was knocked out, the runner ran gasping to the coach's bench and said, 'He doesn't know who he is or where he is.' Grumpy sent him back with the message: 'Tell him he's Bob Skilton and we're playing at the Lakeside Oval.'

Shepparton United has produced about a dozen VFL/AFL players, among them 2001 Norm Smith medallist Shaun Hart. It was partly out of deference to Hart that the Lions took the premiership cup to his old club. In the event, only ten people turned up to see it. The star of the travelling roadshow, Kevin 'Bulldog' Murray, arrived with a Brownlow Medal around his neck and an amazing collection of old trophies and guernseys in a bag, smiling enthusiastically. Kevin Murray had tatts before they were chic. He took the field with a slightly gummy mouth, having taken out his false teeth, played half a size bigger than he actually was and went all day, every day, like a motor. He chased a football in the way that greyhounds chased hares. He protected his smaller team-mates and he protected some of his bigger ones too. For a time, he was Fitzroy. Hearing him talk footy—he remembered the scoreline for every match mentioned involving Fitzroy and Brisbane, both seniors and reserves—I realised this was a man who was not only wholly for the merged club but wholly for the game. Is the game as good as it was? I asked him. 'Oh yes,' he grinned. 'It's still a great game'.Would Voss be a great player in any era? 'Oh yes.'Another grin. So who's the Lions' next best player? He wouldn't answer.'Remarks like that don't help a team.'

Half an hour or so before Murray arrived, a stoutly built, boyish-looking young man in a Fitzroy guernsey recognised me. Giving his name as Wayde Petersen, he began by asking questions about journalism. He had an unusual way of speaking, squinting as he did and leaning back, eyes working quickly as he computed my responses, but the questions he asked were consistently thoughtful and intelligent. The conversation moved on to the effect of city journalism on country living. 'With respect,' he said, 'some of your colleagues wouldn't know clay from excrement about the work we do.'

Two weeks later, I drove up to his family's farm at Dhurringile, half an hour's drive from Shepparton. It was a day when rain had been forecast but instead, almost as a cruel joke, nature sent a huge dust storm, an orange fog covering the paddocks.At my request, Wayde showed me the dairy where he begins his days around 6.30 am. He said it was important the cows be relaxed which means he can't listen to cricket, football or Triple J while he's milking. The cows like old-time music. Outside, lying on his side, was the bull who recently charged and almost got him.'He would have tossed me like a salad,' he said, laughing. I noticed he was remarkably precise in his use of words. At one time, he told me, he thought of being a librarian.

The family took over the property in 1993, having moved from Hurstbridge on the edge of the city, and three years later the worst drought since Federation hit.'History threw us a curve ball,' is how Wayde, a former baseballer, put it, but he also quoted his father saying there's always people worse off than yourself. Farmers in north-eastern Victoria had been burned out in the recent fires. Even those whose homes weren't burned lost what feed they had in their paddocks. After seeing the dairy, we went back to the family home, a large house built in the homestead style. I noticed on a wall in the living room the framed words of nineteenth century Australian poet Adam Lindsay Gordon:'Life is mostly froth and bubble,/Two things stand like stone,/Kindness in another's troubles,/Courage in your own.' I met Wayde's parents and sister, then we went to another room and continued talking.

He told me he had mild autism; the condition had made his high school years 'very difficult'. We both laughed at the idea of schooldays being the best of your life, and there was a moment of silence. That became the pattern of the conversation. He started at Dookie Agricultural College but there were too many variables for him in the lifestyle, too many mental balls to hold in the air, and he had to withdraw. 'It was hard not to feel a failure after that.' Silence again. Farm work was good for him since it was highly ordered. He made a chopping motion with his hand like he was slicing bread to indicate the way tasks were defined and done. 'That's good for me.'He liked the space of country living.At the same time, he appreciated the fact that nearby Shepparton had a similar range of ethnic groups and nationalities to a Melbourne suburb like Brunswick. His best mate, Xhuma Kutrolli, was the son of Muslim Albanian farmers, the same community

Melbourne footballer Adam Yze comes from. At Xhuma's twenty-first, his mate's father thanked Wayde for being a good friend to his son. 'I was really stoked that he thought enough of me to say that,' he said.

Wayde wanted to put something back into the local community.To this end, he was on the committee of the Murchison Football Club and doing a course to become a trainer. That would save the club having to pay for one. He played cricket for the Murchison second XI and helped with the preparation of the club's turf wicket. I said I'd come back up and watch Murchison play a game. He told me a number of the football grounds in the area were so hard and parched they were unplayable. He went on,'The drought affects the lives of people up here in so many ways.'

Twice in the course of our conversation Wayde used the word 'sad', a small word of large consequence when used with precision. Once was in relation to an Iraqi fruit picker who had been spat on in Shepparton. 'Everyone up here always got on,' he said. 'After September 11, it was like a poisonous mushroom appeared.' He didn't want to sound like he was preaching, 'but I'd be a real hypocrite if I made out I didn't know what it was like being treated as an outsider'. He paused, then added,'These people came here because they detest Saddam.'

The other time he used the word sad was in relation to a local farmer, a family man, who killed himself. Everyone in the district knew why because they were all in the same boat, trying to remain positive after six years of drought. If the rains don't come this year, the Petersens will lose the lot.

'We're not whingeing,' said Wayde. 'Everyone says

people in the country whinge. If this place goes bottom up, we'll know we did our best. Every year we improved our herd.' He quoted his father again, saying it's circumstances that will have beaten them 'and that's not failure'.

When I spoke to his father, George Petersen, he said there were worse things in life than going broke. Smaller than his son and bearded, he looked like a deeply weathered philosopher. Outside, orange soil was sweeping off the sparsely grassed paddocks. Could this become desert? I asked.'Easily,'he replied. He admitted some days he stands in the middle of a paddock and curses the heavens. If it makes him feel better, why not? Once I started him talking, it was hard to stop him. He said that as a result of the United States and the European union countries dumping dairy produce, milk prices had dropped thirty per cent over a twelve month period while overheads kept rising. They spent the last of their money, his retirement savings, two months ago on feed for his cows. George Petersen's pride now was the condition of his cattle, but that investment meant selling the new house in which we were sitting and moving to an old weatherboard elsewhere on the property. I asked Wayde's mother how she felt about that. 'A home is what you make it,' she replied. And that's how I left them, a family waiting for rain, waiting together.The next day the war began.

Facing The Future

For someone of her age and many experiences, Georgia Savage is almost unreasonably glad of life. I know people who would be wrecked by what she has been through but her eyes continue to gleam like a child's as she tells me what she has seen and learned. In the event of her death, she once told me, I can find her by looking at the grass in the back straight at Flemington during the Spring Carnival. Imagine a brush of sun-touched green with maybe a rustle of wind in it. And that is why, the week before the season began when I was asked to speak in a pub on the topic 'Facing the Future', I thought I would take Georgia along. I wanted to say something green, something that had life, but was nonetheless real.

There were about eighty or so mostly older people in the pub. I basically told two stories. I told how, a week or so after September 11, I spoke at a testimonial dinner for Bob Brown in Melbourne. Afterwards, he and I had a talk about whether the human experiment could ever achieve any sort of enduring stability for all the peoples of the earth or whether it would end in chaos and destruction. 'I don't know that it won't end in chaos,' he said. 'But I choose to act as if it won't.' Bob Brown believes an act of defiance, within ourselves, is necessary if we are to resist the logic of our times.

The second story I told was about meeting Rainsy Sam, the leader of the democracy movement in Cambodia, in 2002. At the time we met, the number of his party workers murdered for trying to establish democracy in their country was twelve. His wife told of a legally authorised march they participated in; turning a corner, they were met by a line of soldiers, rifles levelled. Her husband continued walking towards the soldiers; so did those behind him. When he finally reached the tip of the barrel of the first gun, presumably belonging to the commander, the military stood back and the marchers passed. Where do you get your courage from? I asked. Rainsy Sam told me that if you have a choice between right and wrong, take the right way without hesitation, because if you pause for a moment your fear will get you. He also told me—with a trace of regret, I thought—that once people believe in you, you don't have a choice.

No War

The AFL issued a press release saying players were not permitted to make statements about the war after a Western Bulldogs player, Robert Murphy, arrived for his team's official 2003 photo with 'No War' written on his forearm. His captain, Chris Grant, defended Murphy, saying he thought the lack of freedom of speech in Iraq was one of the reasons Australia was fighting the war. Go Dogs!

Richmond V. Collingwood, MCG, 28 March 2003

I chose to end this book as I began it, by going to a game.The Ponsford Stand was still missing which prompted Waleed, who was with me, to say it felt like suburban footy. He meant you could see the world outside the game—in this case, the overpass connecting Yarra Park to the National Tennis Centre, the black outline of the trees around Olympic Park. It was a Friday night game and the first of the season, and the stadium, or the three-quarters of it that remained, was filled to capacity. While we were waiting in the queue, Waleed took a mobile phone call from his brother Ahmad, already inside and sitting in the Great Southern Stand. The teams were on the ground, along with their mascots.

Ahmad said it wasn't Jeff in the Tiger suit. I've never met Jeff but there's a theory that Jeff is more Jeff when he enters the personality that goes with wearing a black and yellow outfit with the big tiger's head and tail. Waleed said this was correct. Jeff was out of the game. The opportunity to be the Richmond mascot for the third time had been given to Waleed but he had chosen instead to come with me. By now,Waleed was a father. His daughter will be a Muslim who traces her descent back to the First Fleet and barracks for Richmond.

I gave the Tigers a chance. Collingwood had been smashed by Adelaide in the final of the pre-season competition in a way that exposed distinct limitations in their team, besides which Richmond were crazy and this occasion might just appeal to their crazi-ness—big night, big audience both here and around Australia, the adrenalin of a new year.And Richo was playing, every limb fit and functioning, which in itself was a sign of hope. At one time or another, Richo had snapped just about every bone in his body. Rory Hilton was playing, too.The game wasn't ten minutes old before Rory had put his signature on it, taking a big mark at centre half-back and collecting two Collingwood players, one of them Nathan Buckley. Rory shirtfronted the Collingwood captain at the first opportunity, sending Buckley sprawling. Handed the ball by the umpire, Buckley gave his head a vigorous shake, ran back and played on.

Buckley was best on ground by so much it didn't matter.To me, he played like a man willing his team to go one step further than it had the previous year. Unfortunately, I didn't see his team-mates taking that step with him. How many games could he play with this sort of ferocious hunger? He was thirty now; how much would his body stand? In the second quarter, after a disputed decision, I saw him arguing with an umpire. The Tigers were in the game then. 'The signs are good,' Waleed had said, nodding his head. He was referring to an incident in front of us in which a sequence of Richmond forwards cannoned into a pack to keep the ball from being rushed away by the Collingwood defence. At that stage, Richo was in everything. He took one mark in which his body was taken from beneath him by his opponent after he had left the ground. His torso turned in the air, his long legs rising upwards like the hands of a clock, yet throughout this strange flight he kept his eyes unerringly on the ball so that his hands received it surely. With quiet intensity,Waleed said,'Great mark.' How did Waleed Aly see the game of Australian football? In a sharp, analytical way. And he did something only the quickest eyes and minds can do, simultaneously both watching the game and looking ahead of it, so that he could predict what was going to happen next. 'Look here,' he'd say, pointing.

Doffan came at half-time. Darkness having fallen on what was now the Sabbath day, he had to walk. Knowing his beliefs, I had been reluctant to ask him to the game but had noted in his wonderfully mad football story that he had attended matches at least twice on the Sabbath to see Collingwood grand finals. But it did mean that he had to come to the game, and go home, on foot. Once seated, Doffan applauded all good play, regardless of which side performed it, clapping his hands to express his appreciation. He was far less focussed than Waleed on the detail of the match and was soon telling me his favourite football story. When Doffan's mother was seventy-two, he took her to her first game. At half-time, she said that the team in the brown and yellow had done very well when they had their turn with the ball and the team in black and white had done very well when they had their turn, but the other team hadn't been given a turn. The other team?

asked Doffan, understandably bemused. Yes, said his mother, the ones in white. As a supporter, Doffan was louder than Waleed, calling out to criticise what he deemed unethical play.

My brother Tim, also known as the Big Boy, happened to be passing through Melbourne and came to the game too. He threatened to bring some yollas—Tasmanian mutton-birds—but they were out of season. Probably just as well. When he brought a couple a few years earlier to a game at the G their smell cleared a space around us, a considerable feat at the football. The Big Boy likes to make a game within the game, find a couple of stories within the story.That night his attention had gravitated towards a man of about thirty with dyed blond hair and one of those faces that is both pretty and ugly. He was spewing hatred from the start but went absolutely berserk when an umpire tripped and fell; for some reason, the umpire triggered his deepest rage. The Big Boy, who is good at giving names, called him Rostov, after the town in eastern Europe where the neo-Nazis were then rallying.

I was glad when Tim told me he was coming. It was a big night for me in my footy life, and he'd been the person I first went to the footy with, initially on the north-west coast of Tasmania, then later at the North Hobart oval where Dad played in the 1930s. When Dad was in his eighties, I took him back to a game at his old home ground. The glory days of Tassie footy were long gone and there was no-one there but he saw hundreds of ghosts as we walked around the ground, eventually camping in the old Ryder Street stand where the fiercest North Hobart supporters had sat.That was the day he told me about the best game he ever saw, the 1935 state final between Hobart's New Town, led by Roy Cazaly, and Launceston, which had won the title the previous three years. He recounted the first ten minutes and I saw every kick, every goal, every blow. In Tassie footy, the great rivalry was between the north of the island and the south; the north had tried to secede in the early colonial days and it had been on ever since.

Dad and I still talked footy.We talked about lots of other things too. The war in Iraq had got to him in a way I had not seen before. He joined up in 1940 because he thought there was a war that had to be fought. The madness of fascism was loose in Europe, an army of invasion was on the march in Asia. Now we were doing the invading. 'Master politician,' Dad said of Howard. 'Seventy-five per cent of the population wanted a republic. Didn't get one. Seventy-five per cent didn't want this war and got it.' The night I spoke in the pub, an old digger who had been in New Guinea during World War II expressed similar thoughts to me. He told me you never forget the smell of a battlefield, the stench of those shortly before living now dead. The conversation caused me to think again on the story of the Bloodbath, the game in which those who hadn't been to war were so eager to prove themselves to those who had. I heard a US Republican senator who won two Purple Hearts in Vietnam point out that a lot of key people in the Bush White House had never been to war. He was a tough-looking dude who had opposed the Kyoto Protocol, but he said that when the subject of war arose he was always more interested in the opinions of people who had seen the horror than those who hadn't.

So am I. Meanwhile, back in Australia, waiting for the world to beckon, was John Winston Howard.

At three-quarter time, Waleed and Doffan made a conscious effort to engage one another.Yes, I'd set up the meeting—no, it didn't happen of its own accord—but the sight of two good men trying to find a civilised path through the mayhem otherwise dividing them still moved me so sharply I had to look away. But theirs was also the sort of talk you have at the footy which meant it stopped as soon as the game resumed and Collingwood, more or less as Waleed predicted during the break, kicked a Buckley-inspired burst of goals. Later, I put it to Waleed that he was happier once Richmond had no realistic chance of winning. The idea brought a smile to his face.

As far as Richo was concerned, it was, in Waleed's words, the complete performance: he kicked one goal, six behinds and one out of bounds on the full. In the third quarter, he made it late to a contest, up-ended his opponent, beat the Collingwood player with a superior second effort, won possession beneath a weight of bodies and was penalised by the umpire for holding the ball.That was it! Richo went off, punching the ground not once but twice, threw his head, swore and drew a dark tide of jeers and hooting from the Collingwood supporters in the crowd of sixty-odd thousand. I felt for Richo. I honestly did. What he had done was almost faultless. Almost.That word summed up Richo's career. That word sums up most of our careers.

A few weeks later, I actually met Richo. He had just missed a match through a fractured cheekbone and the right side of his face was puffed up, literally, like a football and tinged the colour of a plum. He had the genial manner of the much older man he would shortly become and, looking at me through one bloodied eye, said he would have played that day had the swelling in his face gone down. I thought he was joking but then realised he was serious. That's why the Tiger fans loved Richo. He was so transparently human, a walking barometer of the difference between what we are and what we could be. In Richo's case, the needle fluctuated between triumph and disaster with not much in between but in spite of everything, the wild inconsistency, the broken bones, the ridicule from smartarses like me, Richo kept coming back. He was a man for the times, a hero even. Go Richo! Go Tigers! Go the whole fucking lot of you! Go whatever mourns in man, whatever shares the eternal, go the wild green song of living, go the first kick of the season.Why not? At the footy, I'm allowed to be as absurd as the next man. What about outside the ground? That's a whole new world to me.What can I do? I hear a voice ask, and in my head an old football coach booms, 'Just do something, just *do*!'

Collingwood won by twenty-eight points.

Richmond's Ty Zantuck had a shot after the siren—had he goaled, the difference would have been twenty-three, but he missed. Waleed, who has won the tipping competition in which he participates for the past two years, had tipped Collingwood by twenty-three. It was apparent to all by now that in any school for students of the Australian game, Waleed Aly would be in the advanced class. We parted from him outside the ground with handshakes all round. As Doffan had to walk home, it seemed only good manners for the Big Boy and I to accompany him.

A distance of about ten kilometres, it took us a bit over two hours. Doffan, you may recall, runs marathons. His walk I would describe as a highspeed shuffle. He went ahead like a husky, talking quickly over his shoulder. I guided him towards the story of David so the Big Boy could hear it, saying, 'David is Doffan's biblical hero.' Doffan immediately corrected me, saying, no, Jonathan was. Jonathan is the young man who sacrifices himself for his brother; later, translating the story into old Australian, the Big Boy described Jonathan as 'the bloke who doesn't rat on his mate'. Moving ahead, Doffan told us he is criticised for seeing too much good in people. So am I, I said. It irks me deeply as a journalist when people expect me to dislike someone they dislike, when I know how offended they would be if I cut loose on the basis of such scant evidence against someone they admired. I am obliged to take people as I find them. As a journalist, I can at least do that much.

When the Big Boy and I finally got home after midnight, my wife kept asking, 'What was it like? How did it go?', and I found I had to think. It was like a night at the footy with a few good mates. I woke next morning to the news on the radio that the war was now expected to take longer than first thought, an American commander in the field saying the enemy was not the one they had war-gamed against.

TOM WILLS: CONFESSIONS OF A GHOST WRITER

You're back in the news, Tom. Not all the news has been good – e.g. page 3 of the Weekend Australian: AFL's Native Roots a Seductive Myth. I was named as the seductive myth-maker. You were named as the seductive myth, or, rather, the novel I wrote about you. I'm not re-writing the novel each time there's an attack to defend either myself or you. But I do now see it was a curious thing I did. People always think a novelist knows his or her characters. I didn't know you. How could I? You saw things I've never seen. Like war. You knew things I'll never know, like the native language of the place you were from. I reported on you like I report on people for the newspaper. I went round talking to people who knew you, recording what they said. Some of those people were actual, some came out of my head. Most were a bit of both. I finished the book but you didn't go away, Tom. Ours is an odd association. I guess you could say I'm your ghost writer. One question above all others to do with you intrigues me.

Tom Wills was native born. The question is how native?

I'm a journalist. Your principal foes were journalists who also happened to be members of the Melbourne Cricket Club - Englishmen, Cambridge men. I'm not making out this is a story about goodies and baddies, but it is a story about place. You spoke an Aboriginal language, you knew Aboriginal songs, you played with blackfellers as a kid. There are white historians who want to argue that you didn't know their games. I find it hard to take them seriously. You were a player. It was your nature to play. The Aboriginal moiety running through Moyston, the place you grew up, was black cockatoo/white cockatoo. That was the big rivalry in local Aboriginal footy - black cockatoo versus white cockatoo. Like Collingwood split in two, black one side, white the other. You played cricket for Collingwood, Tom. There's two things about you everybody seems to have agreed on - you'd drink with anyone and you'd play with anyone.

He played with blacks after his father was murdered by blacks.

The two English gentlemen journalists with whom you clashed were JB Thompson and William Hammersley. They scored well in the AFL's official history released in this, the 150th year of the game. You didn't, Tom. You were described as prickly, self-indulgent, overbearing, undisciplined. It said that, after your father's death, you ran Cullin-la-ringo, the family property in Queensland, inefficiently. That's the line that would've stabbed the deepest, I reckon. At the time, you wanted to invest. Your mother back in Geelong was just learning the extent to which her husband's last great adventure, setting off one more time as a pioneer, had threatened the family's fortunes. You were replaced, first by an administrator sent from Geelong, then by a younger brother. You were seen to have failed as the eldest son. You played some big roles in your life, Tom. One is Hamlet, haunted by your murdered father's ghost.

> I speak as if I know him. Do I? When I think of him, I never see his face. Like I don't see Ned Kelly's. The secret to the power of Sidney Nolan's Ned Kelly paintings is that we never see Ned's face. We never get to see him as a man. To see his horror, his rage, his hope, his fear, his tears, his lust, his love. We see a helmet with a slit for eyes.

Look at the picture of Tom Wills and the Aboriginal cricketers at the MCG on Boxing Day 1866. Historians argue over whether the photo was taken in Melbourne or Sydney, but I'm more interested in Tom's face. It's a mask. It looks like a river bed after a decade of drought. He's 31 but he could be 51. He's like a Vietnam vet. Everyone thought they knew about the Vietnam War because it was on television. To the men who'd been in the war, they knew shit. Tom Wills had been in the war being fought at the Australian frontier when this photo was taken. I reckon he passed beyond understanding, his own or anyone else's. Except maybe the blackfellers in that they understood what it was to lose brothers, sisters, mothers, fathers, in the frontier war. His demons were their demons, if not necessarily the same shape and color.

Former Liberal Prime Minister Malcolm Fraser once told me he couldn't see himself – he meant he couldn't explain to me, when asked, how or why he had become the person he is. Fraser is highly unusual for his absence of racism given his background and generation. I reckon there's a bit of Tom Wills in Malcolm Fraser and vice versa. Both western district boys, both sons of squatters, both sent to England as young gentlemen to finish their education. I fancy Tommy sounded like Malcolm – that curious English edge to his speech. Tommy's accent changed during his years at the Rugby school. His aunt who was in London wrote that he was becoming more gentlemanly which to my ears means more like those around him. Tommy was captain of the Rugby XI the year after the Charge of the Light Brigade in which four old boys of the school died. He was also drinking and having a mighty good time. When he got back to Australia, he was in his pomp. Arrogance may not have been a quality he lacked. He was a young leader. Creating leaders was what Rugby was then about.

If Tom Wills is the young man who thought he could fly to the sun, who believed he could do as he wished, if Tom Wills is Icarus, then his father Horatio is Daedalus. He also flies. But he is Daedalus with a difference. Horatio crashed before Tom did. The Cullin-la-ringo massacre in which Horatio Wills and 19 others are killed occurred in 1861, the same year Burke and Wills perished in the desert. These are large dramas played out in a land which the painter Sidney Nolan saw as a pitiless, ancient stage. Nolan painted Burke and Wills. Had he learned of Tom Wills and the Aboriginal cricket team, I have no doubt he would have painted them, both together and apart. I can see them - scribbly, blurred figures standing in a hot yellow land,

Wills with piercing eyes and blank face leaning forward like a man about to fall. A cricket ball, red as a cherry, spins in the empty blue sky above him. Tragic? I'd say so.

> He was a sportsman whose first language was action.

I haven't always liked you, Tom. I didn't like you the day at Ballarat you told Geelong to kick the ball out of bounds every time they got it in the quarters when the wind was against them. The game ended in near riot when Geelong won. There was a dark edge to your reputation as a sportsman. A bit like W.G. Grace, perhaps, to whom you were sometimes likened. There's an undercurrent in the journalism of JB Thompson and William Hammersley that you're a cheat. I like to think your idea was more along the lines of we'll make up the rules as we go along. Like EJ Ted "Mr Football" Whitten with the flick pass. When you're the best, you don't follow the game, the game follows you. EJ Whitten was a lair. So were you. You turned up to play your first game at the MCG in the colours of the I Zingari club, the gypsy lords of English cricket renowned as much for partying as playing. The morally earnest saw you as a model of the muscular Christian. You may have seen yourself as such. Under your captaincy, the Victorian XI beat NSW for the first time. Around this time you declared of football that we should "have a game of our own".

Did you later argue for the game of the Rugby school? Maybe, although the statement was made by William Hammersely with whom you had a violent falling-out. You were 37 and making a living as a professional cricketer. Hammersley was comfortably ensconced as the sporting editor of the "Australasian". He implied you turned up pissed to captain Victoria in an Intercolonial cricket match. Your letter in reply ridiculed Hammersley, saying a bigger old woman had never held the captaincy of Victoria. He responded in hurt tones, claiming that you had once bowled short and deliberately hit him on the arm when you could not dismiss him as a batsman by any other means, leaving him with an injury from which he suffered "to this day". He also said that if ever there was a selfish captain who put "self" first and "the match" second, that captain was Tommy Wills. Having read Hammersley on a range of subjects, I reckon he wasn't a bad journo - honest within his limitations. I tend to think, therefore, there's something in what he says about your character, Tom. Then I remember one of your brothers saying after your death that you were the most generous man he'd met. There's always two sides to your story, Tommy. At least two. Like Ned.

Gary "Buddha" Hocking told Tony "Libber" Liberatore you've done well in footy if you leave the game with a different name to the one you started with. You did, Tommy. You were the first gentleman sportsman on first name terms with the mob. They loved you. They were the ones who called you Tommy; to the gentlemen of the MCC, when you first came home from Rugby, you were "TWW". Tommy Wills played with anyone, even the slum boys from Collingwood. I'd love to have spoken to some of them about you. Later you played with the blacks even though your father was murdered by blacks.

You never accepted the white version of the Cullin-la-ringo massacre. It's hard to over-state what that means. I've read Queensland views of the massacre recorded in 1961, one hundred years after the event, that are full of the sort of hostility and bitterness then being expressed by white men in South Africa about the blacks in that land. In the 1990s when I visited Cullin-la-ringo and asked a local if there were still Aboriginal people in the area, he said, "Yes, but there's people around here who'll tell you we should have cleaned them out when we had the chance". This conversation was had around the time of ethnic cleansing in Kosovo. You got caught up in all that, Tom. After your father's death, you vowed to kill any black who came back on to the property but within two years you were accused of having done so. Five years after your father's death, you're captaining the Aboriginal cricket team, speaking to them in their language. That's when the team photo I talked about earlier was taken.

The tragedy of your sporting career was that you didn't tour England with the Aboriginal cricket team in 1868. I assume it was because by then you were a hopeless alcoholic. Had you played, the Aboriginal team would probably have defeated the mighty MCC (they led them on the first innings) and Tom Wills would be remembered as the first Australian cricket captain to win at Lord's. Your life would have made some sort of sense. Instead, there were years of despair and neglect and alcohol-induced DTs. You died in 1880, the same year as Ned Kelly, but in different circumstances. They hanged Ned. You stabbed yourself in the heart. Both of you were dumped in unmarked graves to be forgotten.

I wanted you remembered, Tom. I wanted your name to be up there with Les Darcy and Bradman and Ned and Burke and Wills and Truganini and the young men at Gallipoli, all the ones who represent the Australian experience at its most vivid and intense, whose memory lives in the landscape in a special way so that if you go the places where they trod a story ignites in your brain. I will always be grateful to Bruce Myles for adapting my novel "The Call" to the theatre. For three weeks in late 2004, an Aboriginal dancer from Queensland named Earle Rosas danced the spirit of Australian football on the stage of Melbourne's Malthouse Theatre. How good was he? How good was Gary Ablett in the 1989 grand final? I say he was that good. He lit up the entire stage. He had power, technique, precision, and he had what Aboriginal people call spirit.

Moyston, where Tom Wills played with the children of the Tjapwurrung, has a black cockatoo/white cockatoo moiety. Marilyn Miller, the play's indigenous choreographer, gave the play a black cockatoo/white cockatoo dance. Tommy Wills was the white cockatoo. Earle Rosas danced the black cockatoo. My book left you in a suicide's grave, Tom – if you had a memory, it was in this beautiful bastard of a game that continues to unfold and develop behind you, this dangerous dance with a funny shaped ball. Earle Rosas gave the play a different ending. In the play, the black cockatoo returned for the white cockatoo after it had fallen and the pair danced off back into the land, back into the place they were from. You're out there, Tommy. And that's why I want to end by thanking Ruth Brain, the president of the Moyston Willaura Football Club, for insisting that the AFL, in the commercial hoo-ha surrounding its 150th year, recognize Moyston as a special place in the dreaming of our native game.

Martin Flanagan,
Melbourne, June 2008.